THE *Silver* ERA

✿☆✿☆✿☆✿☆✿☆✿☆✿☆✿☆✿☆✿☆✿☆✿☆✿☆✿☆

IN AMERICAN JEWISH ORTHODOXY

Aaron Rakeffet-Rothkoff

THE *Silver* ERA
IN AMERICAN JEWISH ORTHODOXY

✡☆✡☆✡☆✡☆✡☆✡☆✡☆✡☆✡☆✡☆✡☆✡☆✡☆✡☆☆

Rabbi Eliezer Silver and his generation

YESHIVA UNIVERSITY PRESS

FELDHEIM PUBLISHERS
Jerusalem / New York

First published: 1981
Revised edition: 1988
New edition: 2000

ISBN 0-87306-274-4

FELDHEIM PUBLISHERS
POB 35002, Jerusalem, Israel 91350
200 Airport Executive Park, Nanuet, N.Y. 10954

www.feldheim.com

Printed in Israel

In memory of our dear parents

Ceil Grund

זיסל נעמי גרונד ז"ל

נפטרה י"ט חשון תשנ"ג

בת

פייגע זאהן בריל ז"ל

ומנחם נחום בריל ז"ל

and

Sam Grund

שמחה גרונד ז"ל

נפטר א' כסלו תשנ"ט

בן

שרה בתיה גרונד ז"ל

ויוסף חיים גרונד ז"ל

Dedicated with love by
Malkah and Aaron Rakeffet

Contents

☆☆☆☆☆☆☆☆☆☆☆☆☆☆☆☆☆☆☆☆☆☆☆☆☆☆☆

List of Illustrations

Preface

During my doctoral research on Rabbi Bernard Revel, the founder of Yeshiva College, Rabbi Eliezer Silver's letters and viewpoints constantly came to light. At that time I already felt that Rabbi Silver's life would be an excellent topic for a major research project, leading to a biography. Years later I met his son, Rabbi David Silver of Harrisburg, at the Western Wall in Jerusalem on a wintry Friday night. I enquired about his late father's archives, and we soon arranged for a complete photocopy to be made and transferred to me in Jerusalem. Once I began my research in earnest I was fortunate enough to discover additional archives and sources in the Holy City. This volume is the result of more than seven years of investigation and examination of the life and era of Rabbi Eliezer Silver.

Many individuals encouraged and aided me during these years. First and foremost I am most indebted to Rabbi David Silver for his constant help and cooperation. He gladly fulfilled my requests and bridged the gap of research between Israel and the United States. May he and his family derive satisfaction and cheer from this portrayal of their unforgettable father and grandfather.

I am most thankful to Rabbi Yehudah Copperman, dean and founder of *Michlalah*, the Jerusalem College for Women, for his constant aid and interest in my scholarly research. A portion of this study was accomplished as a research project sponsored by the *Michlalah*, where I have taught since 1971. My neighbor Rabbi Yehoshua Hutner, head of the Talmudic Encyclopedia Institute, was most helpful in interpreting rabbinic documents.

My relative Mrs. Leah Schoen assisted in the reading of Yiddish correspondence. Gratitude is expressed to Mrs. Louis Katz Engleberg for supplying copies of her father's papers in the litigation against Solomon Goldman. Mr. Moshe Gewirtz of the Agudat Israel World Organization was most generous in making available historic photographs.

While engaged in this research I was most cognizant of the pitfalls of rabbinic hyperbole. I was therefore most judicious in my use of such documents and publications. I also attempted to be as faithful as possible to the original Hebrew or Yiddish in the many documents which I rendered into English for inclusion in the text and appendix of this volume. For transliterations I have generally followed the system utilized by the Encyclopedia Judaica. At times this was modified in accordance with the norms of scholarship.

Dr. Norman Lamm, President of Yeshiva University, was particularly gracious to me. After reading the manuscript, he authorized its publication under the imprimatur of the Yeshiva University Press. The Rabbi Eliezer Silver Memorial Publication Fund, consisting of devotees of Rabbi Silver from Harrisburg, Springfield and Cincinnati, aided towards the publication of this volume with a generous grant. Mr. Yaakov Feldheim of Feldheim Publishers, Jerusalem, has spared no effort in producing an attractive book. Mr. Moshe Sussman copy-edited the volume in a most thorough fashion. My dear student Rabbi Joseph Epstein assisted in the reading of the proofs.

This work is dedicated to the blessed memory of Reuben Gross, a cherished friend and kindred spirit. Ruby, a pioneer of Orthodox Judaism in Staten Island, was at the forefront of the contemporary campaigns and struggles for Torah on both the American and Israeli scenes. He was constantly at the battle lines for the sake of his principles while upholding his ultimate principle of *Ahavat Klal Yisrael*, the love of the entire Jewish people. May his memory be a source of constant blessing and inspiration to his family and friends.

While the preparation of this volume was in its final stage, my beloved father, Max Mordechai Rothkoff, was called to his eternal rest. Born in New York City, he was privileged to spend his final years in Jerusalem, surrounded by children and grandchildren. May his memory be a source of constant guidance and dedication. May the Almighty spare my mother, Jennie Yehudit Rothkoff, for many more years in health and happiness. May she find solace in the family's continued commitment to those ideals which have sustained our people since the dawn of the Jewish community.

The last, in accordance with the rabbinic dictum, is the dearest. My research and study was only possible because of the encouragement and cooperation of my wife, Malkah, and our daughters, Teyna, Raye and Ranni. They constantly extended aid and support so that I could continue to explore the Torah world of yesteryear. May He who abides in Zion bless them with a meaningful and glorious tomorrow.

This book was researched and written during years saturated with both joy and sorrow for the Jewish people. Peace and war, laughter and tears, achievement and frustration were among my constant companions during this period. At the conclusion of this project I humbly pray that we may soon be privileged to witness the complete fulfillment of the prophetic vision: "Thus says the Lord of hosts: There shall yet sit old men and old women in the streets of Jerusalem, every man with his staff in his hand due to his many years. And the streets shall be full of boys and girls playing in its avenues" (Zechariah 8:4-5).

A. R.

Jerusalem
Hanukkah, 5741
December, 1980

1

The Immigrant Rabbinate in 1907

Rabbi Eliezer Silver was among the mass of Eastern European Jews who arrived in the United States in 1907. This was the peak period of this immigration which began as early as 1821 but did not become particularly noteworthy until after 1870. The intense interest with which the American Civil War was followed in Europe resulted in a more concrete awareness of the new country, soon leading to an ever increasing Jewish emigration to the New World. Following the anti-Jewish riots of 1881 in Russia at Yelizavetgrad and the later pogroms in Kiev and other South Russian cities, this emigration began en masse. During the decade before World War I, these newcomers averaged over 76,000 a year.[1]

The large majority of the new arrivals were not thoroughly steeped in Talmudic knowledge and rabbinic texts. Their Jewish commitment was not fortified with a penetrating understanding of the Torah civilization and perspective.

The true *talmid hakham* did not easily leave his native surroundings. Despite the persecutions and difficulties, he still had his local houses of worship and study, teachers, and fellow scholars. While the masses moved on to new horizons, the rabbinical scholars remained behind. This line of action had always characterized Jewish emigration. The *Sefer Ha-Kabbalah* (The Book of Tradition) claimed that the first great scholar to reach Spain was Rabbi Moses. This only happened because while at sea he was captured by pirates in the service of the Muslim king of Spain. The commander of the privateers reached Cordova where the nascent Jewish community redeemed Rabbi Moses. Attending the local synagogue he heard the teacher explain the rabbinic term for the "immersion of the finger in the pan containing the blood" as the "immersion of the entire body in the ritual bath." The chronicle then relates:

> Thereupon, R. Moses, who was seated in the corner like an attendant, arose before R. Nathan [the Teacher] and said to him: "Rabbi, this would result in an excess of immersions!" When he and the students heard his words, they marveled to each other and asked him to explain the law to them. This he did quite properly. Then each of them propounded to him all the difficulties which they had and he replied to them out of the abundance of his wisdom.[2]

That same day the former spiritual leader declared:

> I am no longer judge. This man, who is garbed in rags and is a stranger, is my master, and I shall be his disciple from this day on. You ought to appoint him judge of the community of Cordova.

Rabbi Moses thus became the spiritual head of Cordova and introduced proper rabbinic scholarship throughout Spain and the Maghreb. Centuries later this Jewry produced master Torah spirits such as Maimonides, Nahmanides and the Rashba.

Scholars likewise were not among the early arrivals to the United States. They did not readily discard the European environment which nurtured and sustained them. Such *talmidei hakhamim* resolutely read the advice proffered by Moshe Weinberger, a scholarly East European immigrant who, in describing the disarray and religious deviations within the immigrant community in 1887, wrote:

These words have been written for our scholarly brethren in

Russia, Poland, and Hungary who, because of their current despair and poverty, might be considering seeking their fortune in the United States. You are advised to honor your scholarly status by remaining in your native country.

Do not listen to those who mislead you with their descriptions of America. Do not become a wanderer for the rest of your life. There is no need for you to travel such a long distance across the seas and to endanger your soul. You have no need of America. Trust in God and He will sustain you in the place of your forefathers, brethren, and acquaintances. There, they know how to appreciate and honor *talmidei hakhamim* who remain in the tent of Torah. There, continuous study is basic to Orthodoxy and you can be certain that your fame and name will be known in accordance with your achievements. Such a decision will be for the good of your soul, your children, and posterity for all generations.[3]

The large majority of those who did reach the American shores had been raised as Orthodox Jews. Reform Judaism had barely influenced them in Europe, although many had been attracted to radical causes. Those who were observant were so in the Orthodox fashion. The two hundred immigrant *shtiblach* and synagogues in Manhattan in 1900 were all Orthodox in the East European tradition.[4] These devotees were nevertheless not learned Jews. Their piety has been termed *Milieu-Fromigkeit* and it was this folk religion which they brought to the United States.[5] Indicative of this era is a conversation recorded by Morris Raphael Cohen who later became a naturalist philosopher and professor at the City College of New York. Cohen arrived in America in 1892 at the age of twelve. Although his father was strictly observant, the younger Cohen left Orthodoxy. He reminisced:

A more important factor, however, in my drift from religious Orthodoxy, was provided by a conversation which I overheard between my father and a certain Mr. Tunick, in the fall of

1892. Mr. Tunick's brother had been a neighbor of ours in Minsk, and my father had helped him to come to this country. Our visitor challenged my father to prove that there was a personal God who could be influenced by human prayers or deeds, or that the Jewish religion had any more evidence in favor of its truth than any other religion. To this challenge my father could only answer, "I am a believer." This did not satisfy my own mind. And after some reflection I concluded that in all my studies no such evidence was available. After that I saw no reason for prayer or the specifically Jewish religious observances. But there was no use arguing with my father. He insisted that so long as I was in his house I must say my prayers regularly whether I believed in them or not.[6]

Many of the immigrants had already been exposed to antireligious viewpoints in "the old country." Socialistic and anarchistic ideals were also brought by the newcomers to America. Here these teachings found unlimited expression in the immigrant ghettos of the politically free United States. The leading European Jewish revolutionary group was the General Jewish Workers' Alliance, popularly known as the Bund. Its sympathizers maintained branches in America which numbered some sixty by 1906.[7] These groups fostered enmity toward tradition through their publications and public meetings. The editor of the *Freie Arbeiter Shtimme*, for example, attacked religion for splitting mankind. He wrote:

Borne, Lasalle, Marx
Will deliver us from the diaspora
The world will recognize no distinctions
All will be free, whether Turk, Christian or Jew
Every age has its sacred message
Ours is freedom and justice.[8]

Abraham Cahan, himself a product of the East Side and later the founder and longtime editor of the *Jewish Daily Forward*, described the awakening of Reb Nehemiah in his story, "The Apostate of Chego-Chegg."

> I had ears but could not hear because of my ear-locks; I had eyes and could not see because they were closed in prayer. . . . I am Rabbi Nehemiah no longer, they call me Nehemiah the atheist now.[9]

This constant and vociferous anti-religious propaganda further weakened the religious perseverance of many immigrants.

During the earlier German Jewish period of immigration, the first ordained rabbi arrived in the United States. Abraham Rice came in 1840 after having studied with Rabbis Abraham Bing in Wuerzburg and Wolf Hamburger in Fuerth. Rice became the spiritual leader of Congregation Nidchei Yisroel of Baltimore. Constantly frustrated by the increasing lack of Torah observance among his co-religionists, Rice contemplated returning to Europe. In a letter to his mentor, Rabbi Wolf Hamburger, he revealed his intentions:

> And one more thing I wish to disclose to you, my revered master and teacher . . . and my soul weepeth in the dark on account of it, namely, that the character of religious life in this land is on the lowest level; most of the people are eating non-kosher food, are violating the Shabbos in public . . . and there are thousands who have been assimilated among the non-Jewish population, and have married non-Jewish women. Under these circumstances, my mind is perplexed and I wonder whether a Jew may live in a land such as this.
>
> Nevertheless in my own home — thank God — I conduct myself as I did in days of old in my native country. I study Torah day and night, and my devoted and God fearing wife is always standing by and helping me with all her strength, in spite of privation and difficulties. Yet in spite of all this, life has lost all meaning here on account of the irreverence and low estate of our people. Alas, therefore, my master and teacher, impart to me of your wisdom, and let me have your august

opinion in the matter; for oftentimes I have made up my mind to leave and go from here to Paris and to put my trust in the good Lord.[10]

Rice did not bring these plans to fruition. He was too caught up with the American scene, and continued to minister to the needs of the growing Baltimore community.

Years later, the widely revered Rabbi Israel Meir ha-Kohen Kagan of Radun, Poland, also concluded that Jews should return to Europe. After watching the incessant emigration and increasing religious infractions, Rabbi Kagan penned *Niddehei Yisrael* in 1894. Universally known as the *Hafetz Hayyim* after the title of his first work, he planned his new volume for the "dispersed and wandering Jews in distant lands." His goal was to strengthen their religious tenacity. In forty-five chapters the *Hafetz Hayyim* detailed the rudiments of Torah philosophy and observances. He pleaded for careful conduct in the areas of *Kashrut*, Sabbath, and Family Purity. His distant brethren were exhorted to devote time to Torah study and in particular to properly educate their children. Albeit, Rabbi Israel Meir ha-Kohen also concluded that the only actual solution was for the Jew to remain in Europe. He ended:

My brethren, after all that I have written in this volume to strengthen those who dwell in distant lands, there is still only one proper solution. Whoever wishes to live properly before God must not settle in those countries. Even if he has already emigrated due to his economic distress, he must return to his home where the Lord will sustain him. He must not be misled by thoughts of remaining away until he is financially wealthy. . . . A proper person should curse the day of his arrival in a land where he must constantly witness desecration of the Torah. All his expectations should be directed towards God's helping him go free and return home. Certainly he must vow never to bring his children where they, God forfend, may be lost among the gentiles. . . . The choice is given to the individual who truly fears the Lord to return to his homeland where he can inculcate his children with Torah values. Then he will be blessed in this world and the next. God will not forsake the righteous who observe His covenant and commandments.[11]

Because of the paucity of learned Jews and proper rabbinic leadership, self-styled reverends soon became numerous among the immigrant masses. They became *mohalim*, *shohatim*, *Kashrut* supervisors and marriage performers. Numerous errors were committed by these "Rabbis without learning or piety" due to their ignorance of *halakhah* or for financial gain.[12] Eliezer Silver later described some of the apocryphal escapades of these religious functionaries.[13] A reverend permitted a daughter-in-law to marry her father-in-law after the death of her first husband. When queried how he could allow this incestuous relationship, the reply was that the Bible related that Judah wed his daughter-in-law, Tamar (Genesis 38:1-30). Another reverend was himself a *kohen* married to a divorcee. When asked how he could transgress an explicit Biblical law, the justification was that the first husband had died after the divorce and she was therefore a widow (Leviticus 21:7). *Gittin* were administered by these clergymen without proper witnesses to endorse the bill of divorcement and even without the consent of the husband. There were equally negligent *shohatim* who did not finish slaughtering before the advent of the Sabbath and continued working into the night. There was one *shohet* who even kept a store he owned open on *Yom Kippur*. Another *shohet*, who could no longer judge whether his slaughtering knife was properly sharpened, would habitually have his wife check it. Among those reverends who became spiritual leaders of congregations there were many whose wives did not observe the laws of *mikveh*. There was even an instance of such a rabbi stipulating with his congregation that he be allowed to continue his desecrating the Sabbath.

Amidst all the religious infractions and problems in the

immigrant community, the first Russian-American synagogue was organized in 1852. Known as the Beth Hamidrash Hagadol, its initial services were held in an attic at 83 Mott Street on New York's East Side. This place was rented for eight dollars a month. It became the leading East European Synagogue for the next four decades.[14] Among its founders was Rabbi Abraham Joseph Ash who arrived in New York that year. Born in Siemiaticze, in the district of Grodno, Poland-Lithuania, he became the spiritual leader of the new congregation in 1860. Ash served intermittently as its rabbi until his death in 1888, although he periodically attempted—unsuccessfully—to engage in business. There was constant discontent with Ash because he alternated between the rabbinate and commerce, and also due to his hassidic inclinations.[15] In 1879, during such an interregnum, the first attempt was made to bring in a leading European scholar to serve as the Chief Rabbi of the Beth Hamidrash Hagadol and other immigrant congregations. Their choice was Rabbi Meir Loeb Malbim, a noted Talmudist and biblical exegete, who had encountered hardships in his European communities due to the opposition of Reform Jews, *maskilim*, and *Hassidim*. Later that year, while still in Europe, Rabbi Meir Loeb died and Rabbi Ash was again reappointed spiritual leader of the Beth Hamidrash Hagadol. The first attempt to elect a chief rabbi thus ended without fulfillment.

This venture, however, did effectuate a new awareness of the dearth of proper rabbinical leadership in the New World. In 1880, Rabbi Abraham Jacob Gershon Lesser, a native of Mir, in the Grodno District, was brought to Chicago to become the spiritual leader of its Beth Hamidrash Hagadol U-Bnai Jacob Synagogue. The congregation proudly published a proclamation in a local paper which stated:

> It is well known to all that many disruptions and troubles were caused between families and quarrels in some congregations by men who call themselves rabbis, who for the sake of a few

dollars will divorce a husband who is in America from a wife in Poland, which brings ruination and misfortune to helpless and innocent children. And these self-styled rabbis, for the sake of a few dollars, will . . . authorize men to be *shohatim* who know nothing of *shehitah*. And for the purpose of abrogating these shameful deeds, and to save the name of Judaism from disgrace, we, the Polish Congregation, Beth Hamidrash Hagadol and others of our brethren in Chicago have brought Rabbi Lesser from Poland . . . a man who, besides the salary that he receives, does not want to take anything from any parties. . . . If a man is capable and worthy to be a *shohet* he gives *kabbalah* gratis and the same in the case of *gittin*.[16]

Rabbi Lesser remained in Chicago until 1898 when he accepted an invitation to head the Beth Tephila Congregation, the largest Orthodox synagogue in Cincinnati. Organized in 1866 by Shakhne Isaacs, the congregation was popularly known as "Reb Shakhne's Shule." Rabbi Lesser remained there until his death in 1925 at the age of ninety-one. He was widely acclaimed as one of the senior members of the American Orthodox rabbinate.

Rabbi Abraham Eliezer Alperstein came to the United States in 1881. Previously he studied with the well-known Rabbi Jacob David Willówski-Ridbaz in their native Kobrin, White Russia, and afterwards in Kovno and Vilna. In the States he served immigrant congregations in New York, Chicago, and St. Paul, and in 1901 he returned to New York where he died in 1913. In all these communities Alperstein devoted his efforts to aiding the recently arrived religious functionaries find their proper niche. An eminent scholar, he published his commentary on the Jerusalem tractate of *Bikkurim* in Chicago in 1887 with the approbation of Rabbi Joseph Baer Soloveitchik of Brisk (Brest-Litovsk).[17]

In 1886 another prominent scholar, Rabbi Moses Simon Sivitz arrived in America. Born in Zittawan, in the Kovno district, he received his education in Telshe and Kovno. His initial rabbinate was in a small Lithuanian community and at the advice of Kovno's chief rabbi Isaac Elchanan Spektor, he emigrated to Baltimore. Two years later he moved to Pittsburgh where he remained until his death in 1936. He published no less than seven rabbinic volumes during his American sojourn, and his work on the Jerusalem Talmud entitled *Mashbiah* went through three editions.[18]

Despite these arrivals the Torah scene remained disorganized and each individual rabbi was soon struggling with the quagmire of religious deviations and indifference. Above all, the vast New York immigrant community was still in total disarray. It was estimated that New York City possessed a Jewish population of 100,000 to 120,000 families by 1887.[19] The majority were East European immigrants residing on the Lower East Side. Their native communities' spiritual leaders were now increasingly aware of the religious maelstrom across the sea. Jacob Halevi Lipschitz, the secretary and representative on public affairs for Rabbi Isaac Elchanan Spektor, wrote from Kovno in 1887:

> For some years, many leading rabbis who are greatly concerned with the welfare of their people and the Torah have turned their attention to their American brethren. The temporal and spiritual lives of our American brothers are totally interconnected with our brethren here, in matters of aid and support, and family purity as reflected in the laws of marriage and divorce. When the latter are executed by nonvalid rabbis and ignoramuses the results are grievous. . . . To deal with these problems the leading *geonim* held three conferences two years ago (1885) in Telshe and Ponevez to seek ways and means of elevating religious life in America.[20]

When the European rabbinical leaders learned of the death of Rabbi Ash on May 6, 1887, they urged that the New York congregations select a "well-known *gaon* to be their undisputed leader." They considered such action the best and most proper advice they could extend to their New York brethren. Similarly the directors of the Beth Midrash Hagadol concluded that official measures should be undertaken to engage a chief rabbi. Its Minute-Book detailed such a suggestion at a meeting on May 23rd:

> It is the duty of our synagogue to seek out ways and means of bringing a chief rabbi for New York. The president [Dramin Jones] comments on the suggestion favorably and orders the secretary to send notices or letters to presidents of some sister congregations of New York, that the day after Shavuot, all presidents shall assemble for a meeting in this synagogue to discuss the matter under what conditions and where a chief rabbi should be invited.[21]

Over fifteen immigrant congregations soon united to form the Association of American Orthodox Hebrew Congregations and twenty-five hundred dollars per annum was pledged for the support of the venture. Leading European rabbis were contacted for their recommendations for the position. By Sukkot of 1887 the Association chose Rabbi Jacob Joseph of Vilna and formally invited him to become its chief rabbi. The latter was at that time the *maggid mesharim* (communal preacher) and a *moreh tzedek* (ecclesiastical judge) in Vilna. This city, popularly known as "the Jerusalem of Lithuania," had abolished the office of chief rabbi since the final decades of the eighteenth century. At that time there had been intense controversy over the last official incumbent, Shmuel ben Avigdor. Rabbi Joseph previously studied in the Volozhin Yeshivah and afterwards became a disciple of the Mussar movement devoted to ethical self-improvement. Rabbi Joseph's aptness as a student earned him the title of *harif* or sharp-witted. He successively became rabbi of Vilon, Jurburg, Novy Zhagare, and in 1883 was selected as the *maggid* of Vilna where he was held in high esteem. This fondness and respect was expressed in a letter from Michael Beirack of Vilna to his nephew Abraham Cahan in New York. Beirack wrote:

> Reb Yankev Yoisef is very dear to us. He is a sagacious scholar and a rare, God fearing man. Our hearts are heavy with pain because we have had to part with him. One does not want to lose such a precious treasure.
>
> See to it, Alter [Abraham Cahan], that the Jews in New York know what a diamond they have taken from us. See that he is properly appreciated. I know that you don't attend a synagogue, but you have a Jewish heart. So tell everyone that Vilna was proud of him and that New York should appreciate the precious crown it has now acquired.[22]

Rabbi Joseph accepted the Association's proposal and arrived at the American port of Hoboken, New Jersey, on July 7, 1888. He was greeted by the lay leaders of the United Orthodox Congregations who were ecstatic with the arrival of such an eminent rabbinical figure. Proudly they recited the traditional benediction upon seeing a great scholar, confident that a new dawn was beginning for American Orthodoxy. On the Sabbath of Consolation, Sabbath Nahamu, July 21st, the Chief Rabbi preached his first sermon. A vast overflow crowd had gathered at the Beth Hamidrash Hagadol and its entrance on Norfolk Street was completely blocked. A vanguard of four policemen was needed to clear a narrow path so the Rabbi, accompanied by four leaders of the Association, could enter the synagogue. Rabbi Joseph delivered a masterful sermon in the rabbinic homiletical tradition which included a reasoned plea for loving-kindness among his adherents. Nevertheless, Abraham Cahan, noting the obstacles awaiting the European trained scholar, commented on one of the early sermons:

> It was only his second or third sermon since his arrival and already he was making a clumsy attempt to accommodate

himself to his audience by using American Yiddish. Once he used the word "clean" for "rein" and it was easy to see this was purposely done to show he was not a greenhorn. His efforts to acquire social polish failed.

At one point he reached for a handkerchief in his pocket. It began to come out, long and blue. He was suddenly embarrassed and struggled to put the handkerchief back into his rear pocket. It twisted around his hand. In desperation, he put the handkerchief on the lectern and soon had both his hands entangled in it. His American words sounded unnatural. It was a pity. . . .

Reb Yankev Yoisef was like a plant torn out of the soil and transplanted into a hothouse.[23]

Rabbi Joseph undertook energetic steps to organize New York's kosher meat business. This step, he felt, was essential if a proper Torah community was to thrive in America. The leaders of the Association felt that the costs of this supervision should be borne by those who directly benefited from it. They therefore levied a tax of one cent upon every bird slaughtered in the abattoir under the Chief Rabbi's supervision. This poultry was stamped with a *plumba* (lead seal) with the words "ha-Rav ha-Kollel R. Jacob Joseph" in Hebrew on it. The purchasers were cautioned that "the fowl bearing seals should not be sold for any higher price than others, except one cent on each fowl for the seal." Intense opposition soon developed once this *Kashrut* program began to function and the lead seals appeared on the chickens. Many butchers and *shohatim* resented the strict control, and some rabbis feared the loss of *Kashrut* supervision income. They were joined by the radical press which was now able to protect the housewives against price gouging and to simultaneously attack organized religion. *Karobka*, a tax imposed by the Russian government on kosher meat, became the war cry of these groups. The very mention of the *karobka* conjured up all the evils and persecutions of Czarist Russia. The front page of the weekly *Der Volksadvokat* featured a poem in bold type entitled *Karobka*. It read:

> Dance, Orthodox chickens;
> Make merry, have no fear
> For the Rabbi an order has issued
> Shiny lead medals you'll wear.
> You'll wear them after your slaughter
> That the Chief Rabbi may live;
> They flay the skin off the worker
> A fat salary the Great One to give.[24]

Public meetings were staged by religious officials opposed to Rabbi Joseph. At one such assembly the main address was delivered by the Reverend H. Brodsky, "marriage performer, *mohel*, and preacher." He contended that the Vilna *maggid* was not in fact the Chief Rabbi since only a few congregations elected him, and these were not even truly concerned with Judaism. He claimed that Rabbi Joseph was simply a convenient pawn for the laymen of the Association who were utilizing him for their own financial gain. There was soon an anti-Chief Rabbi rabbinic court which supervised thirty-one butchers. Each week a list of these butchers appeared in *Der Volksadvokat*.

These constant attacks rapidly weakened and eroded the position and authority of the Chief Rabbi. By the middle of 1889 Rabbi Joseph was little more than a figurehead with virtually no real power. His salary was assumed by the butchers who remained under his jurisdiction. When European Jews learned of Rabbi Joseph's tribulations, they sent letters expressing sympathy for his plight and anger against his detractors. Simon Strashun and Hayyim Berlin, the lay leaders of Vilna's *hevrah kadishah*, wrote:

> It is not possible for us to set upon paper the depth of our sorrow and grief because of the pain and suffering of such a great rabbi, renowned for his learning and piety. We never

would have believed that this could happen to him after the honor and glory which was previously accorded to him in this community.[25]

Although Rabbi Joseph retained the title of Chief Rabbi and maintained his position in dignity and integrity, his influence on the American scene was insignificant. There was a vast difference between being the leader of an active Association of Congregations and merely eking out a livelihood from the supervision of butchers. In the spring of 1895 his status further deteriorated when the retail butchers banded together and rejected the Chief Rabbi's supervision. Two years later Rabbi Joseph took ill and remained a bedridden invalid until his death on July 28, 1902. Even his final tribute was marred by tragedy as a mass riot ensued when the funeral cortege passed a factory which manufactured printing presses. Many anti-Semitic workers bombarded the mourners with stones and pieces of metal. In the confusion the coffin was dropped while the Jews fought back and sought cover. Later that day the Chief Rabbi was finally laid to rest in the burial ground of the Beth Midrash Hagadol. Even this act was not without its shameful aspects since earlier the congregations bid for this honor. Each felt that having the Chief Rabbi interred in its cemetery would increase the value of the neighboring plots. Once again the Beth Midrash Hagadol outstripped the others, paying the widow fifteen hundred dollars in cash and promising fifteen dollars per month for life.

Despite the failure of this venture there were still some constructive results. The portals of America now attracted many more spiritual leaders of scholarship and integrity. If the *maggid* of Vilna could emigrate to the United States then others could follow. Rabbi Israel Kaplan arrived shortly after Rabbi Joseph to serve as an ecclesiastical judge in the Chief Rabbi's Court. An East European scholar, Rabbi Kaplan had previously refused to emigrate to America. He changed his mind only because Rabbi Joseph "cleared the way."[26] In 1889 Rabbis Shalom Elchanan

Jaffe and Moses Zebulun Margolies arrived. Jaffe, a graduate of the Volozhin Yeshivah, ministered to synagogues in Saint Louis and afterwards served as the rabbi of New York's Beth Midrash Hagadol.[27] Margolies became the head of Boston's Orthodox community and in 1906 rabbi of New York's prosperous and influential Congregation Kehilath Jeshurun.[28] Rabbi Bernard Louis Levinthal came in 1891 after receiving ordination from Rabbi Isaac Elchanan Spektor and Bialystok's Rabbi Samuel Mohilever. Settling in Philadelphia, Levinthal became the head of its United Orthodox Hebrew Congregations and was considered "the most Americanized of the strictly Orthodox rabbis in the country."[29] Also arriving in 1891 was Rabbi Judah Leib Levine, after previously studying in Volozhin and Kovno. He served congregations in Rochester, New Haven, and Detroit.[30] Rabbi Asher Lipman Zarchy came in 1892 and became a spiritual leader in Des Moines and Louisville.[31] In 1893 the "Moscower Rav," Rabbi Hayyim Jacob Vidrowitz, arrived in New York after his expulsion by the Russian government for not possessing the right to dwell in Moscow. Widely known for his learning and wit, he headed a few small East Side *shtiblach.* Outside his residence a shingle hung which declared him to be the "Chief Rabbi of America." It was reported that when asked "who made you the Chief Rabbi?" he whimsically replied, "The sign painter." When further questioned why the head of all America, he replied with a chuckle, "Because it would be well nigh impossible for all of American Jewry to join together to depose me."[32]

Despite this increase of reputable rabbinic leadership the American religious scene still remained fraught with difficulties. Each rabbi was isolated, and rarely was joint cooperation possible on a worthwhile undertaking. The rabbis were further frustrated by their inability to truly become part of the American milieu.

While their congregants were exposed to the New World's

method and perspective at work and at leisure, the rabbis remained in the timeless and eternal world of Torah study and tradition. Arriving at a mature age, they rarely mastered the English language and remained Yiddish-speaking. They gradually grew out of contact with their immediate followers and the general community. While the East European masses were constantly Americanizing, their rabbis and the synagogues of these rabbis stood pat.[33] Rabbi Margolies, well acquainted with these problems, thus described the situation:

> For many years, the gravest problem of the Orthodox rabbi in America was his isolation. His traditional and time-honored function, that of "Rov" or elder, of the man who stood sponsor for all the spiritual needs of his community, was continually being undermined by forces over which he had no control. This pathetic helplessness was still more aggravated by the fact that he stood alone. . . .
>
> What I wish to emphasize here is the fact that for many years past, the Orthodox rabbi found himself a spiritual recluse, a harrowed man defending a principle of life, of Jewish life, amidst indifference or laughing scorn.
>
> The "gathering of the dispersion" which this country became to the Jews during the last two decades, wrought great havoc with our old established conceptions of Jewish religious life. All the old standards were upset in the hurly-burly of economic adjustment and he, who in the midst of that new Babel of tongues, ideas and habits, would stand alone, was doomed to destruction.[34]

Religious life and standards did not notably improve and even many of the children of the rabbis were swept away by the tides of change. An anonymous rabbi described the dismal American scene in a 1902 letter to the Orthodox monthly, *Ha-Peles*, of Poltava-Berlin:

> The rabbinate has become a business. This one sells a permissible ruling while the other peddles a prohibitive

decision. Void *gittin* are granted and illicit marriages are performed. . . . I have not seen one of their sons competent enough to study the Talmud, and even the Torah with Rashi's commentary remains unknown to them. The rabbi's daughters work in their places of employment on the Sabbath. They do not act thus because of pressing monetary needs but rather to purchase another kerchief or colorful dress. If these are the examples before the lay people then what can be expected of their children![35]

In a subsequent issue, Rabbi Solomon Jacob Friederman of Boston came to the defense of his colleagues. He hardly contested the facts contained in the previous letter, although he felt that most properly ordained rabbis were not like this. He rather protested that such information was publicized. He feared that the American rabbis would now be blackballed and no longer considered for any European positions. Rabbi Friederman stated:

My heart grieves because the path of escape is now closed for the American rabbis. We can no longer hope to save ourselves by returning to our native countries. We will no longer be considered for important rabbinical posts when available among our people and family. The American rabbis have been disgraced before the Jewish community in all its countries of dispersion. A member of the fellowship has maliciously slandered his colleagues by declaring that they willingly trample the sacred tenets of Judaism. He even claimed that the rabbis are the cause of the dissolution of Torah life in America.[36]

There were, however, some initial rays of light on the American Torah scene, particularly in the field of Jewish education. In many communities there were Talmud Torahs and *hedarim* which were organized by the *rabanim*. More important were the pioneer yeshivot which were established under their tutelage. These became the forerunners of the Jewish Day School movement in the United States. The first was the Yeshivat Etz Chaim which opened in New York in 1886. While stressing Torah study, it also enabled students to attain an elementary school secular education. In 1896 the Rabbi Isaac Elchanan Theological Seminary opened an advanced yeshivah for the graduates of Etz Chaim. In 1915 these schools combined, and one year later opened the Talmudical Academy High School. Later this complex evolved into Yeshiva University. Among the *rabanim* active in the school's administration during its nascent period were Rabbis Alperstein, Levinthal, and Margolies. Another elementary yeshivah was organized by the followers of Rabbi Jacob Joseph in 1901. Located on New York's East Side, it was later renamed the Rabbi Jacob Joseph School in memory of the Chief Rabbi.[37]

During this period individual rabbis began to probe the possibility of forming a national organization to improve the religious situation. Reform rabbis had already united in the Central Conference of American Rabbis in 1889 and the Conservatives in the Rabbinical Assembly in 1900. This notion was initially broached by Detroit's Rabbi Levine and Des Moines' Rabbi Zarchy. Meeting in Detroit, they jointly sent out a letter to their colleagues, dated *Rosh Hodesh* Ellul (August 16) 1901, pleading the cause of unity. They wrote:

When we met together and reviewed the current status of Judaism in the United States, we heard the Heavenly voice proclaiming: "Woe to the people for the disregard of the Torah!" [Avot 6:2]. We are particularly distressed by the cry of the true rabbinic leaders mourning the constant desecration of Torah. The new generation is rapidly assimilating without knowing about their Divine heritage. We have decided to undertake a major step in the hopes that with your acquiescence it will be successful. . . .

We are obligated to unite and form a union of Orthodox rabbis. Together we must decide what is to be jointly executed and what we should abstain from. We will evolve the basic concepts of this organization through our correspondence. Now is the proper time to publicly lead the way in the service of our religion.[38]

These initial efforts elicited numerous positive responses among the rabbis. During February of 1902 there was a Zionist convention in Boston which was attended by some of the leading rabbinical figures. At the Boston home of Rabbi Margolies, the discussions continued and an organizational committee was formed. Margolies was selected as the temporary chairman and Philadelphia's Rabbi Levinthal as his assistant. A formal organizational convention was later planned for July 29, 1902. Immigrant rabbis from all over the Eastern seaboard and the Western United States eagerly reached New York. Their expectations soon turned to sorrow as they learned that Rabbi Jacob Joseph was on his deathbed. Many participated in his funeral and the initial proceedings of the new fellowship were under the pale of his demise. The very day of his burial the *Agudat Harabanim* or the United Orthodox Rabbis of America was officially formed. Its English name later became the Union of Orthodox Rabbis of the United States and Canada. The deliberations continued for five days and through ten sessions. The participants decided to open membership only to spiritual leaders who were ordained by recognized European rabbinical leaders. The candidates also had to be actively engaged in the New World rabbinate. Fifty-nine founding members were chosen, including thirteen from New York City. The remainder ministered to immigrant communities in cities such as Baltimore, Boston, Buffalo, Chicago, Cincinnati, Detroit, Denver, Montreal, New Haven, Philadelphia, Pittsburg, Portland, and Toronto. A constitution was adopted to chart the course of the new organization. Its most important goal was to intensify the education of the youth. The teachers were "to be supervised by the rabbis and to be certified by well-known pedagogues." The language of instruction was to be Yiddish, with English the secondary tongue. The constitution stated:

The teachers are to translate into Yiddish, the native language of the children's parents. When necessary for the clarification of the topic, the teachers may also utilize English. In areas where only English is spoken, then it may be the basic tongue.[39]

The rabbis were also to campaign for Sabbath observance, and to encourage the unions to demand the exemption of Jewish workers from Sabbath work. The members of the new group were to support each other in their quests to organize proper *Kashrut* facilities. They were also to encourage the building of new *mikvaot* in outlying communities and to repair the non-valid ones in established areas. All *gittin* were to be administered by their members and congregants influenced to engage only competent rabbis for marriage ceremonies. The national organization was also to safeguard equable relations among its members. No rabbi was permitted to encroach upon his colleague's domain. The constitution declared:

A member of the *Agudah* called to a rabbinical position in a city where a colleague already resides must appear before the executive committee. Only after they have ascertained that there is no encroachment may the new rabbi move there.

If an unqualified person settles in a community and poses as a rabbi the *Agudah* will attempt to quietly influence him to leave. If this will not be successful then the annual convention of the organization will determine the future of this imposter. . . .

The *Agudah* will not only support its own members but will also assist any competent European rabbinic arrival. He will be assisted in every way even if he does not enter the active rabbinate. All that will concern the organization will be the newcomer's greatness in "Torah and fear of Heaven."

The *Agudah* will attempt to influence Jewish communities to engage bona fide rabbinical leadership to enable them and their children to walk in the path o `Torah and tradition.[40]

Rabbi Lesser of Cincinnati was elected chairman of the executive committee while Rabbi Joshua Israelite of Chelsea, Massachusetts, became secretary. Among the executive committee members were Rabbis Levinthal of Philadelphia, Margolies of Boston, Sivitz of Pittsburgh, Zarchy of Des Moines, Hayyim Silber of Worcester, and Jaffe, Benjamin Rabbiner, and Dovber Abramowitz of New York.[41]

The new organization was soon opposed by those who feared the strength of its unity. Among its opponents were reverends, kosher food purveyors and supervisors, and a few rabbis who felt their dignity was violated by a call to relinquish authority to a national body. One rabbi exclaimed that "he would completely uproot the organization and its executive committee." Others charged that the *Agudat Harabanim* was no more than a rabbinical trade union. At a regional organization meeting in Cincinnati, the rabbis answered this charge in a statement issued on June 11, 1903:

> We are not a union for the sake of business. All those familiar with our constitution and members know that the group has no material or financial aims. Many times our rabbis actually waive monetary gain to observe the organization's guidelines. They do so with a feeling of achievement and purpose since they are thus strengthening Torah Judaism in this country. Their satisfaction is in the knowledge that they are dispelling the darkness and disorder which surrounds contemporary Jewish life.[42]

While the new *Agudat Harabanim* was barely beginning to function, another intense rabbinical conflict developed on the American scene. The Chicago immigrant community invited Rabbi Jacob David Willowski to become its Chief Rabbi in 1903. Willowski, later known as the Ridbaz (Rabbi Jacob David ben

Zev) and popularly called the "Slutsker Rav," was previously a leading European rabbinical figure. His responsa and published commentaries on the Jerusalem Talmud established his reputation in the front rank of rabbinic scholarship. His final European rabbinate was in Slutsk where he established an advanced yeshivah in 1896. This school later transferred to Kletsk, Poland, during the period between the World Wars. It was re-established in Lakewood, New Jersey, in 1943 as the Beth Medrash Govoha of America.[43]

Rabbi Willowski initially visited the United States in 1900 to raise funds to cover the costs of the publication of a new edition of the Jerusalem Talmud with his commentaries. In New York he visited with Rabbi Jacob Joseph and was greatly distressed to find such an eminent *gaon* desolate and forsaken. The "Slutsker Rav" rebuked a public assembly for having emigrated to this "*trefa* land where even the stones are impure."[44] After remaining in America for five months and touring the cities with large Jewish populations, Rabbi Willowski returned to Europe. In 1903, he came to America for the second time to reside in Chicago. At the second annual convention of the *Agudat Harabanim* in Philadelphia, August 16-19, 1903, the Ridbaz was designated as the *zekan harabanim* (elder rabbi) of America. On September 8, 1903 he was publicly installed as Chief Rabbi of a number of Chicago's East European congregations. At the public convocation a letter from the *Agudat Harabanim* was read. It congratulated the community for having selected the Ridbaz as its Chief Rabbi. It pleaded with the community to spare him from strife and vexation. The letter concluded by informing Chicago Jewry that "the Union of Orthodox Rabbis will not recognize any rabbinical certification on food products from Chicago unless the Ridbaz approves the *hekhsher.*"[45]

Rabbi Willowski soon set about organizing the community's religious facilities. He began by attempting to become the

guiding force in the massive local meat industry. Kosher abattoirs were conducted by the four largest meat-packing houses in
Chicago: Armour and Company, Schwartz-Shield and Sulz-
berger and Company, Libby, McNeil and Company, and Swift
and Company. A supervising rabbi was not engaged by these
slaughterhouses since their owners felt their sole obligation was
to employ *shohatim*. It was rather the *shohatim* who voluntarily
agreed to accept a rabbi as their supervisor. Previously their
rabbi was Rabbi Lesser; after 1898 Rabbi Tzvi Shimon Album
assumed their supervision. Trained in the Volozhiner Yeshivah,
Album was later considered "the foremost champion of Orthodox Judaism in Chicago."[46] Album refused to allow the Ridbaz
into his slaughterhouses since he felt the latter was encroaching
upon his status and position in the community. He claimed that
"suddenly the Ridbaz came to Chicago to rob my rights, trespass
upon my property, and cut off my meager sustenance."[47] In turn,
the Ridbaz castigated Album's relationship with the *shohatim*
which did not permit other "Jewish eyes to observe their acts of
ritual slaughter."[48] The controversy soon embroiled additional
rabbis, *shohatim*, and lay-leaders of Chicago's East European
Jewish community. The dispute left the arena of purely *halakhic*
considerations and degenerated into malevolent polemics. The
help of the *Agudat Harabanim* proved of little consequence to
the Ridbaz. With the intensification of the dispute he despaired
of achieving constructive and lasting results. During the summer
of 1904, Rabbi Willowski resigned his position. Afterwards, he
traveled extensively throughout the United States to lecture,
preach, and sell the remaining sets of his Jerusalem Talmud
edition. In 1905 the Ridbaz settled in Palestine where he became
rabbi of Safed's Ashkenazic community. He continued to reside
in Safed until his death on the first night of *Rosh Hashanah*,
October 1, 1913.

While the East European rabbis were struggling with
limited success, there was a sole immigrant hassidic *Rebbe*

enjoying even less spiritual accomplishment. The first man who crossed the Atlantic with the intention of establishing himself as a *Rebbe* was Rabbi Eliezer Hayyim Rabinowitz, the son of Rabbi Baruch of Yampol, and a descendant of the *Ba'al Shem Tov*, the founder of Hassidism. He arrived in New York around 1892, but never really succeeded in attracting a following among the immigrant *Hassidim*. A few years later Rabinowitz returned to Europe. A contemporary thus described his American venture:

> The undertaking was successful in a way; that is, ere long the new *Tzaddik's* coffers were bulging with money, given him by sorrowing and heartbroken women who flocked to him, asking for his divine intercession in their behalf. He also found a number of followers among the rabble. However, he never succeeded in attracting the real *Hassidim*. It is possible that at that early period of Eastern European immigration there were too few real *Hassidim* in this country to form a permanent following. Again, an explanation may be found in the fact that he was not a *Tzaddik* in his own right, but merely a "grandson" of a *Tzaddik*. His ultimate abdication may also be ascribed to the hostile attitude of the Yiddish press, which persecuted him relentlessly.
>
> Be this as it may, the seed surely fell on barren soil. After sojourning a few years in this unfriendly environment, Reb Eliezer Chaim renounced his "holy post" and left America to become merely a "grandson" [of a *Tzaddik*] once more.[49]

This was the spiritual state of the immigrant community and its rabbinate which greeted Eliezer Silver upon his arrival in America.

Notes

1. Samuel Joseph, *Jewish Immigration to the United States: From 1881 to 1910* (New York; Columbia University, 1914), pp. 98-104; Hyman B. Grinstein, "The Efforts of East European Jewry to Organize Its Own Community in the United States," PAJHS 49, no. 2 (December 1959), 73-74; and for the general period consult the "Bibliographical Note" in Moses Rischin, *The Promised City: New York's Jews, 1870-1914* (Cambridge, Mass.: Harvard University, 1962), pp. 275-282.

2. Abraham Ibn Daud, *Sefer Ha-Qabbalah: The Book of Tradition*, trans. Gerson D. Cohen (Philadelphia: The Jewish Publication Society, 1967) p. 65, and see the footnotes for the appropriate rabbinic sources.

3. Moshe Weinberger, *Ha-Yehudim Veha-Yahadut Be-New York* (New York, 1887), pp. 28-31.

4. Grinstein, "The Efforts of East European Jewry to Organize Its Own Community in the United States," pp. 75-76; Peter Wiernik, *History of the Jews in America* (New York: The Jewish Press, 1912), p. 274; and Louis Lipsky, "Religious Activity: New York" in *The Russian Jew in the United States*, ed. Charles S. Bernheimer (Phila.: John C. Winston Co., 1905), pp. 148-156.

For additional details of the Orthodox immigrant community cf. the author's *Bernard Revel: Builder of American Jewish Orthodoxy* (Philadelphia: The Jewish Publication Society of America, 1972), pp. 3-26 and "The American Sojourns of Ridbaz: Religious Problems Within the Immigrant Community," PAJHS 57, no. 4 (June 1968), 557-72.

5. Cf. Charles S. Liebman, "Orthodoxy in American Jewish Life" in AJYB: 1965 (Philadelphia: The Jewish Publication Society of America, 1965), pp. 27-30; and his *The Ambivalent American Jew* (Philadelphia: The Jewish Publication Society, 1973), pp. 77-78.

6. Morris Raphael Cohen, *A Dreamer's Journey* (Boston: Beacon Press, 1949), p. 69.

7. Irving Howe, *World of our Fathers* (New York: Harcourt, Brace, Jovanovich, 1976), p. 292.

8. *Freie Arbeiter Shtimme*, September 19, 1890, cited and translated by Moses Rischin, *The Promised City: New York's Jews, 1870-1914* (Cambridge, Mass.: Harvard University Press, 1962), p. 155.

9. Cited by Rischin, *ibid.*, p. 154.

10. MS in the library of the Jewish Theological Seminary cited by Israel Tabak, "Rabbi Abraham Rice of Baltimore: Pioneer of Orthodox Judaism in America," *Tradition*, 7:2 (Summer 1965), pp. 102-103.

11. Israel Meir Ha-Kohen, *Niddehei Yisrael* (Warsaw, 1894), pp. 129-130.

For an analysis of this work see Lester Samuel Eckman, *Revered By All* (New York: Shengold Publishers, 1974), pp. 85-88.

12. Hutchins Hapgood, *The Spirit of the Ghetto* (New York: Funk and Wagnalls Co., 1909) p. 62; and cf. the author's *Bernard Revel*, pp. 13-14 and Rischin, *The Promised City*, pp. 147-148.

13. Eliezer Silver, *Anfei Erez* (New York, 1960), I:11-12; and *Sefer Ha-Yovel Shel Agudat Harabanim: 1902-1927* (New York: Agudat Harabanim, 1928), pp. 125-127.

14. For its history see Judah David Eisenstein, *Otzar Zikhronothai* (New York, 1929), pp. 246-251.

15. For Ash's biographical details see *ibid.*, pp. 20-21, 253; Hyman B. Grinstein, *The Rise of the Jewish Community of New York: 1654-1860* (Philadelphia: The Jewish Publication Society of America, 1945), pp. 93, 253, 486, 488, n. 12; and Abraham J. Karp, "New York Chooses a Chief Rabbi," PAJHS 44, no. 3 (March, 1955), 130-131.

16. For Lesser's biography see Judah M. Isaacs, "Abraham Jacob Gershon Lesser," in *Guardians of Our Heritage*, ed. Leo Jung (New York: Bloch Publishing Co., 1958), pp. 347-359. The newspaper citation is quoted on pp. 348-349.

17. For Alperstein's biography see *Toldot Anshei Shem*, ed. Oscar Z. Rand (New York, 1950), p. 3.

18. For Sivitz's biography see *Toldot Anshei Shem*, p. 48.

19. Weinberger, *Ha-Yehudim Veha-Yahadut*, p. 1.

20. The Hebrew letter is cited by Eisenstein, *Otzar Zikhronothai*, pp. 253-254. The English translation is a revision of that of Karp, "New York Chooses a Chief Rabbi," p. 133. The ensuing details of the Rabbi Jacob Joseph venture are from these two sources. Also cf. Harold P. Gastwirt, *Fraud, Corruption and Holiness* (New York: Kennikat Press, 1974), pp. 55-80.

For biographical details of Kovno's Rabbi Isaac Elchanan Spektor see Ephraim Shimoff, *Rabbi Isaac Elchanan Spektor* (New York: Yeshiva University, 1959) and Jacob Ha-Levi Lipschitz, *Toledot Yitzhak*

(Warsaw, 1897). For the European aspect of this period see Lipschitz's *Zikhron Ya'akov*, 3 vols. (Kovno, 1924-30).

21. Translated from the Yiddish Minute-Book of the Beth Hamidrash Hagadol by Karp, "New York Chooses a Chief Rabbi," p. 135. Cf. p. 131, n. 6.

22. *The Education of Abraham Cahan*, trans. Leon Stein, Abraham P. Conan, and Lynn Davison (Philadelphia: The Jewish Publication Society of America, 1969) p. 395.

23. *Ibid.* p. 396.

24. *Der Volksadvokat*, August 31, 1888; translated from the Yiddish by Karp, "New York Chooses a Chief Rabbi," p. 164.

25. The letter was dated Adar 3, 5649 (1889). The translation is based upon that of Karp, "New York Chooses a Chief Rabbi," p. 177. For the Hebrew original of this and other letters see Eisenstein, *Otzar Zikhronothai*, p. 269.

26. Karp, "New York Chooses a Chief Rabbi," p. 187. Kaplan's son Prof. Mordecai Menahem Kaplan, of the Jewish Theological Seminary of America, became the founder of the Reconstructionist movement.

27. For Jaffe's biography see *Sefer Ha-Yovel Shel Agudat Harabanim: 1902-1927*, p. 147.

28. For Margolies' biography see *Kehilath Jeshurun Year Book: 1946*, p. 26; Gilbert Klaperman, *The Story of Yeshiva University: The First Jewish University in America.* (Toronto: The Macmillan Co., 1969), s.v. index; and Samuel Gottleib, *Ohalei Shem* (Pinsk, 1912), pp. 304-305.

29. Wiernik, *History of the Jews in America*, p. 282. For Levinthal's biography see *K'vod Chachomim* (Philadelphia: Jubilee Volume in Honor of Bernard Levinthal's Seventieth Birthday, 1935), pp. 74-82; Alex J. Goldman, *Giants of Faith* (New York: The Citadel Press, 1964), pp. 160-176; and *The Brooklyn Jewish Center Review*, October 1952, pp. 5-10.

30. For Levine's biography see *Sefer Ha-Yovel Shel Agudat Harabanim: 1902-1927*, p. 141, and Ben-Zion Eisenstadt, *Hakhmei Yisrael Be-America* (New York, 1903), pp. 65-66.

31. For Zarchy's biography see Eisenstadt, *Hakhmei Yisrael Be-America*, p. 52, and Gottlieb, *Ohalei Shem*, pp. 301-302.

32. Eisenstein, *Otzar Zikhronothai*, p. 77; and Karp, "New York

Chooses a Chief Rabbi," pp. 174-175, n. 128. Cf. Hapgood, *The Spirit of the Ghetto*, pp. 68-69.

33. Cf. David de Sola Pool, "Judaism and the Synagogue," in *The American Jew: A Composite Portrait*, ed. Oscar I. Janowsky (New York: Harper and Bros., 1942), pp. 37-41; and the author's *Bernard Revel*, pp. 15-16.

34. Margolies, M.S., "The Union of Orthodox Rabbis of the United States and Canada," *The Jewish Communal Register: 1917-1918* (New York: Kehillah, 1918), pp. 1180-1181.

35. *Ha-Peles*, ed. Elijah Akiva Rabinowicz, 2, no. 7 (Nisan, 1902), pp. 477-478.

36. *Ibid.*, 2, no. 11 (Av, 1902), p. 688. For Rabbi Friederman's biography see Gottlieb, *Ohalei Shem*, p. 295. For additional reaction to the original article see *Sefer Ha-Yovel Shel Agudat Harabanim: 1902-1927*, pp. 18-19.

37. For details of the early yeshivot see *The Jewish Communal Register: 1917-1918*, pp. 395, 1201-03; and Alvin Irwin Schiff, *The Jewish Day School in America* (New York: Jewish Education Committee Press, 1966), pp. 32-34.

38. *Sefer Ha-Yovel Shel Agudat Harabanim: 1902-1927*, pp. 19-20.

39. *Constitution of the United Orthodox Rabbis of America* (New York: Zion Printing, 1902), p. 7. Portions of this constitution were published in *Sefer Ha-Yovel Shel Agudat Harabanim: 1902-1927*, pp. 24-29. For an English translation of the constitution see Appendix I to this volume.

40. *Constitution of the United Orthodox Rabbis of America*, pp. 16-18.

41. AJYB: 5663 (1902-1903), pp. 140-141; and cf. *Sefer Ha-Yovel Shel Agudat Harabanim: 1902-1927*, pp. 29-30.

42. *Sefer Ha-Yovel Shel Agudat Harabanim: 1902-1927*, pp. 32-33.

43. For Rabbi Willowski's biography see the author's "The American Sojourns of Ridbaz," pp. 557-572; and for a detailed history of the Yeshivah see Hillel Zeidman, "Yeshivat Etz Hayyim of Kletsk," *Mosdot ha-Torah be-Europa: be-Vinyanam uve-Hurbanam*, ed. Samuel Mirsky (New York: Histadrut Ivrit of America, 1956), pp. 229-242.

44. Tzvi Shimon Album, *Sefer Divrei Emet* (Chicago, 1912) 2:69; and Moshe Davis, "Jewish Religious Life and Institutions in America,"

in *The Jews: Their History, Culture and Religion*, ed. Louis Finkelstein (Philadelphia; The Jewish Publication Society of America, 1960), 1:539.

45. Zev Kaplan, *Edut be-Yaakov* (Warsaw, 1904), p. 53.

46. For this statement and Album's biography see Morris A. Gutstein, *A Priceless Heritage* (New York: Bloch Publishing Co., 1953) pp. 129-130. Cf. Gastwirth, *Fraud, Corruption and Holiness*, pp. 90-92.

47. Album, *Sefer Divrei Emet*, 1:6a.

48. Jacob David Willowski-Ridbaz, *Nimukei Ridbaz al ha-Torah: Bereshit and Shemot* (Chicago, 1904), p. 4.

49. Isaac Even, "Chassidism in the New World," *The Jewish Communal Register: 1917-1918*, p. 343.

2

Early European and American Years

There was joy in the Silver household on Shevat 23, 1881. In the hamlet of Abel, Kovno province, Lithuania, a son, Eliezer, was born that day to Rabbi Bunim Tzemah and Malkah Silver. The lineage of both parents included history's most noted rabbinic scholars. Their ancestry could even be traced back to David, King of Israel. Eliezer's paternal grandfather, Rabbi Nuta, was the spiritual leader of a nearby town, Dusat, for close to fifty years. Rabbi Bunim Tzemah, however, chose to support his family through business endeavors. Utilizing every spare moment for Torah scholarship, he studied late into the night and was distinguished for his diligence. But after his business interests suffered reverses, Rabbi Bunim Tzemah consented to enter the rabbinate and succeeded his father in Dusat.[1]

This rural Lithuanian area was still basically unaffected by the *Haskalah* at this time. While the major cities such as Vilna and Kovno were already hotbeds of enlightenment and philosophical ferment, the smaller communities remained essentially stable until World War One. In the Kovno province there were many small towns such as Dusat, Abel, and Rogachov. In Dusat there were some two hundred and fifty Jewish families, mainly engaged in business. There were also some gentile families in the town, and many more lived on the surrounding farms. Dusat

43

served as the business center for all those roundabout.[2]

Among the Dusat Jews from young to old there were none who publicly desecrated the Sabbath. At night the men returned to the house of study where there were numerous classes on various levels. These included the study of tractates of the Mishnah, Talmud, *Ein Yaakov*, and *Hayei Adam*. The classes were conducted by the town's rabbi, *shohet*, and other learned residents. There were one large central *Ashkenaz* synagogue and a smaller *shtible* for the few local hassidic families. Jewish communal life evolved around the rabbi, who was its spiritual arbiter and temporal guidepost. No newspapers reached Dusat and there were no daily connections with the happenings in the greater world.

Eliezer Silver received his earliest education from his father in these provincial surroundings. His home was steeped in the Lithuanian Jewish tradition of intellect and logic. Ritual, emotion, and rational reasoning were blended into the path before the Lord. Uppermost in this way of life was the prime commandment of Torah study which the sages considered "the equal of all the other Biblical precepts."[3]

When Eliezer was nine years old his father began to introduce him to the intricacies of the Talmud. Soon enthralled with this new world of study, the youngster began to devote endless hours in its pursuit. The blissful years of childhood fell behind him as he began to emulate his father's practice of rising at midnight to concentrate on his learning.

This idyllic life was sporadically interrupted by stark reminders of the precariousness of Jewish existence in Russian controlled Lithuania. One event which left an indelible impression upon the youngster was the kidnapping by gentiles of an eight-year-old Jewish girl of a neighboring village. The girl's aunt, posing as a non-Jew, went from house to house in the neighboring villages until she located and returned with the child. A few days later, thousands of enraged townsmen accompanied by their priests forcibly took the girl once again. Rabbi Bunim Tzemah organized the local Jewish youth in vain efforts to regain the child by force. Afterwards, he led the community in legal proceedings. At numerous meetings with judges and police officers, munificent bribes were distributed. The girl was finally released six months later and the rabbi then arranged for her to live with relatives in Vilna.

On another occasion a pogrom ensued right outside the Silver residence. Earlier there had been a major conflagration in Dusat. A rumor spread among the gentile community that the *shohet*'s son had kindled the blaze. Jewish residents were soon brutally attacked and for hours the disturbances raged on.

Despite these harsh interruptions, father and son continued their incessant study sessions. The bonds of mutual understanding intensified between them as they mastered folio after folio of rabbinic literature. When Eliezer became sixteen, his father felt that he was prepared to study with the pre-eminent Torah luminaries of the generation. In 1897 the younger Silver traveled to Dvinsk, a Torah center in Vitebsk province. The census of 1897 revealed that Dvinsk had a population of 72,231, the Jews numbering 32,369.[4] The pride of the Jewish community were its two spiritual leaders, Rabbi Meir Simhah ha-Kohen of the *Mitnagdim* and Rabbi Joseph Rozin of the *Hassidim*. Here Silver found scores of brilliant students from all the surrounding communities. The study halls were filled from morning till late into the night and the Dvinsk atmosphere was permeated with Torah learning. Eliezer joined a group of seven select young men who ate dinner together every day. They limited their repast to fifteen minutes to minimize the time away from formal study. Even during the meals they took turns delivering discourses on Torah topics.

The high points of Silver's stay in Dvinsk were the opportunities to discuss Talmudic topics with the rabbis. Rabbi Meir Simhah achieved fame for his incisive commentary *Or*

Sameah on Maimonides' compendium of Jewish law, *Mishneh Torah*. His *Meshekh Hokhmah* on the Pentateuch appeared one year after his death. He began his rabbinate in Dvinsk in 1887 and was joined by Rabbi Joseph Rozin in 1889. The latter was acclaimed throughout the Jewish world as the "Rogachover Gaon" after his birthplace. His erudition and profundity were legendary. His many works appeared under the title *Tzafenat Pa'neah*. The relationship between these two geniuses was exemplary although they were totally different in temperament and disposition. Rav Meir Simhah was completely composed, sedate in his deportment, and he always attempted to appease and calm those who approached him. The "Rogachover" was rather quick, impatient, and highly critical of other rabbinical scholars who did not measure up to his own unequaled standards. Silver related that Rav Meir Simhah had said of the "Rogachover":

> People say that Rabbi Rozin possesses a phenomenal memory.
> This assessment is completely incorrect. A person can only be
> described as having an excellent memory when he recalls that
> which he studied many years before. The "Rogachover,"
> however, is able to constantly review and study the entire
> range of rabbinic literature.[5]

A year later Silver moved from Dvinsk to Vilna, the center of Lithuanian Jewry. The census of 1902 showed about 80,000 Jews in a total population of 162,633.[6] Vilna was popularly described as the "Jerusalem of Lithuania," a term which probably originated with Napoleon I when he led his Grand Army through in 1812. In Vilna Silver came into contact with Rabbi Hayyim Ozer Grodzenski, the individual who had the greatest influence on his life and ideals. Born in 1863 in Ivia, a small city near Vilna, Rav Hayyim Ozer later studied at the advanced Volozhin Yeshivah. This school was then enjoying its golden period prior to its forced closing by the Russian government in 1892 because

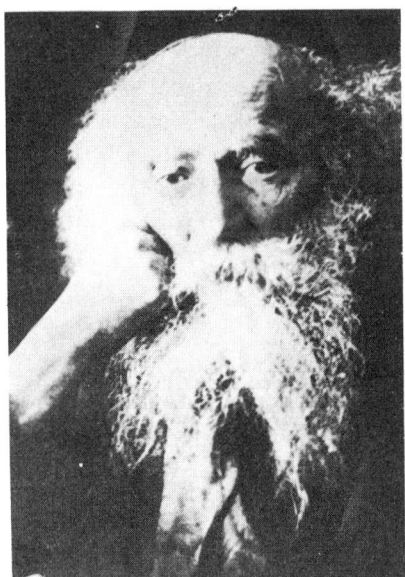

Leaders of European Jewry who had a profound influence on the life of Rabbi Eliezer Silver. *Clockwise from upper left-hand corner*: Rabbi Hayyim Ozer Grodzenski of Vilna; Rabbi Hayyim Soloveitchik of Brisk; Rabbi Meir Simhah ha-Kohen of Dvinsk; Rabbi Joseph Rozin of Dvinsk

Rabbinical delegation which visited President William H. Taft in 1912.
Left to right: Reverend Glushok of Washington, D.C.; Rabbis Isaac Siegel
of Bayonne; Abraham Alperstein of New York; Gedaliah Silverstone of
Washington, D.C.; David Ginsburg of Wilkes-Barre; Jacob Redelheim of
New York; Eliezer Silver of Harrisburg

Rabbis Dovber
Kahane-Shapiro
of Kovno and
Eliezer Silver

it refused to introduce secular study. In 1887, upon the demise of his father-in-law, Rav Hayyim Ozer was invited by the Vilna community to succeed him as one of its three *dayanim*, judges of the community's ecclesiastical court. The other members of the *Bet Din* were the well-known Rabbis Shlomo ha-Kohen and Betzalel ha-Kohen, popularly called the "Kohanim ha-Gedolim." Both men were famed for their knowledge and their ability to render decisions on the most complicated of *halakhic* questions. Nevertheless, it was felt that the twenty-four year old Rabbi Grodzenski would be a worthy colleague for these scholars. With the passage of time, it became apparent that Rav Hayyim Ozer was more than just one of the Vilna *rabanim* but rather the chief rabbi of Vilna. Upon the death of Rabbi Isaac Elchanan Spektor of Kovno in 1896, Rav Hayyim Ozer was gradually acknowledged as Rabbi Spektor's successor as the leading scholar-respondent-statesman of the Orthodox Jewish world. The Vilna community later decided to officially elect him as its Chief Rabbi. However, he refused since he desired to continue the Vilna tradition of not officially designating a chief rabbi. Instead he retained his previous title of "Moreh Tzedek," teacher of righteousness. The three volumes of Rabbi Grodzenski's published responsa, *Ahiezer*, were later to become basic tools of rabbinic research and decision-making.

Following the closing of the Volozhin Yeshivah, Rav Hayyim Ozer organized study sessions for advanced yeshivah students in Vilna. His lectures were soon attended by leading young rabbinical scholars, and the school became known as the *kibbutz* of Rav Hayyim Ozer. Among the foremost students studying in the group at this time were future rabbinical leaders such as Yehezkel Abramsky of Slutsk, London and Jerusalem; Moshe Avigdor Amiel of Antwerp and Tel Aviv; Shmuel Yitzhak Hillman of London and Jerusalem; Reuven Katz of Bayonne and Petah Tikvah; and Shlomo Polachek, widely known as the "Illui of Meitshet" and later of Lida, Bialystok and New York. Eliezer

Silver joined this select group in the *kibbutz*. To avoid the meddlings of the Russian government, Rabbi Grodzenski divided his school into four less conspicuous study groups. Each studied in a different Vilna synagogue with one group being particularly noted for its extraordinary diligence. Silver chose to join this unit since he studied from fifteen to eighteen hours a day, and devoted three entire nights a week to study. At times Rav Hayyim Ozer advised him to decrease his study hours so that his health would not be impaired. Silver, nevertheless, continued at his own intense pace. Blessed with a phenomenal memory, he soon earned a niche among the pre-eminent scholars in the *kibbutz*. For about half a year, Silver did curtail his Torah learning to about twelve hours a day. He devoted the remaining time to mastering the Russian and Hebrew languages and cognate subjects. He also found time to keep up with the latest *Haskalah* literature which abounded in Vilna which was also a center of Jewish Enlightenment. Silver read the poetry, essays, and belles-lettres of the foremost Hebrew literary figures of the age. Years later, he could quote from memory the poems of Bialik and analyze what he considered the errors in Ahad ha-Am's essays.

Silver's emphasis in his Torah studies was unique. The rabbis had always stressed the superiority of the Babylonian Talmud over its Jerusalem counterpart. The former was considered the more reliable since it was redacted at a later date so that its editors also had the Jerusalem version before them. Thus any decision contrary to that of the Jerusalem Talmud meant that the latter was rejected. As a result of this approach a myriad of commentaries were composed on the Babylonian Talmud, while the Jerusalem text remained comparatively obscure. Silver, however, devoted almost equal time to both versions and mastered the two branches of the Talmud. In addition, he daily studied all four divisions of the *Shulhan Arukh* and its commentaries. On one occasion Rav Hayyim Ozer questioned how his student could daily concentrate on so many different subjects. When the seventeen-year-old youngster responded with his latest Torah insights and novellae, the rabbi of Vilna kissed him in front of the other scholars and communal leaders then present in his office.

Rabbi Grodzenski was more than just a teacher for his disciple. His rabbinic deportment and selflessness were also a constant example and source of guidance. Silver observed how his mentor always retained his calm and composure despite the continual vexatious communal problems and difficult *halakhic* questions brought before him. Even when his only child, a teenage daughter, became seriously ill with a disease which later claimed her life, Rav Hayyim Ozer retained his composure. He comforted others, continued his public work, and unremittingly answered the ever-increasing amount of inquiries he received.

Silver also beheld his teacher's harmonious relationships with his colleagues. During this period there already was much dissension among the leading rabbis regarding consequential topics such as Zionism and secular endeavor. Although himself a non-Zionist, Rav Hayyim Ozer refused to allow into his home any pamphlets or periodicals which vilified the Mizrachi, the religious Zionist movement, and its idealistic forerunners. Once he abruptly cut off an acquaintance who was mocking Rabbi Isaac Jacob Reines, one of the founders and first head of the Mizrachi movement. Rabbi Grodzenski declared that such defamation was an affront to Reines who was a rabbinic scholar and graduate of the Volozhin Yeshivah. On the other hand the Vilna rabbi would swiftly and energetically act to aid those who requested his help. In particular, he outdid himself when the supplicant was an erudite student of the Talmud.

In 1900 Silver's father advised him to go to Brisk to acquaint himself with the new method of Talmudic study advocated by Rabbi Hayyim Soloveitchik.[7] This system stressed incisive analysis, exact classification, critical independence, and emphasis on

Maimonides' *Mishneh Torah*. Rabbi Soloveitchik had begun to instruct the outstanding students of the Volozhin Yeshivah in its final decade of activity. After its forced closing, Rav Hayyim joined his father in Brisk (Brest-Litovsk), where the latter was the rabbi. After his father's death in 1892, the younger Soloveitchik succeeded him and became widely known and revered as "Rav Hayyim Brisker."

Together with his closest colleague, Shlomo Polachek, Silver arrived in Brisk.[8] The *Meitsheter* had already studied with Rabbi Soloveitchik and was his most beloved pupil. Rabbi Polachek was later to become the head of the Talmud department in the Lida Yeshivah which Reines organized in 1905. In 1922 Polachek emigrated to the United States to serve as the senior *rosh yeshivah* in the Rabbi Isaac Elchanan Theological Seminary, the forerunner of Yeshiva University. Silver and the *Meitsheter* remained close friends until the latter's untimely death in 1928.

In Brisk Silver not only studied with Rav Hayyim but also observed his deportment and concern for the less fortunate. When he first arrived Silver went to Rabbi Soloveitchik to present a letter of recommendation from Rabbi Grodzenski. Rav Hayyim was then in the *Bet Din Shtible* in conference with the Brisker *Av-Bet-Din*, Rabbi Simhah Zelig Reguer, and the other *dayanim*. While Silver awaited the end of their conference, he saw a pauper enter their room. Completely ignoring the presence of the rabbinic luminaries, the poor man sat down at the table and ate his bread and apple. Afterwards he took a nap on the couch in the anteroom. All the time Rav Hayyim cautioned his colleagues not to rebuke or hinder the down-and-out individual.[9]

After his stay in Brisk, Silver returned to Vilna to continue his studies at Rav Hayyim Ozer's *kibbutz*. He periodically visited with his other teachers and continued his incessant learning. Silver later received his rabbinic ordination from Rabbi Grodzenski and the senior member of the Vilna *Bet Din*, Rabbi

Shlomo ha-Kohen.[10] He was also ordained by Rabbi Meir Bassin, the spiritual leader of the Vilna suburb, Shnipershuk, and a future Vilna *dayan*.[11]

In 1906 the young rabbi met Bassia Aranowitz. Unlike the then contemporary practice it was not a prearranged match. With his customary independence of character, Silver chose his own mate. Bassia, from a poor but eminent Vilna family, was related to both Rabbis ha-Kohen of the *Bet Din*. Later that year the young couple married. Their union was eventually blessed with four children. David, born in 1907, graduated from the Rabbi Isaac Elchanan Theological Seminary and became the rabbi of Harrisburg. Yetta, born in 1910, married a member of Yeshiva College's first graduating class of 1932 who later became a physician, Dr. Louis Izenstein of Springfield. Twins, Bessie and Nathan, were born in 1912. Bessie later married a widely known rabbinic scholar and author, Rabbi Yehuda Gershuni of Grodno, Jerusalem, and New York. Nathan studied in the Rabbi Isaac Elchanan Theological Seminary and later became a cardiologist in Cincinnati.

After his marriage, Silver was called to serve in the Russian Army. As was the common practice he could have arranged for an exemption through the good offices of Rav Hayyim Ozer, but instead chose to emigrate to the United States. In Vilna he constantly heard about the rabbinic scholars who previously emigrated to the New World. In particular, he knew about the many disciples of Rabbi Isaac Elchanan Spektor who were already in America. In addition, Bassia had relatives who were successfully integrated into the American scene. The challenge of the distant American shores also appealed to Silver's self-directing spirit. Above all, his mentor Rav Hayyim Ozer concurred with his decision and gave him a hearty letter of commendation for his future endeavors:

The erudite Rabbi Eliezer Silver, the son of the *gaon* Rabbi

Bunim Tzemah of Dusat, has studied in our *kibbutz* for exceptional students these past few years. His diligence was superb and he became expert in the entire Talmud and cognate literature. His high level of knowledge is only equaled by his deep love for Torah.

It is superfluous for me to declare how grateful I will be for assistance extended to this Torah personage. I will cherish and honor those who seek the welfare of Torah and its adherents.[12]

The young couple arrived in New York in early 1907. Aided by his wife's family during his initial adjustment, Silver worked for her uncle as a salesman in the garment industry. Later he sold insurance. Gradually he contacted his colleagues to plan his proper role on the American scene. Silver also visited the Lower East Side's Rabbi Isaac Elchanan Theological Seminary. Popularly known as the Yeshiva, this school was the first advanced American Torah institution. It continued the tradition of the European yeshivot in teaching Torah *lishmah*, the study of Talmud and its commentaries solely for their own sake. By 1907 many of the students were already European trained rabbinical scholars who continued their studies at the Yeshiva during their initial period of adjustment. During one of his visits, Silver discussed intricate Talmudic topics with the students. After he left, one of the group remarked, "What a shame that such a fine scholar chose to emigrate here. America will destroy him while in Europe he would have become a Torah sage."[13]

The new arrival's abilities were brought to the attention of Professor Solomon Schechter of the Jewish Theological Seminary of America and the founder of Conservative Judaism. Schechter, who constantly sought to attract new talent to his institution, invited Silver to the Seminary and offered him a teaching fellowship. He expected Silver to master the scientific approach to Talmudic scholarship during this period. While Silver had only the foggiest notion of the Seminary's ideals at that time, his interview convinced him that it was not the place for him — Schechter sat without his head covered during their meeting.

Silver began to visit communities along the Eastern Seaboard. Tens of vibrant communities were already organized by East Europeans who were constantly moving from the main immigrant centers to outlying areas. When he came to Worcester, Massachusetts, Silver encountered an entire group of *landsleit*, people from his own area in Lithuania. They were so thrilled that the son of the "Dusater Rav" was in America that they immediately offered him the rabbinate of one of their synagogues. Rabbi Silver, however, rejected this position since he considered it an infringement upon the community's Rabbi Hayyim Silber.

Finally, towards the latter part of 1907, Rabbi Bernard Levinthal of Philadelphia brought Silver to the attention of the Jewish community in Harrisburg, Pennsylvania. Within the immigrant community it was not generally the norm for an individual synagogue to engage a rabbi. It was rather the leading laymen who banded together to choose a spiritual leader. They provided him with a meager salary through their individual contributions. The rabbi supplemented his income with the gifts and fees received for his rabbinic functions. The rabbi did not associate with only one congregation, but instead serviced all the immigrant synagogues. Rabbi Silver thus became the Orthodox spiritual leader of Harrisburg. His salary was six dollars per week. This sum was raised by some individuals donating a quarter a week or on alternating weeks. One of the group accepted upon himself the meritorious deed of weekly making the rounds and collecting the quarters.

The first Jewish settlers in Harrisburg were German and English immigrants. They arrived in the 1840s and regularly assembled for Sabbath and Festival services. In 1852 this group formed the first synagogue Ohev Shalom. It was Orthodox until 1867 when it adopted the Reform ritual. The main Orthodox houses of worship at the time of Silver's arrival were Chizuk Emunah (1884), Kesher Israel Congregation (1902), and Machzike Hadas (1904). By 1907 the Harrisburg Jewish community numbered about 2,000.[14]

Scattered among the newcomers at this time were proficient European trained Talmudists. Some also reached Harrisburg and despite their rapid Americanization they were the backbone of the local synagogues. These men gave Silver his early lessons in the realities of American life. He organized a *Hevrah Shas*, a daily study group for the Mishnah and Talmud. The learned men attended even though most had already become Sabbath desecrators in Harrisburg. When their young rabbi questioned how they could deviate from Torah norms, they pointed to the most learned layman in town. He was a former student of Rabbi Naftali-Tzvi Yehudah Berlin, popularly known as the *Netziv* (from the initials of his names), in the Volozhin Yeshivah. In Harrisburg he not only transgressed the Sabbath and *Kashrut* laws but also rarely attended the synagogue.

When the study group completed its first Talmudic tractate, Rabbi Silver arranged for a public celebration of the *siyyum*. With all their religious infractions, there still was a deep rooted folk love for Torah within the immigrant community. Many came to the festivities, including the former Volozhin student. He was mesmerized by the rabbi's *pilpul* and soon became Silver's devotee and confidant. He gradually returned to the observance of Torah and sat closest to the rabbi at the daily Talmud class.

Silver continued his own studies at an unabated pace. The community was small and there were only limited demands upon his time. In addition to the hours eked out by day, he also studied late into the night. He rose early in the morning and devoted the time before the morning prayers to learning. In Harrisburg, Silver particularly added to his knowledge of the Jerusalem Talmud and cognate literature.

The reaction to his preoccupation with study by the more ignorant portion of his community heightened Silver's awareness of the local scene. While most of the Harrisburg residents were proud of their rabbi's dedication to scholarship, for it reminded them of the competent rabbinical scholars of their native European towns, others were skeptical. One of these challenged the assertion of a more erudite immigrant that the new rabbi was an eminent scholar. He asked, "If he is so learned, then why must he continue studying?"

On another occasion, Rabbi Silver was forced out of a synagogue by its president. Since Silver resided, at that time, in rather cramped quarters, he studied by day in one of the local synagogues. Its president considered it disgraceful for the gentile passers-by to hear the rabbi's sing-song voice of study. The president thereupon shut off the synagogue's electricity so that the rabbi could not study there. Silver never forgave this uncouth behavior; he never returned to this particular house of worship.

Silver also began to concern himself with the temporal well-being of his community. He organized a *Gemilat Hesed*, free loan society. This organization made interest free loans available to Harrisburg residents for both personal and business needs. Silver gradually supplemented the transactions of this society by personally helping the many people turning to him. At times he would himself borrow money in order to lend it to others. Silver also organized a local *Hakhnasat Orehim* hospitality association. Harrisburg was then a major railroad terminal and many itinerants stopped off there. It was common for immigrants to journey from city to city to seek a livelihood. Some were headed for distant locations in the Midwest where they hoped to settle through the aid of relatives or *landsleit*. Often the travelers did not have the means to purchase a train ticket directly to their destination. They rather moved along from one Jewish community to the next, being helped at each stopover to reach their next goal. Silver founded the *Hakhnasat Orehim* to aid these transients with lodging, meals and finances.

Rabbi Silver also began to acquaint himself with the communities beyond his own. As the rabbi in Harrisburg, he found himself being called upon by Jews far beyond the confines of his own immediate synagogues. There was no qualified spiritual leader between Harrisburg and Pittsburgh, although many Jewish communities existed in between. Each had its own small synagogue and *shohet*. The same situation also prevailed southward between Harrisburg and Baltimore, eastward to Philadelphia and northward to Rochester. Time and again Silver traveled to these communities to guide the *shohatim* and to check the validity of the existing *mikvaot*. Silver particularly aided with the upkeep and support of the ritual baths. When queried why he so resolutely served this cause, Silver responded:

> There are certain *mitzvot* which are neglected and orphaned in the United States. The rabbis considered "the *Bet Din* . . . the father of orphans."[15] Therefore, I deem myself the guardian of this *mitzvah* which is so neglected on the American scene.

At times the lay leaders and would-be religious functionaries came to him to check on their qualifications or to resolve disputes.

Silver's self-confidence and courage also increased with his growing involvement in the American scene. At first he continued the conventional rabbinical practice of a beginner's not administering *gittin*. The strictest care must be taken with the formula of the document of divorce, which is mostly in Aramaic. Any deviation in the text or the procedure may void the *get* and leave the woman in her prior matrimonial status. After he had sent previous parting couples to the elder rabbis in either Philadelphia, Pittsburgh, or Baltimore, another difficult case developed in Harrisburg. A young husband was ill and faced a perilous and unsure operation. If the husband died the childless woman would be required to receive the *halitzah* release from his brother who was still in Europe. To avoid this possible entanglement, Rabbi Silver had a colleague administer a conditional divorce to which the husband reluctantly agreed. However, the elder rabbi erred in the condition and Silver had to plead with the husband to grant a second divorce. He finally agreed but only after receiving five hundred dollars from his wife's family. After this incident Silver began to administer his own *gittin* and no longer sent the couples before other rabbis.

Silver was also becoming aware of the overall American rabbinical scene. A lasting impression was left upon him by the strength of an organized rabbinate when the *Agudat Harabanim* scored an early partial success. In the year of Silver's American arrival, Levinthal led the organization in a campaign against the newspaper *Die Wahrheit*. Founded in 1905, it stressed socialism and secular Jewish national aspirations, yet it enjoyed a large circulation among the observant immigrant element due to its pro-Zionist policy. Rabbi Levinthal insisted that it cease publishing on the Sabbath. Vilified and attacked by the newspaper, Levinthal stood his ground, supported by all his colleagues. Although the Sabbath edition continued, the paper was denied advertisements and financial support by Orthodox Jews.[16]

Rabbi Silver began to attend assemblies and conventions of the *Agudat Harabanim*. It was customary for each session to open with a learned discourse on a difficult Talmudic passage. The chairman would call upon one of those present, and as no one knew who would be chosen, each came prepared to discuss the topic of his choice. Before officially joining the organization, Silver attended a meeting in Boston. The chairman, Rabbi Shalom Jaffe, honored the newcomer with the lecture. Silver delivered a masterful one hour discourse on the Talmudic topic: "Living creatures are important and cannot be neutralized."[17] The elder rabbis listened with rapt attention and afterwards eagerly invited the young scholar to join their ranks. A few years later Silver was once again honored in this fashion by Rabbi Levinthal at a convention in Philadelphia. During the many addresses Silver later delivered within the *Agudat Harabanim* forum, he extended this practice by always beginning with a Torah discourse. In 1912 he was elected to the organization's executive committee and a year later became the committee's vice chairman.

During this period Silver participated in his first national function for the immigrant rabbinate. On June 12, 1912 he was part of a delegation which called upon William Howard Taft, the twenty-seventh president of the United States. It was the first time that such a group of rabbis was received by a president. Their intent was to encourage the president to pursue a more vigorous policy of protest against Russia because of its intense persecution and discrimination of its Jewish citizens. They also wanted to add their voices to the protests over the lingering passport controversy. The Russian government deemed it an offense when its subject became a citizen of another country without its consent. Upon returning to Russia, the violator was subject to arrest and punishment unless he previously obtained permission to enter. Jews, whether they were formerly Russian citizens or not, were not admitted into Russia unless they obtained prior permission from the Czarist government. As a result of this policy the American Department of State would not issue passports to former Russian subjects or to Jews with intentions of entering Russian territory unless it was assured that there was consent to their admission. The American Jewish Committee, led by Louis Marshall, had demanded revision of this policy. Now the East European newcomers were likewise adding their dissent.[18]

After meeting at the Union Station terminal, the group headed for the White House. On the way they debated whether they should keep their hats on in the presence of the president.

Silver insisted that they leave them on so they could honor the president with the recitation of the blessing, "Who hast given of Thy glory to mortal man." When the rabbis finally were received by the president, Taft quickly donned his hat out of respect to his guests. Greatly relieved at the president's gesture, they recited the blessing and translated it into English. Rabbi Silver then blessed the president in Hebrew, and the cantor of a local Washington congregation translated his words into English. Their meeting with President Taft continued in a cordial and relaxed atmosphere. This visit began a warm relationship between Silver and the Taft family which later found expression in his kinship with the president's son, Senator Robert A. Taft, "Mr. Republican" of Cincinnati.

While Silver gradually mastered the subtleties of American life, he constantly thought about his parents and mentors on the other side of the ocean. He had promised his father a visit once he became established in his new home. After becoming a naturalized American citizen, Silver once again crossed the seas following Passover of 1914. In Dusat he found his aged parents ministering to the needs of a now rapidly changing community. The tensions preceding World War I were already substantial. Silver was still there when the conflict formally broke out on August 1, 1914. During this period a local Jewish soldier returned for rest and recuperation following an injury sustained in battle. The wounded soldier testified that another local boy, the son of the butcher Zalman, was killed in the same fray. When Zalman came to ask the rabbi whether he should sit *shivah* for his son, the younger Silver urged his father to advise him not to. Silver was apprehensive lest the soldier who was himself seriously wounded during the battle be mistaken. While many of the local scholars differed with his ruling, months later a letter arrived from the butcher's son. A few years afterward the young man returned home and all recalled the ruling of the rabbi's visiting son.[19]

While in Europe Silver also sought out his teachers. He visited Dvinsk where Rav Meir Simhah and the "Rogachover" were gratified to see him once again. Rav Meir Simhah questioned Silver about the American scene at length. He particularly enquired about Rabbi Album of Chicago who had been his study partner in his youth. When informed of Album's American difficulties, Rav Meir Simhah remarked:

> Had Rabbi Album remained in Lithuania, he would by now be acclaimed as a leading *gaon* and Torah luminary. However, your United States devours its true rabbis and belittles greatness.[20]

Silver also observed his mentors laboring to assist the greater Jewish community. While he was in Dvinsk a request arrived from Warsaw for ten thousand rubles in order to provide kosher food for the Jewish conscripts. The wealthy lay leaders desired to divert the sum from local communal funds. The "Rogachover" emphatically declared that this money belonged to the local poor and his affluent followers soon donated the entire amount.

Silver also visited Vilna and was reunited with Rav Hayyim Ozer. Here he observed his master daily preoccupied with sustaining the hundreds of war refugees streaming through Vilna. On one occasion close to two thousand needy and distressed migrants had to be provided for. Within hours Rabbi Grodzenski made all the necessary arrangements for their food and lodging. Every spare moment was utilized by teacher and disciple to discuss Talmudic topics. Silver was also privileged to deliver a public lecture in the main Vilna synagogue.

Although Silver was scheduled to return to America during the fall, the war now subverted his original plans. The Russian government reinforced its previous stand and refused to recognize an American passport held by a Jew. So, Silver remained stranded in his native environs for another seven months. During this period he attempted to inform his wife and congregants of his critical situation. Apprehensive lest Russian censorship authorities confiscate his letter, Silver finally sent an enigmatic message. It was in the form of a postcard addressed to the New York Orthodox daily, *Judisches Tageblatt*. The contents of this communication discussed the unavailability of certain volumes. Silver requested that the recipients inform the yeshivah head and students in Harrisburg and the judges of the *Agudat Harabanim* of his lack of success. Silver claimed that these missing books were titled: *The Proper Path, At The Crossroads*, and *The Illuminated Way*. He also made intricate references to appropriate Talmudic topics and commentaries. He referred to the prohibition against crossing the *tehum*, the boundary beyond which one must not walk on the Sabbath. He also cited the *Milhamot Hashem* ("Wars of the Lord") of Nahmanides. Silver indicated that he could not be more precise because of the need to guard one's tongue as indicated in the *Shemirat Ha-Lashon* of the *Hafetz Hayyim*. He also stated that "all the gates are locked except for the gate of tears."[21]

The editorial staff of the *Tageblatt* could not understand the postcard. They were fearful lest the rabbi of Harrisburg had become incoherent due to his dire European circumstances. A staff member brought the card to Rabbi Jaffe, then the president of the *Agudat Harabanim*. He carefully studied its contents and soon deciphered its message. Silver's wife, community, and colleagues were immediately informed of his plight. There was general relief that he was still alive since rumors already began to spread that he had perished in the fighting. In 1915 Silver managed to cross the border from Russia into Norway under an assumed name. He supposedly had been called to officiate at High Holyday services in Norway. Once on neutral soil, Silver readily made his way back to the United States.

Arriving at the Jaffe home in New York, Silver telegraphed Harrisburg. In order not to shock his wife, he wired a lay leader of the congregation to break the news to her. The congregant was not in, and his children instead rushed to the Silver home shouting, "Rebbitzen, your husband has returned." She fainted on hearing their cries. Neighbors revived her, and the rest of the telegram was read. It requested that Jaffe's home be called. They then quickly walked two blocks to the closest store which had a telephone. Within minutes, Silver was speaking to his wife. A few days later the rabbi of Harrisburg was reunited with his family and community.

The war situation so influenced Silver that henceforth he dedicated much effort to alleviating the plight of Jewish refugees and war victims. He was particularly concerned for the scholars and students of the yeshivot located in the zones of open hostilities and combat. Silver supported the fund raising activities of the Central Relief Committee, formed during his absence by Orthodox Jewish leaders on October 4, 1914. Louis Kamaiky, publisher of the *Jewish Morning Journal*, was its president. Harry Fischel, a prominent New York builder and realtor, served as treasurer. The funds raised by this group and other American relief committees were distributed overseas by the American Jewish Joint Distribution Committee. Popularly known as the "Joint," or JDC, this umbrella group was formed on November 27, 1914. Its help during the war was paramount toward strengthening the standing and survival of the European Jewish community.

With all that the Central Relief Committee and the Joint were accomplishing, Silver was still concerned about the tribulations of the rabbis and scholars. He knew that many would be ashamed to actually request help and others would be overlooked due to their modesty and reticence. While in Europe, Rav Hayyim Ozer already urged him to form a charity to aid these individuals. Silver wrote:

When I finally succeeded in departing from Europe, I took

leave of the *Gaon*, Rav Hayyim Ozer. He requested that upon
my return to America I should propose that the *Agudat
Harabanim* form an Ezras Torah. I thank the Lord that when I
arrived the rabbinical leaders were already discussing such a
plan. Two prophets both envisioned the same need.[22]

In 1915, Rabbi Silver aided his colleague Rabbi Israel
Rosenberg in forming the Ezras Torah. Rosenberg was a pre-
eminent Talmudic scholar who arrived in the United States in
1902.[23] He also worked jointly with Silver in many subsequent
endeavors. The Ezras Torah gradually expanded into a general
charity, distributing hundreds of thousands of dollars to many
needy persons. Particularly it reached out to those who were not
being helped by the other more prominent charities. Due to the
guiding hands of its rabbinic leadership, only Ezras Torah truly
comprehended the heartbeat of the overseas Torah scholars.
Rosenberg became the new organization's chairman while Silver
served as vice chairman. The *Agudat Harabanim* and the
American Mizrachi Organization were the main supporters of
the Ezras Torah. The seventh of Adar, the traditional anniversary of both the birth and death of Moses, was designated as the
focal date for public appeals for this charity. Another colleague,
Rabbi Joseph Elijah Henkin, a leading graduate of the Slutsk
Yeshivah, became the executive director of Ezras Torah in 1925.
He remained in this post, in close cooperation with Rosenberg
and Silver, until his death in 1973.

Silver also played a central role in salvaging a foundering
venture to publish the first American edition of the entire
Talmud. Distressing reports were received in the United States
that the large printing plants in Vilna, Warsaw, and Lemberg
were destroyed during the fighting. It was feared that there
would be a scarcity of Talmudic volumes due to the loss of the
printing plates. This undertaking was originally sponsored by
the *Agudat Harabanim* and the Rabbi Isaac Elchanan Theological Seminary of New York. They selected the Eagle Publishing

Company of Montreal, Canada, to print the massive twenty-volume set. The company proudly announced in late 1918 that it was moving to larger premises due to this project. The declaration stated:

> The printing establishment in Vilna, where it has hitherto been published, has, owing to war necessities, been closed. Montreal will henceforth be the only place in the world where the Babylonian Talmud will be published. The work will be in the hands of the Union of Orthodox Rabbis of the United States and Canada, assisted by the Rabbi Isaac Elchanan Theological Seminary.[24]

Rabbi Bernard Revel, the president of the Yeshiva, was chosen honorary chairman of the Talmud Publication Fund while Rosenberg became chairman and Silver was elected secretary. Soon after the committee started to function, antagonism to the venture developed among some of the lay leaders of the Yeshiva. They felt that the project would be capitalized on by some of the rabbis. It was therefore not befitting the dignity of the rabbinical school to be involved in such a business venture. Revel was then in Tulsa, Oklahoma, assisting his wife's family in the petroleum industry. As the project started to break down, Silver reacted effectively by organizing a rabbinical committee to visit Revel in Tulsa.

On December 9, 1918, Rabbis Silver, Rosenberg, and Joseph Konvitz arrived in Tulsa. The latter, the son-in-law of the Ridbaz, had settled in America in 1915. He was then the rabbi of Elizabeth, New Jersey.[25] Together with Revel the group agreed that the project would be concluded solely by the rabbinical organization. The Yeshiva was to receive thirty sets of the published Talmud in return for its three thousand dollar investment. The printing was finally completed in 1920. The venture was a financial failure and the *Agudat Harabanim* lost much money. Nevertheless it did succeed in alleviating the pressing demands for Talmudic volumes throughout the Jewish world. Many sets were distributed gratuitously to yeshivot and rabbis in Europe and Palestine. The prestige of the organization and its leaders was greatly enhanced with the conclusion of this undertaking.

By the end of this turbulent decade, Silver had become widely known in American rabbinical circles. As a result of his many endeavors for his brethren, the rabbi of Harrisburg was now a public figure. In 1917 Silver was elected national treasurer of the *Agudat Harabanim*, and in 1923 a member of its presidium. Except for a brief interlude, Silver continued as the organization's president or presidium member until his passing away in 1968.

Notes

1. For the full details of the Silver genealogy see Menahem Glickman-Porush, *Ish Ha-Halakhah Veha-Maaseh* (Jerusalem, 1947), pp. 7-12; Eliezer Silver, *Anfei Erez* (New York, 1960), 1:9-10, and the diagram at the conclusion of the introduction to volume two of *Anfei Erez* (New York, 1965).

The details of Rabbi Silver's life in this entire volume are primarily based upon these sources; interviews with his son, Rabbi David L. Silver, on October 4, 1972 and July 24, 1974; and an unpublished MS by the latter.

2. Dusat was described by its native, Rabbi Joseph Morduchovitz (b. 1901) in an August 4, 1974 interview.

3. Peah 1:1, cf. Shab. 127a. For further description of the Lithuanian milieu see A. S. Sachs, *Worlds That Passed* (Philadelphia: The Jewish Publication Society of America, 1928), pp. 248-252; Benjamin L. Gordon, *Between Two Worlds* (New York, 1952), pp. 80-82; and Solomon Simon, *In The Thicket* (Philadelphia: The Jewish Publication Society of America, 1963), pp. 69, 86-88, 190-191.

4. For details of the Dvinsk community at this time see *The*

Jewish Encyclopedia, ed. Isidore Singer (New York: Funk and Wagnalls Company, 1904), 5:22.

For biographical studies of its two spiritual leaders see the author's "Rabbi Meir Simchah Ha-Kohen of Dvinsk," *Jewish Life*, January 1973/Shevat 5733, pp. 51-58, and Saul Silber, "The Gaon of Rogatchov," in *Jewish Leaders*, ed. Leo Jung (New York: Bloch Publishing Company, 1953), pp. 393-404. Cf. the analyses of their methods in Shlomo Joseph Zevin, *Ishim ve-Shitot* (Tel Aviv: Bitan Ha-Sefer, 1952), pp. 133-165 (Rabbi Ha-Kohen); pp. 71-131 (Rabbi Rozin).

5. Related in the name of Rabbi Silver by Rabbi Menahem Kasher in a July 16, 1974 interview.

6. See *The Jewish Encyclopedia* 12:530 for details of the Vilna Community at this time. For biographical studies of Vilna's Rabbi Hayyim Ozer Grodzenski see Aaron Sursky, *Ahiezer*, 2. vols. (Bene-Brak: Netzah, 1970), and the author's "Chaim Ozer Grodzenski," *Jewish Life*, May-June 1967/Sivan-Tammuz 5727, pp. 40-49.

7. For details of Rabbi Hayyim Soloveitchik and his method see Zevin, *Ishim Ve-Shitot*, pp. 39-70 and Eliezer Leoni (ed.), *Wolozhin* (Tel Aviv: The Wolozhin Landsleit Associations of Israel and the United States, 1970), pp. 209-214; and Joseph B. Soloveitchik, *Be-Sod ha-Yihud Ve-ha-Yahad* (Jerusalem: Orot, 1976), pp. 212-235.

8. For details of Rabbi Polachek's life see the author's "The Meitsheter Illui," *Jewish Life*, November-December 1967/Kislev-Teveth 5728, pp. 29-35, and *Bernard Revel*, pp. 115-118.

9. Related in the name of Rabbi Silver by Rabbi Samuel Chill in a February 26, 1974 interview. Cf. Silver, *Anfei Erez* 2:6.

10. Hayyim Greenberg (ed.), *Kovetz Rabbani Torani*, Nisan-Ellul 5729-1969, p. 5. Cf. the eulogy on Rabbi Silver by Rabbi Yehiel Michal Feinstein of Tel Aviv, *ibid.*, pp. 3-4, and the pamphlet, *Yemei Shenotai: Madbah Shel Avraham*, by Rabbi Abraham Ephraim Rosing (1971), p. 35.

11. Interview with Rabbi Bassin's son-in-law, Rabbi Israel Gustman, on October 22, 1972.

12. The original Hebrew document located in the Silver Archives at the home of Rabbi David Silver, Harrisburg. All subsequent cited documents are from these Archives unless otherwise noted.

13. Related to Rabbi David Silver by Rabbi David Rackman. The latter, an instructor at the Yeshiva during this period, later became a

successful businessman. His son, Rabbi Emanuel Rackman, became the assistant to the president of Yeshiva University and the spiritual leader of Manhattan's Fifth Avenue Synagogue and subsequently became president of Israel's Bar-Ilan University.

For David Rackman's biography see his *Kiryat Hanah David* (New York: Shulsinger Brothers, 1967), pp. 24-28.

14. *The Jewish Encyclopedia* 9:588 listed the Jewish population at 1200 in 1904. *AJYB:5686* (1925-1926) stated that its 1917 population was 4000.

15. Baba Kamma, 37a.

16. *K'vod Chachomim*, p. 23. Cf. Glickman, *Ish Ha-Halakhah Veha-Maaseh*, pp. 21-22, and Silver,*Anfei Erez* 1:11.

17. Zevahim, 73a; cf. Silver, *Anfei Erez* 1:13.

18. For details of this controversy see "The Passport Question," *AJYB; 5672* (1911-1912), pp. 19-128. The visit of the East European delegation with President Taft was detailed by Eliezer Silver, *They Fought For Our Cause* (The Influential Taft Family and their Attitude to Jewry), ed. Z.H. Wachsman (Toronto: Daily Hebrew Journal, 1946), pp. 5-7.

19. Eliezer Silver, "Talmudic Novellae" to Hayyim Eleazar Wachs, *Nefesh Hayah* (New York: Shulsinger Brothers, 1946), p. 6.

20. Silver, *Anfei Erez* 1:10-11 and clarified by Rabbi David L. Silver in the October 4, 1972 interview.

21. Cf. Baba Metzia, 59a. Details of the postcard are contained in a November 1914 Jewish newspaper clipping. Also see Glickman, *Ish Ha-Halakhah Veha-Maaseh*, pp. 29-30 and Silver, *Anfei Erez* 1:13-14.

22. *Sefer Ha-Yovel Shel Agudat Harabanim*, p. 69.

23. For Rabbi Rosenberg's biography and his association with the Ezras Torah see *Eduth LeYisroel*, ed. Oscar Z. Rand (New York: Ezras Torah Fund, n.d.), pp. 3-14. Cf. *Sefer Ha-Yovel Shel Agudat Harabanim*, pp. 64-71.

24. Press clipping dated October 23, 1918.

For details of this venture from the Rabbi Isaac Elchanan Theological Seminary point of view see the author's *Bernard Revel*, pp. 60-61.

25. For Rabbi Konvitz's biography see his *Divrei Joseph* (New York, 1947), 1:13-50. For his role in the Talmud venture see p. 23.

3

Springfield and Cincinnati

☆☆☆☆☆☆☆☆☆☆☆☆☆☆☆☆☆☆☆☆☆☆☆☆☆☆☆☆

Rabbi Silver accepted a call to the larger community of Springfield, Massachusetts in 1925. Unlike the circumstances in 1907 when Rabbi Levinthal had pressured the Harrisburg laymen to engage a rabbi, the Springfield group appealed to Silver. Jews had already settled in this city before the Civil War. With the increase of the East European immigration during the final decades of the nineteenth century, the Jewish community rapidly increased. The first synagogues, Bnai Jacob and Beth Israel, were organized in 1891-92. Within a decade five other small Orthodox congregations were established and there were 3,000 Jews in Springfield by 1907. The community numbered 6,000 by 1917 and 12,000 by 1927.[1] In 1921 the first Conservative synagogue was established and a Reform temple opened in 1932. Springfield was also an integral component of the over-all active Massachusetts Jewish community. Some of the other towns and cities with important Orthodox congregations included Worcester, New Bedford, Brockton, Boston and its adjacent areas such as Chelsea and Malden.

When four Springfield synagogues formed the United Orthodox Congregations in order to bring Silver to their city, they were facing chaos in the local *Kashrut* situation, and a strong personality was sought to rectify the situation. The community was gratified with Rabbi Silver's acceptance and over one thousand people attended his installation ceremony at the Beth Israel Synagogue. Silver soon succeeded in raising the local *Kashrut* standards. He formed a *Vaad Hakashrut* board to aid in this undertaking. In many communities only a few kosher butcher shops were truly reliable and the rest were granted questionable certification. In Springfield all such stores became trustworthy. Silver was later involved in a vehement local controversy because of his stringent standards. A local resident, who desecrated the Sabbath, was a partner in his brother's meat shop until 1929. The brother was a Sabbath observer and the store was therefore certified by Rabbi Silver. After the partnership dissolved, the non-observant brother opened his own shop. Silver refused to endorse this butcher and ordered the local *shohatim* to refrain from slaughtering cattle for him. The controversy intensified as the Council of Orthodox Rabbis of Massachusetts, of which Silver was chairman, supported their leader. The butcher, meanwhile, obtained the supervision of a nearby rabbi, a recent graduate of the Rabbi Isaac Elchanan Theological Seminary. Nevertheless, the new meat store suffered financial reverses due to Silver's prohibition. The proprietor challenged the legal authority of a rabbi "to interfere with his business and injure his property rights." On December 2, 1931 the Court ruled in Silver's favor. The judgment upheld the right of the rabbi and the *Vaad Hakashrut* to set standards for their supervision. It was found that:

> . . . the plaintiff has at different times and in diverse ways violated the Hebrew law with respect to the Sabbath and that he has refused to answer a summons to a *Din Torah* touching a controversy with his brother.

The decision stated:

> The plaintiff, by becoming a member of an Orthodox Jewish congregation and seeking to conduct a business with respect to kosher food which plays a highly important part in the Hebrew faith, must conform to the canons of that faith touching that subject if he desires to continue that business under

religious sanction. He cannot hold or gain that kind of
commercial advantage unless he complies with all requirements of the rules established by that religious sect as
prerequisite therefore, and he must also abide by the decisions
of the tribunals erected and constituted for the determination
of controversies concerning that subject. He cannot claim the
benefits of the business without accepting the burdens
attached to it. Incidental to his membership in the religious
organization and his undertaking to do this particular kind of
business, he impliedly consented to be governed in all essential matters by the decisions of boards established to end
disputes and contentions of this sort. Courts do not sit in
review of decisions thus rendered even though it may appear
that there has been an error of judgment, an innocent mistake
or failure to make a searching investigation. Courts are especially reluctant to interfere in a controversy which, like the
one at bar, rests largely upon ecclesiastical dogma and canon-
ical practices. As to matters of that nature, religious organizations are themselves entitled to a relatively free hand under
settled principles of law.[2]

Silver protested the contrary action of the Yeshiva graduate
in certifying the miscreant butcher. His letter to the heads of the
Rabbi Isaac Elchanan Theological Seminary was suggestive of
the then evolving discord between the elder European trained
rabanim and the younger American rabbis. Silver wrote:

In the name of the rabbis and *geonim* who comprise the
Council of Orthodox Rabbis, I am issuing this violent protest
against the graduate of the Yeshiva . . . who desecrated the
name of God and ruined himself when he publicly contra-
dicted with the insolence of a prostitute all the rabbinical
members of our Council, and permitted that which we have
forbidden . . . stating that our rulings are foolish and that he
is well acquainted with all the laws. . . . And when asked if he
knows the Chairman of our Council, he acted as if the
Chairman wasn't worth knowing and he boasted that he had

Rabbi Eliezer Silver, 1925

Installation of Rabbi Eliezer Silver in Springfield in 1925. *Front row, left to right:* unidentified; Rabbis Samuel Friedman; Bernard Revel; Israel Rosenberg; Moses Z. Margolies; Eliezer Silver; Bernard Levinthal; Sheftel Kramer; Baruch Epstein (author of *Torah Temima*). Between Rosenberg and Margolies is Rabbi Meyer Berlin. Between Levinthal and Kramer is Rabbi Judah Levenberg. In the back row, at the extreme right is Rabbi Solomon Polachek, with Rabbi Judah Forer to the left of him

Rabbi Eliezer Silver speaking at the dedication of the new Kesher Israel synagogue in Harrisburg in 1949

Agudat Harabanim convention in 1926. *Left to right*: Rabbis Eliezer Silver; Israel Rosenberg; Moses Z. Margolies; Ezekiel Libshitz of Kalish, Poland; Bernard Levinthal; Isaac Siegel; Joseph Konvitz

no desire to be a member of an organization such as the *Agudat Harabanim.* . . .

It is understood that the Yeshiva became a laughing stock when he stated that his rulings were correct and the rulings of our Chairman were incorrect. . . . We decided at our meeting that if the Yeshiva doesn't publicly revoke his ordination and bring him up on charges, then we will present the entire case before the next convention of the *Agudat Harabanim* and demand that they publicly disqualify him.

Silver's victory was hailed beyond the borders of Springfield. A headline in New York's Yiddish daily, *Jewish Day*, declared it a "Great Victory for the Council of Orthodox Rabbis of Massachusetts." Because of this triumph, the Sioux City, Iowa, Jewish community later turned to Silver for guidance in initiating legal proceedings against a local butcher. A Sioux City attorney thus described their problem:

The Jewish people of Sioux City are experiencing a very difficult situation in reference to the distribution of kosher meat by a butcher who does not comply with the Jewish faith and traditions . . . the fact being that he has married a woman who has not had a Jewish divorce.[3]

Due to the close mutual relationship between the Massachusetts Jewish communities, Silver also became involved in state-wide *Kashrut* supervision. Time and again he was called upon to mediate in the greater Boston area where there was constant *Kashrut* strife. In 1929 the national *Agudat Harabanim* and the local rabbinical council requested that Silver raise the standards in the Boston abattoir. One of the supervising rabbis objected to Silver's intrusion into his domain. Although a recognized scholar, this rabbi had long been in conflict with his local colleagues. Silver refused to be intimidated and instead wrote to his recalcitrant associate on October 28, 1929:

I love and honor all rabbinic scholars, and particularly such an eminent sage such as yourself. Nevertheless, the other rabbis of Massachusetts are likewise dear to me, and many of them are also scholars. I am certain that you all seek peace, and the contention is caused by laymen. I am determined to establish harmony between the rabbis. Why should Judaism and the rabbinate continue to be desecrated? Why should the enemies of Torah continue to rejoice in Boston? In all my accomplishments I will be concerned with your welfare and that of the other rabbis. I have therefore consented to the requests of the *Agudat Harabanim* and the Council of Orthodox Rabbis to undertake this task . . . .

I will be in the Boston slaughterhouse next Wednesday. I have heard that the *Kashrut* standards there are below that which we have achieved in New York, Chicago, Newark, and Philadelphia. I am sure it is not your fault but rather the result of the propietor's negligence.

Please meet me in the slaughterhouse, but not in a contentious and quarrelsome mood. Let us join in peace and dedication. Let us display to the greater Boston community that scholars are the true builders of peace.

Although Silver succeeded in raising the Boston *Kashrut* standards, the city still remained a center of rabbinic dispute. In his own city, however, his innovations fared well. When Silver later left Springfield in 1931, he recorded his *Kashrut* regulations for the community's continued achievement. Among these were his insistence that the local butchers and delicatessens only be allowed to purchase meat outside Springfield from sources with the same high level of *Kashrut* observance. Only slaughterhouses where at least two *shohatim* and a supervisor worked together were acceptable. The local *Vaad Hakashrut* was subject to the rulings of the rabbi of Springfield. He was to be selected by the Orthodox synagogues in consultation with the *Agudat Harabanim*. The city was to continue to employ the six *shohatim* who already possessed established claims to their positions. A *shohet* could only be removed for delinquent behavior following a *Din*

Torah before a rabbinic court of law. The *Vaad Hakashrut* in consultation with the rabbi could engage additional *shohatim* if the community expanded. Silver concluded his statement of regulations with the "hope that all will be observed and that there will be no *Kashrut* controversy in the future."[4]

Silver also built a new *mikveh* in Springfield and started a campaign for a new Talmud Torah building. He announced a $40,000 drive and circulated a letter issued by the *Agudat Harabanim* supporting his initiative. Dated February 11, 1929, it was hopeful that:

> ... the members of your community will appreciate and properly evaluate your efforts to achieve this goal. They will answer your call and emulate your example of love for your people and its Torah. The laymen will generously provide the temporal stones and bricks to construct the home of the people and its Torah. This institution will thereafter be firm as a cliff in the midst of the sea.

Despite Silver's efforts this campaign did not succeed. The prosperity of the 1920s came to an abrupt end in September 1929 with the stock market crash. The severe depression which ensued greatly curtailed the funds available for charitable drives. Silver nevertheless felt that his congregants could have contributed more generously despite the difficulty of the times. His lingering resentment later contributed to his decision to leave Springfield.

Silver came in contact with collegiate Jewish youth who attended the various institutions of higher learning in the greater Springfield area. In these relationships Silver perceived the enmity displayed by some students toward their religion. He also sensed the difficulty of a European trained rabbi such as himself in communicating with sophomoric young adults. On April 19, 1928, Silver wrote to the Yeshiva's Rabbi Revel to enlist his aid in this matter. Silver stated:

> I seek your counsel in a subject which concerns the essence of

Judaism. In the Springfield area there are a number of colleges . . . at which hundreds of Jewish youth study. I and Rabbi Forer [Judah Leib Forer of Holyoke] have discerned that they are inculcated with hatred for Jews and Judaism. Many are the children of observant Jews. Yet once they cross the portals of these schools they no longer wish to associate with the Jewish community. They insist on eating unclean meat even though they have been offered kosher facilities. We have not been successful in our addresses before the students since there are always a few among them who agitate against us. It would be very helpful if the Yeshiva sent us a young intelligent student for one week . . . one who will be capable of communicating with the collegiate youth. He should be able to attract them to Torah and unity under the Jewish banner. Perhaps the students will then improve their ways.

In 1929 the Kodimah congregation, a founding member of the United Orthodox Congregations, received Rabbi Silver's permission to engage a Yeshiva student to assist in conducting the High Holy Day services. Silver requested that the assistant be "scholarly, a capable preacher in the English language, and a gentleman."[5] A year later Kodimah broke away from the Orthodox Congregations to engage its own English speaking rabbi. Malicious gossip and whispers abounded in the Springfield community regarding Silver's resentment towards Kodimah and its future rabbi. Many felt that the community would now become a hotbed of controversy similar to that in other areas where Americanized spiritual leaders encroached upon the elder rabbis. Silver restrained this discord by his unadorned and direct letter to the president of Kodimah, Harry Ehrlich. Dated January 26, 1930, it read:

I hear that some laymen are spreading rumors that I will be against the new rabbi of Kodimah. They claim that I have petitioned the Yeshiva and Rabbi Levinthal [of Philadelphia] to demand that the new rabbi only be chosen with my consent and under my jurisdiction. . . . The people should realize that such petty behavior is not at all characteristic of me. I therefore clearly state to you that you can engage any rabbi you wish. I will not interfere or intrude into his rabbinate. If you do not wish to recognize me as the local Chief Rabbi, I will not even enter your synagogue in the future. I do not want any of my actions to be interpreted as constraining the new rabbi. . . .

You are free to do whatever you wish. When you think all this over, you will appreciate my position. I will not emulate the practice of elder rabbis in other cities who vehemently protest and cause endless controversy in similar circumstances. I leave all decisions in this matter to you. I will not involve myself further in this trivial matter.

You, your family and all the members of Kodimah have my blessings for continuing success.

In addition to his local involvements and activities, Silver also had much to do with the greater Massachusetts rabbinic scene. In his capacity as chairman of the State's Orthodox rabbinical council, he opposed cantors officiating at weddings in lieu of rabbis. Silver petitioned the legislature of Massachusetts not to recognize them as "ordained rabbis" as required by the State law for a "religious marriage ceremony." In a detailed memorandum he outlined the history of the rabbinate and their exclusive authority in performing weddings "in accordance with the law of Moses and Israel." He explained that cantors were honored by the rabbis to sing certain verses under the canopy. These verses, however, did not comprise the actual marriage ceremony and might be left unsaid. Only the rabbis could be relied upon to oversee the marriage proper and the writing of the *ketubah* marriage contract. Silver described many instances where cantors officiated at marriages which were either adulterous or illegal according to Mosaic or Talmudic law. He further wrote:

Often because of his musical compositions, the cantor forgets the most important part of the marriage ceremony: the formula which the groom must say when placing the marriage ring on the bride's finger; or even [forgets] the placing of the ring itself, and the couple is therefore not legally married.

The reason for the cantors' negligence is because the vaudeville stunts and the singing are most important to them and they even disregard the protests of the parents of the bride and groom. And in order not to find themselves in any predicament and in order to avoid the protests of the rabbis for the manner in which they are conducting themselves, the cantors or the ignorant marriage performers and hall proprietors began to do without the rabbis — in disobedience of the religious law. And in order to satisfy the formality of the law, they begin to sign themselves as rabbis, being fully aware of their falsity. . . .

Jewish clergy, like those of other faiths, have their diplomas—*Semikhah*. The Union of Orthodox Rabbis of the United States and Canada, as well as all Jews, recognize as a Rabbi only one who has received *Semikhah* from a great and widely recognized rabbinic authority, one who received it either by studying in a rabbinical seminary (yeshivah) or one who studied by himself and passed certain examinations. The Reform or Conservative rabbi has his diploma from his seminary. . . .

The title "Rav" — "Rabbi," only designates a Rabbi — one who has been ordained. No Jew calls the cantor "Rabbi," not even a member of his own congregation. They have been falsely designated so by some congregational presidents, thereby deceiving the governmental authorities. . . . Our cantors are like the choir singers in any Church. And we therefore ask of the State not to "ordain" those who have not studied the religion, or to permit them to officiate at religious ceremonies where a rabbi is needed.[6]

Silver also supported the efforts of the Boston Association of Jewish Congregations to strengthen the ranks of the *mohalim*.

The latter complained to the Association that "some non-Jewish doctors" circumcised Jewish children in hospitals. "In one case a Jewish doctor who does not observe Jewish laws and tradition does the work." The Association thereupon formed a committee of certification for the *mohalim* which was to supervise and safeguard the performance of this *mitzvah*. Nathan Isaacs, an Orthodox Jew and professor of law at Harvard University, was selected to serve as chairman. A rabbinical committee also was planned to "certify the *mohalim* from a Jewish and rabbinical standpoint." Silver pledged the support of his council of rabbis on condition that only Orthodox rabbis be selected. He was, however, willing to accept any Jew on the general committee. He wrote:

> We are grateful to you for your endeavor to systematize and arrange the *mohalim*, to rule out from hospitals those who are unfit, and to have the basic *mitzvah* carried out according to Jewish law by the proper persons. We also wish to thank Prof. Isaacs for his efforts in this behalf, and we are glad to learn that he is chairman. We are indeed willing to cooperate with all who try to establish order in this matter.
>
> We also beg to remark that in regard to certifying *mohalim* from the religious and rabbinical standpoint, we insist that the committee to decide on religious matters should consist only of Orthodox rabbis, neither Conservative or Reform, for different fundamental religious opinions exist between the religious factions. We therefore suggest that the *Vaad Harabanim* appoint three rabbis to decide on all religious and rabbinical matters. But we have no objection as to who should be a member of the general committee and supporters.[7]

In the midst of his local activities, Silver was sent to visit Cincinnati by the *Agudat Harabanim*. The second largest city in the state of Ohio, the city's organized Jewish community was the oldest west of the Allegheny Mountains. Cincinnati proper had a population of 23,500 Jews by 1927 which dropped to 18,500 by 1934 as Jews moved into the surrounding suburbs.[8] Its first known Jewish inhabitant was Joseph Jonas, an Englishman who arrived in Cincinnati in 1817. He led twenty other Jewish settlers in organizing the Bene Israel Congregation in 1824. Bene Yeshurun Congregation was organized next in 1841. Both later adopted the Reform ritual as Cincinnati became the center of this faction with the founding of the Hebrew Union College. This seminary for Reform rabbis was established in 1875.

Orthodoxy also thrived in Cincinnati with its oldest congregation being Beth Tefillah, organized in 1886. By the 1930s there were about ten Orthodox synagogues located in the West End, Price Hill, Walnut Hills, and Avondale sections. Congregation Adath Israel was started as an Orthodox institution in 1847. It later became a stronghold of the Conservative movement under the guidance of Rabbi Louis Feinberg.

The last spiritual leader of Cincinnati's Orthodox community had been Rabbi Hayyim Fishel Epstein. An erudite graduate of the Volozhiner Yeshivah, Epstein arrived in the United States in 1923. He was in Cincinnati from 1926 to 1928, and from 1930 until his death in 1942 was the chief rabbi of the United Orthodox Jewish Community of St. Louis. Epstein left Cincinnati because of incessant quarrels within the Orthodox community and its irresolute and apathetic approach to local *Kashrut* standards. Cincinnati remained without a central rabbi during the ensuing years with a resulting impairment of its religious standards. The *Agudat Harabanim* was further distressed by the city's continued prominence as the home of American Reform Judaism. Rabbi Silver, then the organization's president, was delegated to take stock of the Cincinnati situation and to propose a course of action.

Silver discovered that there were many learned Jews in the community. Some earned a living through door to door installment selling. They worked mornings and devoted their afternoons to Torah study. In synagogue after synagogue such individuals taught the *daf yomi*, a system of learning a page of Talmud daily. The community, however, lacked leadership. On Saturday, May 2, 1931, Silver preached at the Knesseth Israel and Tifereth Zion synagogues. On Sunday, he addressed a mass meeting at Knesseth Israel, the leading congregation which was popularly known as the "Washington Avenue Shule." The next Friday an interview with Silver appeared in Cincinnati's *Every Friday*, a weekly, pro-Zionist and traditionalist newspaper appearing from 1927 through 1965. Silver stressed that the Orthodox community could not succeed without the proper leadership. The congregations were urged to unite and engage a rabbi or the *Agudat Harabanim* should "place a rabbi in Cincinnati until the difficulties were overcome." He emphasized that for Orthodoxy there could be no compromise with other groups. Silver stated:

> Orthodoxy may tolerate other religious forms, but it can never agree to them. The difficulty in Cincinnati, perhaps, is aggravated by the undue Reform influence which the presence of the Hebrew Union College generates. It is further aggravated by the unwillingness of a few individuals, members of the Orthodox community, to cooperate. All these difficulties will be smoothed out under the proper leadership.

Under Silver's direction a committee was appointed by the local congregations to work for the creation of a *Vaad Ha-Ir*, an Orthodox City Council. They agreed that each synagogue would have equal representation regardless of its size or wealth. Once a rabbi was selected a *Vaad Hakashrut* would also be formed. The City Council would select five members and the rabbi three. Under the supervision of the rabbi, this *Vaad* was to revamp the city's *Kashrut*. The synagogues also concurred to work towards a more favorable image for Orthodoxy.[9]

The synagogues began in earnest to seek a spiritual leader.

However, every candidate or proposal fell through. The image of Rabbi Silver's zest, dedication, and plans remained with the community's leaders. Other rabbis paled by comparison. Following the High Holy Days of that year, the community decided that only Silver would succeed as its rabbi. The position was officially offered to him. The lay leaders also appealed to the other heads of the *Agudat Harabanim* to pressure him into accepting this position. Silver was hesitant due to his commitments to the greater Springfield community and its relative proximity to New York. This facilitated his activities for the *Agudat Harabanim* since its office was in New York. Nevertheless, the lure of the Cincinnati challenge and the pleas of its lay leaders and his colleagues won out. That fall Silver moved to his new community. His installation was held at the old Beth Tefillah Congregation on Sunday, November 22, 1931. Popularly known as "Shachna's Shule" since it was founded by Shachna Isaacs, it had been the main synagogue until its neighborhood changed. On Monday, a banquet in honor of Rabbi Silver was celebrated at the Hotel Alms. Concurrently with these events, the *Agudat Harabanim* held its semi-annual convention in Cincinnati. The elder Rabbi Sivitz of Pittsburg thus expressed the feelings of Silver's colleagues when he addressed Cincinnati Jewry:

> In this city there is the constant allure of the gold and silver which veils the Reform philosophy. Many are led astray by these devious ornaments. You, however, have done the opposite. With the election of Rabbi Eliezer Silver, you have created a golden cover to place on the Torah scroll. Fortunate is the Torah community of Cincinnati.[10]

Rabbi Silver soon implemented his earlier recommendations for his new city. The *Vaad Ha-Ir* became a vibrant body and a *Vaad Hakashrut* was designated. Communal standards were raised and supervision tightened. Silver was not just concerned with conditions within the Orthodox element, but also struggled for his ideals on the general communal scene. He began to campaign for *Kashrut* in Jewish institutions. In particular, Silver was appalled by its absence in the Jewish Hospital of Cincinnati. On January 26, 1932, Silver wrote to the hospital's superintendent, Dr. Walter List:

> In the several months that have elapsed since my coming to Cincinnati, I have had occasion to become acquainted with the many humanitarian activities of the Jewish Hospital, its admirable service to the community, and the excellent reputation it enjoys among all classes of local Jewry. I have indeed at various times visited Jewish hospitals in the large cities, such as those of New York, Philadelphia, and Baltimore, and with them all may the local Jewish Hospital be most favorably compared.
>
> I wish to remark, however, that in these hospitals kosher departments have been instituted in consideration of the religious observances and sensibilities of many of their patients. I was therefore greatly surprised to learn that no such provision has been made here. Besides the hygienic value of kosher food, I urge you to consider the religious affiliations and beliefs of many who enter the portals of the hospital. Indeed, many patients, while appreciative of the fine attention they receive, have complained about the non-kosher food of which they cannot partake. Furthermore, during the building fund campaign of the hospital the local Orthodox Jews were promised that a kosher department would be instituted. . . . I realize the difficulties and inconveniences involved in setting this up, yet I am certain that thereby you will but enhance the great humanitarianism of the Jewish Hospital.

Dr. List answered Silver's request by simply stating "just how impossible it would be for us to establish a kosher kitchen as a part of our centralized kitchen service at the present time."[11]

Silver did not desist and he next contacted Maurice Pollack, the president of the hospital. Pollack responded that "with our present set-up, we have no available space whatsoever for the installation of this activity."[12] Silver next attempted to enlist the support of the Reform rabbinate to advance his position. Here too, cooperation was not forthcoming. Some utilized the opportunity to hit back at Rabbi Silver's snubbing of Reform clergy. James Heller and Samuel Wohl were then the spiritual leaders of Bene Yeshurun which had been officially renamed the Isaac M. Wise Temple. Heller was widely known as a Zionist leader who later served as president of the Reform Central Conference of American Rabbis (1941-43). On March 22, 1932, Heller wrote to Silver:

> I am informed by Rabbi Wohl that you refused to take part in the conference this last week on World Jewish Affairs, on the plea that an Orthodox rabbi cannot enter a Reform Jewish edifice. I am ignorant of any passage in the Jewish law which contains such a provision. Moreover, if an Orthodox rabbi is unable to enter our edifice, why should Orthodox people go into a Jewish hospital maintained almost exclusively by Reform Jews? It seems to me that the proper action on your part is not to urge that the Jewish Hospital have a kosher kitchen, but that you start a hospital of your own. . . . I want you to know that I resent expressly your reply to our invitation.

Although his initial efforts did not achieve the desired results, Silver did not let the issue rest. Finally, with the construction of new hospital facilities in 1939, a kosher kitchen was instituted. Silver raised twelve thousand dollars for this purpose. In turn he was assured "that the *Kashrut* provisions will always be under the Rabbi of the United Orthodox Congregations (the *Vaad Ha-Ir*)."[13]

Silver's most noteworthy local accomplishment was his construction of a new *mikveh* building. The ritualarium which served the community upon his arrival was run down and located in the old Jewish neighborhood. In a circular letter, Silver admonished the "precious Jewish daughters of Cincinnati" to continue utilizing this *mikveh* until he could construct a new one in the Avondale section. Silver wrote:

> The *mikveh* on 9th and Mound Streets, has been newly remodeled and reenameled. The rooms have been repainted and are now clean, pleasing and comfortable. The water is fresh and clean for every woman.
>
> The law governing the *mikveh* is fundamentally sound and based on facts. The Almighty blesses the mothers and children who observe this purification law which cannot be substituted by bathtubs or irrigations. . . .
>
> In the near future we intend to build a new *mikveh* in Avondale but until then do not fail to make use of the above one.
>
> The *mitzvah* of *mikveh* is one of the greatest in the Torah. It is even more important than attending synagogue services on the High Holy Days or maintaining a kosher home.[14]

A lot was acquired at Hickory and Burnet Avenues in the Avondale section. This was a side street close to a citadel of Reform Jewry, the Bene Israel or "Rockdale Avenue Temple." The neighbors of this location, including many Jews, banded together to challenge the erection of the proposed *mikveh*. The Building Zone Code did permit "any building, structure, or premises" in this district "to be used for churches and other places of worship." The challengers claimed that a *mikveh* was not a "place of worship." The properties fronting on "the lot in question have been developed primarily for residence purposes, in full compliance with the use requirements of the Building Zone Code." They therefore objected to the planned *mikveh* structure. The litigants were represented by Murray Seasongood, a leading Jewish attorney and the city's former mayor. Seasongood was one of the organizers of the Charter Movement which successfully reformed Cincinnati municipal politics. He was the first mayor under the new city manager charter, and served from 1926 through 1930. The Zoning Board ruled in favor of Seasongood and refused to grant the *Vaad Ha-Ir* a permit to erect the *mikveh*. The Board announced three conclusions which guided its May 18, 1932 decision:

> First: That, The Code of Jewish Laws, Customs and Rules bearing on personal Hebraic practice, require the use of a private or public bath, referred to as a *mikveh* in said Laws:
>
> Second: That, a *mikveh* is an institution devoted to the observance of a religious rite, whereas, a Synagogue is a place of worship, the services of which do not require the use of a *mikveh*;
>
> Third: That the use of premises in Residence Districts for a public or quasi public *mikveh* is not necessary to conserve the public health, safety, convenience, comfort, prosperity and general welfare;
>
> Therefore, be it resolved, that . . . the Board of Appeals does interpret . . . the Building Zone Code . . . as not permitting the property in question to be used for a public or quasi public *mikveh*.[15]

While many of his followers were disheartened and ready to seek an alternate site, Silver decided to intensify his position. To their amazement, he sought the aid of a leading non-Jewish attorney and Cincinnati citizen. Robert A. Taft of the prestigious Taft, Stettinius, and Hollister firm agreed to support his friend and well-wisher, the city's new Orthodox rabbi. Taft, the son of the twenty-seventh president of the United States, had already served in both the Ohio House of Representatives and Senate. In 1938, he was elected to the United States Senate, where he remained until his death in 1953. At first, Taft was hesitant about taking the case since he considered himself solely a corporation lawyer. Silver, however, insisted that a question of religious freedom was at stake. Taft then agreed to take the case to court and advised Silver that their case would rest upon the definition of a "place of worship." Taft wrote:

> If you wish to erect a *mikveh* in a residence district, your only recourse will be through the courts. The question whether a *mikveh* is a "place of worship" within the meaning of the zoning ordinance is a somewhat doubtful question, although I think the argument in favor of its being so considered is somewhat stronger than the contrary argument. It is primarily a question of definition and interpretation of the English words "place of worship" and decision as to the exact nature of the ritual performed at the *mikveh*.

Silver prepared a detailed scholarly memorandum for Taft outlining the importance of the *mikveh* for Jewish observance. Among the reasons he listed were the need to immerse newly purchased kitchen utensils; the indispensable immersion of a convert upon his conversion to Judaism; the custom of pious Jews to immerse themselves before the Sabbath and Festivals; and the widely observed tradition of immersion before each of the High Holy Days. The last reason explained by Silver was the prohibition against marital relations until the wife immerses herself at the appropriate time, usually a monthly ritual. After reading the list, Taft correctly remarked to Silver, "The last reason is undoubtedly the most important."[16] When it became known that Taft was representing the *Vaad Ha-Ir* there was dismay and consternation among the obstructionists. Seasongood soon withdrew and the objections to the proposed *mikveh* were retracted. Taft later sent Silver a bill for $4,000 for services rendered along with a receipt for the same sum.

The *mikveh* controversy, featured in the local press, engendered additional debate between the Reform and the Orthodox. David Philipson, one of the four who formed the first class ever graduated from the Hebrew Union College, had been the rabbi of the "Rockdale Avenue Temple" since 1888. He remained in this pulpit until his death in 1949. In a letter published in Cincinnati's *Enquirer* on May 6, 1932, Philipson attacked both Silver and the concept of *mikveh*. Philipson wrote:

> In the first place, the individual who styles himself Chief Rabbi of the United States and Canada presumes too greatly. There is no such dignitary in this country as a Chief Rabbi. The person in question was, as I understand, the presiding officer of the Association of Orthodox Rabbis for a time. He is therefore now an ex-president of that organization. This and nothing more. . . . I question whether this self-appointed spokesman represents the sentiment of even all the Orthodox Jews of Cincinnati or any of the so called Conservatives. He surely does not and cannot speak for the liberals.
>
> For example, this institution of the *mikveh* or ritual bath which he is now championing is entirely foreign to our modern interpretation of Jewish faith and practice. . . . [From this negation] there will not be any dissent on the part of the large body of Jews who have given Cincinnati so prominent a position among the Jewish communities of the United States during so many years and who have been so largely instrumental in creating and maintaining that entente cordiale between Jews and non-Jews for which our city is so justly famous. In the name of that not negligible sector of Jews which I have had the honor of representing for so many years I have felt it incumbent upon myself to shed light upon a rather muddled situation.

Philipson's letter in the local press created a storm of protest even among some of his own followers. If anything, it helped create a more favorable climate for Silver's position. Aaron Isaacs, the chairman of the *Vaad Ha-Ir*, was among those who defended Rabbi Silver in a subsequent letter to the *Enquirer*. Isaacs wrote:

> Had Dr. Philipson made any attempt at all to find out the true facts, he would have learned that Chief Rabbi Silver not only

has been the president of the Union of Orthodox Rabbis of the United States and Canada for the past three years, but is the president at the present time. . . .

As to his remarks regarding the *mikveh*, that this institution is entirely foreign to our modern interpretation of Jewish faith and practice, this is not the time and place to enter into a discussion of the *mikveh*, which has been a basic law of the Jewish religion from its very beginning. Modifications of the *mikveh* have been adopted by both the Christian and Mohammedan religions and I wish simply to call his attention to the fact that there are thousands of *mikvehs* in the world today. . . .

The early Jewish settlers of Cincinnati, among whom were my grandparents, were Orthodox Jews and these Jews were the ones who laid the foundations for the remarkable good will between Jews and non-Jews in Cincinnati.

As the debate faded and the *mikveh* plans were approved, Silver set about raising the funds and overseeing its construction. It was not until four years later, on May 24, 1936, that the new *Beth HaTvilah* ritualarium was formally dedicated. The event was described as a holiday for Cincinnati Orthodoxy as they "turned out en masse last Sunday to the dedication of the *Beth HaTvilah*, Hickory at Burnet Aves."[17]

Silver also successfully championed the rights of Orthodox Jews in a 1934 dispute with the University of Cincinnati Medical School. This quarrel centered around his younger son Nathan and his future son-in-law Louis Izenstein. Both were students in this medical school and did not attend any Sabbath classes. During their first year they encountered no obstacles. Their teachers were duly considerate, allowing them to do their lab work on alternate days and only scheduling exams on weekdays. However, in their sophomore year, their pathology professor refused to cooperate. At times acting as an obstinate anti-Semite, he purposely scheduled labs and exams for the Sabbath.

These students thereupon requested his permission to make up the course the following summer at either Harvard or the University of Michigan medical schools. They knew that failing students had been allowed to redo this course at these schools. The pathology professor, nevertheless, refused this request. He claimed that their reason for not meeting the requirements of his course was not valid enough to allow for its make-up during the summer. At this point Rabbi Silver became involved as he appealed to the dean of the school to overrule this teacher. The dean replied that the entire faculty would have to make the decision. When they met they refused to vote down their colleague.

From here on the fight became intense and unpleasant. Rabbi Silver rallied the most prominent citizens of Cincinnati to champion the cause of religious freedom inherent in this case. Both Jew and non-Jew, clergy and laity supported him. Silver also wrote to every governor and many prominent officeholders in the United States. Typical was his March 14, 1934 letter to the Commissioner of Education in the United States Department of the Interior:

I hereby wish to call your attention to a grave injustice that is being committed against multitudes of Orthodox Jewish young men and women by our institutions of higher learning. Particularly is the injustice evident in the case of medical schools and colleges whose curricula, almost everywhere, necessitate the violation of the Sabbath, since required courses of study, laboratory work, and examinations are invariably held on Saturday. Because of this phenomenon, multitudes of young Jews are either swayed to forego their religious principles or are compelled to deny themselves, despite ability and aptitude, the pursuit of medical studies. This state of affairs involves discrimination against a certain group because of their religious scruples. . . .

Silver elicited strong approval of his stand from many of

these public figures. Much communal pressure was thereby engendered and this matter finally reached the University's highest authority, its board of trustees, who overruled the Medical School teachers for the first time in its history. The faculty was directed to allow the two students to make up the course during the summer in an accredited medical school. Too much of that school year had already passed to enable any other course of action. In the future, the Sabbath observing Jews were to be fully accommodated within the University of Cincinnati Medical School itself. Immediately after the trustees met, the president of the University phoned Rabbi Silver to inform him of the favorable decision. The one sour note came the following morning when the dean approached the two young men. He pledged in anger that he would never again approve the admission of a yeshivah graduate to the medical school. Over the years this threat was forgotten, and Sabbath observing students benefited time and again from Silver's adamant stand for their rights.

While these issues confronted segments of the entire Jewish community, Silver also busied himself with matters affecting primarily the Orthodox group. The local afternoon Yeshivah Eitz Chaim which functioned after the students attended public school was expanded. It moved to a new building at Maple and Knott Streets in the Avondale section and also maintained a downtown branch. Rabbi Silver aided the local *Sephardic* community to construct its own synagogue. This group, comprising about fifty Jewish families from Constantinople, had attempted to raise sufficient funds for their own house of worship for close to twenty years. The new synagogue, Beth Shalom, located in the Price Hill section of Cincinnati, was dedicated by Rabbi Silver on March 18, 1934.[18] Rabbi Silver also succeeded in having the Ohio Senate amend the General Code, in regard to kosher meat, by declaring it a misdemeanor for a kosher establishment to:

. . . sell or expose for sale in the same place of business both kosher and non-kosher meat or meat preparations either raw or prepared for human consumption.[19]

There also was a challenge to Silver's authority by three Orthodox congregations which refused to join the *Vaad Ha-Ir*. This group centered around Rabbi Betzalel Epstein and formed the *Hisachdus Hakehilos* ("The United Congregations"). Soon the *Vaad Ha-Ir*'s *Kashrut* was challenged. The *Every Friday* newspaper supported the *Vaad* and Rabbi Silver in an editorial on April 5, 1935, which stated:

We understand that the new organization has already imported a *shohet* from Chicago who will *shecht* chickens for a couple of pennies less than the prevailing price and the organization has promised to have two butcher shops where meat will be sold for a couple of pennies less than the price which is charged by the present butchers. We fail to see how that will raise the standards of traditional Orthodox Judaism.

The bringing of outside *shohatim* to this community will hardly contribute towards peace in our midst. We feel that the time has come when it becomes our duty as a publication sincerely interested in the welfare and betterment of traditional Orthodox Judaism, to challenge the qualifications of the men heading the *Hisachdus Hakehilos* to lead a movement which undertakes to improve upon the status quo of the existing *Vaad Ha-Ir* and its spiritual leadership. . . .

We are . . . convinced that Rabbi Silver's honesty and integrity are unquestionable. And no matter what one's attitude to Rabbi Silver's methods and personality may be, no one will deny the fact that he is one of the most outstanding rabbis in this country as far as Talmudic learning is concerned. We feel that the rank and file of our Orthodox population possesses enough innate reverence for Talmudic scholarship to remain steadfast on the side of Talmudic prestige.

Silver stood firm and within the year the new group disbanded.

There was also much personal joy and sorrow for Silver during his initial Cincinnati years. In 1932 his eldest son, Rabbi David Silver, became the spiritual leader of the Kesher Israel Congregation of Harrisburg. Great was the joy of the father that his son was following in his path. At the weekend celebrating the new rabbi's installation during February 1933, the elder Rabbi Silver stayed in Harrisburg for the Sabbath. There was hardly a dry eye in the synagogue during the sermon as the father blessed the Lord, paraphrasing the words of King David upon the anointment of Solomon:

> Blessed be the Lord, the God of Israel, Who hath given one to sit on my throne this day, mine eyes even seeing it.[20] Great is my joy that my son has come to the very community where I was the spiritual leader for eighteen years.

A few years later deep sorrow enveloped the rabbi of Cincinnati as his wife passed on. On Sunday evening, September 15, 1935, Bassia Silver died of diabetic complications and pneumonia. Funeral services were held the next day as the *Rebbetzin* was eulogized in both the Yeshivah Eitz Chaim building and afterwards at the "Washington Avenue Shule." The community later perpetuated her memory with the Bassia Silver Memorial Fund, a loan without interest and benevolent society.[21] Silver thereafter submerged himself more and more in his communal undertakings to mitigate the pain. To his colleague Rabbi Israel Rosenberg, he later wrote:

> I have been sad since the day my wife died. She was the soul and joy of my life. Perhaps I should be ashamed to tell you this. However, I cannot bid her soul farewell since mine was bound with hers. . . . At times I find temporary respite by studying around the clock. On other occasions I simply devote

fifteen hours a day to my communal endeavors. . . . Yet I am still alone, forlorn, and dispirited.[22]

In 1939 joy was restored to the Silver household upon his marriage to Pearl Berkson. The ceremony took place at Rabbi Levinthal's home in Philadelphia with the host and Rabbi Rosenberg officiating. When the newlyweds returned to Cincinnati a large group of devotees met them at the railroad station to express their good wishes. She remained his dedicated helpmate and confidante until his death some thirty years later.

With all his activities, Silver established Cincinnati as a focal point on the map of Torah. A few years later when a European *talmid hakham* corresponded with Silver, he could not conceive of his residing outside New York. The salutation of the rabbinic style letter read, "In honor of the outstanding *Gaon*, Rabbi Eliezer Silver, the *Av-Bet-Din* of New York in Cincinnati, Ohio."[23]

Notes

1. For statistical details of Springfield see *AJYB: 5686* (1925-1926), p. 386; *AJYB: 5692* (1931-1932), pp. 279-280; and Sidney Goldstein, "Springfield," *Encyclopedia Judaica*, ed. Cecil Roth and Geoffrey Wigoder (Jerusalem: Keter Publishing House, 1971), 15:318-19.

2. "Henry Cohen v. Eliezer Silver et al.," Hampden (Mass.), December 2, 1931 (Silver Archives). Cf. *AJYB: 5692* (1931-1932), p. 46, and *Bernard Revel*, p. 171.

3. Letter from Joseph A. Guttelman, Attorney at Law, to Rabbi Silver, January 27, 1933. Guttelman declared that he wrote to Silver after learning of the latter's legal victory.

A Jewish woman who does not receive a *get* or bill of divorcement in addition to her secular divorce is still considered married to her first husband. Her remarriage to the butcher was therefore adulterous from the vantage point of Jewish law.

4. The *Kashrut* regulations, dated October 12, 1931, were written for the "benefit of the Springfield community" when Rabbi Silver was already in Cincinnati.

5. Letter from Rabbi Silver to Samuel Sar of the Yeshiva, September 8, 1929.

Sar served as secretary of the Yeshiva during this period, and was Revel's main adviser and confidant. See *Bernard Revel*, s.v. index.

The policy of the Yeshiva was that no student or graduate be sent to a community unless the elder rabbi agreed in writing to his coming. Silver's letter was in response to Sar's request for his approval of the Kodimah application.

6. There is no date on the seventeen page memorandum. Rabbi David Silver fixed its date as being during the late 1920s.

7. Letter from Rabbi Silver to M. Mishel, president of The Boston Association of Jewish Congregations, April 22, 1931. The earlier letter from Mishel to the rabbinical group is dated April 13, 1931.

8. For Cincinnati's statistical details see *AJYB: 5692* (1931-1932), p. 279; *AJYB: 5696* (1935-1936), p. 356; and David Philipson, "Cincinnati," *The Universal Jewish Encyclopedia*, ed. Isaac Landman (New York, 1941), 3:205-210.

9. The document, signed by the representatives of ten synagogues, was dated May 3, 1931. The interview with Rabbi Silver appeared in the May 8, 1931 edition of *Every Friday*.

10. A copy of Rabbi Sivitz's speech was located in the Silver Archives. Also see *Hapardes*, ed. Samuel Aaron Pardes, November 1931, pp. 2-3.

11. Letter from Dr. Walter E. List to Rabbi Silver, February 4, 1932.

12. Letter from Maurice Pollak to Rabbi Silver, March 7, 1932.

13. Letter from Rabbi Silver to Maurice Pollak, June 22, 1939. Also see *Every Friday*, July 7,1939.

14. The circular letter, undated, contained Yiddish and English sections. The last paragraph is translated from the Yiddish portion of the letter.

15. Letter from Walter Dobert, engineer-secretary of the Zoning Board of Appeals of the Cincinnati Department of Buildings, to Bernard Pepinsky, appellant for the *Vaad Ha-Ir*, May 20, 1932. A copy of the resolution adopted by the Zoning Board was enclosed.

16. These incidents were related in the name of Rabbi Silver by Rabbi Jehiel M. Feinstein of Tel Aviv in an interview on August 12, 1971. Also cf. a clipping from the New York rabbinic journal, *Ha-Ma'or*, in the Silver Archives.

17. *Every Friday*, May 29, 1936. Also see *Hapardes*, July, 1936, pp. 21-22.

18. *Every Friday*, March 9, 16, 1934; September 18, 1936.

19. Letter from State Senator William E. Handly to Rabbi Silver, February 28, 1935. Handly drew up the legislation under Silver's direction. It was State Bill No. 253 to amend section 13111-1 of the General Code, relative to kosher meat.

20. I Kings 1:48. The installation ceremonies were described in *Hapardes*, March, 1933, pp. 2-4.

21. *Every Friday*, September 20, November 8, 1935; December 4, 1936; and *Hapardes*, October, 1935, pp. 3-5.

22. Letter from Rabbi Silver to Rabbi Rosenberg, May 8, 1937. This letter is located in the Rosenberg Archives of the Jewish Theological Seminary of America. Copies of these papers are also located at the Hebrew University's Institute of Contemporary Jewry.

23. Letter from Rabbi Barukh Ginzburg of Jonava, Lithuania, to Rabbi Silver, August 30, 1940.

4

President of the *Agudat Harabanim*

Silver was elevated to the three-man presidium of the *Agudat Harabanim* in 1923, joining his elder colleagues Rabbis Bernard Levinthal and Israel Rosenberg. In 1929 the organization decided to have only a single president and Silver was selected. These were the golden years for the *Agudat Harabanim* as a fellowship of pulpit rabbis. Its members were generally accomplished Talmudic scholars, and their deportment was that of the traditional European *rav*. These *rabanim* were then still in demand in numerous communities where there were many Yiddish speaking residents. The *rabanim* had also mastered the basic rudiments of the American life style by now.

The American trained Orthodox rabbi also began to gain prominence during this period. The Rabbi Isaac Elchanan Theological Seminary was graduating an ever increasing number of rabbis at its triennial ordination convocations. In 1921 there were twelve ordainees, sixteen in 1923, twenty-two in 1926, and twenty-seven in 1929. These graduates soon were in demand when the younger, American born generation began to clamor for English-speaking spiritual leaders, as Harris Selig, the director of the Yeshiva College Building Fund Campaign, keenly noted:

"Speak English!" Is it not the curse of almost all of our American synagogues and congregations? A rabbi, may he be ever so great a scholar, possessing a knowledge of the Talmud and the Codes to an unusual degree, what is his standing alongside of the English-speaking rabbi? While the rabbi who is able to speak a fluent English, may he be ever so empty and ignorant, is yet recognized as a leader, as an authority on things Jewish!

Rabbis Isaac Elchanan, Josef Baer Soloveitchik,[1] Chayim Soloveitchik, Joseph Zechariah Stern,[2] Meir Simchah, and others of the great celebrated European scholars and leaders who were the pride of and object of worship to our fathers, were no speakers. The great rabbis of the Jewish communities in our old home spoke but seldom from the platform. They usually preached only on *Shabbos Hagadol* and occasionally also on *Shabbos Teshuvah.* Their public did, however, respect the scholarship and great Jewish knowledge embodied in their person. . . .

The respect that we formerly paid to scholarship has been lost to us after our arrival in America. The stature of a rabbi is not measured any longer by his knowledge, but by his speechmaking ability. Let him but be a good speaker, no matter how ignorant he may be, he has no difficulty in becoming the leader of his community and its ruler. My late father, of blessed memory, who in his day had been the rabbi of several leading Russian communities, said to me once that he felt certain Moses would never have obtained a rabbinical position in America, because he stammered a bit, and an American rabbi must above everything, be a good speaker.

Our people are showing an exaggerated respect for the English speaker. The content of the speech is of little consequence to them. It may be poor and superficial, but if the language is smooth and the speaker fluent, he becomes at once the pet of his community. . . . But in America, we have exchanged study for mere speech, and all that we expect of the rabbi is that he should speak and again speak to us, and employ his leisure hours not in study, but in calling upon his members and their wives, and to found Brotherhoods and Sisterhoods in order that they too may meet and indulge in speechmaking.[3]

Upon assuming the presidency, Rabbi Silver was desirous of unifying the entire Orthodox rabbinate under the aegis of the *Agudat Harabanim.* Shortly afterwards he undertook the first survey of this rabbinate to properly appraise the situation. On July 12, 1929, the following letter was sent by Rabbi Judah Seltzer, the executive director of the organization, to all its members:

We are honored to inform you that our distinguished member, the well-known *gaon,* Rabbi Eliezer Silver unanimously has been elected the president of the *Agudat Harabanim.* We are confident that all our members will rejoice in this excellent selection for the future success of our group.

Rabbi Silver is desirous of learning of the viewpoints of our members. I have therefore been directed to send you these questions in the expectation that you will reply promptly.

1. What can we do to overcome the constant fighting among the *rabanim* which disgraces Judaism and the rabbinate? How can we engender unity and brotherhood among them and increase their association with the *Agudat Harabanim?*

2. What tasks should the *Agudat Harabanim* immediately undertake? What are the most pressing needs of Judaism on the contemporary scene?

3. Are there any personal matters in which the organization can aid you? Do you have any criticisms or compliments regarding the group's past functions?

4. Do you have any suggestions regarding the improvement of the status of the rabbinate? What can be done with the communities which do not possess rabbis?

5. The organization is annually short over five thousand dollars for its operating budget. Do you have any suggestions how this deficit can be overcome?

6. Are you prepared to devote time to the *Agudat Harabanim's* activities and to aid in raising funds?

7. What should the relationship of the national organization be to local rabbinic councils?

8. Should the organization form an auxiliary group of laymen to aid in its activities?

9. Should we undertake the publication of a journal to advocate our ideals?

The respondents all agreed that there was ample "controversy in the name of Heaven" on the American scene. While the sages alleged that such contention "is destined to result in something permanent," in the United States it was simply a permanent occurrence.[4] However, the solutions proposed ranged from the naive and upright to the daring and resolute. A Bronx rabbi suggested that the organization's members undertake at a public convention to study daily the classic ethical literature such as the *Hovot ha-Levavot* of Bahya Ibn Paquda and the writings of the *Hafetz Hayyim*. After daily meditations in these texts perhaps there would be "peace among the rabbis and sages." Another rabbi suggested that a *Vaad Ha-Shalom* be established to "exert a moral influence upon an aggrieved member to abandon his resentment." Another rabbi answered:

Among the true *rabanim* there is good will and brotherhood. However, we should have nothing to do with the other rabbis since they are no more than sextons and cantors.

A *rav* on New York's East Side suggested that an attempt be made to bring all the European trained *rabanim* in the United States into the organization. The other rabbis should form an association of preachers and spiritual leaders. This new group would function under the guidance of the *Agudat Harabanim* for the advancement of Orthodoxy. A Brooklyn scholar went even further and proposed that all the spiritual leaders be welcomed into the fellowship. He felt this was the most advisable plan "even if the *Agudat Harabanim* will have to compromise on some of its principles."

The *rabanim* pointed to many areas of religious infractions where they felt the organization should take a public stand. Among these were the low level of *Kashrut* observance and supervision; the need for yeshivot and day schools; and intensified propagation of Sabbath observance. One *rav* suggested that the group insist that only *rabanim* officiate at weddings by stressing the difference between them and the reverends. Another rabbi felt that the organization should strongly oppose the widespread practice of renting theaters and cinemas for High Holy Day services. "This conduct destroys ethical standards and financially harms the established synagogues and its rabbis." Other *rabanim* held that raising their stature and financial standing was of prime importance for the *Agudat Harabanim*. A *rav* wrote:

> Much effort must be exerted by the *Agudat Harabanim* to improve the status of its members. Their lot is generally in a bad way. Some are so poor that they lack for bread and clothes. Others eke out a meager sustenance. But even this is illusory since their employment resembles the gourd of Jonah. They have their positions today, but tomorrow the masses dismiss them without pity.

Many held that this was the main area in which the organization must improve its past record. There should be concern for the widely dispersed *rabanim* who constantly struggle against the fads of innovation. A *rav* stated:

> The sons of Korah have not died. They are rather found in every town and hamlet. They curse and swear at the rabbis while the *Agudat Harabanim* stands at a distance.

Others advised the organization to refrain its members from becoming involved in questionable *Kashrut* supervision. These *hekhsherim* caused endless controversy and detracted from the group's reputation.

In order to place *rabanim* in new communities it was

suggested that the *Agudat Harabanim* send its best orators to visit these cities. They should impress upon the lay people the necessity for engaging proper rabbinic leadership. These *rabanim*, however, must be among those:

> . . . who spent days and nights in the study of Torah and are masters of *Shas* and *Poskim*; *rabanim* who have sacrificed their strength in the tent of Torah. Only such spiritual leaders will enhance the prestige of the *Agudat Harabanim* and not those who permit that which is forbidden.

Once unity was achieved among the organization's widely dispersed members, the laymen would be able to set up an auxiliary group. Under the guidance of the *Agudat Harabanim*, the laymen would aid in strengthening Orthodoxy and obtaining financial support for their endeavors. With the expanded monetary sources the *Agudat Harabanim* would then be able to publish a rabbinic journal. The rabbis felt that this publication would strengthen the bonds between them. A *rav* wrote:

> Such a journal will strengthen the rabbis and their influence. It will also unite all the *rabanim* who are so widely spread out throughout the United States and Canada. It will be a source of guidance and inspiration for the laymen.

Another rabbi suggested that perhaps the privately published *Hapardes* rabbinic monthly could become the organization's official publication. Edited by Rabbi Samuel Aaron Pardes of Chicago, it had previously been published by him in Europe since 1913. In 1927 he began the American series and it indeed became the unofficial organ of the *Agudat Harabanim*.

Rabbi Silver next turned to the American trained Orthodox rabbinate. In a detailed questionnaire dated April 1930, he attempted to ascertain their level of Torah study and rabbinic activities. Silver wrote:

As the president of the *Agudat Harabanim* I am desirous of learning about the spiritual and temporal status of every Orthodox rabbi. I am particularly interested in the graduates of the American yeshivot. All our hopes rest upon them and we constantly pray that they will follow in our path. This is the way the great rabbis of all generations have conducted themselves. They completely dedicated themselves to Torah study and educated their followers in the authentic Torah tradition.

I therefore request that you answer each of the following questions:

1. When were you ordained?

2. How many years have you been in the active rabbinate?

3. Do you daily study *Shas* and *Poskim*?

4. Is there a *hevrah Shas* in your community and are you its teacher?

5. Do you occasionally discuss Torah topics with an elder *rav*?

6. If you do not, would you desire the *Agudat Harabanim* to designate a *rav* to be your mentor?

7. Do you write *hiddushei Torah* and *pipulistic* novellae?

8. Have you studied the laws of *mikvaot, Shulhan Arukh: Even ha-Ezer*, and the laws of *gittin*?

9. How many tractates of the Talmud have you studied in depth, and do you consult the responsa literature?

10. Is there a Hebrew School in your community under your supervision? How many teachers and students are there in the school, and is Talmud studied?

11. Is there a *mikveh* in your city? How has it been constructed? Who administers *gittin* in your community?

12. Do you supervise *Kashrut* and are the *shohatim* under your guidance?

13. What are your other communal activities?

14. Does your synagogue have a balcony for the women or

are they separated from the men only by a partition? Or do the men and women sit together, Heaven forfend!?

15. Do you conduct late Friday night services?

16. Do social dancing or card games take place in your synagogue?

17. Does an elder *rav* occasionally preach in your synagogue?

18. What is your relationship with Conservative and Reform spiritual leaders? Do you jointly officiate at weddings with them?

19. Are you a member of any rabbinic group?

20. What is your attitude towards the *Agudat Harabanim*?

21. Do you wish to become truly proficient in Torah knowledge like the well-known *rabbanim*?

22. Do you intend to remain in the active rabbinate?

While no rabbi answered all the questions there were many general responses to Silver's inquiry. The tone of these answers ranged from the respectful to the polemical. Many expressed their happiness that the *Agudat Harabanim* was finally displaying interest in the American trained rabbis. One rabbi wrote:

I am extremely happy to notice this new trend in American Torah life. The elder pious *rabanim* are beginning to concern themselves with the welfare of the American trained rabbis. Until now the *rabanim* paid no attention to them and even drove them away from the Lord's inheritance. Many times they exclaimed to the young rabbis, "You worship a different God!" It may be that your letter signals the start of a new era in which we will jointly devote ourselves to the sacred work which must be accomplished for Judaism in this country.

Others expressed their desires to become truly proficient in Torah knowledge and requested that "Rabbi Silver guide them along the wellsprings of Torah and wisdom." Many were already members of the rabbinic alumni organizations of the Rabbi Isaac Elchanan Theological Seminary and Chicago's Hebrew Theological College. The latter school, established by Rabbi Saul Silber in 1922, was patterned after its New York counterpart. These rabbis still expressed their desires to become members of the *Agudat Harabanim*. All the respondents declared their disdain for the Conservative and Reform movements. Many were nevertheless on good personal terms with these spiritual leaders. A rabbi stated:

> We do not officiate at weddings together. However, our private relationships are good and even friendly. At times we jointly appear in public dialogues or debates.

Few of the rabbis were able to report that their Hebrew School curriculums included Talmud. Similarly only a handful conducted Talmud study groups for their congregants. One rabbi described how the laymen could no longer follow the intricacies of this study:

> For about two years I was able to teach the *daf yomi* in the synagogue. Then some of the elder learned members died. Others moved away from this area. Those who remained are not capable of studying the Talmud. I therefore now conduct classes in *Mishnayot* and *Ein Yaakov*.

Other rabbis responded to Rabbi Silver in more strident terms. They refused to answer most of the questions since they considered them an "intrusion of their privacy." One rabbi declined to answer the questions about his studies, claiming that "such questions are for kindergarten children." Some mocked the *Agudat Harabanim*. A rabbi wrote:

> I have heard about this organization. I also know that its members destroy each other and are involved in constant strife. As a result, Judaism is disgraced and humiliated, and the laymen have lost all respect for the rabbinate.

Who are the expert rabbis in the United States? I know a few, but I am certain that the other rabbis will not acknowledge them. After all, each member of the *Agudat Harabanim* is a great *Rav* and *Gaon*!

Following this survey, Silver attempted to unify the Orthodox rabbinate. His plan called for full membership in the *Agudat Harabanim* to remain open only to knowledgeable *rabanim*. These scholars had to possess both the *yoreh yoreh* and *yaddin yaddin* degrees of ordination. The former empowered the recipient to decide matters of ritual, while the latter permitted the more advanced student to adjudicate all areas of Jewish law. The other rabbis would only be associate members with the right to elect but not to be elected to office. Once they successfully mastered the necessary texts and attained the *yaddin yaddin Semikhah* they would be granted full membership.[5] Silver took the lead in proposing this plan with his colleague Rabbi Israel Rosenberg in agreement. The alumni of the Yeshiva were also active in these negotiations. They were represented by three of their scholarly graduates, Rabbis Yehiel Charlop, William Drazin, and Solomon Reichman. At their request, Silver delineated the course of study for the advanced ordination:

In my opinion students desiring to obtain the full ordination must know the majority of the tractates in the *Nezikin* and *Nashim* sections of the Talmud. In addition to the first volume of *Shulhan Arukh: Yoreh Deah* and the laws of *niddah* and *mikvaot*, they must also know *Even ha-Ezer*. They should be particularly proficient with the laws relating to marriage, *ketubah*, and divorce. They must also know the laws of Passover in *Orah Huyyim*, especially the section devoted to the purging of vessels for this holiday. They should also master the laws of mourning in *Yoreh Deah*.

Rabbi Revel of the Yeshiva was particularly pleased with this proposal since he had constantly sought to have the *Agudat*

Harabanim accept the Yeshiva's graduates as members. He acted on Silver's proposal and arranged lectures covering the advanced program of study for the rabbinical graduates.

Silver's plan met with only partial success among the Yeshiva's graduates. Some did qualify and were accepted into the *Agudat Harabanim*. The majority, however, were not satisfied with this policy. They felt that as ordained rabbis ministering to Jewish communities they were entitled to full membership from the outset. This position was later expressed by Rabbi Simcha Levy, an erudite Yeshiva graduate. He wrote:

> The leaders of the *Agudat Harabanim* claim that the young rabbis cannot be accepted as members since their knowledge is not adequate. However, not all the members of this organization are equally learned and competent. If they feel the American graduates are not properly prepared, then they should demand that the *yeshivot* improve their curriculums. In no way should the young rabbis be rejected. They should rather be accepted immediately as members. Disunity will only weaken the strength of Torah and tradition against the deviationist trends.[6]

The cleavage between the older and the younger rabbis continued to increase as their interests conflicted. The Alumni Organization of the Yeshiva merged with the Rabbinical Council of the Union of Orthodox Jewish Congregations in 1935. They formed the Rabbinical Council of America which became the influential voice of the spiritual leaders who were not members of the *Agudat Harabanim*.

As the president of the *Agudat Harabanim*, Silver was constantly caught up in the discord between the *rabanim* and the rabbis. In 1929 a graduate of the Yeshiva was engaged by a Far Rockaway synagogue. When it was announced that Revel would represent the Yeshiva at his installation ceremonies, *rabanim* immediately complained to Silver. They felt that the synagogue's partition between the men and women was not sufficiently high. Silver wrote to Revel on August 26, 1929:

> We heard that you might attend the installation of the new rabbi of the Far Rockaway synagogue. It is known to all that for the last few years this congregation has been Conservative, with men and women praying together. We therefore inform you of these facts and are certain that you will not enter such a synagogue which is constructed in a fashion which transgresses a basic law of Orthodoxy.

After receiving this letter, Revel assured Silver that there was a smaller but acceptable partition in this synagogue. He had the Yeshiva's secretary, Samuel Sar, wire back to Silver on September 4, 1929:

> Far Rockaway Congregation same as Rabbi Jung's [the smaller partition of New York's Jewish Center where Rabbi Leo Jung was the spiritual leader]. *Agudat Harabanim* and Yeshiva should do everything possible to gain congregation. Your letter to Doctor Revel regarding Rabbi's installation incomprehensible. Will you dear Rabbi reconsider your decision so the *Agudat Harabanim* and Yeshiva do not suffer by it.

On another occasion that year a *rav* from New Bedford requested Silver's help in controlling a Yeshiva graduate who was being engaged by another local synagogue. The rabbi was needed:

> ...to lead responsive readings in English from sheets distributed among the worshippers. He also had to read portions of the *mahzor* in English although they could themselves read these passages from their own prayerbooks. It is even doubtful if most of the congregants understand English.[7]

The *rav* wanted to be certain that the rabbi would be submissive to his authority "just like the relationship between

New York's Rabbi Margolies and his assistant." The *rav* wrote to Silver that "Rabbi Dr. Revel already promised me that he would inform his student of his insistence upon such an association with the *rav*."

In 1931 Silver was called upon to ban a rabbi who infringed upon the *rav* of Portland. The young rabbi, a recent graduate of the Yeshiva, was engaged by a congregation for the Passover season. Arriving in Portland, he arranged for the traditional pre-Passover sale of *hametz* and answered his congregants' inquiries concerning the holiday. These activities provoked the *rav* who considered them an encroachment upon his authority and income. The *rav*, like most *rabanim*, was not paid a salary, but rather depended upon honoraria for his rabbinic services. The *rav* wrote to Silver:

> I plead with you to come to my aid. For months I have had little income and all my hopes centered on this pre-Passover period. Now this cursed youngster comes along to take away even this remuneration from me. He too is arranging for the sale of *hametz* and answering questions concerning the holiday. This young chick whose eyes have not yet opened has pushed me aside after my ten years in the community. Please declare his rulings void and his ordination nullified in an advertisement in the *Jewish Morning Journal*. Do not allow the rabbinate to be a lawless world in which anarchy reigns. Do not allow strangers to encroach upon the true *rabanim* and desecrate the name of God.[8]

A few years later, a *rav* justified his controversy with a neighboring rabbi because of the latter's sinful behavior. In a letter to Silver, the *rav* thus described the rabbi's impieties:

> The rabbi eulogized the wicked Spinoza at a Friday night forum. Those who understand English repeated to me the rabbi's assertion that the *rabanim* of Spinoza's era were incorrect in excommunicating such a saintly individual.

The rabbi also utilized vulgar and uncouth jokes in ridiculing the Yiddish language during his *Kol Nidrei* sermon. He invited speakers to his Friday night forums who drove to the synagogue. Cards are played in the sanctuary by a mixed crowd of men and women. Before Purim, he permitted in the same place of worship a masquerade in which each sex dressed up like the other.

The rabbi became angry when one Sabbath, before the prayers began, an elder pious Jew rebuked him for his permissiveness. Later, during the sermon, the rabbi called this noble Jew "a great *sheigetz*." The fishmonger Cohen soon demanded that this Jew leave the synagogue. Only through the intervention of some other worshippers was Cohen restrained and the service finally concluded.[9]

There was generally little that Silver could do to ameliorate the problems of the *rabanim* as circumstances beyond their control engendered hostility between the generations. There were likewise instances of discord among the *rabanim* themselves. In 1933, the *rav* of the West Philadelphia area requested that Silver keep out another *rav* who was entering his locale. The *rav* wrote:

All know that I have always been content with a minimum of income. My main desire has been to daily study Torah and enhance its observance among young and old. I have never troubled the heads of the *Agudat Harabanim* during the twenty years I have been a member. Now, however, I am compelled to request your help. Another *rav*, a member of our organization, is cutting off my meager sustenance. He is infringing upon my rabbinate and becoming the *rav* of a new congregation only half a square from my house. This new synagogue has only been formed to cause disunity after I have been the *rav* of this neighborhood for over ten years. . . .

Our mutual friend, the *rav* and *gaon* of Philadelphia, Rabbi Bernard Levinthal, will support me and do whatever he can for me. However, he must first receive an official request from you in this matter as the president of the *Agudat*

Harabanim. I therefore ask that you immediately write to Rabbi Levinthal so he can forbid the other *rav* from doing this grave injustice to me.[10]

The arguments between the *rabanim* were also intensified by their counter interests and disagreements in the field of *Kashrut* supervision. This constant bickering in the Orthodox rabbinate was so extensive that a visiting European rabbinic leader considered it the *Agudat Harabanim's* most conspicuous feature. At the organization's 1930 convention Rabbi Silver proudly introduced Rabbi Abraham Dovber Kahane-Shapiro, the chief rabbi of Kovno. Rabbi Shapiro declared:

The individual becomes more cynical as he becomes older. He despairs of change and accomplishment. This is not so of the community which never grows old. The *Agudat Harabanim* is not simply a professional organization to protect the narrow interests of its members. Its main goal must be to enhance the status of Torah and tradition in the entire community. . . . However, you have not achieved this goal. The constant quarrel and strife among the rabbis instead saps the foundation of Judaism. It permits for anarchy and disorder on the American Torah scene. Your disunity hinders your attempts to correct this lawless situation.

I have also noticed another major flaw on the American scene. Rabbinic greatness is no longer commensurate with proficiency in Torah scholarship. The *Agudat Harabanim* must educate the masses as to the true nature of the rabbinate. Once this is accomplished then proper Torah life can be structured in the United States.[11]

While the Orthodox rabbinate was caught in its own difficult situation, the Conservative rabbinate was constantly forging ahead. Time and again the *rabanim* informed Silver that if their differences could not be resolved, the younger element in the community would turn to the Jewish Theological Seminary. The *rav* of Brockton enlisted Silver's help in uniting synagogues in a neighboring community so that there would be sufficient income to engage a *rav* there. If they did not succeed, the *rav* was certain:

> The younger members will take the initiative in building a new synagogue which will be Conservative. They are clamoring for a modern rabbi and will undoubtedly choose a Seminary man. Such a rabbi will then become the city's spiritual leader and guide.[12]

Another *rav* was concerned that a breakaway synagogue in his community would soon engage a Seminary graduate. Such a rabbi would acquiesce to their demands for reforms in the synagogue. Among these were their desires for:

> Late Friday night services with a choir of both men and women assisting the cantor. . . . They also object to the rabbi preaching with his hat on as is customary among *rabanim* and *benei Torah*. They rather want the rabbi to wear only a small skullcap during his sermons.[13]

These demands for religious innovations, which only could be met by Conservative rabbis, were pointedly impressed upon Silver by a November 12, 1930 letter written by an attorney in Savannah. It presented an incisive description of an ever increasing trend among the children of East European immigrants:

> On a number of occasions in the past ten years or more, there have been sporadic movements by the Orthodox Jewish young men and women of this city to create a more attractive form of religious worship in our local Orthodox synagogue, in order to bring into the synagogue hundreds of young men and young women of the strict Orthodox faith who have shown little or no interest in our religious worship.
>
> Within the past thirty days, these young people have proven their sincerity by forming an organization called the Judaic League of Savannah, with the purpose of using our

present Orthodox synagogue on Friday nights after supper to worship according to the form used at regular Maariv Services excepting such changes as are necessary to differentiate the incoming of the Sabbath Day and similar minor omissions. It was also the program of this group to have both sexes seated together during these Friday night services and on the Holy Days. It was our further plan to have a choir, and in all other respects to worship strictly and according to the tenets of our forefathers, with the exception of the changes described. Upon the Holy Days our synagogue is overcrowded, and this congestion makes it uncomfortable and creates confusion and noise which we had hoped to eliminate by asking the officers of our synagogue to rent a Hall in the residential section of this city where those persons who prefer this modern form of Orthodox service may attend and worship.

I might state that our Orthodox synagogue is most inconveniently located in the business section, at a very considerable distance from the majority of the homes of the members of the synagogue. A branch opened for the Holy Days would practically assure all worshippers of the opportunity of walking to the services in accordance with our faith, instead of riding in automobiles as some are now compelled to do because of distance. Many of the members of the synagogue are of an age which prevents them from walking several miles as they had to do in the past.

Opposition has arisen among a very few of the older members to the use of the synagogue on Friday nights after supper for worship by the younger people, along the lines I have described. We are further informed that our Rabbi could not be a party to countenancing these changes of worship because it is charged that such changes are not Orthodox and are a violation of the traditions and tenets of strict Orthodox Jewry.

We, speaking for the 175 young men and young women who are zealous and enthusiastic in our desire to give devotion to our God in keeping with the faith of our forefathers, respectfully seek your counsel and advice, and ask:

1st: Whether it is proper that men and women sit together on Friday nights after supper at regular Orthodox Services, using as our prayer book, the [Conservative] United [Synagogue] Prayer Book.

2nd: Whether it is right and proper that during the Holy Days, we use the United Prayer Book at a branch of our Synagogue, having both sexes seated together.

3rd: Whether the Orthodox Rabbi of our Synagogue would be permitted, under the Orthodox Rabbinical practice, to lead and participate in these services.

Please understand that we do not expect to use musical instruments of any kind, nor do we wish to offend or violate the wishes of the elderly members of our Synagogue who will continue to use the present building.

We simply wish to save these hundreds of young men and young women from estranging themselves and their children from Orthodox Jewry.

Silver could not agree to these changes and he soon joined issue with the Conservative movement and its rabbinate. In 1927 Silver took a central role in the lawsuit initiated by the Orthodox members of Cleveland's Jewish Center against their spiritual leader, Solomon Goldman. Led by Abraham Katz, a committee of one hundred was formed to safeguard the synagogue's Orthodoxy. Goldman, born in Volhynia, Russia, was brought to the United States as a child. He studied at the Yeshiva and at the Seminary where he was ordained in 1918. A die-hard Conservative rabbi, Goldman initiated ritual changes in his Cleveland congregation which had formerly been Orthodox. These included the mixed seating of men and women during services, late Friday evening services, forbidding the rising of the worshippers when the Ark was opened, and abolishing the kneeling during the High Holy Day services. Goldman also omitted the ritual washing of the hands before meals at congregational dinners and permitted eating with uncovered heads. He carried books through the streets on the Sabbath on the way to the services and kissed the brides after the marriage ceremonies. Goldman also expressed non-Orthodox views regarding the Bible and traditional Jewish sources. The offended members challenged Goldman's right to introduce these radical changes in an Orthodox synagogue. Silver was called upon as an expert witness to establish proper Orthodox ritual and dogma. In his testimony Silver marshaled many rabbinic sources to establish the Orthodox tradition. Among the questions he was asked were:

Q. Is the rabbi permitted to forbid the ceremony of kneeling during the services on the Day of Atonement?

A. This is contrary to traditional customs and no custom can be changed. While this is not a law in respect to the synagogue, it was a law in respect to the Temple. In the Temple the law provided that kneeling should take place on the Day of Atonement, and that insofar as the synagogue is concerned, Jewry through the centuries have adopted the law as a custom found in the Temple — and therefore, insofar as the synagogue is concerned it has become a custom with the force of law. That at least the cantor and the rabbi shall kneel — and that no custom can be changed — and this is in *Chasam Sofer*, Yoreh De'ah, 107.

Q. Suppose a Rabbi says from his pulpit to his congregation that the story of the flood is a myth, has no foundation in fact, and that a twelve-year-old boy would not believe it: is that considered within or without?

A. I view this as heresy.

Q. [How do you view the] kissing of brides by the rabbi during marriage ceremonies?

A. It is said that when a man does this we cannot believe him even as a witness — this is according to Maimonides, *Hilchos Sanhedrin* 19, and in *Shoel Umeshiv* Book 4, Part 3,

Chapter 132, and according to all the *Poskim* [his conduct] is contrary to the Mosaic law.[14]

As a result of this determined opposition Goldman later left Cleveland in 1929. He then became the rabbi of Chicago's Anshe Emet Synagogue where he remained until his death in 1953.

With the continued expansion of the Conservative rabbinate, Silver faulted their discharging functions which he considered beyond their competence. At the 1932 convention of the *Agudat Harabanim*, Silver declared in his presidential address:

> We now must contend with the Conservatives who consider themselves Orthodox. They have begun to seize for themselves the duties of the authentic rabbinate. They engage in the sale of *hametz* and grant *kashrut* supervision. We must oppose them and display to the masses exactly who are the genuine and learned rabbis. Only in their hands may Judaism be entrusted. Only they will be able to improve its contemporary situation.[15]

Silver joined the other leaders of the *Agudat Harabanim* in 1935 in publicly interdicting an attempt by the Conservative Rabbinical Assembly to solve the vexatious *agunah* problem. A married woman who is separated from her husband and cannot remarry is termed an *agunah*. Many times this is due to her inability to obtain a *get* from her recalcitrant husband or because it is unknown whether he is still alive. The problem of such an unfortunate woman is one of the most complex in halakhic literature. Throughout the ages the foremost rabbinical scholars dedicated much effort to alleviating her plight within the framework of Jewish Law. Rabbi Louis Epstein, a 1913 graduate of the Jewish Theological Seminary and the spiritual leader of Brookline's Kehilath Israel, proposed a radical solution in 1930. According to Epstein, at the initial marriage ceremony the groom was to sign a formal document authorizing his wife to

have a rabbinical court write a *get* on his behalf. The husband
was to authorize:

> ... a messenger to deliver the *get* to my wife in case I shall
> desert her for three consecutive years or civilly divorce her. I
> swear that I shall not annul this authorization or the
> subsequent *get* which will be issued.[16]

By 1935 this innovation was accepted by his colleagues but
was later abandoned because of the total opposition of the
Orthodox rabbinate and of some members of the Jewish Theological Seminary's faculty. Epstein's proposal was declared hala-
khically unsound since the husband might always verbally
nullify the *get* prior to his wife's receiving it, regardless of any
earlier commitment not to do so. It was also felt that such an
authorization would be automatically canceled when the newlyweds took up residence together.[17] There was also much
resistance to universally lessening the marriage bonds at the very
onset of matrimony. On May 29, 1935, the heads of the *Agudat
Harabanim* issued a *herem* (rabbinic ban) against the
Conservative innovation stating:

> As the emissaries of the rabbinic courts throughout the ages,
> we declare this *herem* against anyone who will dare to change
> the practice of the sages in the marriage ceremony. Parti-
> cularly those who would have the groom authorize his bride to
> be his messenger to later attain a divorce for herself. One who
> officiates at such a marriage, the witnesses, and the bride and
> groom, will be totally excommunicated and separated from
> the Jewish community. They will be designated for eternal
> castigation.
>
> We are confident that all those whose ancestors stood at
> the Mountain of Sinai will not follow those attempting to lead
> the people of God astray.[18]

In addition to Rabbi Silver, some of the other signatories to
the *herem* were Rabbis Konvitz, then the president of the

Agudat Harabanim, Levinthal, Margolies, Revel, Rosenberg, and Seltzer.

Years later Silver was once again involved in litigation concerning Jewish Law. In 1957 Orthodox members of Congregation Chevra Thilim of New Orleans, led by Harry Katz, sued to prevent the violation of its charter as an Orthodox synagogue. The defendants were the newly elected officers of the congregation who replaced separate seating with mixed seating of the sexes at religious services. The trial before the Civil District Court for the Parish of Orleans, State of Louisiana, lasted from June 27th to July 11th. The plaintiffs, aided by the Union of Orthodox Jewish Congregations of America, obtained affidavits from leading rabbis in the United States, Israel, and Great Britain, declaring mixed seating as contrary to Jewish Law. Four experts also confirmed this viewpoint in their testimony before the court. The first to testify was Rabbi Silver, then the chairman of the Presidium of the *Agudat Harabanim*. In his testimony, Silver established the basic and fundamental differences between the Conservative and Orthodox factions. He showed that the elimination of the partition between men and women was a deliberate manifestation of a schism which touched the very core of the belief in the Divine origin of both the Written and the Oral Laws. In a decision later upheld by higher courts, the Civil District Court ruled in favor of the Orthodox litigants. It found that Orthodox Judaism prohibits worship without separation of the sexes. Mixed seating therefore violated the charter and trust of an Orthodox Synagogue.[19]

Silver later penned a responsum which even forbade a woman's entering a synagogue which did not possess a proper partition. He compared contemporary houses of worship to the two Temples where there was a special Women's Court. Only when they enter their own properly designated area may women participate in public worship.[20]

In his capacity as the president of the *Agudat Harabanim*

Silver was also called upon to adjudicate internal disputes within the Orthodox community. The halakhic scholars and communal leaders constantly stressed the prohibition against litigation in the gentile courts. It was laid down that there was to be no resort to the gentile courts even when their law on a particular matter did not differ from that applied in the Jewish courts.[21] The Jew was rather encouraged to settle his disputes in what was popularly termed a *Din Torah* before a rabbinic court. While this institution was widely neglected in the United States, there were still occasional *Dinei Torah*. These generally reached the *Agudat Harabanim* and came before Rabbi Silver as its president. In 1930 he had to settle a dispute between the Diskin Orphan Asylum Society of Jerusalem and its New York representative. This controversy made headlines in the Jewish press due to the fame of the orphanage. The largest of its kind in the Holy Land, the institution had been established by Rabbi Moses Joshua Diskin in 1880. The orphanage was supported by appeals made throughout the Jewish world. The directors were about to close its New York office in 1930 since they felt the income received from this source did not cover its operating expenses. Their representative at this location, however, refused to surrender his responsibilities. He instead claimed the support of Rabbis Margolies and Rosenberg as being worthy of his position. The Jerusalem directors wrote to Silver on July 27, 1930:

> As those responsible for the support of the orphans, we cannot stand by and see their funds dissipated. If we allow the New York office to continue to drain funds it will bankrupt our institution. If our emissary still feels we are obligated to him, we shall be happy to have a *Din Torah* with him in Jerusalem. Since we have supported his family here in his absence, we feel that Jerusalem is the proper place for such a *Din Torah*.

After this communication, Rabbi Silver met with the New

York representative and another agent of the Diskin orphanage.
They accepted his decision that the New York office be closed,
and the previous emissary was granted severance rights.[22]

Another dispute which was indicative of this period came
before Silver later that year. It concerned the teachers and
directors of the Rabbi Jacob Joseph School. Founded by Rabbi
Jacob Joseph in 1900 as the Beth Sefer Yeshiva, it was renamed
in his memory upon his death. The school which previously flour-
ished on New York's East Side was now caught up in the web of
the economic depression. Salaries were cut, payment was in
arrears, and fifteen teachers were dismissed or retired. The
faculty responded with a strike which brought home the controversy to the disrupted classrooms and student body. The quar-
reling factions finally agreed to a *Din Torah* before the *Agudat
Harabanim*. Sitting as the *Av-Bet-Din* was Rabbi Silver,
assisted by Rabbis Rosenberg, Seltzer, Hayyim Bloch of Jersey
City and Isaac Siegel of Bayonne. The tribunal ruled that nine of
the teachers were to be reinstated immediately since there was
no dissatisfaction with their teaching abilities. The other six
teachers against whom there was dissatisfaction were to be
evaluated within one week by a joint committee of the rabbis and
the teachers. Their dismissal would then be final or they would
be reinstated. The directors were obligated to arrange for a
monthly wage of one hundred and eighty dollars for each teacher.
Every effort was to be exerted to meet the payroll on time. The
Bet Din also expressed its anguish that the teachers saw fit to
strike stating:

> We must express our indignation that the teachers introduced
> the strike weapon into the yeshivah. If the teachers have a
> claim against the directors, why must the innocent students of
> Torah suffer! The faculty must not utilize these methods in
> the future.

Rabbi Silver pledged the support of the *Agudat Harabanim*

in sponsoring a campaign to raise funds for the school. He urged the teachers and directors to establish amicable relations. Thus "the love of Torah and the will to sacrifice for it" will be enhanced.[23]

On another occasion Silver was called upon to render a decision concerning the heads of an advanced yeshivah. The New Haven College of Talmud, organized in 1923, was transferred to Cleveland in 1929. Among its founders and instructors were Rabbis Sheftel Kramer and Judah Levenberg. In 1930 they were joined by Kramer's erudite son-in-law, Rabbi Jacob Ruderman, widely known as the "Dolhinov *illui*" after the place of his birth, and leading graduate of the Slobodka Yeshivah. Soon after he took his place as an inspiring teacher of Talmud in the school, contention erupted among part of the faculty and directors regarding the exact division of functions within the yeshivah. In 1933, during the Passover intersession, Silver issued the following ruling:

> With the permission of the Almighty I have come to Cleveland as the president of the *Agudat Harabanim* to aid its yeshivah, popularly known as the Yeshivat New Haven. All its faculty and directors have agreed to accept my rulings as to the exact positions each should occupy within the school. . . .
>
> Each of the principal heads is to be assigned in accordance with his abilities. Rabbi Sheftel Kramer is to be in charge of the daily administrative functions. He will call meetings of the faculty and directors and enforce their decisions. He will guide his colleagues in directing and managing the school.
>
> Rabbi Jacob Ruderman will be the *rosh yeshivah*, the instructor of the highest Talmud class. He will supervise the curriculum and will test prospective students. He will also examine the student body and supervise their promotion to higher classes.

Rabbi Judah Levenberg will be the *mashgiach ruhani* or spiritual director of the school. His task will be to influence the students to be diligent in the study of Torah and *Musar*. He is to guide them in the fear of God and love of Torah. He is to meet with them individually or in small groups so his influence will be maximal.

No student may be expelled without the concurrence of all three heads of the Yeshivah.[24]

After this decision, Levenberg requested that Silver take on a permanent role in the school so that good relations would be maintained. He wrote:

In my opinion lasting peace will be established if you play a more active role in the school. You should either be chosen honorary president or national president. Another solution might be for you to become the senior *rosh yeshivah* or honorary *rosh yeshivah*.

Before the High Holy Days of 1933, Rabbi Ruderman organized the Ner Israel Rabbinical College in Baltimore. This new school soon replaced the Cleveland Yeshivah. Under Ruderman's guidance it gradually became one of the leading yeshivot of America.

This constant involvement with *rabanim*, rabbis, and Orthodox institutions throughout the United States was now an integral part of Silver's role in the *Agudat Harabanim*.

Notes

1. Rabbi Joseph Baer Soloveitchik (1820-92), the spiritual leader of Slutsk and Brest-Litovsk, was the father of Rav Hayyim. The elder Soloveitchik penned the *Bet ha-Levi*.

2. Rabbi Joseph Zechariah Stern (1831-1903), the spiritual leader of Shavli, was the author of *Zekher Yehosef*.

3. Harris Selig, "Is a Union of Orthodox Committees Possible?" MS located in the Revel Archives at the home of Mrs. Bernard Revel, New York.

Selig was engaged to direct the Yeshiva's multi-million dollar campaign to construct a new campus for the Yeshiva and its proposed liberal arts college. See *Bernard Revel*, s.v. index.

For additional material on the conflict between the *rabanim* and rabbis see *Bernard Revel*, pp. 167-178.

4. Avot 5:17, interpreted thus by Rabbi Nathan Pecker of the Bronx in his reply.

5. Interviews with Rabbi Solomon Reichman, an early Yeshiva graduate, August 6, 1974 and Jacob Hallerstein, secretary of *Agudat Harabanim* (1928-1972), April 30, 1974. Also see the letters from Rabbi Seltzer to Rabbi Silver, January 29, 1931; and from Rabbi Revel to Rabbi Charlap, August 23, 1931.

6. Simcha Levy, *Simhat ha-Levi* (New York: Shulsinger Bros., 1967), p. 105, citing his correspondence on this subject in 1940.

7. Letter from Rabbi Tzvi Hayyim Papkin to Rabbi Silver, October 3, 1929. Also see his letter of September 12, 1929.

8. Letter from Rabbi Moshe Shohet to Rabbi Silver, March 24, 1931. Also see his letter of March 25, 1931.

9. Letter from Rabbi Eliezer Gorelick to Rabbi Silver, March 19, 1933.

10. Letter from Rabbi David Swiren to Rabbi Silver, September 15, 1933.

11. Minutes of the 1930 *Agudat Harabanim* convention, p. 3. Rabbi Shapiro addressed the opening session on May 6, 1930.

12. Letter from Rabbi Abraham Borvick to Rabbi Silver, October 9, 1929. Also see his letter of September 29, 1930.

13. Letter from Rabbi Zevi Hayyim Papkin to Rabbi Silver, October 3, 1929. For additional description of Conservative inroads upon Orthodoxy during this period see *Bernard Revel*, pp. 163-167.

14. Deposition of Rabbi Eliezer Silver, November 3, 1927, supplied by Mrs. Louis Engleberg of Cleveland Heights, Ohio. Mrs. Engleberg's father, Abraham Katz, was the leading plaintiff in the case against Goldman. In her letter of August 6, 1975, she recalled that the verdict stated that the "civil courts take no jurisdiction in ecclesiastical questions." This decision was later reversed by the Court of Appeals which

declared that "the change from Orthodox to Conservative synagogue ritual was a violation of a trust." Finally, in 1929, the Ohio Supreme Court reversed the decision of the Appeals Court and upheld the initial verdict of the lower court. Rabbi Silver's deposition is reproduced in Appendix II to this volume.

Also see *Sefer Ha-Yovel Shel Agudat Harabanim: 1902-1927*, p. 105.

For Goldman's biography see Jacob J. Weinstein, *Solomon Goldman: A Rabbi's Rabbi* (New York: Ktav Publishing House, 1973).

15. *Hapardes*, June 1932, p. 20.

16. Epstein's proposal first appeared in his 1930 *Hatza'ah Lema'an Takanot Agunot* and was reprinted in greater detail in his *Leshealat ha-Agunah* (New York, 1940), pp. 79-80. Also see his *Marriage Laws in the Bible and the Talmud* (Cambridge, Massachusetts: Harvard University Press, 1942), s.v. index.

For an historical analysis of the Epstein proposal see Abraham Hayyim Freimann, *Seder Kiddushin ve-Nissuin* (Jerusalem: Mossad Harav Kook, 1945), pp. 385-97.

17. Following the viewpoint of Maimonides in his *Mishneh Torah, Hilchot Gerushin*, 9:25.

18. For the complete text of the *herem* see the volume which the *Agudat Harabanim* later published against Epstein's proposal, *Ledor Aharon* (New York, 1937), pp. 22-23. Cf. Konvitz, *Divrei Joseph* 1:38-39. Silver already negated Epstein's proposal as early as July 2, 1931 in a letter to Seltzer.

19. The full details of this case are contained in Baruch Litvin, *The Sanctity of the Synagogue* (New York: The Spero Foundation, 1959). Silver's role is described on pp. 67, 73.

20. Rabbi Silver's responsum was published in *Shealot U-teshuvot Ha-Maor*, ed. Meir Amsel (New York, 1967), pp. 40-41. Cf. *Noam*, ed. Menahem Kasher, 17:223.

21. *Gittin* 88b. Also see Maimonides, *Mishneh Torah, Hilchot Sanhedrin*, 26:7 and Ramban to Exodus 21:1.

As early as the middle of the ninth century it was declared permissible to institute proceedings in a gentile court against a party which refused to accept the results of a *Din Torah*. It was therefore permissible for the previously described disputes in Cleveland and New Orleans to be brought before secular courts since the defendants refused to be bound by the *Din Torah* of rabbinic tribunals. Cf. the ruling of Paltoi Gaon in

Binyamin M. Lewin (ed.), *Otzar ha-Geonim* to Baba Kamma, Responsum no. 227, p. 69.

22. Also see the letters of the directors of June 10, 1930 to Rabbi Seltzer, and of July 30, 1930 to Rabbi Silver; and the letter of Rabbi Silver to the directors, September 14, 1930. Cf. the article in *The Jewish Day*, August 1, 1930.

23. The signed acceptance of the decision of the *Din Torah* is dated October 28, 1930.

24. Silver's decision is not dated, but the following correspondence from Levenberg to Silver is dated April 6, 1933.

5

Kashrut

✿☆✿☆✿☆✿☆✿☆✿☆✿☆✿☆✿☆✿☆✿☆✿☆✿☆✿☆

Despite all the difficulties faced by Orthodoxy on the American scene, *Kashrut* standards and regulations still remained the single most invidious problem for the rabbinate. Silver dedicated major efforts during his initial years as president of the *Agudat Harabanim* to this basic area of Jewish ritual.

Due to the mass immigration and the dramatic increase in the East European Jewish population in the United States by the 1920's, *Kashrut* became a most significant enterprise. Meat purveyors, *shohatim*, and supervising rabbis constantly struggled with the business necessities of this industry while at times the religious and doctrinal aspects were neglected. An editorial in the May 1928 issue of *Hapardes* rabbinic journal decried this situation. It compared the attitude of the European *shohet* of yesteryear to his American counterpart:

> In many ways Jewish life has undergone radical change in the United States. Nothing has been altered more than the position of the *shohet*. In the old home this profession was considered a sacred calling. The *shohet* was granted clergy status as a dedicated individual properly discharging his holy task. The European *shohet* did not view his profession as simply a "business" to enable his earning a living. He rather completely dedicated himself to Torah and Tradition, carefully following the dictates and rulings of the rabbis. Never did the *shohet* act on his own without rabbinic approval.

Here in America the situation is completely different. The *shohet* simply considers his vocation a means of attaining a livelihood. It is simply another profession among many. His fondest wish is to join a union so his salary will be increased. In many cities the *shohatim* have already organized and work together with the union bosses.

What are the results of this new attitude? The *shohatim* no longer wish to be under rabbinic influence. They rather desire to function at the whims of the union. In these cities the rabbis are now unable to properly control the *Kashrut* situation.

In the smaller widely dispersed towns and hamlets throughout the United States the *shohatim* have usurped the role of the rabbi. They constantly issue incorrect rulings which contradict Torah and Tradition. Just recently in Albany a *shohet* performed a marriage ceremony for a man and his sister-in-law, although she already had children with his late brother.

Against this background of neglect and vested interests, Rabbi Silver, as the president of the *Agudat Harabanim*, was constantly called upon to give guidance and resolution to local disputes and halakhic infractions. In 1932, Rabbi Yehudah Braver of the United Synagogues of Greater Kansas City requested Silver's aid in his vehement disputes with a local *shohet*. Braver accused the latter of having been forbidden to slaughter by prominent rabbis due to his halakhic transgressions in his previous positions. The *shohet*'s arrival in Kansas City was also illegal, Braver said, since he encroached upon the employment of the city's previous *shohatim*. Braver also claimed that the *shohet*:

. . . engaged in additional base and sinful acts. He officiated at the wedding of a *kohen* and a divorcee. He also allowed a convert to immerse herself in a swimming pool instead of a *mikveh*. When this became known, the few women from surrounding communities who previously utilized the Kansas City *mikveh* stopped coming. They explained that they too have swimming pools in their local communities.[1]

Braver, in a reprimand to Silver for the *Agudat Harabanim*'s lack of activity outside of New York which permitted such an embroilment, wrote:

All your activities are centered around the greater New York area. The organization completely neglects the almost two million Jews living outside of this metropolis. There are communities where there is not even a *shohet* or Hebrew school teacher. These Jews are rapidly losing their Jewishness, eating all types of forbidden foods, and residing where there are no *mikvaot*. The Reform and Conservative rabbis enter these communities, build congregations, and completely uproot the last vestiges of authentic Judaism. While this goes on, the *Agudat Harabanim* concerns itself solely with the New York area.

In response, Silver wrote that he was not overly impressed with the complaints against the rabbinical organization:

You constantly fault the *Agudat Harabanim* and its leaders. Nevertheless, we always do what we can for you. . . . When it comes to helping my colleagues, there is practically no week in which I do not travel to aid them. This past winter I visited Norfolk, Worcester, Cleveland, Columbus, Louisville, Youngstown, Akron, Dayton, Atlanta, Los Angeles, Springfield, Minneapolis, and a few cities in Canada. In each community I aided the rabbi and raised the level of observance.

Silver urged Braver to mitigate his controversy with the *shohet* since public polemics harmed Orthodoxy's image. Silver promised to aid in solving the problems with the *shohet* in a forthcoming visit to Kansas City.

An aged *shohet* from Akron, Ohio, wrote to Silver at the

request of the *Vaad Ha-Ir* to describe the status of local *Kashrut*. In his faltering handwriting the *shohet* apologized for not being able to improve the situation "since he was old and ill." There was no rabbi in Akron at the time, but there were four other *shohatim*:

> Two have previously been prohibited from slaughtering by outstanding rabbis. Nevertheless, they slaughter whenever they wish. There are also another two *shohatim*. One is excellent and a real scholar. The other one is not capable of feeling whether the knife is properly sharpened. He is also an ignorant boor, but still answers inquiries regarding *Kashrut*. These *shohatim* also determine the status of slaughtered fowl, mixtures of meat and milk, and minglements of permitted and forbidden foods. Although I shout in the streets that they have no right to determine questions of Jewish Law, my protests are unheeded.[2]

The letter closed with the request that Silver aid the community in attaining proper rabbinic guidance. Silver placed Rabbi Elijah David Stampfer in the community. Under Silver's guidance, the new rabbi succeeded in instituting properly supervised *Kashrut* in Akron.

Silver was also informed when there was discontent with *Agudat Harabanim* members. At times there were accusations that their supervision was essentially for financial gain and *Kashrut* standards were therefore minimized. Rabbi Carl Manello of Youngstown thus described the reputation of the *rabanim* in the Ohio area in a May 20, 1930 letter to Silver:

> The honest rabbis join with charlatans who claim membership in the *Agudat Harabanim*. There are factories where delicatessen products are produced while non-kosher meats are sold under the same roof. Yet rabbis supervise these establishments. . . . A few months ago I straightforwardly asked a *rav* why he supervises questionable products. I also

inquired about his colleagues who lend their names to products they have never seen or investigated. He answered that the rabbis lack for bread and therefore must earn a living in this fashion. The *rav* also explained that it is better for the people to eat the non-kosher food in error, thinking it is supervised, than to eat it on purpose. My heart dropped when I heard these answers. How can *rabanim* sell their souls for a few cents? I therefore am angry at the honest members of the *Agudat Harabanim* for not condemning these acts of deceit.

After Silver moved to Ohio, Manello worked with him in both raising *Kashrut* standards and propagating the concepts of the dietary laws throughout this area.[3]

During 1932 Silver was drawn into a local conflict in Buffalo. A native Palestinian *shohet* came to Buffalo in 1923 where he also conducted a synagogue in his home. He later sought to organize a *Vaad Hakashrut* to centralize the supervision of the local slaughterhouses. He was opposed by a recent European arrival who was a member of the *Agudat Harabanim*. The *shohet* claimed the European *rav* minimized the shortcomings of Buffalo *Kashrut* so the lay people would not organize such a *Vaad*. The *shohet* wrote to Silver:

I thought that the *rav* would aid me in the meritorious deed of forming a *Vaad Hakashrut*. I was shocked when the *rav* declared before the committee that Buffalo *Kashrut* standards are outstanding. He actually said that in New York there are more *trefot* in one corner than in the entire city of Buffalo. I could not believe that a member of the *Agudat Harabanim* would speak in this fashion![4]

In a second letter, the *rav* was accused of not wishing to join the *Vaad* so he could retain his own *hekhsherim*:

The only reason the *rav* does not wish to join is because he wishes to remain the sole rabbinic authority in the city. Everything will then continue to be under his jurisdiction. I wonder how one rabbi can handle such a grave responsibility in our large city. He already supervises one slaughterhouse. He is also the chaplain in two nearby prisons where he spends the majority of the daytime. At night he takes courses in English. I can also testify that he attends his English classes on Friday nights, even though he does not write then. His attendance is still a desecration of the Divine Name. Where will he have the time to devote to proper *Kashrut* supervision and the other needs of the city?

I can now inform you that another slaughterhouse has turned to him. He has joined together with a non-married individual who claims to be a rabbi since he has a certificate from the Yeshiva Rabbi Isaac Elchanan. This youngster is engaged to the daughter of one of the leading *shohatim* in the slaughterhouse which they are now supervising. He is completely afraid of his fiancee's father who in reality is supervising him. This has ended any hope for a proper *Vaad Hakashrut* here.

The *rav* responded to these accusations by claiming that the *shohet* and his followers were "among the children of Korah who did not perish." He wrote:

The learned people refuse to accept them since they are ignoramuses. They treat them like *hametz* on the eve of Passover.[5]

The *rav* also declared that he was not happy with having a young American rabbi assist him. He suggested that the *Agudat Harabanim* demand that he be given sole authority.

It is beneath my dignity to be associated with this young rabbi. Local conditions, however, forced me into this situation. I have a suggestion which could solve this problem and also aid the *Agudat Harabanim*. If the organization will utilize its good offices to demand that I be given sole authority, I will remit half my salary to its central office. This will gain between five hundred to six hundred additional dollars a year for the *Agudat Harabanim* which is currently in such dire financial straits.

Silver later visited the community but was unable to accomplish much in solving its internal *Kashrut* problem.

During this period Rabbi Silver was also involved with a troublesome and hard-fought *Kashrut* conflict in a large New England city. A recent American arrival who was a scion of a preeminent Lithuanian rabbinical family became the *rav* of a group of Orthodox synagogues in this city. The new *rav* was himself a renowned *gaon* who was warmly hailed by the *Agudat Harabanim* upon his arrival. Advertisements were published in the Jewish daily press declaring:

> How great is this day of the *Gaon*'s arrival for us and all American Jewry. A new bright light is being revealed — the light of Torah and Judaism. We are confident that this sage will illuminate the entire house of Israel in America. He will become the greatest force for the teaching and dissemination of Torah in this country.[6]

Silver installed the *rav* in his new position on December 11, 1932. The president of this city's *Vaad Ha-Ir* wrote to Silver in anticipation of this event:

> I was urged by the entire committee to beg you in the name of the *Vaad Ha-Ir* to honor us with your presence at the installation. . . . We want you to install the Rabbi, that is part of our program; and we are looking forward to seeing you on December 11th.

Silver developed a warm friendship with the *rav* which continued until the former's death. However, some of Silver's colleagues were resentful of the newcomer and his sterling reputation. Already upon his arrival they complained that the *rav* was beardless.[7] In his new position the *rav* soon became involved in *Kashrut* supervision in his area. The local branch of the Swift slaughterhouse which previously had been supervised by Silver when he resided in the area was now supervised by the *rav*. Some nearby, elder *rabanim* took offense at this development. Their resentment was intensified when the *rav* did not immediately join their Council of Orthodox Rabbis. The local butchers were also drawn into the conflict, siding with either the new *rav* or the *rabanim*. A majority agreed to support the *rabanim* and refused to use the meats under the supervision of the *rav*. The executive director of the United Kosher Butchers Association wrote to Silver on June 6, 1933:

> You may be interested to know that Messrs. Rose and Craig, managers of the Swift slaughterhouse here, just left our office. We had a conference in which we thoroughly discussed the conditions in these slaughterhouses. We insisted that we could not use meats prepared under the supervision of a Rabbi who did not belong to the Council of Orthodox Rabbis. . . .
>
> I told Mr. Rose that we could take out an injunction against the Rabbi's supervision, but that we do not wish to make trouble yet.
>
> The result of the conference was that we flatly refused to use meat whose *Kashrut* is not certified by a seal bearing the words "Council of Orthodox Rabbis." We are sending him a letter to that effect, and he is going to take it up with you and with Chicago and let us know in about a week. We are giving him two weeks, at the most, and after that we shall do what must be done.

An elder *rav* in the area wrote to the *Agudat Harabanim* demanding that they:

> . . . uproot the idol planted by the young *rav*. . . . They must warn him to repent.
>
> If the result is the desecration of God's name, the leaders of the *Agudat Harabanim* will be the cause of it.[8]

Rabbi Silver was deeply tormented by this controversy. He saw justice in both positions. He felt that the young *rav* was being influenced by gossip which abounded in this area as the result of earlier controversy. Silver wrote to Rabbi Rosenberg on February 24, 1933:

> The young *rav* refuses to meet with many of the *rabanim*. He believes all the stories which are circulating about them since the earlier conflicts in this city. They are accused of declaring all types of *nevelot* and *trefot* to be kosher, and constantly disgracing God's name.

He also felt that the older *rabanim* were overly inflexible in their opposition to the young *rav* with their threats of injunctions and prohibitions against his supervision. Silver expressed his quandary in a June 9, 1933, letter to Rabbi Seltzer:

> I am in doubt as to the proper course of action. Should I ignore the entire matter and simply allow them to fight it out. Once it is over there will be a winner although the controversy will undoubtedly engender desecration of God's name. Or should I take the side of the young *rav* since those who oppose him constantly oppose my efforts to improve standards as well.

Silver finally did side with the young *rav* while constantly attempting to bridge the gap between the factions. Nevertheless, *Kashrut* friction remained constant in this community.

These communal *Kashrut* conflicts harmed the image of Orthodoxy and the *Agudat Harabanim* in the greater Jewish community. Hitler's rise to power in Germany, for example, and his subsequent ban on *shehitah* moved Silver to write to members of the Reform rabbinate, urging that they reinstitute *Kashrut* observance to demonstrate Jewish solidarity in protest of the Nazi decrees. Among the answers he received was that of Rabbi Max Raisin of Congregation B'nai Jeshurun of Paterson, New Jersey, dated May 9, 1933:

> Unfortunately, the cause of real *Kashrut* is hurt by its supposed friends. The Orthodox Rabbis of the community, in

Paterson, New York, and it would seem everywhere, fight among themselves on this very question. What one Rabbi declares to be kosher the other Rabbi will declare to be *trefa*. The ordinary people stand bewildered at a sight like this, and many of them make up their minds that there is no real *Kashrut*, and that the Rabbis have invented it as a source of income or "graft."

Here is a chance for your organizations to clean out the vineyard of the many thistles and briars.

Years later, an editorial in *The Commentator*, the undergraduate newspaper of Yeshiva College, declared on March 19, 1941:

That the driving force . . . is the leadership of the *Agudat Harabanim* is no surprise. The record of anarchy in *Kashrut*, and the dire danger of a barren future to Torah-true Judaism are eloquent testimony to the hegemony of the *Agudat Harabanim* in American Orthodox life.

Rabbi Silver achieved greater success when he was personally called into a community to officially organize or improve its *Kashrut* system and standards. Many times Silver acted on his own or headed a committee appointed by the *Agudat Harabanim*. In 1930 the United Orthodox Jewish Community of St. Louis requested aid in strengthening its *Kashrut* regulations. This central Orthodox community was organized in 1924. At that time it had already decided that only the official committee would collect the fees for *Kashrut* supervision. They in turn would employ the supervising rabbis and *shohatim*. By 1930 there was no chief rabbi in the community, and this basic guideline was being altered for the worse. Silver headed a committee appointed by the *Agudat Harabanim* which visited St. Louis. The other members were Rabbis Joseph Rosen of Passaic and Ben-Zion Notelevitz, then of Harrisburg. The group thoroughly investigated the religious standards in the community and interviewed all the concerned parties. Their decisions were later announced at a public meeting. They cited the need for the strict observance of the original ban against private individuals receiving payment for *Kashrut* tasks. *Shohatim* were enjoined from also being involved with the sale of meat as butchers. The ritual slaughterers were also prohibited from worshipping in non-Orthodox temples. Above all, the community was urged to seek a new chief rabbi so that the United Orthodox Community would benefit from proper spiritual leadership.[9]

Leon Gellman, the editor of St. Louis' *The Jewish Record*, later described the positive impact of the rabbinic committee in an August 29, 1930 letter to Silver:

> I cannot adequately detail the strong impression which the committee made in our city. The public meetings, the decisions, the public assembly in the Shaare Zedek Congregation, the careful investigations, the neutral attitude, the constant energy and work in so few days — all these factors have inspired and reunited local Orthodox Jews. . . .
>
> It is due to your merit and that of your colleagues that God has blessed this venture. Everything is being reorganized as it originally was and there is practically no opposition. Everyone now recognizes how much a united community can achieve.

But even Gellman had to inform Silver months later that one influential person later "publicly cursed and called down evil upon the heads of the *Agudat Harabanim* because he did not agree with their conclusions."[10] Nevertheless, the basic religious problems were totally solved toward the end of 1930. Rabbi Hayyim Fishel Epstein was then engaged as chief rabbi at Silver's suggestion. Under Epstein's guidance, the St. Louis community became a model of *Kashrut* standards and reliability.

In 1932 Silver visited Cleveland at the head of an *Agudat*

Harabanim delegation in an attempt to strengthen and centralize local *Kashrut* conditions. Here their efforts met with less success than in St. Louis. Most informative about the feelings of a concerned layman was the letter sent by Joseph Mellen, an attorney at law, to Rabbi Silver on February 14, 1932:

As you perhaps know by this time, word has been forwarded to you in your official capacity as President of the Union of Orthodox Rabbis of North America that the local *Vaad Hakashrut* has requested and at the same time extended an invitation to your organization to send to Cleveland at the earliest possible convenience a delegation of outstanding Rabbis for the purpose of hearing our grievances [insofar as they pertain] to the existing evils in our community and all of which have a direct bearing on matters pertaining to our religion. I hope you can find the time to come along with the others that you may see and hear for yourself that our grievances and our complaints are true, sincere and honest in every respect and that we would like to rebuild and re-establish what has been ruined and to all intents and purposes destroyed. . . .

All of this I say because I am about to offer a suggestion and I am hopeful that you will receive and consider it, in the light and in the spirit in which it is offered. It is my earnest wish and desire that when the delegation of rabbis come to Cleveland that they will disregard everything and everyone in Cleveland; that they will call a spade a spade; that they will not permit themselves to be blinded by sweet words and compliments, nor guided by words spoken in haste or by persons who have personal interests to defend, or by those who are aiming to profit financially or otherwise in the outcome of the hearing and that the delegation go about rendering the services for which they are coming, without fear or favor. . . .

From my experience in the past, I have found that the Rabbis who have come here, have tried to find favor in the eyes of the local Rabbis and at the same time try to find favor with the *shohatim* and with our organizations and even with those who are engaged in both the sale of meats and meat products, whether it be wholesale or retail. This cannot be so because these various interests conflict, and from my point of view, this has been primarily the reason why the evils existed and why these problems now confront us. In my humble judgment when the words that are to be spoken by the delegation are spoken frankly and freely and are the voice and sentiment of the Union of Orthodox Rabbis of North America, they will be received, I am sure, with a most profound respect and will carry with them the prestige that they ought to have.

When the words of the Rabbis of this delegation will go out into our community, uttered in the name of your organization, I am satisfied in my own mind, that no one in the city will have the audacity to challenge them, because they will be sincere words spoken by sincere men, leaders and outstanding Rabbis of the highest authority in North America on behalf of Orthodox Judaism.

In Cleveland, the local members of the *Agudat Harabanim* were split into two rival groups. One formed the *Misrad Harabanim* or Rabbinical Council of Cleveland. The other faction centered around Rabbi Judah Levenberg who was brought to the community by a number of congregations in the expectations that he would organize a formal Orthodox *kehillah*. The newcomer indignantly complained to Silver about the *Kashrut* conditions in Cleveland. Levenberg claimed that:

. . . non-Jews stand right next to the *shohatim*. While the latter slaughter, the former kill the chickens. Time after time the dead chickens are mixed up. Those killed are sold as kosher while the slaughtered are mistakenly considered non-kosher.

The salaries of the *shohatim* vary in accordance with their speed. They average about thirty-five dollars a week. There is one who actually earns over one hundred dollars a week. This *shohet* employs his own rabbi to supervise him.[11]

The previously established rabbinic group countered with charges that Levenberg and his followers were primarily concerned with financial gain:

> Their only goal is money, and coins are their rock of salvation. . . . They supervise butchers who have continuously sold *nevelot* as kosher. Many of their butchers publicly desecrate the Sabbath. They authorize *shohatim* who were previously prohibited by outstanding rabbis. All this they will do for two additional cents.
>
> They constantly speak against the other *rabanim* in the presence of the community's laymen. "Their deeds are those of Zimri but they expect the reward of Phineas," claiming they are sacrificing themselves for the sanctification of God's name![12]

While Silver attempted to bring about unity among all the Cleveland *rabanim*, discord and contention recurred intermittently during the ensuing years.

One important city which was permanently aided by the *Agudat Harabanim* was Toronto. As early as 1926 a committee consisting of Rabbis Israel Rosenberg, Joseph Konvitz, and Alter Pfeffer of New York's East Side visited the community and established its *Kashrut* regulations. During April of 1940 the organization once again sent a rabbinic delegation to Toronto. This time Rosenberg was joined by Rabbis Silver and Joseph Dov Soloveitchik of Boston.[13] The latter, both a Lithuanian Talmudic scholar and the recipient of a doctorate in philosophy from the University of Berlin, was then gradually gaining acknowledgment for his singular scholarship and vision. The visiting rabbis did not limit their suggestions to only *Kashrut* matters but issued detailed guidelines for a unified Toronto *kehillah*.

They stressed the urgency for the Toronto *rabanim* to form a local unified rabbinic group. This body was to have sole jurisdiction over all the *gittin* administered within Toronto. The *rabanim* were also to attempt to regulate the local marriage ceremonies so that only qualified personnel would perform them. The rabbis were to be the ultimate authority in the various *Kashrut* areas. All *shohatim* were to be subservient to their authority and in the employ of the *kehillah*. The suggestions continued:

13) The *kehillah* is obligated to pay a decent salary to the *shohatim*. We have designated a proper salary for each *shohet* for the time being. The *kehillah* may not decrease this sum.

14) The *kehillah* must also designate a budget which will sustain the *rabanim* in honor and dignity. Each *rav* is to receive his specified salary without delay from the *kehillah*.

15) No *rav* is permitted to accept any payment for the supervision of slaughterhouses, butcher shops, or *shohatim*.

16) The rabbinate and the *kehillah* are obligated to establish proper supervision in the many chicken abattoirs where currently lawlessness reigns. Why should the supervision of poultry be less stringent than the supervision of meat?

17) Any controversy or doubt regarding our suggestions and rulings will be adjudicated by the executive of the *Agudat Harabanim*. No *rav* may act on his own without the consent of the organization. The *kehillah* will also submit any dispute before the *Agudat Harabanim*.

18) The members of the *kehillah* are to properly render honor to the scholars, *rabanim*, and *shohatim* in their community. Their reverential regard enhances the status of the entire *kehillah* and its allegiance to Torah. A sacred obligation rests upon the leaders of the *kehillah* to enhance and glorify the Torah and the prestige of its standard-bearers. The *rabanim* must also aid in this task by working for unity within the community. They must cooperate in a total spirit of candor, peace, and faithfulness to uproot any ill will in their midst.

We are confident that the Toronto community which

possesses so many outstanding *rabanim* and dedicated laymen will accept this responsibility. The house of the Lord will be repaired, *Kashrut* strengthened, and the honor of the rabbinate restored.

After Rabbis Rosenberg, Silver, and Soloveitchik issued their detailed ruling, unity was achieved in Toronto. The *rabanim* joined together and a *kehillah* formed. This community later became a prime example of united Orthodox accomplishment.

While constantly stressing the need for unity whenever consulted, Silver still limited the participation of the non-Orthodox rabbinate. He insisted that the actual supervision of *Kashrut* can only be entrusted to the *rabanim*. In a December 14, 1934 letter to the Boston rabbinate Silver declared:

I totally agree with those who oppose placing the Council of Orthodox Rabbis under the jurisdiction of the lay body. Such an act can jeopardize the independence of the *rabanim*. The laymen could then insist on the appointment of Conservative rabbis to aid in *Kashrut* supervision. I could never agree to such an arrangement. Even some of the *rabanim* might try to curry additional favor with the lay people by being too lenient in their rulings.

My suggestion would be for the laymen's committee to agree that they will not interfere with the actual *Kashrut* supervision. They must agree to leave this solely in the hands of the *rabanim*. . . .

Rabbi Silver was centrally involved in the major *Kashrut* issues which challenged the entire *Agudat Harabanim* during this era. One such topic was the prohibition against having kosher and non-kosher factories under the same ownership. As early as 1905 the *Agudat Harabanim*, under the leadership of Rabbi Leventhal, removed their certification from a kosher factory which belonged to the proprietor of a *trefa* factory. This step was taken after kosher tags were discovered on *trefa* meat and also in the non-kosher factory. This problem periodically reappeared and became widespread in the mid-twenties. By this time even non-kosher firms recognized the profitability in the kosher food industry. They began taking over or setting up plants for the processing of kosher smoked meats and delicatessen. Religious personnel and even respectable rabbis were engaged to supervise and vouch for the products of the kosher departments. Many *rabanim* assumed that these setups would be conducted above reproach. Silver, nevertheless, instructed his *Kashrut* supervisors to carefully check shipments from such factories. While he was still in Springfield, in the latter half of 1927, a shipment of supposedly kosher frankfurters from a New York firm was found to include non-kosher ones. Silver undertook a thorough investigation and even brought the supervising rabbi of the kosher branch to Springfield. The evidence was shown to him and the rabbi admitted that there must have been some chicanery in the factory. The rabbi attempted to get to the bottom of the mix-up at the factory but was unsuccessful. The owner of the plant later informed the heads of the *Agudat Harabanim* that he filed criminal charges against the employee responsible for the fraudulent act. Upon further investigation even this was found to be untrue.[14]

Another incident which convinced Silver of the need for a ban against joint ownership took place in the Boston area. A kosher and non-kosher plant were owned by the same person. They were located in separate areas of the city, each having a different United States government meat inspection number. Silver was called upon to investigate the reliability of this situation. Together with a highly regarded local *rav*, he took a taxi to the non-kosher plant. Upon entering the building, Silver asked the receptionist if the kosher plant manager happened to be in this factory. When she replied in the affirmative, Silver did not wait for her to ring him. Instead Silver and the *rav* immediately proceeded to the manager's office. When they entered, the manager looked up aghast upon seeing the *rabanim*. Without further ado, Silver proceeded to open the drawers of the manager's desk. In one he found a supply of kosher labels. Silver explained to the *rav* that the firm evidently resorted to this kind of fraud when they ran short of an adequate supply of meat in their kosher division.

This conduct was typical of Silver's attitude towards *Kashrut* supervision. He often said that a rabbinic supervisor must not only be learned and scrupulously honest, but also exceedingly shrewd and resourceful. Above all, he was not to be too credulous and trusting of those standing to profit from the kosher production.

After these events and similar episodes throughout the United States, Silver brought influence to bear upon his colleagues to ban such establishments. Finally, on November 19, 1930, a resolution prohibiting joint ownership was adopted at the semi-annual convention of the *Agudat Harabanim*. The official English translation of this resolution which was publicized by the organization reads as follows:

Whereas, we already are acquainted from facts long existent that many swindlers, proprietors of factories that manufacture *trefa* smoked meats that defraud and fool Jews by selling them *trefa* instead of kosher, under the guise of kosher, and

Whereas, they maintain together with their *trefa* factories a supposedly kosher department or factory in order to bring into Jewish homes *trefa* and

Whereas, we have proven to ourselves that they falsify the kosher department, bringing therein *trefas*, and

Whereas, they falsify the tags and employ various schemes to deceive the *mashgihim*, (supervisors), and

Whereas, their *Kashrut* is worth nothing, and

Whereas, even though there are present *mashgihim*,

always, we have found many deceptions and frauds and that *trefa* is being sold by them instead of kosher products from their supposedly kosher departments with symbols intimating that the same is kosher, to the detriment and pain that such a thing brings in our day even though the scandal shrieks to us from every corner and by reason thereof, *trefa* is being consumed even in the most pious homes, while they are being deceived and defrauded by such methods.

This, therefore, brought about that the Union of Orthodox Rabbis of the United States and Canada at its convention was aroused to action and came forth with all its strength and cried out that in every place where there are to be found factories that call themselves kosher but are conducted by proprietors who also have *trefa* factories or departments, are banned in the same manner as *trefa* and *nevelah* and it is the duty of every Rabbi and every Jew to whom this ban reaches to the heart, to make public this ban in order that Jews shall not eat *trefa* and thereby sin without knowledge and one should himself understand that no Jew is permitted to give a *hashgahah* (supervision) in his name in such places, for if he does he merely brings about that Jews shall sin.

Be it further resolved that the factories are saturated through and through with *trefa* instead of kosher and that they are under the supervision of irresponsible and ignorant people and that by reason thereof they are deceiving and misleading people into eating *trefa* instead of kosher and that their products are banned for every Jew and it is prohibited for every Jew to bring the same into their houses. We also place it upon every synagogue president as a duty to proclaim this decree from their pulpits and to mention all the factories that are supposedly [but not truly] kosher — [as being] *trefa*, over the entire land. Be it further resolved that a standing committee of the Union of Orthodox Rabbis of the United States and Canada shall be existent for the purpose of devising ways and means of eliminating this evil and for the purpose of publishing from time to time all over the land the

ban of *trefa* and for the further purpose of educating the
people to the importance of the institution of *Kashrut*, which
unworthy persons are attempting to tear down; persons who
are not Rabbis and who have no authority in matters
concerning *Kashrut* but undertake to interfere with *Kashrut*
and to bring much havoc among our Jewish people.

Silver and the *Agudat Harabanim* were soon caught up in
fierce controversy. Other *rabanim* claimed that there was
nothing inherently wrong in certifying a kosher plant just
because its owner also possessed a non-kosher factory. Two small
Orthodox rabbinical organizations, the *Knesset Harabanim* and
Degel Harabanim, at a joint convention resolved that it was
permissible to supervise such factories. Rabbi Isaiah Margolin of
the *Knesset Harabanim* supervised one of these factories. When
the *Agudat Harabanim* advised his synagogue of the ban,
Margolin was fired. He later instituted a $75,000 damage suit
against the *Agudat Harabanim*. Margolin claimed that the ban
was "a foolish and implausible prohibition" and for uniformity
should have likewise been applied to abattoirs which also
handled kosher and non-kosher slaughtering. He accused the
Agudat Harabanim of being swayed by its members who derived
income from the abattoirs but not from the delicatessen plants.[15]
Silver was adamant in his opposition to Margolin. He described
conditions in the plant under Margolin's supervision:

The kosher and *trefa* divisions are under one roof. We found
signed kosher labels in the actual place where the *trefa* meat is
processed. There is no permanent *mashgiah*, and the door to
the kosher region is constantly open. There is practically no
way of avoiding mix-ups under these conditions. Even without
the *Agudat Harabanim*'s resolution, it would be absolutely
forbidden to supervise such a factory.[16]

To a prominent purveyor of kosher meat, Silver wrote on
August 30, 1932:

The *Agudat Harabanim* does not have to justify its rulings before the masses. We will not deviate from the proper Torah path by causing Jews to stumble in the laws of *Kashrut*.

Silver's strong stand was challenged by some members of the *Agudat Harabanim* who felt that under proper conditions there could be certification of the kosher divisions of such plants. These *rabanim* were among those who elected Rabbi Joseph Konvitz to the presidency of the organization in 1934 since he was more lenient in this issue. Konvitz was also supported by his fellow members of the Mizrachi Organization of America while Silver was identified with the Agudat Israel.[17] Konvitz continued in this position until 1939 with Silver serving as one of the honorary presidents during this period. In 1939 the *Agudat Harabanim* once again reverted to a presidium, selecting Rabbis Silver, Rosenberg, and Levinthal.

Silver continued in opposition to the certification of such kosher factories even when he was no longer the president. On September 9, 1935, he wrote to Rosenberg:

> Everyone will admit that I always defend my convictions. You are my dearest friend and most precious colleague. Nevertheless, I will never conceal my feelings from you when the status of Judaism and its observance can be improved. Likewise I do not intend to be silent during this period. I will oppose all those who render decisions against the Torah. I am not concerned with the approval of the masses, but only with the integrity of our tradition and its standard-bearers.

Silver even took issue with the *kashrut* Department of the Union of Orthodox Jewish Congregations of America for granting its kosher seal to some products of the H.J. Heinz company of Pittsburgh. Silver felt that supervising the kosher products of such a large firm which also manufactured *trefa* produce was a violation of the *Agudat Harabanim*'s decision. His feelings intensified when it was claimed that a can bearing the kosher label was found to be *trefa*. Silver held that this possibility was the very reason for the *Agudat Harabanim*'s prohibition. He thus wrote to William Weiss, the president of the Orthodox Union:

All the leaders of our rabbinical organization have warned you to desist from granting supervision to factories which contain both kosher and *trefa* products. You will cause the Children of Israel to eat non-kosher food by such *hekhsherim*. Leave the responsibility for *Kashrut* supervision to the genuine *rabanim* who will know how to avoid making such errors.

I warn you again, saying, "Depart, I pray you, from the tents" of the manufacturers of both kosher and *trefa* produce.[18]

Weiss defended the actions of his organization and pleaded for the cooperation of the *Agudat Harabanim*. On July 24, 1936, he wrote to Silver:

It has come to our attention that you are spreading information concerning the Heinz products endorsed by us, which we consider unwarranted under the circumstances.

At the conference with you and your associates, at which Mr. Koenigsberg and I were present, we asked for the production of the evidence, and up-to-date it has not been produced. Furthermore, a committee of our Rabbinical Council, consisting of Rabbis Charlop, Goldstein, Reichman and Rosenbloom,[19] immediately upon hearing rumors of the incident went to the grocery store in the New Jersey town and purchased other cans of beans and found all of them to be in proper condition. The Heinz Company representatives do not concede the mislabeling of the *one* can of beans, claimed to be mislabeled, especially as it seems to be conceded that the code mark on the can indicates that the contents were not intended to be kosher beans.

The fact that neither you nor we have had our attention called to more than one questionable can out of millions that are produced indicates that there is no cause for further publication of the incident. The Union of Orthodox Jewish

Congregations of America is conducting its *Kashrut* policy for the benefit of the community on a non-commercial basis, and it is our desire to cooperate with all organizations for the purpose of establishing more kosher products and better supervision in behalf of our people. Our policy has received the approval of the community in general. We believe that the *Agudat Harabanim* should cooperate with us, as we are at all times ready to cooperate with them, for the purpose of creating more friendly relationships between all elements of the Jewish community. In fact, when incidents have been brought to our attention which would tend to indicate some inadvertent situation in connection with *Kashrut* endorsements or supervision of other responsible Rabbinic bodies, we have refrained from publicizing such isolated incidents, knowing that in the many details there may at times occur an oversight which should be remedied by sympathetic cooperation rather than by confusing the public and creating distrust on the part of the Jewish community.

Permit me to assure you that while we do not doubt your sincerity of purpose, nevertheless, we feel that it is to the general interest of the Orthodox leadership and public that the most friendly spirit of cooperation exist among the various organizations, even though complete unity of method cannot be achieved.

The differences between Silver and the Orthodox Union continued during this period. Years later, Silver became more partisan toward the Union's *Kashrut* supervision as their reputation for reliability and exactness grew. He particularly enjoyed a warm relationship with its *Kashrut* administrator, Rabbi Alexander Rosenberg.

Silver also became involved in New York's major kosher poultry controversy. As early as 1931 attempts were begun to correct the many improprieties in this city's massive *Kashrut* industry.[20] A number of local prominent Jews appealed to Mayor James J. Walker. He responded by appointing a Mayor's committee on *Kashrut*. This committee proceeded to organize the Kashruth Association of Greater New York which was chartered in May 1932. Under the energetic leadership of Rabbi Nachman Ebin, a graduate of the Rabbi Isaac Elchanan Theological Seminary, attempts were made to control and centralize supervision. However, due to the many vested and counter-business interests of people in the industry, and that of some rabbis and *shohatim*, little progress was achieved. In the summer of 1934, the kosher poultry industry was thrown into crisis by conflict between the *shohatim* and marketmen. Mayor Fiorello H. LaGuardia appointed Judge Otto Rosalsky to mediate the dispute. Rosalsky, an Orthodox Jew, promptly began hearings and concerned himself more with the religious problems than with the labor issues involved. He discovered widespread faults and shortcomings. The *shohatim* were required to work too fast and to slaughter unequitable amounts of poultry each week. The rabbis did not supervise every kosher poultry market and neither was there an identifying mark on each properly slaughtered chicken. Rosalsky requested the aid of the Kashruth Association in solving these basic problems. In conjunction with the Association, Rosalsky announced among his decisions:

That all kosher slaughtered poultry offered for sale shall have affixed thereto a *plumba* [lead seal] signifying that it is kosher, the same to be placed thereon by a *mashgiah*. The *plumba* shall be supplied by the Kashruth Association of Greater New York.

In order to strengthen this ruling and to convince the Jewish consumers of its importance, the rabbis decided to ban any poultry which did not possess this *plumba*. Such chickens were to be considered non-kosher and the utensils used in their preparation were to require ritual purging. At a mass meeting convened at the Beth Hamidrash Hagadol on November 5, 1934, the ban proper was pronounced:

And, therefore, in accordance with the authority specifically vested in us by the holy Torah, for safeguarding the observance of its dietary laws, we herewith do with the full strength and severity of the law, solemnly declare, pronounce, issue and publish an *issur* (religious prohibition), to go into effect forthwith on poultry not slaughtered in accordance with the above regulations or not bearing an authorized token, as above described, declaring that such poultry is forbidden to be consumed by Jews. Utensils in which birds not killed in accordance with these regulations have been cooked may not be further used without previous inquiry of a Rabbi, who shall determine whether they may be used again.

And every *shohet* who, in contravention of these regulations, will slaughter birds without supervision or without a token of *Kashrut* being affixed, as described above . . . will lose his status of reliability in regard to *Kashrut*, and as a violator of the Jewish Law will henceforth become disqualified to act as *shohet*.

We cherish confidence that no rabbi or scholar versed in Jewish Law will attempt to diminish the force of this prohibition or rule to the contrary, and thus rebel against and separate himself from the entire body of the Orthodox Rabbinate of New York City in which case his ruling shall become null and void as are the rulings of one who is a destroyer of the fence of the law (non-conformist).[21]

In the summer of 1935, the right of the New York rabbis affiliated with the Kashruth Association to ban kosher poultry without their *plumba* was challenged in the civil courts. The S.S. and B. Live Poultry Corporation of the Bronx sued the Association for declaring its poultry *trefa*. The suit claimed that the Association did not have the right to ban chickens not slaughtered under its supervision and that by such action the plaintiff's business was being ruined. The case finally reached the Supreme Court of the State of New York and was heard by Justice Philip J. McCook. Rabbi Silver became one of the central witnesses in this trial. Despite threatening letters which warned him not to appear, Silver was on the witness stand for six hours. He totally upheld the authority of the New York Association to issue the ban. Silver was asked over forty questions by the judge and attorneys regarding rabbinic authority and their enactments.[22] Orally citing all the relevant sources and responsa, Silver's testimony fortified the ban. His appearance was thus described in Cincinnati's *Every Friday* of January 17, 1936:

> Rabbi Silver was on the witness stand for six hours. He withstood a merciless cross examination by Mr. Allen Deutsch, attorney for the S.S. and B. Poultry Company who for two hours tried unsuccessfully to find a flaw in the direct evidence of the witness.
>
> According to the report of H. Ehrenreich, appearing in the *Jewish Daily Forward*, the Yiddish newspaper, Rabbi Silver made the strongest impression of all the witnesses who appeared at this trial to date. To quote Mr. Ehrenreich: "Of all the rabbis — many of them renowned in the rabbinical world — who appeared on the witness stand thus far, no one has made such a strong impression as did Rabbi Silver. It was not necessary to be a pious Jew to be impressed with a feeling of deep reverence and respect and amazement while listening to passage after passage from the Talmud which the learned rabbi cited from memory without any notes whatsoever, giving the volume, number of the page, paragraph and in many instances the line where the cited passages appeared. For such a powerful memory, even the agnostic must bow his head."

Judge McCook later ruled in favor of the New York rabbis and upheld the ban. His decision was welcomed by all of organized Orthodoxy. *Every Friday* declared, in an editorial headed "A Gratifying Decision" (February 7, 1936):

> Orthodox Jewry as well as American Jewry in general has every reason to feel elated over the recent decision which

Justice Philip J. McCook of the New York Supreme Court handed down in favor of the New York City Kashruth Association. While the decision has directly strengthened the authority of the Orthodox Rabbinate it has also added much to the prestige of traditional Judaism in general.

The beginning of the now famous *Kashrut* trial threatened to bring disrepute and chaos to Orthodox Jewry, but it turned out to be a blessing, due to Justice McCook's decision which is full of wisdom and sympathy. As a non-Jew, Justice McCook was able to view the entire case with all its complexities in an objective manner and his decision may now serve as an object lesson to all Jewry in its attitude to Traditional Judaism and to the Orthodox Rabbinate. . . .

Despite this ruling, opposition to the Kashruth Association continued. McCook's ruling enabled the Association to declare non-kosher any poultry slaughtered without its supervision. However, it did not legally prevent poultry markets from continuing to engage private rabbis as supervisors. By early 1939 a group of butchers formally united in opposition to the Association. They were certified by a group of rabbis known as the Beth Din Tzedek. In an attempt to terminate this new public dispute, the Kashruth Association and the Beth Din Tzedek agreed to accept the decision of three prominent *rabanim* residing outside New York City. Rabbis Silver, Levinthal, and Soloveitchik were chosen. After careful investigation and hearings, the *rabanim* issued their *pesak din* on April 26, 1939. The original ban of 1934 was declared to still be valid and only this *plumba* could be used to certify poultry. The Beth Din Tzedek was therefore to surrender its *hekhsherim* to the Kashruth Association. On the other hand, the authority of the Association was limited to the poultry industry. It was not to interfere with the supervision of other rabbis in areas such as the cattle abattoirs. In order to insure lasting good relations the *rabanim* suggested:

1) The members of the Beth Din Tzedek should join the Kashruth Association. They should aid in its administration and attempts to strengthen the observance of Torah. We are confident that the leaders of the Kashruth Association will appreciate this aid and will properly honor the rabbis of the Beth Din Tzedek.

2) It is desirable that the heads of the Kashruth Association constantly consult the leaders of the *Agudat Harabanim*. Thus they will successfully resolve the important issues before them.

We are confident that the New York rabbis and lay leaders, famed for their Torah knowledge and good deeds, will establish amicable relations. This will raise the prestige of Torah and enhance the honor of the rabbinate throughout the city and the country. Respect will be rendered to Orthodoxy and the Name of God endeared through the actions of its leaders and helmsmen.[23]

Later that year on November 21, 1939, a public convocation was held at the Hatam Sofer Synagogue on New York's East Side. Once again the ban was renewed on poultry slaughtered without the *plumba* of the Kashruth Association. Rabbi Silver was the main speaker and stressed the importance of ritual observance at a time of ever increasing tribulations for the House of Jacob. He called upon New York Jewry to insist upon this symbol of the Kashruth Association. Thus they will be assured of proper supervision.[24]

Despite all Silver's efforts and those of his colleagues, it was approximated that the *plumba* of the Kashruth Association was affixed to only eight percent of the so-called kosher poultry slaughtered in New York City in 1940.[25] *Kashrut* remained a constant subject of dispute during the ensuing years. Even as late as 1960, Silver was publicly attacked in an editorial which supported the Conservative rabbinate in its attempts to enter the field of *Kashrut* supervision. Trude Weiss-Rosmarin wrote in *The Jewish Spectator*, which she edited:

Even more important, however, is provision for more effective supervision of the *Kashrut* of meat. This supervision is so complex that not infrequently some of the most revered pillars of the Orthodox Rabbinate have found the task confronting them too much. Thus, to cite but one instance, Rabbi Eliezer Silver, eighty-year-old dean of the "European-type" American Orthodox Rabbis, has found himself on several occasions in the embarrassing situation of being summoned before the "Kosher Law Enforcement of the Food Control of the New York State Department of Agriculture and Markets" for charges that meats which he certified as "kosher" were not properly washed (*hadahah*) en route from the slaughtering houses . . .[26].

These accusations could not possibly have been valid, since meat under Silver's supervision arrived in New York City long before *hadahah* was required. Yet those who opposed Orthodoxy continued to attack Rabbi Silver.

Kashrut remained a problem. In addition, by the late 1930's, Silver became involved with the other acute and desperate problems which were then engulfing the Jewish people.

Notes

1. Letter from Rabbi Braver to Rabbi Silver, May 30, 1932. Silver's response is dated June 2, 1932.

2. Letter from Reverend Nathan Danzig to Silver, n.d. However, a letter from the new rabbi, Elijah David Stampfer, is dated June 29, 1932.

3. Manello's later letters to Silver are from 1935. Among the ideas discussed are the dissemination of pamphlets in English stressing the religious and scientific importance of the dietary laws.

4. The first letter of the *shohet* to Silver is dated December 5, 1932, and the second letter is dated August 31, 1933.

5. The letter of the *rav* to Silver is dated December 8, 1932.

6. Undated clippings in the Silver Archives.

7. Letter from Rabbi Seltzer to Rabbi Silver, August 31, 1932. Seltzer described how the *rabanim* who greeted the *rav* at the pier on the day of his arrival rebuked him for being beardless.

8. Letter from Rabbi Boruchoff to Rabbi Seltzer, July 28, 1933. The letter was forwarded by Seltzer to Silver.

9. *Hapardes*, August 1930, p. 1, and letter from Rabbi Samuel H. Klibansky of St. Louis to Silver, August 17, 1930.

For details of the St. Louis United Orthodox Jewish Community see *Brocho L'Mnachem*, ed. Norman Paris (St. Louis, 1955), pp. 24-40. This volume was published on the fifteenth anniversary of Chief Rabbi Menachem H. Eichenstein's association with the United Community and its own thirtieth anniversary.

10. Letter from Gellman to Silver, May 23, 1932. Gellman, an organizer of the U.S. Mizrachi movement, later served as its president (1935-39). He moved to Israel in 1949 and became chairman of the World Mizrachi Organization in that year.

11. Letter from Rabbi Levenberg to Rabbi Silver, September 26, 1932.

12. Letter from Rabbi Mordecai Schwartz to Rabbi Silver, January 30, 1933. Also see the letter from the *Misrad Harabanim* to Silver, February 8, 1934. The quotation cited in the text is from Sotah, 22b.

13. The details of the 1926 regulations were contained in an August 27, 1929 letter to Rabbi Silver from the Rabbinical Council of the Orthodox Rabbis of Toronto. The decisions of the 1940 delegation were announced on April 11, 1940, and published in *Hapardes*, May 1940, pp. 6-7.

14. The background to the kosher and non-kosher joint ownership problem was contained in an English fact sheet issued by the *Agudat Harabanim* in 1930, and the unpublished MS by Rabbi David L. Silver.

15. For the details of the Margolin controversy see Gastwirth, *Fraud, Corruption, and Holiness*, pp. 145-46.

16. Letter from Rabbi Silver to Rabbi Pardes, January 10, 1932.

17. For the reasons for Silver's defeat in the 1934 elections see the letters from Rabbi Judah Forer of Holyoke, Mass., to Rabbi Silver, January 30, 1934, and the clippings from the Yiddish press of February 5, 1934.

18. The quotation is from Numbers 16:26. Silver's letter to Weiss is undated.

19. The earlier reference was to Benjamin Koenigsberg, then a lay vice-president and a member of the administrative council of the Orthodox Union.

The rabbis referred to were Rabbis Jehiel Charlop, Herbert S. Goldstein, Solomon Reichman, and Ben Zion Rosenbloom.

20. For the history of the New York controversy see Jeremiah J. Berman, *Shehitah* (New York: Bloch Publishing Co., 1941), pp. 339-347; and Gastwirth, *Fraud, Corruption, and Holiness*, pp. 131-186.

Also consulted were the plaintiff's and defendant's moving papers presented to the Supreme Court, "S.S. and B. Live Poultry Corporation, plaintiff-against-the Kashruth Association of Greater New York, defendant."

21. The ban is cited from Exhibit "D," "English version of the Hebrew text of *Issur*" in defendant's moving papers.

22. For the questions asked of Rabbi Silver and the sources cited in reply see *Hapardes*, February 1936, pp. 5-7.

23. *Hapardes*, June 1939, pp. 4-5. Also see *Hapardes*, July 1939, p. 6.

24. *Hapardes*, December, 1939, pp. 12-13.

25. Berman, *Shehitah*, p. 347.

26. "Kashruth and Conservative Rabbis," *The Jewish Spectator*, September 1960, pp. 6-7. The requirement for washing the meat before seventy-two hours elapse since its slaughter is detailed in *Shulhan Arukh: Yoreh Deah* 69:13.

6

Agudat Israel

Silver remained in close contact with his main spiritual mentor, Rabbi Hayyim Ozer Grodzenski, during all these years. The master and disciple overcame the physical distance between them through constant correspondence. Torah insights, mutual aid, advice and guidance were the themes of their communications. Rav Hayyim Ozer often related to his confidants that he was glad that his student was in the United States. From there Silver could aid his brethren throughout the world.[1]

Silver was particularly influenced by Rabbi Grodzenski's total involvement with the Agudat Israel movement. Organized in 1912, this association united German neo-Orthodoxy, Hungarian extreme Orthodoxy, and the hassidic and erudite Jewries of Poland and Lithuania. Its main goal was to safeguard the *halakhah* as the basic principle governing Jewish life and society. Agudat Israel presented a viable counterforce to the inroads made by the Reform, assimilationist, and socialistic trends. It was also opposed to Zionism, considering it sinful to revive Jewish nationhood in the Land of Israel through human agency. There was also opposition to the secular trend of the Zionistic movement and its irreligious leadership. To protect the authority of its prominent rabbinical leaders, a Council of Torah Sages was formed by the Agudat Israel. Known as the *Mo'etzet Gedolei ha-Torah*, its decisions were accepted as binding and they were considered the guiding force of the movement. Rav Hayyim Ozer became the chairman of this council.[2]

155

Several attempts made to organize an American branch of the Agudat Israel during the twenties and early thirties failed since there were few American Jews interested in its viewpoint. During this period the Mizrachi Organization of America was rapidly gaining ground.

The Mizrachi was founded in 1902 as a religious faction in the World Zionist Organization. Its American branch was founded in 1911 and became effective in 1913 when Rabbi Meyer Berlin, later Bar-Ilan, settled in New York. He was the youngest son of the famed Volozhin *Rosh Yeshivah*, Rabbi Naftali Tzvi Judah Berlin. Resourceful and energetic, Meyer Berlin turned the Mizrachi into a vibrant force on the American scene.

While loyal to the Agudat Israel commitment of his mentor, Rabbi Silver was a fellow companion of the Mizrachi movement. He attended many of its conferences and conventions, raised money for its drives, and referred to the Mizrachi as his "younger sister."[3] Silver proposed that steps be undertaken to bring about a merger between the Mizrachi and Agudat Israel. In his address before the *Agudat Harabanim* at its annual convention on November 13, 1933, Silver declared:

> We must bring about a meeting in Eretz Israel of all the heads of world Orthodoxy. In cooperation with the rabbinic and lay leaders, we should unify the Mizrachi and the Agudat Israel. Perhaps we can arrange for a central authority for all Orthodoxy. We must no longer suffer from disunity.[4]

Silver soon corresponded with Rav Hayyim Ozer regarding his ideas for a merger between the two organizations. Rabbi Grodzenski, however, felt that it was still premature for such an approach. He wrote to Rabbi Silver:

> You have asked my opinion regarding your idea . . . to call a meeting this summer in the Holy City of Jerusalem in order to unify all the Orthodox factions. I feel it is still too early for such a step. The exact viewpoints of the Mizrachi and Agudah

must be clarified. Until now, the Agudah has insisted that the Mizrachi leave the World Zionist Organization. Only then can they work together for the good of the *yishuv*. The Mizrachi, however, has not agreed to this step. Already at the Agudah's first Great Assembly in Vienna [in 1923] this idea was unsuccessfully broached. The Agudah likewise requested that the Mizrachi leave the Jewish Agency's education and culture committee. This too was rejected by the Mizrachi. Nevertheless, it is worthwhile for the leaders of the *Agudat Harabanim* to correspond with the heads of the Mizrachi in order to clarify positions. Once this is accomplished, then we can consider a general assembly. Only after much preparation will such a gathering succeed. Otherwise, an assembly without the necessary arrangements will result in more harm than good.[5]

Despite Silver's efforts, he did not succeed in achieving unity. Rabbi Grodzenski later invited his disciple to participate in the Agudat Israel's third *Kenesiyyah ha-Gedolah* or Great Assembly, scheduled for August 1937 in Marienbad. This Assembly attracted representatives from all the local branches and exercised "the ultimate political authority of the association." Silver willingly undertook the voyage at his mentor's request. There was some opposition among his colleagues who totally identified with the Mizrachi movement. Levinthal and Konvitz were apprehensive lest he commit the entire *Agudat Harabanim* to the ideals of the Agudat Israel. In response to their criticisms, Silver wrote to Rosenberg on July 30, 1937:

I informed Rabbi Levinthal that I am not going as an official representative of our organization. I am rather a *rav* who was the president and am now the honorary president of the *Agudat Harabanim*. I will not speak in Levinthal's name and certainly not for the entire rabbinate.[6]

Silver arrived in Vilna where he was warmly received by Rav Hayyim Ozer. Silver thus described his reunion with his *rebbe*:

I arrived in Vilna and even the gentiles knew where Rabbi Grodzenski was. They directed me tc his summer residence which was outside the city proper. The *gaon* received me with great joy. He declared that his delight in being reunited with his student actually improved his physical health. I accompanied him on his walks, and he enquired about all the *rabanim* and scholars in the United States. He particularly praised the undertakings of the Ezras Torah and the Central Relief Committee.

. . . He also explained the inner workings of the Agudat Israel and delegated me to represent him at the meeting of the Council of Torah Sages and the *Kenesiyyah ha-Gedolah.* Every spare moment was utilized for Torah discussion and Talmudic analysis. My greatest joy was on the Sabbath when I spent the entire day with him. Late into Saturday night, I sat at his table, enthralled by his knowledge, insight, and joyful spirit.[7]

The high point of Silver's visit came at the *Kenesiyyah* itself which was held from August 17th through August 23rd. Here he saw the last massive gathering of European Orthodoxy before the Holocaust. There were hundreds of delegates and thousands of guests representing all spectrums of Torah commitment. These included Polish *Hassidim,* Lithuanian scholars, Hungarian pietists, and German devotees of Torah and modern civilization united under the Agudah banner. The presidium-dais, filled with many of the generation's leading rabbis, presented an awesome picture of dignity and sanctity. Rabbi Silver was given a place of honor at this dais as the leading American representative in attendance. He also addressed a plenary session of the *Kenesiyyah* and a meeting of the Council of Torah Sages. His public address began with a Talmudic discourse. Afterwards Silver demanded that the Torah leaders of European Jewry extend greater spiritual guidance for their American brethren. He stated:

Now I must speak for my American colleagues. My words have the approval of the *gaon*, Rav Hayyim Ozer. For the first time I will make a request from you. We of the United States are constantly answering your appeals for financial aid. We support your charity funds, Talmud Torahs and Yeshivot. Now we request that you start to repay us by inspiring us with your spirit. Let each of the Torah leaders visit us once not to raise funds, but rather to intensify American Torah life.

Why have you deserted almost a third of your people? . . . We have sowed and planted yeshivot and other Torah institutions. We have fought for *Kashrut* and Family Purity. However, we are now weak. Come and implant a new spirit within us. Nevertheless, only send us Torah leaders steeped in learning and fear of God. Only such *geonim* can be influential in the United States. With such an approach you will repay us for what we have done for you over the years.[8]

Silver proposed that an international rabbinical committee be organized to strengthen Torah observance throughout the world. He stated:

This international rabbinic body should consist of two or three pre-eminent Torah scholars from each country, regardless of whether they are affiliated with Agudah or Mizrachi. They should confer on how to strengthen Torah observance and the yeshivot. They should also express their viewpoints regarding Eretz Israel. The first assembly should be in Vilna, and from there a committee should be sent to visit all the Palestinian and diaspora Talmudical schools. An international fund should be established for these institutions.

These meetings should take place from time to time, although the group will not be an official world rabbinical organization. Rav Hayyim Ozer and many of the other *roshei yeshivah* have agreed to this suggestion.

On the Sabbath of the *Kenesiyyah* Silver visited with the leading hassidic *rebbe* present, Rabbi Abraham Mordecai Alter of Gur (Gora Kalwaria), Poland. Together with Rabbi Elhanan

Bunim Wasserman, the head of the Baranowicze Yeshivah, Silver entered the Gurer *Rebbe*'s reception room. They found the hassidic leader completely engrossed in Torah study. As was his practice, Rabbi Alter did not indulge in secular talk on the Sabbath, but rather only discussed Torah and Talmudic topics. For the next hour, Silver enjoyed every moment as he posed question after question concerning difficult Talmudic passages to the *rebbe*. Many were resolved on the spot by Rabbi Alter who was both a celebrated scholar and the charismatic leader of tens of thousands of *Hassidim*. An hour later, which seemed like fleeting minutes to Silver, they parted in joy as a large crowd of *Hassidim* stood outside waiting to be received by their *rebbe*.

Silver spent the rest of his stay continuing his discussions with the other rabbinic leaders present. He pledged the aid of his American followers for many worthwhile projects. He also made the acquaintance of Rabbi Menahem Zemba, a unique Warsaw *gaon*. The latter's method of Talmudic study was an amalgam of both the dialectical approach common in Poland and the logical and penetrating system of the Lithuanian yeshivot. Silver encouraged Zemba to edit his novellae entitled *Mahazeh la-Melekh* on Maimonides' *Mishneh Torah* and pledged to sponsor its publication. These plans were not to be realized, however, as Zemba later died a martyr's death in the Warsaw Ghetto in 1943. His manuscript and many of his other important works were subsequently lost in the Holocaust.[9]

When the time came for Silver's departure on August 23rd, a large group of rabbinic and yeshivah leaders accompanied him to the railroad station. As his train left, the assembled group burst into song, chanting: "With joy shall you go forth, and in peace shall you be led."[10]

After his return to the States, Silver intensified his efforts to revitalize the American branch of the Agudat Israel. Rav Hayyim Ozer supported his student in these endeavors since he

Farewell to Rabbi Eliezer Silver at the railroad station, following the *Kenesiyyah ha-Gedolah* in Marienbad in 1937. *1*, Rabbi Yitzchak Weinstein; *2*, Rabbi Hillel Liberman; *3*, Rabbi Meir Karelitz; *4*, Rabbi Eliezer Silver; *5*, Rabbi David Tzvi Zilberstein; *6*, Rabbi Meir Scziransky. The other personalities have not as yet been identified

Kenesiyyah ha-Gedolah in Jerusalem in 1954. *Left to right:* Rabbis Eliezer Silver; Israel Alter of Gur

Rabbi Eliezer Silver speaking at an Agudat Israel of America convention. *Left to right:* Rabbis Nahum Mordecai Perlow of Novominsk; Moshe Feinstein; Mordecai Shelomo Friedmann of Boyan; Eliezer Silver; Abraham Joshua Heschel of Kopzynce; Mordecai Shalom Joseph Friedmann of Sadgora

Rabbi Joseph Konvitz

Rabbi Israel Rosenberg

Rabbi Aaron Kotler

Rabbi Mendel Zaks

felt the time had arrived for American Orthodoxy to undertake a central role in the Agudah. Silver urged his rabbinic colleagues to join with the leading rabbis and scholars he met in Marienbad. In an open letter, dated November 18, 1937, Silver stated:

> I was privileged to visit with the leading *gaon* of our generation, the prince of the Torah, Rav Hayyim Ozer, in Vilna. I also saw the glory and holiness of all the assembled scholars and *geonim* in the Council of Torah Sages and at the *Kenesiyyah*. Happy are the eyes that have seen such sights!
>
> How much longer will we separate ourselves from these leaders of the Torah? How can we continue to stand apart as our masters are opposed and censured by those outside the Agudah camp? Can it be that we do not choose to be with Rav Hayyim Ozer, Rav Menahem Zemba, and the Gurer Rebbe?
>
> The time has come for us to declare our allegiance to Agudat Israel. This is the organization to which "the cedars of Lebanon, the nobles of the Law, and the masters of Torah and fear of God"[11] belong. Is there any other sanctity in our time outside of this encampment of the Lord?
>
> My brothers, the time has come to overcome our hesitations, and to unite with the *geonim* of the world. Many in America will now publicly declare their joining with us. We will not attack or contend with other political parties. Numerous members of another organization [Mizrachi] are dear to us. Our main concern will rather be to raise the prestige of Torah and its standard-bearers. . . .
>
> The dawn is breaking and the time has come to unite with the guardians of the Torah. Whoever is for God and His Torah and wishes to honor his teachers will join us. Please write to me declaring your acquiescence to be a member of Agudat Israel. We will form a special rabbinic body, and later a local council of Torah sages will be organized. Groups of young, observant lay people will also be formed. Agree, sign, and answer me in the affirmative.

There was favorable response to Rabbi Silver's appeal. Over sixty rabbis declared their willingness to join the Agudah. But there was also vigorous opposition by the Mizrachi who feared the possible divisiveness in Silver's proposal. To assuage their feelings, Silver published an open letter in *Hapardes* in which he stressed his "peaceful intentions."[12] His main goal was to "unite and join the American *geonim* with the European scholars."

Preliminary meetings continued throughout 1938 with the American branch of Agudat Israel being formally organized in 1939. Silver drafted its platform which stated:

1. Agudat Israel of America is an integral branch of the international Agudat Israel movement. It will participate in its institutions such as the *Kenesiyyah ha-Gedolah* and executive committee. Its highest authority will be the World Council of Torah Sages and its American branch.

2. Any observant Jew in the United States may join the organization. Likewise, groups from synagogues, *hevrot shas*, yeshivot, and Talmud Torahs may join.

3. The American branch will concern itself with all the matters affecting world and American Jewries. Its goal will be identical to that of the world Agudah — to solve all problems which daily challenge the Jewish people, in accordance with Torah and tradition.

4. The founding of Agudat Israel is no longer subject to negotiations or debate, but is rather an accomplished fact.

5. The initial acts of Agudat Israel of America will be to spread Torah knowledge and fear of God. The study of Torah will be encouraged among both young and old.

6. Every attempt will be made to enhance the prestige of Torah and its sages in the United States, Eretz Israel, and all the other countries of our dispersion.

7. American Jewry should be encouraged to build Eretz Israel in accordance with Torah and the guidance of the Sages. The institutions of the old *yishuv* and its leaders must be supported.

The labor division of the organization, Poalei Agudat Israel, must be strengthened. The dedicated efforts of its *kibbutzim* and settlements to observe the sabbatical year will be supported.

8. The American branch will remain in constant contact with the World Council of Torah Sages, the international executive committee, and the *Agudat Harabanim*.

9. In all its American attempts to strengthen Torah observance, the Agudat Israel will cooperate fully with the *Agudat Harabanim*.

10. The auxiliary Agudah groups such as *Tzeirei Agudat Israel* [Agudat Israel Youth], *Benot* [Daughters], and Poalei Agudat Israel will be encouraged to expand their American activities.

11. Special efforts will be made to aid the refugees now arriving in the United States. Our organization will particularly aid the newcomer rabbis and observant Jews.[13]

The first convention of the new organization was held in Far Rockaway from July 9th through July 11th, 1939. Rabbi Silver was elected president, with Rabbi Shlomo Heiman, the senior *rosh yeshivah* of Mesifta Torah Vodaath of Brooklyn, and Rabbi Mordecai Shelomo Friedman, the Boyaner Rebbe, selected as vice presidents. In his keynote address, Silver stressed that the new group was intimately concerned with the welfare of the *yishuv* in Eretz Israel. He listed the many Palestinian institutions founded and supported by the Agudat Israel. Silver asserted once again his desire to cooperate with the Mizrachi in their common goal to strengthen Torah life in America and Eretz Israel. Silver, impressed with the large group in attendance, thus wrote to Rav Hayyim Ozer on July 17, 1939:

I can joyfully inform you that we succeeded in our first Agudat Israel conference. The crowd was much larger than expected, and the assembly hall could not accommodate all those present. Among them were the leading *rabanim*, hassidic rabbis, lay leaders and numerous reporters. Despite the determined opposition of the Mizrachi, all these people attended.

With the continued influx of European Orthodox refugees, Agudat Israel expanded its American activities. Finding employment for the newcomers where Sabbath observance was possible became a pressing goal. Many of those who worked were unfairly penalized for leaving early on Friday and being absent on Saturday. The executive board adopted Silver's proposal that the Agudah open an employment agency so that Sabbath observing employers could advertise among the newcomers. This agency aided many Sabbath observers during this period.[14] The Agudah also began to campaign with government officials for the welfare of Sabbath observers. Silver later received a request for help from Sabbath observers in the Civil Service of New York. Dated July 3, 1941, the letter read:

> You are aware, doubtless, that the greatest difficulty besetting Sabbath observers is the economic one, that of "making a living." This is the chief reason why a great number of Jewish youth are forsaking the Sabbath, forsaking Judaism, with the fancied excuse of *pikuah nefesh* [saving one's life].
>
> The solution to this difficulty is, of course, to make it easier for Sabbath observers to acquire gainful employment. One of the most promising fields for this, and one to which Agudat Israel has not paid much attention to in the past, is the field of Civil Service.
>
> I am a member of the above organization, a group of Sabbath observers employed in Civil Service. For a number of years we have been doing what we could to make it easier for other Sabbath observers to enter and obtain fair treatment in the Government Service. Last year we were able to obtain pay for summer Saturdays from the New York City Department of Welfare where many of us are employed. At present we are negotiating with the Federal Civil Service Commission regarding allowances in taking Saturday examinations. We are also in the last stages of a successful claim against the New

York City Comptroller and Corporation Counsel regarding annual increments for Sabbath observers.

We have been able, with the aid of God, to accomplish quite a lot through hard persistent work. However, to really make it possible for Sabbath observers to take examinations (which are usually scheduled for Saturday), and to be appointed to permanent positions, without having to face the individual difficulties which we have had to face, would require the community support which only an organization with your prestige can get.

Silver and the Agudat Israel did extend their aid. However, during this period only limited success was achieved. It took another twenty-five years for Orthodoxy to possess enough authority to gain almost total recognition on the governmental scene.

Silver sensed that a dynamic change was now taking place in American Jewish life. The new immigrants were determined to retain their previous Torah life-style. These newcomers had not come to America out of choice, but rather to escape from European oppression and outrages. Many were determined not to suffer the religious erosion that befell the previous waves of immigrants. Silver supported their resolution and decided to visibly display the arrival of this Orthodox element on the American scene. He approached many of the prominent new arrivals and requested that they join the Agudah. Silver even visited with the Lubavitcher Rebbe, Rabbi Joseph Isaac Schneersohn, who had arrived in America on March 19, 1940. Silver later reported to the Agudah's executive that he:

> . . . visited the Rebbe and discussed at length his joining the Agudat Israel in America. The Rebbe replied that he was also approached by the leaders of Mizrachi. He totally rejected their proposal, but the Rebbe agreed to work with the Agudah for the advancement of proper Torah life in America. He expressed love, affection, and great sympathy for the

Agudah's goals. Nevertheless, the Rebbe felt that he could not
yet become an official member of the organization.[15]

Silver continued his efforts to put Agudah on the map. He
called for the second convention of the Agudat Israel to be held in
Cincinnati. Here, in the heartland of the United States and the
home of Reform Judaism, Silver wanted to raise the Agudah's
banner. At an executive committee meeting he broached this
suggestion. There was some opposition on the part of those who
feared that the masses of New York's Agudah branches would
not be able to assemble in Cincinnati. Nevertheless, the majority
went along with Silver and his city was selected.

While arrangements for the convention were in full swing,
the Agudah was cast into deep mourning with the demise of Rav
Hayyim Ozer Grodzenski on August 9, 1940. The death of his
mentor and the intensifying tribulations of European Jewry only
strengthened Silver's determination. The convention was
intentionally planned to include the Sabbath so the delegates
could publicly consecrate the day together in Cincinnati. It was
held from Thursday through Monday, August 22nd through
August 26th, 1940. The first session opened with the kindling of a
memorial light for Rabbi Grodzenski. The recitation of Psalms
was led by the Novominsker Rebbe of Brooklyn, Rabbi Judah
Perlow. Rabbi Silver later delivered the main address, which set
the tone for the convention's sessions. He called upon the
Agudah to disseminate Torah knowledge throughout the United
States. Silver stated:

> The main goal of Agudat Israel must be to spread the study of
> Torah throughout the land. Both the young and old should be
> educated. They must learn to appreciate the true Torah elders
> and sages. The organization also should engage in the
> praiseworthy task of teaching women and young ladies the
> rudiments of Jewish observance. To accomplish this, the Beth
> Ya'akov network of schools for girls must be expanded.

Throughout the United States, the Agudah must strengthen the influence of the scholars and men of action.

"Light is sown for the righteous" (Psalm 97:11). There is much Torah light for us to sow and plant. "And joy for the upright in heart": Our children will only discover true joy in our efforts and not in those of strangers. "Enlarge the place of thy tent" (Isaiah 54:2): We must enlarge the tents of Torah. We will thereby create "a ladder set up on the earth with its top reaching to heaven" (Genesis 28:12). "The angels of God will ascend and descend on it": Our nation has long been accustomed to having angels of the Lord accompany them. However, our people can only merit such an escort when they act like a "kingdom of priests" (Exodus 19:6). Priests must be enrobed in their priestly garments. For the Jewish people the proper priestly garments are Torah study and commitment.[16]

The Sabbath was an inspirational experience for the almost two hundred delegates assembled. Lithuanian *Mitnagdim* and Polish *Hassidim* joined together in prayer and song. Many of the *Hassidim* were dressed in their characteristic festive garments, black silk coats and fur hats. The Sabbath meals were served on the lawn of the "Washington Avenue Shule." This area was partially blocked from public view by the canvas from Rabbi Silver's *succah*. The sight in the synagogue was thus described in *Hapardes*:

The main synagogue was filled beyond capacity. The *rabanim* and hassidic leaders sat in front of the Eastern wall. Their patriarchal look and venerable rabbinic garb cast an aura of sanctity throughout the entire sanctuary. The regular worshippers rejoiced in the sight. The Jewish people have not been left leaderless even in this derelict generation. The congregants blessed the Lord for having spared illustrious spiritual leaders for our times.

On Saturday afternoon Talmudic discourses were delivered by Rabbis Shlomo Heiman, Moshe Feinstein of New York's

Mesifta Tifereth Jerusalem, and Hayyim Korb of Chicago's Hebrew Theological College. The largest crowd of the convention attended Sunday evening's public session dedicated to the memory of Rav Hayyim Ozer. Silver opened the gathering with a description of his teacher's unique ability in all facets of Torah knowledge and leadership. The high point of the evening was reached with the eulogy delivered by Rabbi Joseph Dov Soloveitchik. He vividly portrayed the total leadership provided by the late rabbi of Vilna against the background of the unprecedented tribulations and dissolution of the European Jewish community. Soloveitchik stated:

> Two aspects of the High Priest's garments were stressed by the Torah: the plate of pure gold placed upon his forehead, and the breastplate of judgment. "And thou shalt make a plate of pure gold, and engrave upon it like the engravings of a signet: holy to the Lord" (Exodus 28:36). On the breastplate were the twelve precious stones representing the twelve tribes. "And Aaron shall bear the names of the children of Israel in the breastplate of judgment upon his heart, when he goeth in unto the holy place, for a memorial before the Lord continually" (Exodus 28:29).
>
> Each vestment had a different function. The gold plate, entirely sacred, was placed upon the forehead, the seat of wisdom and knowledge. The breastplate was placed upon the heart of Aaron, the center of love and affection for the Jewish people. The gold plate, entirely holy to the Lord, guided the Jews in purely ritual matters. . . . The breastplate, on the other hand, answered inquiries of a political and social nature. Throughout the millennium, the true heads of the Jewish people were their spiritual leaders. They provided guidance in both spiritual and temporal matters. Rav Hayyim Ozer was the prime example of such total leadership in our times.
>
> Recently a new viewpoint is being foisted upon the Jewish community. The claim is now being made that rabbis only decide purely ritual questions. Other areas are the prerogative

of the political leaders of the Jewish people. . . . Rav Hayyim Ozer valiantly fought against this standpoint during his lifetime. At this moment of eulogy for him, we likewise must demand that political leadership be returned to the true heads of our people, the principal rabbis of our generation. The breastplate must once again be reunited with the plate of pure gold.[17]

The convention ended on Monday with the adoption of resolutions and the election of officers. The resolutions stressed the continued evolvement of the Agudah in the United States, and aid for the Eretz Israel Agudah settlements and refugees from the Nazi persecutions. Silver was once again elected president, with Sam Travis, a prominent lay leader, joining Rabbi Heiman and the Boyaner Rebbe as the vice-presidents. Rabbi Soloveitchik was selected as the chairman of the national executive committee.[18]

After the convention, Silver issued a press statement in which he stressed the success of the Agudah in the home of Reform Judaism. He also called upon the Mizrachi to cooperate with the Agudah for the advancement of Torah observance. Silver stated:

A miracle took place in Cincinnati. The capital of Reform Jewry and assimilation became a center of dedicated and uncompromising Torah Judaism. Agudat Israel conquered the city. Reform Jews were surprised when they saw so many bearded Jews with *peyot* wearing long black coats. The singing and the dancing on the lawn of the synagogue upset their complacent sense of assimilation. . . .

The time has come for the Agudah and Mizrachi to declare a truce. Although the Agudah is daily gaining strength in the United States, we still publicly stress our peaceful intentions. We should together advocate the study of Torah and the observance of *mitzvot*. Our mutual commitment unites us and we should rather oppose those who entirely uproot our tradition.

I shall remind you that your own distinguished leader, Rabbi Moshe Avigdor Amiel [Tel Aviv's Ashkenazic Chief Rabbi] recently declared that the Mizrachi should separate from those estranged from Torah. They should rather unite with the Agudah with whom they share a common destiny. Listen to your leader, and lasting peace will be achieved.

Irrespective of Silver's plea to the Mizrachi, the rivalry between them continued. As the Agudah expanded its American activities, Rabbi Joseph Konvitz feared lest its rabbinic leadership supplant that of the *Agudat Harabanim*. On November 5, 1940, Konvitz sent a letter to the entire membership of the rabbinical organization. He stated:

When I received an invitation for the next convention of the *Agudat Harabanim*, I felt I must write to my dear colleagues about the dangers that confront us. . . .

The Council of Torah Sages of the United States and Canada which is being formed will uproot the authority of our organization. They claim that they are the true leaders of the nation, while the other rabbis are not worthy of heading the Jewish people. They will soon declare that only their rulings are authoritative since they are the trustworthy saints of the Jewish nation.

This rivalry between the Agudah and the Mizrachi viewpoints intensified during the ensuing years. It even interfered with the relief work of the American branch of the Agudat Israel. The Central Agudat Israel branch of Eretz Israel pleaded with Rabbi Silver for additional financial support. With the spread of the war all other channels of aid were blocked. However, they cautioned Silver to be certain that any help obtained was not sent directly to the Ashkenazic Chief Rabbi, Isaac Herzog, an ardent Zionist. On July 9, 1940, the director of the Central Agudat Israel wrote to Silver:

We must caution you to ensure that the funds obtained for the

Torah and charitable institutions in Jerusalem be sent directly to them. If this cannot be arranged, then the sums should be sent to both Rabbis Duschinsky [Joseph Tzvi of the separatist Orthodox community of Jerusalem] and Herzog. We have learned from experience that any money sent only to Rabbi Herzog is turned over to the Mizrachi. These funds are utilized for narrow party purposes. The refugee European rabbis who were Agudist in the diaspora are then forced to turn to the Mizrachi for their meager sustenance.

Silver was exhorted along the same lines by the newly organized *Vaad ha-Yeshivot* in Eretz Israel. The original *Vaad* was formed by the *Hafetz Hayyim* and Rav Hayyim Ozer in 1924 for the spiritual and material support of the East European yeshivot. With the forced closure of these schools and the increased *aliyah* of their students and deans, the *Vaad* was reorganized in Eretz Israel in 1940. Chief Rabbi Reuven Katz of Petah Tikvah warned Silver that the Mizrachi was trying to alter the traditional atmosphere of these schools. In a February 21, 1941 letter Katz wrote:

The money recently raised by Rabbi Herzog in his South African visit was forwarded to Rabbi [Meyer] Berlin and Rabbi [Judah Leib] Fishman [later Maimon, the first Minister of Religions]. They insist upon dividing the aid only among those yeshivot which will accept the Mizrachi influence. They wish to undermine the importance of the recently formed *Vaad ha-Yeshivot*, and have caused us much aggravation and vexation.

When we became aware of the grave spiritual and material dangers facing the yeshivot here, we organized the *Vaad ha-Yeshivot*. We must make certain that no secular and alien trends enter these schools. We must also guarantee that they will not be financially dependent upon any political party. The yeshivot must retain their independence as in the past. To safeguard these goals, all the advanced yeshivot have joined the *Vaad*. The chairmen are the *geonim* Rabbis Isser

Zalman Meltzer [of Jerusalem's Etz Hayyim Yeshivah] and Isaac Herzog. The other members of the executive are myself, Rabbi Jehiel Michel Tykocinski of the Etz Hayyim Yeshivah, Rabbi Ezekiel Sarna of the Hebron Yeshivah, and Rabbi Yaakov Sankevitz of the Sefat Emet Yeshivah of the Gurer Rebbe. The executive director is Rabbi Zalman Sorotzkin, previously the spiritual leader of Lutsk, Poland.

The *Vaad ha-Yeshivot* will be conducted along non-political lines. The yeshivot will not be subject to any political party, and Agudat Israel has also agreed to this policy. The *Vaad* will enhance the prestige of Torah and its institutions in Eretz Israel just as it did in Vilna. . . . It will be conducted in the same fashion that our great master, Rabbi Hayyim Ozer, led the Vilna *Vaad*.

Silver heeded these requests and particularly supported the efforts of the *Vaad ha-Yeshivot* to remain free of political influence and dominion. The American Agudah continued relief activities for its European branches. Silver was particularly sensitive towards their dietary needs due to the many *halakhic* stringencies they followed. He helped arrange for *matzot* baked by hand for those who did not utilize machine *matzot* on Passover. Silver also aided in supplying coconut oil for those who abstained from oils derived from legumes on this holiday.[19] In order to facilitate these and other relief activities, the Agudah made use of its international organization to transfer money to branches already under Nazi conquest. These activities brought Silver and the Agudah into conflict with the anti-Nazi boycott movement. In protest against the Nazi excesses, an organized boycott developed throughout the Jewish world in the mid-thirties. This movement reached its peak in the United States with the formation in 1936 of a Joint Boycott Council by various Jewish organizations. The council was chaired by Joseph Tenenbaum, a prominent physician, writer and communal leader.[20] When the Boycott Council learned of the Agudah's activities, the organization was accused of aiding the enemy. On July 1, 1941, Rabbi Benjamin Hendles, the Agudah's executive director, wrote to Silver:

> I already informed you that the Joint Boycott Council insisted that we stop sending the care packages to Europe. Today I met with their chairman, Dr. Tenenbaum. He insists that our packages are confiscated by the Nazis, and that he has documents to prove this. I tried to convince him that in the Agudah office there are hundreds of thankful letters from the recipients. Nevertheless, he insisted that the packages are reaching the Nazis and not the addressees. When I asked to see his proof, Tenenbaum claimed that this was unnecessary. We should comprehend the situation on our own.
>
> I am apprehensive that the Joint Boycott Council will harm us by placing pickets around our office. Their heads have nothing better to do at this moment. Since they are collecting fabulous salaries from the public, they must come up with such petty matters to justify their employment. . . .

The Council did boycott the Agudah and on July 15th pickets appeared for about an hour. Silver advised Hendles to contact the editors of the Jewish press to utilize their influence for the good of the Agudah. Despite some favorable publicity for the Agudah's activities, the picketing continued. On August 5th, Tenenbaum issued a harsh statement against the Agudah:

> After three weeks of continuous picketing, the Agudat Israel of America still continues in the sorry role of being the only organization breaking the British blockade and Jewish solidarity.
>
> Recent investigations undertaken by the Council show that, in addition to non-delivery of food packages in Nazi Poland, the German fiscal system has developed a new means of exploiting the sympathies of those sending food packages, by charging the full amount of the American price of the packages as duty, before allowing the package to go to the

unfortunate to whom it is addressed. It is to be deplored that
the Agudat Israel of America, a sickly weed transplanted from
foreign soil to the liberal American environment, should
continue to poison the atmosphere without regard for the
consequences to the entire Jewish people.

Shortly after the public airing of this conflict, the Agudah
yielded. An announcement by its World Executive stated that
the organization would be guided by the wishes of the Joint
Boycott Council. The Agudah still claimed that their earlier
deliveries reached their ultimate destinations. The organization
only regretted that the Council had "made a national issue of a
problem which was on the verge of amicable settlement."
Tenenbaum soon confirmed that "the sending of food packages
to Poland seems to have ceased completely."

Later that summer the third convention of the American
Agudah took place from August 21st through August 25th, 1941.
Following the successful choice of Cincinnati for the previous
convention, another city outside of New York was chosen. This
time it was Baltimore, which had become a center of Orthodoxy
due to its many synagogues and the Ner Israel Rabbinical
College. This convention was graced by the presence of leading
European *roshei yeshivah* who succeeded in reaching the shores
of the United States that year. Among them were Rabbis Aaron
Kotler of the Kletsk Yeshivah, Reuven Grozovsky of the
Kaminetz Yeshivah, Mendel Zaks of the Radun Yeshivah,
Abraham Joffen of the Novorodok Yeshivah, and Elijah Meyer
Bloch and Hayyim Mordecai Katz of the Telz Yeshivah. Also
present was Jacob Rosenheim, president of the World
Organization of Agudat Israel. He was to remain in the United
States until 1950 when he settled in Israel. All the new arrivals
praised Silver repeatedly during their addresses for his foresight
in having organized the American branch. In his speech, Silver
stressed the opportunity now confronting American Jewry. In
this period of upheaval and destruction of the previous Torah

centers, American Jewry must take its rightful place on the world scene. Silver declared:

The leading *geonim* and disseminators of Torah knowledge in the world are now in the United States. We must build centers of Torah and fear of God in this country. "Light is sown for the righteous." We have enough light to properly sow and plant in this country. There will be "joy for the upright" as the results are achieved and the status of Torah enhanced. . . .

"*Bezot*, with this, shall Aaron come into the holy place" (Leviticus 16:3). It is only due to the merit of the Torah which is also called *zot* — "*vezot ha-torah*, And this is the Torah" (Deuteronomy 4:44) — that Aaron may enter into the holy place. We shall succeed in turning America into a holy place due to the merit of the Torah. In the past, great saints and sages were called upon to establish Torah life in new countries. Today this task falls upon us, although we are spiritually weak and inadequate. Nevertheless, we shall succeed due to the virtues of Torah observance. We must cease to despair of progress. Instead, we should organize, build and achieve our purpose.[21]

At the election session, Silver suggested that an energetic layman be elected president. Such an individual would be able to devote more time to the needs of the Agudah since Silver was then totally involved with saving European Jewry. The delegates, nevertheless, unanimously re-elected Silver as president, with Rosenheim designated honorary president. The Council of Torah Sages was finally formed, and Rabbis Kotler, Silver, and Heiman were selected as chairmen. Its inner council was also to include Rabbis Bloch, Feinstein, Friedman of Boyan, Grozovsky, Joffen, Soloveitchik, and Zaks. The convention closed with the adoption of resolutions which stressed expanded activities in both the United States and in rescue undertakings for overseas Jews.

Despite his multitudinous activities for his European

brethren, Silver continued to guide the Agudat Israel. He did not simply concentrate on individuals but rather concerned himself with the masses. Silver strongly felt they could be inspired to return to the standards of Torah. Instead of an annual convention, he organized a Special Conference for the Strengthening of the Jewish Religion, at Belmar, New Jersey. It took place from August 20th until August 23rd, 1942. Silver's keynote address was later distributed as an English-Yiddish pamphlet by the Agudah. Silver movingly described the period and stressed the importance of Sabbath observance at this time:

> In opening this special conference of the Agudat Israel we are fully conscious of the frightful Holocaust that has enveloped the world and realize the special grave danger that threatens the whole of our people at the hand of the demon loosened upon the earth. In this fateful and most crucial hour we turn to the Creator in supplication for succor.
>
> Our approach to the Almighty is similar to the manner which we appealed to the State Department, when about two years ago a delegation of venerable Talmudists and patri-archal hassidic rabbis came to Washington to secure special visas for our great leaders and teachers whom we were anxious to rescue from the hell of Eastern Europe. At that time we addressed the heads of our State Department as follows: "We come to you not as great orators nor as astute politicians; not as leaders of worldly influence nor as great lawyers with shrewd arguments. We come to you with millions of bleeding Jewish hearts, with the totality of Israel's great catastrophe, with hands outstretched in silent appeal from hundreds and thousands of our great Talmudic scholars and present day sages, representing the very flower and nobility of traditional Jewish learning and wisdom, who plead for rescue. Our own limited power of speech prevents us from putting this plea in words, nor are we able to put it in writing on paper. We beseech you to receive this silent plea as if it were uttered in words coming from your own hearts."

And thus we humbly approach the King of the Universe. In the past we did possess great pillars of our Torah, *geonim*, who were able to advocate our cause before Him. We did have great *tzaddikim*, men of action who intervened with the Almighty in our behalf. For it is said, "The Holy One, blessed be He, decrees and the *tzaddik* annuls" (Moed Katan, 16b). It may be that there are no such advocates in our midst today, but we hardly need them. Now we may storm Thy gates of mercy, O Lord, with millions of Thy people of Israel who are tortured, disgraced and broken in heart and spirit. We come to Thee with countless disrupted families whose members were slaughtered and killed as martyrs in Thy Name. With the babies at their mother's breast, with the aged and the infirm, with the tots from the elementary schools and with the great scholars from our famous yeshivot. With all these of our brethren who find themselves scattered on the highways and by-ways — on the steppes and on the mountains, hounded like animals, degraded, shattered, and tattered.

With these do we come to the high court of the Creator and we offer our urgent prayer, "Save Us, O Lord, rescue our people, it is high time for our deliverance, O Lord." We pray that the Almighty may designate a year of plenty. May there be no more need to take away children from their parents, neither here nor abroad. Grant a good New Year to Thy people Israel."

However, we must realize that some contrition is also necessary in order to reach the Omnipotent. Let us therefore fill our hearts with penitence and scrutinize our own ways and deeds and that of our religious leaders. It may be that we are disqualified to appear before the Almighty this New Year.

It is written, "On thy walls O Jerusalem, have I placed watchmen" (Isaiah 62:6). We were appointed to guard over the safety of the fortress containing our holy heritage. We are the trustees of that heritage and that trusteeship carries with it definite responsibilities. Let us do some introspection, as we approach the threshold of the Day of Judgment. Have we performed our duty towards our trust? Have we guarded well the protecting walls of that fortress? Was it not because of our own unforgiveable negligence that the enemies of our Torah were able to lay siege to the fortress and to break through the walls and to pilfer the costly fruits of our Tree of Life? It is because we were not faithful to our trust that the vineyard of Israel was defiled.

There is a precept in the Torah, "When thou buildest a new house, thou shalt make a battlement for thy roof; that thou bring not blood upon thy house, if anyone were to fall from there" (Deuteronomy 22:8). We have come to a new land. New houses have we built. We have prospered, but in building our new great houses, we forgot to provide battlements for the roofs, not even for the roofs of the towers in our holy fortress. Behold the great Jewish tower, the Sabbath, and other such towers as Purity of the Family, the study of the Torah, the ritual of Circumcision. From these great towers have we fallen. Without safety rails, without protective guards, it is not so strange that the new generation, the children born in the new houses, fell from the roofs so readily. This is a direct result of our digression from the precept "Thou shalt make a battlement for thy roof."

There is still time to erect battlements, *maakeh*, a protective railing to guard our young, to place a fence about the Vineyard of Israel. Let us turn around and go back to our original start; to the Creator, our Lord and Master. We have none other to turn to. Let those of us who assume the responsibility as shepherds of Israel observe the precept of occupying ourselves with the Torah. It must become our only interest. We must discard all other interests and concentrate upon the Torah. We have no other remedy. "These precepts are our very life." In this way we shall become re-established. We must battle in the name of the Lord and such a battle requires sacrifices for the Torah. It is true, there are some who are ready for self sacrifice in the name of ideals, for the Jewish nation, for Palestine. But, there are *dinim*, specific laws and regulations covering the practice of sacrifices. Not every sacrifice is considered as proper. A sacrifice, in order to be considered as proper and effective, must be pure and unadulterated, without imperfections and without blemish. A sacrifice which is crippled, lacking only the most insignificant joint or organ, is considered as improper, even when the sacrifice is a dove. And such a sacrifice, when placed on the Altar inadvertently, must be removed from the Altar. . . .

We, the leaders of strict traditional Judaism, most certainly must be extremely careful to avoid all imperfections and blemishes. Our leaders must be free from every blemish. They must be strict observers of the precepts of the Torah, only *shomrei dat*. Such leaders will provide battlements, fences for our roofs. Such leaders will be the guardians of our walls. They must be meticulous in their observances, and particularly in that of the Sabbath. Our Sages have promised us: "If the whole of Israel were to observe but two Sabbaths according to the laws thereof, they would at once be redeemed" (Shabbath 118b).

The assembled delegates at this special conference responded to Silver's address by calling for total Torah observance. It was resolved that only Sabbath observers could serve as presidents of synagogues. The rabbis should be encouraged to preach about the Sabbath and its laws. Evening classes should likewise be organized to teach the laws of Judaism with particular stress upon the Sabbath. An American Torah Foundation was also established at this conference to support yeshivah students so they could totally devote themselves to Torah study.[22] This foundation had originally been organized at the first *Kenesiyyah ha-Gedolah* in Vienna in 1923 by Rabbi Meir Shapiro of Lublin. During the years many European Torah institutions and students were aided by it. Silver now felt that the time had come for the American Agudah branch to take over this activity. He stated that only through such financial support would the American yeshivot succeed in graduating "true *geonim*, both excelling in Torah knowledge and fear of the Lord."[23]

Beginning with early 1943, Silver led the American Agudah in its determined stand in what was later termed the "Teheran Children Controversy." Youth Aliyah, a branch of the Zionist movement administered as a department of the Jewish Agency, was founded in 1933. Its purpose was to rescue Jewish youth from hardship and persecution, and to raise and educate them in Eretz Israel. During the early years of World War II very few children arrived from Europe. In 1943, eight hundred youngsters succeeded in getting from Poland to Persia via the Soviet Union. They were accommodated in a refugee camp in Teheran and were soon brought by Youth Aliyah to Eretz Israel. A heated controversy broke out in the *yishuv* over the education of these children, most of whom were orphans. While many were from religious homes, they were generally placed in irreligious *kibbutzim* and educational institutions. Agudat Israel, which did not belong to the Zionist movement, publicly contended with the Agency regarding the education of the youngsters. The Mizrachi element also joined issue in this matter, but within the official channels of the Jewish Agency. On January 25, 1943, Silver received the following telegram from Rabbi Alter of Gur who had settled in Jerusalem in 1940:

> Kindly strengthen demands of Agudah Executive Jerusalem Ben Yehuda St. for Teheran children. Very urgent to help.[24]

Silver organized the Child Refugee Rescue Campaign and began transmitting large sums of money for the support of these children. He served as the chairman of the drive, while Hirsch Manischewitz, a proprietor of the B. Manischewitz Kosher Food Company, was the treasurer. Descriptions of the children who were not placed with religious institutions reached the United States. One such report claimed:

At the first meal served the children were informed that the food was kosher. All sat down to eat, except for one seven year old boy who remained standing in the corner. The cook came over and asked him why he was not eating. Then the boy raised his eyes and asked her whether the food was really kosher. She began to cry together with the lad. . . .

Many of the children sneak away from their irreligious counselors and demand to be taken to nearby synagogues. The other day, while the house of worship was filled, a group of orphans came in. With screams and tears, they threw themselves upon the Holy Ark. The entire congregation cried bitterly at this sight. No talk or lecture had ever moved the people as much as this event.[25]

In June 1943 Silver sent an open letter to American Jewry and its rabbinate. He demanded that they intervene with the Zionist leaders to attain religious education and facilities for these children:

These refugee youngsters are from religious Polish homes. They are now being inculcated with hatred of Torah and its precepts. They are being turned into socialists and radicals. These unfortunate orphans are now becoming Sabbath desecraters, eating defiled food, and denying the Jewish religion. No protest can be too strong under such circumstances. The Torah scholars of Eretz Israel cry out against what is being done to these innocent children. Not only are they enjoined from observing the Torah, but even the Chief Rabbi [Herzog] was not permitted to address them. . . .

Israel, the Jews, and God are one [Zohar to Leviticus, 73b]. Only when the Land of Israel will be built in conformance and loyalty with this ideal, will the achievements be lasting.

By July 12, 1943, Silver received another cable from the leading rabbinical scholars of the Eretz Israel Agudah stating:

Now nearly 100 children with us even we received 32 only

others flew to us from irreligious institutions STOP As known receive no support of Zionists therefore urgently needed money STOP If we should have money enough further lot of children may be saved by us STOP Concerning agency Jerusalem no progress reached on the contrary nearly every day new children arriving and are distributed to irreligious institutions STOP Do utmost efforts sending money STOP Transmit the money on the same address as till now.

The telegram was signed by Rabbis Isser Zalman Meltzer, Isaac Zev Soloveitchik (previously of Brisk), Joseph Kahaneman (previously of Ponevezh), Zalman Sorotzkin, Akivah Schreiber (previously of Pressburg), and Meir Karelitz (the brother of the *Hazon Ish* of Bene-Berak). Silver continued to help both financially and by exerting moral pressure upon the Zionist leaders. The issue continued to rage until 1945 as more refugee children constantly reached Eretz Israel. The Jewish Agency finally issued new operative directives. Young people over fifteen were to decide for themselves whether to be placed in religious or secular surroundings. Younger children were to be brought up according to the way of life followed in the homes of their parents. The Agudah and Mizrachi formed a joint committee to question those under fifteen to ascertain their previous mode of observance. If their homes were conducted with even a slight level of Torah commitment, they were placed in either a Mizrachi or Agudah institution.[26]

After the War, Silver continued to identify with the Agudah. Nevertheless, a new element was coming to the fore of the organization which gradually replaced the founders of the American branch. These new leaders no longer envisioned an ultimate merger between the Agudah and Mizrachi, but rather charted a totally independent course for their movement. Silver was also limited in the time he could devote to the organization. It continued to expand at this time due to the influx of Agudist refugees. On the other hand, even after the cessation of hostilities, Silver was still totally involved with his *hatzala* activities.

Notes

1. For examples of their correspondence see Sursky, *Ahiezer* 1:163-66; 296-97; Glickman, *Ish Ha-Halakhah Veha-Maaseh*, pp. 105-107; and the numerous letters in the Silver Archives.

The quotation from Rav Hayyim Ozer is cited in *Kovetz Rabbani Torani*, p. 4.

2. For the early history of the Agudat Israel and Rabbi Grodzenski's involvement see Sursky, *Ahiezer* 2:625-636; Shmuel Rothstein, *Ahiezer* (Tel Aviv: Netzah, n.d.), pp. 24, 28-29; and *Yaakov Rosenheim Memorial Anthology* (New York: Orthodox Library, 1968), pp. 6-12. For its initial years on the American scene see George Kranzler, *Williamsburg* (New York: Philipp Feldheim Inc., 1961), pp. 242-245; and Shmuel Singer, "His Title was 'Hillel Hakohen,' " *The Jewish Observer* (May 1975), p. 17.

3. Interviews with Rabbi Aaron Pechenik of New York-Jerusalem, September 9, 1975, and Rabbi Mordecai Kirshblum of New York-Jerusalem, October 2, 1972.

4. Copy of the address is located in the Silver Archives. Cf. *Hapardes*, December 1933.

5. The letter, dated November 21, 1933, was published by Sursky, *Ahiezer* 1:296-97.

6. In a September 2, 1937 letter to Rosenberg, Silver also took issue with Konvitz for the latter's opposition to his viewpoints.

7. *Hapardes*, September 1937, pp. 18-19. Cf. the letter from Rabbi Silver to Rabbi Rosenberg, August 18, 1937.

8. *Hapardes*, September 1937, pp. 6-7.

9. Glickman, *Ish Ha-Halakhah Veha-Maaseh*, p. 53. Cf. the letter from Rabbi Zemba to Rabbi Silver, October 26, 1938.

10. *Hapardes*, September 1937, p. 18. The quotation is from Isaiah 55:12.

11. Cf. the *Kinah* in the liturgy for the Ninth of *Av* which begins "The Cedars of Lebanon." See *Kinot for the Ninth of Av*, trans. Abraham Rosenfeld (London, 1965), p. 125.

12. The letter appeared in the December 1937 issue, p. 3.

13. The platform appeared in *Hapardes*, July 1939, pp. 7-8.

14. See the letter from Rabbi Joel Fink, Secretary of the Agudat Israel of America, to Rabbi Silver, May 22, 1940, and the appendixed protocol of the executive committee meeting.

Also cf. the letter from Fink to Silver, June 5, 1940, and the attached letters from Walter R. Hart of the Council of the City of New York to Agudat Israel and from Agudat Israel to Councilman James H. Burke.

15. Protocol of the executive committee meeting on May 22, 1940.

16. *Hapardes*, September 1940, p. 14. For a complete report of the convention see pp. 9-24, and *Every Friday*, August 30, 1940.

17. *Hapardes*, October 1940, pp. 7-8.

18. Travis, the brother-in-law of Rabbi Bernard Revel of the Yeshiva, previously was active in the petroleum industry in Oklahoma. For details of the Travis family see the author's *Bernard Revel*, s.v. index.

The resolutions and list of officers were published in *Hapardes*, September 1940, pp. 20-24.

19. For details of this venture and its financing see the letters from Central Agudat Israel of Transylvania to the American Agudat Israel, February 23, 1941; and from Rabbi Benjamin Hendles, executive director of the Agudat Israel of America, to Rabbi Silver, May 7, 1941.

The machine-made *matzah* controversy is detailed in Hayyim Hezekiah Medini, *Sedei Hemed* 7:396-401. The literature regarding the utilization of legume oil is summarized in Solomon Braun, *She'arim Mezuyanim Be'Halakhah* on the *Kitzur Shulhan Arukh*, 117:4.

20. For the early history of the boycott movement see Moshe Gottlieb, "The First of April Boycott and the Reaction of the American Jewish Community," PAJHS, 57, No. 4 (June 1968), 516-556. Cf. Joseph Tenenbaum, "The Anti-Nazi Boycott Movement in the United States," *Yad Vashem Studies*, vol. 3 (Jerusalem, 1959), pp. 141-159. For the conflict with the Agudah see Moshe Gottlieb, "In the Shadow of War: the American Anti-Nazi Boycott Movement in 1939-1941" PAJHS, 62, No. 2 (December 1972), 146-161. Tenenbaum's stinging statement against the Agudah is cited in this article on pp. 156-157.

21. *Hapardes*, September 1941, pp. 9-11.

22. Details of the conference were contained in *Hapardes*, September, 1942, and in the pamphlet distributed by the Agudat Israel. Entitled "Address delivered by Rabbi Eliezer Silver at the opening of the Special Conference of Agudat Israel for the Strengthening of the Jewish Religion," it contained 17 pages in Yiddish, and 5 pages in English.

23. Cited from an article by Silver entitled "The Torah Foundation in our Country," *Hapardes*, December 1942, p. 8.

24. Telegram published in *Hapardes*, February 1943, p. 7.

25. *Hapardes*, July 1943, p. 8. Also see *Yaldei Teheran Ma'ashimim*, published by Agudat Israel (Jerusalem, 1943).

26. Details of the agreement were published in *Hapardes*, March 1945, pp. 22-23 as an announcement by the Mizrachi Organization of America. In it the Mizrachi took issue with the Agudah, claiming that the latter had turned this issue into a political point of contention with the former.

7

The *Vaad Hatzala*'s Initial Years

✿☆✿☆✿☆✿☆✿☆✿☆✿☆✿☆✿☆✿☆✿☆✿☆✿☆✿☆✿☆

Silver's bond with his mentor, Rav Hayyim Ozer, was considerably reinforced after their 1937 reunion. Their correspondence increased and almost each letter from Vilna contained news of additional restrictions, deprivations and tensions within the European Jewish community. Rabbi Grodzenski sensed and foresaw the approaching catastrophe. In the introduction to the third and final volume of his responsa entitled *Ahiezer*, published in the summer of 1939, he wrote:

> Now is the time to act for the Lord. Great is the responsibility that rests upon those who can aid their brethren at this critical hour. How desperate is the current plight of our people. Even during the Middle Ages, persecution of the Jews did not reach the current level. The entire diaspora is aflame, and houses of study and Torah scrolls are daily burned on every street. New decrees are promulgated by our enemies which seek to completely destroy the Jewish religion. Entire, important and large Jewish communities are uprooted and they cannot find a new haven. Families wander throughout Europe attempting to flee from the ever increasing waves of hatred. We have become an object of derision for our neighbors. Even the light that previously emerged from Eretz Israel is now dimmed since the *Yishuv* no longer knows what

tomorrow may bring. We are completely enmeshed in tribulations, persecutions, expulsions, and murder. The entire Jewish nation is sinking in seas of blood and oceans of tears from those oppressed and tortured. Oh, what has befallen us!

As the Nazi threat to Poland became more imminent, many Polish yeshivah students streamed into Vilna. In that vicinity, further away from the border, they felt safer. There also was a widespread sentiment among these refugees that only Rabbi Grodzenski would be able to sustain them. After the German invasion of Poland on September 1, 1939, an ever increasing number of yeshivah deans, teachers and pupils arrived in Vilna. This migration intensified when Vilna was returned to independent Lithuania on October 10, 1939. Previously, Vilna had been part of Poland since its seizure by the latter in 1920. Rav Hayyim Ozer divided the various schools among the Vilna synagogues and provided for their material needs. He insisted that each yeshivah retain its unique atmosphere and method of study, and that no attempt be made to amalgamate the institutions. Even branches of the Yeshivat Hakhmei Lublin and Tomkhei Temimim of Lubavitch were established since large numbers of hassidic students arrived in Vilna.

On the first day of *Rosh Hashanah* (September 14th), Silver received an urgent telegram from his teacher. In it, Rabbi Grodzenski appealed for desperately needed funds to help care for the war refugees. Silver was informed that they were re-establishing their yeshivot in Vilna and devoting themselves to Torah study despite the difficult circumstances.[1]

Soon after this telegram, Silver convened an emergency meeting in the *Agudat Harabanim*'s office in New York. His rabbinic colleagues and American representatives of the European yeshivot attended. Also present was the well known dean of the Lomza Yeshivah, Rabbi Yehiel Mordecai Gordon, who was then in America to raise funds for his school. Those in attendance decided to publish an appeal for funds so that the study of Torah could continue in the European schools. The appeal declared:

> The latest dispatches from the Sage of our time, Rabbi Hayyim Ozer of Vilna, report that the yeshivot continue to exist. In all the history of the Jewish people our Holy Torah has demonstrated wonderful qualities of endurance, continuing to exist despite all hindrances, despite all harsh decrees. We are convinced that in these trying times, too, the bastions of the Torah under the leadership of the Torah heroes, the teachers who have shown much self-sacrifice and devotion, will continue to exist in their present locations or be transferred to more secure places. In any case, the rescue of the yeshivot and their continued existence will demand tremendous material means and considerable financial assistance. It is incumbent upon us to be ready to offer speedy aid to the yeshivot at their first call.

The executive committee of the *Agudat Harabanim* continued deliberations on the plight of the refugee yeshivah students, and decided to call an emergency conference to step up relief activities. The convention, held November 13-14, was attended by hundreds of rabbis who agreed that unsurpassed action must be undertaken for the European yeshivot. Nevertheless, a debate ensued regarding whether a new organization was necessary for this purpose. Some felt that the existing relief agencies such as the Joint Distribution Committee and Ezras Torah were sufficient. They pointed out that the latter organization was particularly suited since it catered to rabbis and Torah scholars. Others, however, held that the Ezras Torah functioned in a provincial fashion, limiting its appeals mostly to synagogues and hotels patronized by observant Jews. In 1938 its total income did not even reach thirty-five thousand dollars. An observer claimed that during this period Ezras Torah "thought in terms of five dollars, not a thousand dollars."[2] Silver was the main advocate of the creation of an entire new body which could rise to the manifold challenges of the hour. Throughout the debate he pressed for this separate relief fund which would operate beyond the limited funds, means and manpower of Ezras Torah. Silver declared:

> We must not despair; nor let us become weakened in our determination to rescue the remnants of Israel. Many periods in history were considered periods of destruction for the Jewish people and for Judaism, but always our people placed their trust in God and gave their lives to save the treasures of our Torah.[3]

Silver carried the day and the *Vaad Hatzala* (Emergency Committee) for War-Torn Yeshivot was established. The Cincinnati rabbi was unanimously elected president by his colleagues. Rosenberg and Levinthal were chosen the honorary presidents and Lomza's Rabbi Gordon the chairman of the executive committee. While the impetus for its formation came from the *Agudat Harabanim*, the *Vaad*, it was decided, would remain independent. Other Orthodox groups were also invited to participate. Among those from other organizations who became active in the *Vaad* were Irving Bunim of Young Israel, Rabbi Herbert Goldstein of the Rabbinical Council of America, and Michael Tress of Agudat Israel.

The months of Tevet and Shevat (December 13, 1939-February 9, 1940) were designated for a national fund-raising drive. The assembled *rabanim* were called upon to devote at least two weeks a year for this purpose. Silver's proposal to send an emissary to Vilna was also adopted by the convention. Silver felt it necessary for their delegate to ascertain exactly what was happening in Eastern Europe and to establish channels of communication. He also wanted the messenger to work out exact plans with Rav Hayyim Ozer for all that the *Vaad* would undertake to accomplish. Silver chose his disciple and co-worker, Samuel Schmidt, the editor of Cincinnati's *Every Friday*. Born in 1883 in Kovno, Schmidt emigrated to the States in 1895. In 1911 he graduated from the Massachusetts Institute of Technology with a degree in biology and public health. After working in public health, Schmidt moved to Cincinnati in 1926 as an executive of its B'nai Brith branch. He soon founded the *Every Friday* and became an important voice in the community. An active Zionist, Schmidt was a member of the Poalei Tzion movement whose ideology combined secular Jewish nationalism and socialism. He gradually became Silver's devotee and more observant in his religious practice. Schmidt later related, "I would do anything that Rabbi Silver requested since his words are holy to me."[4]

Schmidt sailed on February 8, 1940, and arrived in Vilna nineteen days later. The impact of his initial meeting with Rav Hayyim Ozer, which deeply moved him and inspired him to become completely observant, Schmidt described thus:

After I told Rabbi Grodzenski of my mission, he asked that I tell him about myself. I broke down like a Jew on *Yom Kippur* and told him about my entire life and the causes I previously espoused.

When I finished, Rav Hayyim Ozer gently placed his hand on my shoulder. He asked whether I would permit him to address me as "Reb Shmuel" in the traditional fashion.

I answered that I am not worthy of such an honor. Rav Hayyim Ozer, however, insisted that I am. He claimed that I proved myself by leaving the security of the United States and journeying to a war zone to aid my brethren.

At that moment I became another person — I became "Reb Shmuel."[5]

Schmidt visited the refugee yeshivot in the Vilna area. He also traveled to Kovno where he called upon the Slobodka Yeshivah. He went to the Mir Yeshivah which was then in Keydan and the Kletsk Yeshivah in Janova. All the while Schmidt distributed funds which Silver sent with him. Schmidt also tried to establish a single committee to channel the aid which would be sent for all the schools. His constant letters to Silver were published in *Every Friday*. In a communication printed in the April 5, 1940 issue, Schmidt declared:

The heroism of the yeshivah *bochurim* in fleeing to Vilna to pursue their ideals cannot be overestimated. In general, the way the yeshivot managed to settle here is nothing short of a miracle. The yeshivot themselves as an institution remaining untouched and unblemished, entirely immune to the ravages of time and events, are a miracle. That some 2,400 refugee yeshivah men are studying with devotion and fervor in the various synagogues of towns throughout Lithuania, having but recently escaped from such hell, is a strong manifestation that we are a people of destiny.

By the April 26, 1940, issue, Schmidt's personal connection with Judaism became apparent in his writing:

A Jew with the ordinary five senses can hardly appreciate the Jewish cultural reservoir in such yeshivot. You must possess the true, basic, specifically Jewish sense to be able to comprehend the dynamic Jewish cultural current that is being generated and stored for future generations in these yeshivot. It is this very current which is the driving power in all of us who are working for a positive Jewish life, even though some of us may be removed far, far from the source where this current is being generated.

In the May 3, 1940, issue, Schmidt described his initial meeting with Rabbi Aaron Kotler who later became a focal figure in American Orthodoxy. Schmidt wrote:

I just returned to Kovno from Janova where the Kletzker Yeshivah is now located. Reb Aaron Kotler is the Rosh Yeshivah there. He is indeed a most interesting person and considered the greatest Talmudic master of his own age. He is about 48 years old, with blue smiling eyes, of small stature, powerful determination and penetrating vision.

At the end of May, Schmidt started on his return trip. On June 18th he addressed the key members of the *Vaad Hatzala* in New York. He described the plight of the yeshivot and their students. Schmidt detailed Rav Hayyim Ozer's role as the patron of these refugees and relayed his urgent request to "save the Torah."[6] Silver telegraphed the Vilna rabbi to inform him of Schmidt's safe return and to arrange for the distribution of additional funds among the schools. Schmidt soon reached Cincinnati with a personal letter of thanks from Rabbi Grodzenski in his dossier. It closed on a mundane note: "Please express my thanks to your distinguished wife for agreeing to your journey under such dangerous circumstances."[7]

With Silver's emergence as the head of the *hatzala* activities, an ever increasing amount of desperate requests for help and salvation reached him. The Immigration Act of 1924 greatly limited the arrival of aliens into the United States. It did, however, permit entry as non-quota immigrants for:

> An immigrant who continuously for at least two years immediately preceding the time of his application for admission to the United States has been, and who seeks to enter the United States solely for the purpose of, carrying on the vocation of minister of any religious denomination, or professor of a college, academy, seminary, or university. . . .
>
> An immigrant who is a bona fide student at least fifteen years of age and who seeks to enter the United States solely for the purpose of study at an accredited school, college, academy, seminary, or university.[8]

In accordance with these regulations, Silver had Cincinnati synagogues send contracts to European rabbis. Among those he aided was Rabbi Zalman Sorotzkin of Lutsk, Poland. The latter excelled at the yeshivot of Slobodka and Volozhin, and then became a prominent spiritual and communal leader. Silver arranged for a formal letter which stipulated a salary of one thousand dollars a year and an adequate amount of additional income for rabbinic functions.[9] While negotiating for an American visa on the basis of this offer, Sorotzkin succeeded in arranging his *aliyah*. He later became the chairman of the Israeli *Mo'etzet Gedolei ha-Torah* of Agudat Israel.

Silver attempted to gain acceptance for yeshivah students into American schools. As the race against the European inferno became increasingly hopeless, the tone of the letters became more desperate. Silver telegraphed Yeshiva College on June 28, 1940, regarding the son of a Lithuanian rabbi: "Have received cable from Rabbi Rabinowitz Kibarti [a Lithuanian city]. Why not prepare necessary papers for his son Chatzkel. Providing upkeep I am responsible."

On June 30, 1940, Samuel Sar, the executive secretary of the Yeshiva, answered Silver:

> We have already sent three letters to the American Consul regarding this pupil. We have no idea what is really happening there. As far as we are concerned, we have fully exhausted all the channels open to us.

Silver continued to press the Yeshiva, and on July 11th, Sar wrote:

> I am once again writing to you regarding the student you wish to bring to America.
> I don't know what more I can do. I have already told you many times that we have sent numerous letters to the Consul and we have informed them that we are accepting this student.
> The truth is that the Yeshiva can do no more. It is now entirely up to the Consul. If they choose not to accept our letters, then there is no way to overcome this opposition.

At other times, relatives and students succeeded in obtaining the necessary papers and visas for their kinsmen and colleagues. They then turned to Silver for funds for the transportation. One such instance was the rescue of Rabbi Elyah

Chazan, a leading graduate of Poland's Mir Yeshivah. A Brooklyn rabbi knew Chazan from Poland. Although both were total strangers to Silver, the Brooklyn rabbi decided to approach him for financial aid. Silver responded by pledging the funds for half the price of the ticket. The Brooklyn rabbi called on Silver's New York transportation agent and was immediately given a ticket for half price. The balance was billed to Silver. Chazan soon arrived in the United States and later became a *rosh yeshivah* at Mesivta Torah Vodaath.[10]

Silver was also involved in the successful effort to rescue the renowned hassidic leader, Rabbi Alter of Gur. With the fall of Poland, Silver immediately communicated with Senator Taft to learn of the welfare of the *rebbe*. Taft contacted Cordell Hull, the Secretary of State, and on October 21, 1939, Taft wrote to Silver:

> I have received from the Secretary of State a report on the Polish situation which prevents the Department from ascertaining the whereabouts and welfare of . . . Gurer Rabbi Alter about whom you are concerned.
>
> You will note that the Department is still unable to make the inquiry suggested because communication with Poland has been completely interrupted, but will advise me promptly when this communication is re-established.

It was later learned that Rabbi Alter escaped from Gur to Warsaw. Silver joined with the leading Gur *Hassidim* in the United States who applied international pressure to arrange for the *rebbe* to emigrate to Eretz Israel. Among these were Rabbi Menahem Kasher, the editor of the encyclopedic *Torah Shelemah*, and Rabbi Abraham Selmanovitz, a *rosh yeshivah* in the Rabbi Isaac Elchanan Theological Seminary. Along with Silver, they succeeded in raising the necessary funds, and Rabbi Alter reached Jerusalem in 1940. He re-established his Court there and was later active in the material and spiritual rehabilitation of refugees.[11]

While these initial salvation attempts met with varied success, conditions were worsening in Europe. On June 15, 1940, Lithuania was occupied by the Soviet army and its independence ended. The yeshivot which previously sought refuge there from the Nazis suddenly found themselves under the dominion of the Communists. The yeshivot were soon exposed to anti-religious manias and particularly suffered from the Jewish renegades who continued the traditions of the Yevsektsiya, the Jewish section of the propaganda department of the Russian Communist Party from 1918 to 1930. There was now general realization that the yeshivot had no future even in Vilna. American sympathizers of the various schools began to evolve plans to transfer them en masse to the United States. When the European *roshei yeshivah* learned of these plans, they decided that all the yeshivot should be dealt with as one institution. On July 7, 1940, Rabbi Kotler wrote to Rabbi Silver:

We rejoiced to learn of the noble idea to transfer the sanctuaries of the Torah, the sacred yeshivot, to the United States. These holy intentions can be compared to the deeds of Rabbi Johanan ben Zakkai at the time of the Temple's destruction. For the sake of the soul of our nation and its survival, action must be quickly undertaken. This is an instance when punctilious individuals rush to do the *mitzvah*.

Nevertheless, we all plead with you to act for the salvation of all the schools together. There are many important reasons for this, but above all, the merit of all the yeshivot is greater than the merit of any individual one. We know that your actions will be done in accordance with the Biblical principle of walking modestly before God. We are confident that you will wisely involve influential Jews such as Lehman [Governor Herbert H. Lehman of New York] and others. Perhaps you should also appeal to "the pious ones of the nations of the world." May the favor of the Lord our God rest upon you to succeed in sustaining the Torah.

You will certainly receive similar letters from the other

roshei yeshivah here. We all agree to this course of action. Our hope is that you will do everything in your power to bring these plans to fruition as quickly as possible. We all know of your indefatigable energy and dedication to the Torah and its traditional institutions. We are therefore confident that you will accomplish these goals.

Silver did indeed receive other letters, all stressing that the yeshivot wanted to be treated as one group.[12] He arranged for a delegation to visit Washington to obtain visas for the *roshei yeshivah* and their students. They were received by Assistant Secretary of State Breckinridge Long who requested that they submit an initial list of those they wished to bring over. Two lists were prepared, one of twenty rabbis, and another of one hundred. When they next met with Long, he immediately accepted the bigger list. Long promised to cable the American consuls to grant the visas and advised the delegation to instruct the rabbis to go to these consuls to receive their documents. The delegation, informed of this decision on Friday night, immediately cabled the rabbis in Lithuania. It was unanimously felt that the chance to rescue their overseas brethren overrode the Sabbath prohibitions.[13] Silver also intensified the drive to raise money which was now needed in ever increasing sums. His efforts met with limited success since donors were hesitant to part with substantial sums at a time of uncertainty and darkening war clouds. In an appeal published in the Yiddish press, Silver declared:

I am amazed that at times like this, people are hesitant to contribute because they are fearful for the future. Telegrams, arriving daily from the Lithuanian *geonim* and *roshei yeshivah*, declare that learning continues unabated in the schools. They plead for help so that the Torah can be saved. Yet, their American brethren do not respond and thereby contribute to the possible closing of these Torah institutions. Where is your wisdom and understanding? It is just the opposite. More help than ever is needed now since the yeshivot may have to relocate soon. Appeals must be held and the funds immediately sent to the *Vaad Hatzala*. Whoever impedes these collections is greatly endangering his overseas brethren. We also need these funds to enable the sending of affidavits to start the procedure of bringing the *rabanim* and *roshei yeshivah* to our shores.

We cannot be late in these undertakings. All of us must unite as one individual to quickly aid our brothers. It is literally a question of life or death. Let us not be guilty of not having saved our brethren and the yeshivot.

The *Vaad Hatzala* is now involved in many projects for the yeshivot, their heads, and the leading *rabanim*. The Lord will save us![14]

Despite Silver's efforts, progress was still limited and slow. American representatives and friends of the various yeshivot began to act out of desperation. They started traveling to the large American cities to raise funds on their own for their schools. Silver decried these partisan acts and insisted that the *Vaad Hatzala* supervise all such activities. On July 15, 1940, he complained in a letter to Rabbi Rosenberg:

Yesterday Rabbis [Abraham] Kalmanowitz, [Samuel] Greineman, and [Elazar Simcha] Wasserman visited here in Cincinnati.[15] Today Rabbi Kalmanowitz left for Chicago. In my opinion it is not advisable to visit that city now. It will do more harm than good.

In general I see that each one is going out on his own, speaking, and simply demeaning himself. Little is achieved. It becomes worse when they vainly turn in all directions. The results are very bad for our organized salvation work. It is time that the *Agudat Harabanim* take a strong stand in this matter and force everyone to work only through the organized *Vaad* [*Hatzala*]. Otherwise, irresponsible deeds will ruin all our efforts.

In my opinion, we should inform the representatives of the yeshivot that the *Agudat Harabanim* will expand the

Vaad. We should co-opt all their people of influence and action to the *Vaad.*

While Silver and the *Vaad* struggled with these daily problems, the news from Europe became worse. At these critical moments, the problems were compounded by the grave illness of Rav Hayyim Ozer. The seventy-seven year old spiritual leader had labored feverishly to sustain the refugees and centralize the relief activities in Vilna. In the last days of his life he insisted upon writing a letter with his own hand to Silver. When his intimates saw that writing tired him and caused him pain, they suggested that one of them write the letter and that he only sign. Rav Hayyim Ozer declined, explaining: "Perhaps when Rabbi Silver sees the letter in my own handwriting, he will intensify his efforts in behalf of the Yeshivot." By the time the letter did reach Cincinnati, the Vilna rabbi was dead.[16]

After Rav Hayyim Ozer's demise on August 9th (Av 5th), the news spread rapidly throughout Vilna. A meeting was called at the *Vaad ha-Yeshivot* to arrange the funeral and to notify Jewish communities throughout the world. It was decided to conduct the funeral on Sunday, August 11th, so that proper final respects could be accorded the deceased.

On Sunday morning, despite the Soviet Army ban against public assemblies, tens of thousands of Jewish Lithuanian citizens and refugees crowded around his residence. All stores, even those of non-Jews, were closed during the actual funeral. Late that day, Rabbi Grodzenski was placed at eternal rest in the local Jewish cemetery, between the final resting places of two earlier Vilna rabbinic leaders. The eulogies at the gravesite continued late into the night.

Schmidt described the final illness in the obituary he wrote for the August 16, 1940 issue of *Every Friday*:

Recently, on our trip to Vilna, it was our great honor and privilege to be in frequent personal contact with Reb Hayyim

Ozer Grodzenski. He had been suffering from a malignant
ailment for several years which confined him to bed at
frequent intervals. Never did he complain nor in any way
betray the great pain he must have been suffering. He always
greeted us with a smile and was always full of deep concern
about all those who were engaged in the study of the Torah.
Once he did express his regret to us, that the heavy
correspondence which came to him from all corners of the
world and his being confined to bed so frequently, left him
little opportunity for study of the Torah.

Silver received many letters from Vilna *rabanim* describing
the quick deterioration in their situation following Rabbi
Grodzenski's demise. Rabbi Joseph Shub, the director of the
Vilna *Vaad ha-Yeshivot*, thus described their emotions:

We are frightened that the "wealthy uncle" will now stop
supporting us. At times we think about potentialities that one
should never consider within the bounds of possibility. . . .
Many of us felt that our lives were totally dependent upon
that of our late master. Now we feel like small orphaned
children.

Rabbi Israel Hayyim Kaplan, the dean of the Brisk
Yeshivah then in Vilna, claimed that there was practically starvation in his school. He wrote to Silver:

Our students hunt for bread and we do not have the means to
sustain them. Every hour that our aid from you is delayed
intensifies the danger to life. It also increases the time spent
away from Torah study. All our local sources of income have
been nullified. The aid from the Joint has been cut back to a
negligible sum. The students suffer the reproach of hunger
and poverty. . . . We plead with you to share our sorrow at this
grievous hour. Please see that we receive our monetary grant
promptly while there is still time to save the yeshivah.

The Baranowicze *rosh yeshivah*, Rabbi Elhanan Wasserman, described the poverty among the young married yeshivah

couples. He also detailed their efforts to have Rabbi Yitzhak Zev Soloveitchik, "the Brisker Rav," take over some of Rabbi Grodzenski's duties. Rabbi Wasserman wrote to Rabbi Silver:

> There are many families of *benei* Torah that do not possess enough money to purchase the food for even one meal. . . .
>
> We requested the Brisker Rav to accept the responsibility for our community's correspondence. This was one of the many tasks performed by our late master. The Brisker Rav refuses, claiming that he is not important enough for such a central responsibility. Perhaps you can write to him urging that he not refuse our request. We have no other person on his level. Rabbi Soloveitchik is not only great in Torah but he is a man of truth. He possesses the wisdom of the elder sages which he inherited from his father [Rav Hayyim].[17]

Despite the more difficult situation at the European end, the American side did not lack for new tensions and conflicts. The Mizrachi leaders demanded more formal representation in the *Vaad*, claiming that Silver might be partial to Agudat Israel people. Silver was taken aback by these requests, fearing it would politicize the *Vaad*. Its main goal must be to save the yeshivot and not to question their affiliations. The *Vaad* could certainly utilize additional active leaders. However, Silver insisted that the *Agudat Harabanim* should select the new members and not partisan political groups. He threatened to resign if this new approach was implemented. In a December 29, 1940 letter to Rosenberg, Silver stated:

> I cannot be part of this new proposed arrangement. I will oppose it with all my might. It is not for the Mizrachi, or Agudat Israel, or Young Israel to become the overseers of the yeshivot. I do not want them to introduce partisan strife into the rescue of rabbinic scholars.
>
> In my opinion only the *Agudat Harabanim* has the right to appoint either the rabbis or the laymen to the *Vaad Hatzala*. Those chosen should not be selected as the repre-

sentatives of their own organizations, rather as observant Jews and competent individuals. . . . The *Vaad* must remain a body founded by the *Agudat Harabanim* and responsible only to the *rabanim*.

I am adamant in my point of view. If the *Vaad* is politicized I will resign my position. I will thereby spare myself endless aggravation, grievous contention, and the wasting of endless hours. I can only function in the fashion I was taught by my teachers, the great *geonim* of the last generation. Their path is my path.

An amicable solution was reached with the *Agudat Harabanim* forming a presidium to head the *Vaad*. In addition to Silver, two prominent *rabanim* who were devotees of the Mizrachi were added. They were Rabbis Joseph Konvitz and Jacob Levinson of New York. The latter was the former president of the American Mizrachi and a prominent Brooklyn spiritual leader. It also was decided that henceforth one of the European *roshei yeshivah* who was already in America would attend the meetings of the *Vaad*. The presidium was later enlarged at the end of 1941 to include Rabbis Rosenberg and Gordon of Lomza. With all these additions, Silver still remained the focal figure of the *Vaad*.[18]

While the *Vaad* was reorganizing its leadership, conditions were worsening on the other side of the ocean. Two thousand refugees succeeded in escaping from the Communists and reaching Kobe, Japan, via Siberia. Among this group were many *roshei yeshivah* and almost the entire student body and faculty of the Mir Yeshivah. They arrived at Kobe through the aid of the funds sent by the *Vaad* and the Joint Distribution Committee, and with the collusion of two humanitarians. One was the Japanese temporary-consul in Kovno, and the other the Dutch ambassador in Riga. The latter granted the group obviously fake Curacao (Dutch West Indies) end visas which served as the basis for the former issuing Japanese transit-visas.[19] Once this group reached Kobe an alliance of the *rabanim* and leading *kollel* students was formed. They once again appealed to Silver from their new stopping place. On March 5, 1941, the rabbinical committee of the Alliance wrote:

> Among those who reached Kobe are many *rabanim* and members of *kollelim* from Vilna and Kovno. It is almost impossible to describe the poverty and starvation in which these unfortunate *rabanim* and Torah scholars find themselves. They had to leave everything behind in Lithuania since they were only able to escape with their souls. All their possessions were sold in order to raise part of the funds for the trip from Vilna to Japan. You know full well of the hundreds of dollars it cost each refugee. Now, in Kobe, they are once again penniless. There is no way we can survive without the aid of our American brethren.
>
> We have organized an Alliance of the *rabanim* and leading *kollel* students to represent all those who succeeded in arriving here. We request that you rapidly start to send us funds on a permanent basis. That way we can sustain ourselves until God will complete His help to us.

Silver and the *Vaad* started to transmit funds with the permission of the United States Department of the Treasury. They also kept demanding that the government grant non-quota immigrant visas for the *rabanim* in Kobe. Silver insisted that pressure be applied in Washington, D.C., that the government bring over the scholars as was previously promised. He wrote:

> It is now the time to demonstrate in our capital. We must knock on the doors of the White House to demand that the State Department fulfill its promise to bring over the *roshei yeshivah* and their students. It was only a short while ago that we were promised that the government would be favorably disposed to aiding their immigration. We gave their names to the State Department and looked forward to prompt results. We already started praising the president and his cabinet for

their decency and benevolence. . . . Instead, over six months have gone by and little has been done to effectuate this commitment. The overseas representatives of the United States have hardened their hearts and placed obstacles in the path of the refugees. Instead of bringing about a blessing they are causing a curse. They are deserting our brethren in their moments of intense danger. Let us shout and yell in the streets of Washington. How can our president be so cruel to Torah luminaries and scholars who wander in despair from city to city?[20]

The *Vaad* did succeed in bringing over the Kletsker *Rosh Yeshivah*. Rabbi Kotler, or Rav Aharon as he was popularly known, arrived in San Francisco on April 10, 1941. He reached Rabbi Silver's home on the day after Passover. Silver arranged for a public convocation to welcome the newcomer to Cincinnati. From there Silver accompanied Rav Aharon to New York where a delegation from the *Agudat Harabanim* and *Agudat Israel* greeted them at Pennsylvania Station. Silver published a statement of welcome for the *Rosh Yeshivah* which read:

I heartily greet the great guest whom American Jewry is now privileged to welcome.

My dear friend the great *gaon* is the greatest teacher of Torah in our generation. Rabbi Aaron Kotler and his family have succeeded in leaving the continent of blood and reaching our country. I am certain that he will raise the level of Torah in America. We will now be able to educate great Torah scholars here. May his coming be for peace and success.[21]

Rabbi Kotler immediately threw himself into rescue activities. His first public appearance was at the semi-annual convention of the *Agudat Harabanim*. On April 30th, the second day of the convention, Silver introduced the new arrival to the assembled *rabanim*. Silver called upon them to forget the small matters that divide them and rather unite as one man to greet the *gaon*. In unity they would be able to quench the great fire

which was raging. In response, Rav Aharon stressed the urgency
for saving the yeshivot:

> I must first thank the *Agudat Harabanim* and the *Vaad
> Hatzala* for enabling me to reach these shores. Nevertheless, I
> am the father of many children on the other side of the ocean.
> I have only one goal — to save them. . . . The Lithuanian
> schools remain intact and learning there is stronger than ever.
> The souls of the students are miraculously sustained. My
> departure from them caused me great anguish. I was always a
> source of comfort to them in the past and I love them as a
> father cherishes his children. The moment of farewell was
> grievous for all of us. Nevertheless, they pleaded with me to
> leave so I could inspire American Jewry to labor with added
> dedication to save the Torah and its students.
>
> I, therefore, turn to you with one plea: Remember your
> obligation at this dark hour. The Holy Ark, Torah scrolls, and
> their students are bleeding. Every moment is precious since
> we do not know what the morrow may bring. With all due
> gratitude to the *Agudat Harabanim* and the *Vaad Hatzala* for
> the past, not enough has been done. Little time is left and we
> must immediately act. Everyone must volunteer for this
> sacred task.
>
> Rabbi Silver, you are right. We are the most sinful of all
> generations. Other nations totally sacrifice themselves for
> their survival. We do not do enough. If we only had the
> necessary funds, we could have already saved thousands of
> additional souls.
>
> Everyone must do his share to help attain these means.

Following the *Rosh Yeshivah*'s words, Rabbi Levinson presented an account of the *Vaad*'s financial activities. The amount
raised by them totaled $81,476.36. Out of this $79,671.79 had
been spent to purchase passage for close to six hundred
individuals.[22] Many of them were now reaching the United
States. In addition to the *roshei yeshivah* among this group,
there were also prominent spiritual leaders of European cities.

These included Rabbis Moses Shatzkes of Lomza and David Lifshitz of Suwalki. Both later became senior members of the Yeshiva University faculty. All the newcomers echoed Rav Aharon's sentiments and detailed the need for immediate action to save those left behind. These pleas forced Silver to commit himself all the more in rescue schemes. The Canadian government was also approached and agreed to accept some of the Kobe refugees. The Canadian permits were sent to the Polish government which was to forward them to Kobe. On May 16, 1941, Silver received the following telegram from the Federation of Polish Jews in Canada:

> Polish government sending Canadian permits for Polish Jewish refugees to Polish embassy in Tokyo who together with Jewish committee in Kobe shall select those who have no opportunity emigrating United States or elsewhere STOP Essential you communicate with your committee in Kobe.

More Kobe refugees did succeed in emigrating. Twenty-nine were finally able to reach Canada with these special permits. However, a few months later, the Kobe chapter abruptly ended. Japan was on a total war footing; plans were under way to attack the United States, and their ties with Nazi Germany were closer than ever. The presence of fugitives from Nazi persecution in Japan created an unpleasant situation for its leaders. It was decided to transfer them to the Japanese sector of Shanghai. The removal of the remaining one thousand refugees was completed from August through October 1941. Those unable to emigrate from Kobe now found themselves in Shanghai. On *Rosh Hodesh* Ellul, August 24, 1941, the Mir Yeshivah opened there with its *Rosh Yeshivah*, Rabbi Hayyim Szmulewicz, delivering a Talmudic discourse. He continued his lectures regularly in Shanghai throughout the duration of the war.

Sustaining this community now became a major concern for Silver and the *Vaad*.[23] Particularly active on their behalf was the

Mir Yeshivah's president, Rabbi Abraham Kalmanowitz, who was already in the United States. The salvaging of the school became the consuming passion of his life. It was mainly due to Kalmanowitz's efforts that the entire yeshivah survived and finally reopened in the United States in 1947. Mike Tress of Agudat Israel was also energetic on their behalf. A contemporary described him as:

> The unforgettable Elimelech "Mike" Tress, who devoted every fiber of his being to saving lives — shuttling between Washington and New York on any of the seven days of the week, managing the "immigration office" housed in Tzeirei Agudat Israel headquarters at 616 Bedford Avenue in Williamsburg, Brooklyn, that ground out employment guarantees and documents for affidavits and emergency visas, saving thousands of Jews from the clutches of death.[24]

Together with Silver, they left no stone unturned, whether in Washington, the Vatican, or a dozen other embassies or key locations all over the world, to support and rescue their Shanghai brethren. Farfetched but unsuccessful schemes were devised by these leaders of the *Vaad* after 1942 to bring the rabbinical group out of Shanghai with the aid of neutral countries vis-a-vis Japan, such as Sweden, Spain, and the Vatican. An unbroken line of communication was retained with Shanghai through *Hatzala* representatives in neutral European countries. Particularly helpful in these contacts were the Sternbuch family in Switzerland and Rabbi Shlomo Wolbe in Sweden. Isaac and Rachel Sternbuch were a prominent Orthodox couple who devoted all their resources to rescue activities, while Wolbe was an alumnus of the Mir Yeshivah of Poland.

The *Vaad* was also vitally involved with sustaining the refugees in Siberia. With the Russian occupation of half of Poland and its neighboring countries, their Jewish residents also became subject to Soviet authority. The Russians did not trust the Jews in general, and the "professional religious functionaries" in particular, to dwell near the Russo-Nazi borders. These people were not considered trustworthy in case of hostilities. Tens of thousands of Jews from all over Poland and Lithuania were therefore banished to Siberia. Among them were many well known rabbis, *roshei yeshivah*, and their students. This Siberian exile was at first a cruel decree since it was a cold wasteland and wilderness. Many died there of starvation and disease, with no food and no roof over their heads. The *Vaad* immediately opened channels of communication and supply. These connections became easier after Hitler's invasion of Russia on June 22, 1941. This Siberian banishment ultimately proved to be a blessing for those who survived its hardship. They were spared the Nazi inferno and many were able to emigrate after the cessation of hostilities.[25]

These ever increasing activities of the *Vaad* elicited some negative responses from the Joint Distribution Committee. The latter felt that the *Vaad*'s fund-raising activities were undercutting their own. There was also objection to the *Vaad*'s special concern for rabbinic leaders and yeshivah students. In the spring of 1942, a letter criticizing the *Vaad* was brought to Silver's attention. It had been sent by the Joint to a local community leader in a Midwestern city. He forwarded it to Rabbi Silver who was incensed by its contents. In response, Silver wrote to the Joint on May 11, 1942:

> We read with a great deal of chagrin a copy of a letter sent by the secretary of your Committee on Cultural Affairs to an executive secretary of a Jewish Welfare Federation in a city in the Middle West. One would suspect from the contents of that letter that it is your earnest desire to "pick a quarrel" with the *Vaad Hatzala* and the Orthodox Rabbinate of the United States and Canada. . . . May I say that we notice a tendency on your part to minimize the work of the *Vaad Hatzala*, leaving the erroneous impression that the JDC takes care of everything and everybody.

As you well know we could come out with weighty counter-charges of instances where the JDC has appropriated sums of money originally designated for *Vaad Hatzala*. Those sums far exceed any claims you may have against the *Vaad Hatzala*. We even requested a *Din Torah* at that time. There are other criticisms that should we come out publicly with them would not add to the prestige of the JDC. We refrain from doing so because we value greatly the work of the JDC. With all its faults, the JDC is doing a tremendous job, and we overlook the shortcomings.

However, we feel that we are entitled to the same consideration. You know that the *Vaad Hatzala* reaches places and extends relief and rescue work where the JDC cannot or will not go. Why, then, those letters to the Jewish communities?

It seems to us that this form of destructive criticism is detrimental to both organizations and it has to be terminated. . . . I sincerely feel that no good will come to either organization from such avoidable misunderstandings.

In a later letter, dated June 9th, sent to the Joint under the signatures of Rosenberg and Silver, the *Vaad* explained its special concern for the yeshivot:

One may well understand why we, more than others, are so much concerned about the lot of the yeshivot — the Jewish Academies of old standing — and their individual students and instructors. We see in them the very essence of Judaism, and we see in this element the very perpetuation of Judaism. We could not expect that the JDC or similar national bodies should give special tender attention to this suffering element in the present Jewish tragedy, and therefore we established the *Vaad Hatzala*.

You will surely admit that the special assistance we give to the two exiled yeshivot in Shanghai is a duplication of no other relief work, and you will surely appreciate that our support to several yeshivot in exile in the various Russian provinces (for instance, Siberia, Turkestan, Bukhara, Samarkand, and others) representing important nucleus groups of the former famous yeshivot of Klesk, Bialystok, Radin, Telshe — is essential and is a duplication of no other work.[26]

For a while relationships between the two rescue groups did improve. There was some genuine understanding of the *Vaad*'s unique work. On June 25, 1942, for example, a Joint executive wrote to a Philadelphia community leader:

We feel that the *Vaad Hatzala* has a valid claim for community support since whatever they are doing to extend aid to refugee yeshivot and their students is done on the basis of keeping alive traditional cultural-religious institutions. The funds they make available are over and above the sums which we are able to provide for the maintenance of needy refugees, including the yeshivah groups.

Another Joint leader wrote to Louisville laymen on August 27th, that their work:

. . . has no connection to the purely religious program of the perpetuation of traditional Judaism and the aid to the teachers of the yeshivot who were forced to flee from Poland. To that extent we are not doing what the *Vaad Hatzala* is seeking to do in Siberia in behalf of the yeshivot teachers and students there.

Relations between the *Vaad* and the Joint once again deteriorated towards the end of 1942. The new point of contention remained permanent since it resulted from their basic modes of operation. The Joint would only act strictly within the letter of the law. Their policy was postulated upon the premise that as an American organization, they were obligated to observe all the guidelines of the American government. The Joint felt duty-bound to fully honor the restrictions imposed upon even telegraphic communications by the "Trading with the Enemy

Act." The Joint charged the *Vaad* with transgressing this law every time aid was sent to the Shanghai refugee scholars. In a December 22, 1942, letter, a Joint executive wrote to the manager of a Pennsylvania welfare fund:

As you are doubtless aware, such remittances [to Shanghai] are prohibited by our own Government under war laws, and we, as an American organization cannot be involved in anything that has the remotest color of trading with the enemy. . . . We are debarred from communicating with our own representatives [in Shanghai] by the war regulations of our own Government.

The *Vaad* indeed did not feel bound by the strict letter of the law. The future of the Jewish people, its Torah and scholars, was at stake. Under these conditions, every possible act and attempt to aid the victims of Hitler's inferno were justified. A *hatzala* activist thus described Silver and his colleagues: "They rushed in where others dared not tread; they broke every rule in the book, in frustration and despair, when red tape and legalities blocked move after move."[27]

The perseverance of the *Vaad* later helped effect a change in the United States government's policies. In addition, there was also constantly intensifying pressure on the government following the initial disclosures of the Nazi atrocities. Also influential was the unique relationship which Rabbi Kalmanowitz developed with Henry Morgenthau, Jr., then the Secretary of the Treasury. With Morgenthau's help, Kalmanowitz was also able to influence the State Department. A Joint official later declared "that there was a rabbi [Kalmanowitz] with a long white beard, who, when he cried, even the State Department listened."[28] By December 1943 permission was granted for the resumption of communications with enemy-occupied territory, both in China and in Europe. Sanction was also granted to legally transfer money via Switzerland by the start of 1944.

While the debate between the *Vaad* and the Joint sporadically flared up, Silver concentrated on the essential matter of fund-raising. He once again placed Cincinnati in the limelight when he convened a *Vaad Hatzala* Conference for the Western and Southern parts of the United States there. This gathering met on January 27-28, 1942. Silver brought some of the prominent newcomers to his city to address the delegates. Among these were Rabbis Reuven Grozovsky of Kaminetz, Hayyim Mordecai Katz of Telz, Mordecai Shulman of Slobodka, and Mendel Zaks of Radun. In his address, Silver stressed the change that was taking place in America. He could now invite leading *roshei yeshivot* to his community since the United States was their new home. Large sums had to be raised so that additional scholars could be brought over. The more that would reach America, the greater its Torah environment would be. Silver felt that the *Vaad* could still succeed in bringing them out of Europe once the funds were available. The response to the conference was fairly generous and regional meetings became more widespread among *Vaad* activities.

During this period, Silver also activated a branch of the *Vaad Hatzala* in Eretz Israel. This *Vaad* took on a central role during 1942 since it was easier to send aid to those in Russia from the Middle East than from the United States. Rabbi Hezekiah Joseph Mishkowski, a close colleague of Rav Hayyim Ozer, was chosen as its head. Formerly the spiritual leader of Krinki, Poland, Mishkowski was now in Jerusalem. He was assisted in his tasks by Chief Rabbi Isaac ha-Levi Herzog. The latter utilized all the international connections he had established in his rabbinate and travels for the good of the *Vaad*. Silver had previously met Herzog when the latter visited the United States in 1941. At that time Silver declared:

It is with a joyful feeling that we are privileged to greet the Chief Rabbi of Eretz Israel. The world situation does not permit such happy feelings at this time. Nevertheless, our joy is great because we can now honor this leading Torah personality.[29]

Herzog soon cut short his American visit when he learned that Eretz Israel was in serious danger of a German invasion since Rommel's forces were victoriously advancing through North Africa. He insisted on returning to be with the *yishuv* at this critical juncture, confident that the enemy would not reach the gates of the Holy Land. He remained in contact with the *Vaad Hatzala* and, together with Mishkowski, joined forces with Silver and the American group. During this period, they concentrated on attempts to evacuate the Polish yeshivah students to Eretz Israel. They also sent relief packages to these yeshivah people as long as they remained in the Soviet Union.

Silver still nurtured the hopes that these rescue schemes would work out. Even as late as early 1943, when the dimensions of the European catastrophe were beginning to filter through, Silver was still hopeful. At a *Vaad Hatzala* conference on January 5, 1943, he declared:

Despite our being brokenhearted and crushed as we learn of the magnitude of the afflictions which have overtaken European Jewry, this meeting was called so that we can undertake important new deeds. We must raise the funds for the basic maintenance of our brethren. They must be supplied with food to eat and clothes to wear. Most of all, we need large sums because we have been promised that the transfer of those in Shanghai and Siberia to Eretz Israel and South Africa will be possible. This is our most important goal, and we need one and a half million dollars to achieve it.[30]

At this conference Silver also declared that not enough had been done in the past. After reporting on the *Vaad*'s activities during 1942, Silver condemned American Jewry for not having contributed more generously. He felt that both the rabbis and the entire community were obligated to confess their guilt. They did not do enough to save their brethren, and therefore could not recite with a clear conscience that "Our hands have not shed this blood" (Deuteronomy 21:7). Silver stressed once again that the *Vaad* could have saved more lives if only the funds were available. When they cried for help, "We did not have sufficient means to save them. Together with the entire community we must confess and say we have sinned."

Thus the initial years of the *Vaad* ended with some success, but much failure and frustration. Silver still had not given up hope, and was working impassionedly to save his colleagues and the yeshivah students who were still stranded in Europe.

Notes

1. The early history of the *Vaad Hatzala* is based upon Rabbi Eliezer Silver's English introduction entitled "Disaster and Salvation" to *Divrei Yemei Vaad Hatzala* (New York: *Vaad Hatzala*, 1957); and the unpublished M.A. project of Ephraim Zuroff entitled "Rabbis, Relief, and Rescue: American *Vaad Hatzala*, November 1939-April 1943," Institute of Contemporary Jewry of the Hebrew University in Jerusalem, 1975.

Acknowledgment is extended to Mr. Zuroff for making his project available and permitting its citation.

The *Rosh Hashanah* telegram is quoted by Silver on p. 21 and Zuroff on p. 13a.

2. Rabbi Yitzhak Grozalsky, executive-director of the Northwest region of the *Vaad Hatzala*, cited in Zuroff, "Rabbis, Relief, and Rescue," p. 124, n. 15. For the sums raised by Ezras Torah during this period see *Eduth LeYisroel*, p. 296.

3. *Divrei Yemei Vaad Hatzala*, p. 14.

4. Letter to the author from Herman Landau of Toronto, August 19, 1973. Mr. Landau was a member of the European Executive Committee in Switzerland for the *Vaad Hatzala*. His letter quotes Schmidt's remark on his relationship with Rabbi Silver.

For details on Schmidt see the "Biographical Sketch" in *Every Friday*, July 19, 1940, p. 7, and his obituary in *Hapardes*, February 1966, p. 39.Cf. *Divrei Yemei Vaad Hatzala*, pp.166-177.

5. Sursky, *Ahiezer* 2:716 and *Hapardes*, February 1966, p. 40.

6. *Divrei Yemei Vaad Hatzala*, p. 177.

7. The letter dated April 7, 1940, was published in Sursky, *Ahiezer* 1:228.

8. *Laws Applicable to Immigration and Nationality*, ed. Edwina Austin Avery, under direction of Carl B. Hyatt (Washington, D.C., 1953), p. 413.

9. Letter from Rabbi Sorotzkin to Rabbi Silver, April 7, 1940, acknowledging the proposal made by the Cincinnati synagogue. Sorotzkin was then in Vilna, following the Nazi conquest of Poland.

10. Interview with Rabbi Samuel Chill, February 26, 1974.

11. Moshe Yehezkeli (Prager), *Nes ha-Hatzalah shel ha-Rebbe me-Gur* (Jerusalem: Yeshurun, 1959), pp. 24-26.

12. E.g. the letter from Rabbi Abraham Yitzhak Bloch, the *rosh yeshivah* of the Telshe Yeshivah, dated July 12, 1940.
A copy of this letter was also sent to Rabbi Bernard Revel of the Yeshiva College, who studied at Telshe in his youth. For a more detailed citation of this letter see the author's *Bernard Revel*, p. 213.

13. *Divrei Yemei Vaad Hatzala*, pp. 203-205.

14. *Hapardes*, August 1940, pp. 2-3.

15. Rabbi Kalmanowitz, the rabbi of Tiktin, was the president of the Mir Yeshivah. He succeeded in reaching the United States in 1940 and completely threw himself into the rescue activities. His role in saving the Mir Yeshivah will be detailed *infra*.
Rabbi Greineman was the brother-in-law of the famed *Hazon Ish*, Rabbi Avraham Yeshayahu Karelitz, of Bene-Berak. Rabbi Wasserman was the son of the Baranowicze *rosh yeshivah*, Rabbi Elhanan Bunim Wasserman.

16. Interview with Rabbi Abraham Sher, October 25, 1970. Later the director of the Israeli *Vaad ha-Yeshivot*, Sher was then one of Rabbi Grodzenski's assistants. He mailed the letter to Silver. Cf. *Divrei Yemei Vaad Hatzala*, pp. 24-25.

17. The letter from Rabbi Shub is dated August 26, 1940, the letter

from Rabbi Kaplan is dated September 1, 1940, and the letter from Rabbi Wasserman is dated August 16, 1940.

Of these three rabbinical figures, only Rabbi Kaplan succeeded in surviving the holocaust. He reached the United States in July 1941. He taught at Mesifta Torah Vodaath and later headed its Beth Medrash Elyon Kollel in Monsey, New York.

18. Zuroff, "Rabbis, Relief, and Rescue," pp. 47a, 75. Also see the letters from Silver to Rosenberg, October 16, 1940; and from Rabbi Israel Dushowitz of Brooklyn to Silver, May 8, 1941.

There was also some resentment from Ezras Torah at the initial relief undertakings of the *Vaad Hatzala*. See the letter from Silver to Rosenberg, July 14, 1941.

19. For the details of the escape to Kobe see David Kranzler, "How 18,000 Jews Survived the Holocaust While Europe Burned," *Jewish Life*, Tishrei 5736, pp. 28-39; Chaim Shapiro, "Escape from Europe: A Chronicle of Miracles," *The Jewish Observer*, May 1973, pp. 20-23; and David Kranzler, *Japanese, Nazis and Jews* (New York: Yeshiva University Press, 1976), pp. 309-315, 356.

20. *Hapardes*, May 1941, p. 5.

21. *Hapardes*, May 1941, p. 6. Rabbi Kotler later re-established his yeshivah in Lakewood, New Jersey in 1943. After his death, its name was changed to the Rabbi Aaron Kotler Institute for Advanced Studies. Rav Aharon became the chairman of the World Council of Torah Sages of the Agudat Israel in 1954 and was a guiding force behind its independent Orthodox (*Hinukh Atzma'i*) educational system in Israel. Following the death of Rabbi Isser Zalman Meltzer, his father-in-law, Rav Aharon was nominally appointed his successor as head of Jerusalem's Etz Hayyim Yeshivah. Rabbi Kotler's occasional visits there became major events for the local Jerusalem scholars.

For his biography see Aaron Ben-Zion Shurin, *Keshet Giborim* (Jerusalem: Mosad ha-Rav Kook, 1964), pp. 244-248; Shaul Kagan, "Reb Aharon Kotler," *The Jewish Observer*, May 1973, pp. 3-13; and Liebman, "Orthodoxy in American Jewish Life," pp. 68-69.

22. *Hapardes*, June 1941, pp. 8-9.

23. For the details of the entire Shanghai venture see the doctoral dissertation by David Kranzler entitled "The History of the Jewish Refugee Community of Shanghai, 1938-1945," Bernard Revel Graduate

School of Yeshiva University, 1971. Kranzler cites the following statistics for this group in Shanghai on p. 193 n. 6:

Mir, 238 students; Kletsk, 22; Telshe, 12; Lublin, 35; Lubavitch, 29; Misc. (mostly rabbis), 73; total 409. If we include the families of some rabbis, the figures for the rabbinical groups number somewhere close to 500, thus comprising over half the Polish refugees.

Kranzler later published his dissertation under the title cited *supra*, n. 19.

Also see Joseph Epstein, "Yeshivat Mir," *Mosdot ha-Torah be-Europa*, pp. 116-132; and Aaron Sursky, "Thirty Years Since the Establishment of a Torah City in the Shanghai Diaspora" (Hebrew Article), *Beth Jacob*, January 1972, pp. 10-13.

24. Nissan Wolpin "Never Again," *The Jewish Observer*, May 1975, p. 7. Cf. Gershon Kranzler "Setting the Record Straight," *The Jewish Observer*, November 1971, pp. 9-14.

25. *Divrei Yemei Vaad Hatzala*, pp. 28-29.

Rabbi Dov Berish Wiedenfeld, the "Tshebiner Rav," is an example of one who survived the Holocaust in Siberia. Scion of a prominent Galician rabbinic family, he was the rabbi and *rosh yeshiva* of Trzebinia. During the War he escaped to Lvov from where he was exiled to Siberia by the Russians. Here, under dire circumstances, he still continued his Talmudic studies. He recorded his new interpretations on scraps of paper and pieces of wood. Rabbi Wiedenfeld arrived in Jerusalem in 1946 where he re-established his yeshivah and was soon a central halakhic authority. For his biography see Bezalel Landau, *Ha-Gaon mi-Tshebin* (Jerusalem: Hotza'at Usha, 1967).

26. For a detailed analysis of these letters and the *Vaad*'s relationship with the Joint at this juncture see Zuroff, "Rabbis, Relief, and Rescue," pp. 85-90a.

27. G. Kranzler, "Setting the Record Straight," p. 10.

28. Interview with Joseph J. Schwartz, chairman of the European executive council of the Joint Distribution Committee. This quote is recorded by the interviewer, D. Kranzler, in his "Shanghai," p. 383, n. 62.

29. *Hapardes*, June 1941, p. 8. Also see *Hapardes*, February 1941, p. 3.; May 1941, pp. 2-4; and June 1941, pp. 4-6.

30. *Hapardes*, January 1943, p. 8. For an analysis of this conference see Zuroff, "Rabbis, Relief, and Rescue," pp. 95-98.

8

The *Vaad Hatzala* in Despair and Reconstruction

✡☆✡☆✡☆✡☆✡☆✡☆✡☆✡☆✡☆✡☆✡☆✡☆✡☆✡☆

By the start of 1943, the full impact of the European Jewish catastrophe began to filter through to the United States. At the *Vaad*'s initial conference that year, Silver listened in stunned silence to the alleged deeds of the ninety-three students of the Beth Jacob Teachers' Training Institute of Cracow. These girls, ranging in ages from fourteen to twenty-two, chose to commit suicide rather than submit to the Nazi soldiers.[1] As the year ran its course, the entire scope of Hitler's "Final Solution to the Jewish Problem" became known. What was previously considered impossible and unthinkable was now a harrowing reality. In the course of this year, Silver changed the direction of the *Vaad*'s activities to begin to take an active interest in the plight of all of European Jewry. No longer was the *Vaad* solely concerned with the rabbis and scholars. Now that the grave danger to the life of every Jew was clearly realized, Silver held that ransoming as many of his brethren as possible was the primary concern.[2] He later wrote about this period:

> I will, therefore, confess that in those frightful years, the years of murder and destruction in which scores of thousands of the Jewish people were burned in the crematoria; in those years of horror when the groans of millions of our brethren being led to their doom reached us; when we knew that thousands of

Jewish communities, old and young, men, women and children were placed on the scales, for rescue or for destruction — at such a time I was unable to be among those who were satisfied with whatever little could be done and derive comfort from our achievements.[3]

Silver vigorously denounced the results of the Bermuda Conference which was held from April 19-30, 1943. This Anglo-American Conference on Refugees was called because of Jewish and general public opinion. They urgently demanded that the Allied governments rescue the victims of the Nazi persecution. Only official delegates of the American and British governments were present, and no private organizations or observers were admitted. The delegates were unwilling to refer to the Jews as the Nazis' main victims. The British refused to abandon the White Paper Policy and instead proposed the impractical idea of opening up camps in North Africa as a haven for these refugees. The Conference's few feeble decisions did not save a single Jew from the Holocaust.

Activists among American Jews blamed the British government for causing the Bermuda Conference to collapse. They felt that the last hope of serious massive rescue activities depended upon the United States government alone. Silver now cooperated with a Revisionist group known as the Emergency Committee to Save the Jewish People of Europe. Particularly active in this group was Hillel Kook, an *Irgun Tzeva'i Le'ummi* leader, who functioned in the United States under the name of Peter Bergson. The *Irgun* or "National Military Organization" was an underground armed group in Eretz Israel which did not accept Jewish Agency control. Rejecting the latter's policy of "restraint," the *Irgun* carried out armed reprisals against the Arabs and the British Mandatory authorities. Its sympathizers in the United States were therefore strongly opposed by the other Zionist parties which were part of the establishment. Despite pressure brought upon Silver by the "official" Jewish leadership not to cooperate with this partisan committee, Silver insisted on joining forces. He supported the Emergency Committee's submission of a draft resolution to Congress to establish a special governmental agency to save European Jewry. To add support to this venture, a demonstration of Orthodox rabbis at the White House was organized. This was the first time that such a determined step was undertaken by this group in order to influence the passage of the proposed resolution. Silver later declared:

> The Agudat Harabanim supported this committee, despite the fact that it was sponsored by the Revisionist party and was, therefore, opposed by the other Zionist parties for partisan reasons. But we supported any serious rescue plan, regardless of its source.[4]

On October 6, 1943, over two hundred rabbis, almost all members of the *Agudat Harabanim*, marched from Union Station to the Capitol Building. Rabbis Silver, Rosenberg, and Levinthal led the recitation of Psalms on the Capitol's steps. Silver and a group of his colleagues were introduced by Bergson to the Vice President, Henry Wallace, and some of the Congressional leaders. From the Capitol, the rabbis went to the Lincoln Memorial where prayers were recited in memory of the Holocaust victims. From there they proceeded to the White House. It was later revealed that Roosevelt asked his Jewish counsel and speech-writer, Samuel Rosenman, as to the identity of these demonstrators. Rosenman responded that they were "a group of rabbis who just recently left the darkest period of the medieval world. I unsuccessfully tried to stop their coming since they really represent no one."[5]

Roosevelt did not come out to greet the marchers. Instead they were informed that the president was out of town, and one of his secretaries received their delegation. Silver delivered a Rescue Memorandum on behalf of the *Agudat Harabanim*. He read it in the Hebrew original, while Rabbi Aaron Burack of the Yeshiva faculty read an English ve:sion. The document beseeched the president to hear the cries of those pleading for their very lives:

To the President of the United States, Franklin D. Roosevelt, God protect him:

In the name of God, Almighty Creator of the Universe, Who commanded us in the Holy Torah, "Do not let the blood of your friend be spilled, I am the Lord," we cry out in our misery to the Lord, God of Heaven and earth. A voice is heard aloft, the voice of the blood of our brethren, pure souls in the hundreds of thousands; children, infants, and elders, men and women crying out to us: Save us!

How will we be able to stand and pray on the Holy Day, the Day of Atonement, knowing that we had not fulfilled our duty? Therefore, we come, on the eve of this most Holy Day of ours, to ask you with broken heart, Mr. President, Franklin Delano Roosevelt, to hearken and listen to the sighs of our brethren hovering between life and death under the evil hand of the cruel Nazis, who have declared their intention to destroy and annihilate, God forbid, the whole Jewish people, and have made our brothers and sisters a target for their arrows, and have poured out their wrath on our people with a cruelty unheard of since God created man on earth. Millions have already fallen, put to the fire and the sword. Tens of thousands have perished of starvation, and of the most horrible manners of death — let the earth not cover their blood!

In view of this emergency situation, it is a sacred duty to take urgent measures for saving the Jewish people and especially:

a) to find a way immediately to stop the mass killings by these cruel murderers, and to put an end to this brutality by all possible means;

b) to warn the German people and all the countries under Nazi rule that the murder and plundering of the Jews living there will not be forgotten, while rescue activities and good work that will be done for the oppressed by the local governments or by individuals will be given due recognition;

c) to take all possible steps to send food and medical help to the Jews in the ghettos, to be distributed under the supervision of a neutral commission or through the International Red Cross;

d) to intervene with the neutral countries and influence them to allow the Jewish fugitives from the sword to take refuge, and to assure them haven and sustenance in these lands;

e) to open the gates of the democratic countries for refuge, and to open more widely the gates of our own country and to expedite the entrance of these refugees into the United States;

f) to open immediately the gates of the Land of Israel, the Holy Land of our Fathers, to these fugitives from the sword, the land that was given to Israel as an eternal estate by God Almighty, in covenant and in oath;

g) to establish a special agency for rescuing the remnants of the Jewish people in Europe.

We pray and hope to God Almighty that the President of the United States will recognize this historic moment of great responsibility in which he was chosen by the Creator to save many people together with the remnants of the Eternal People of the Book.

For this, may God Almighty help us to reach a quick victory on all the fronts in the struggle against our enemies and to achieve peace. On the Day of Atonement, we will pray, God willing, for the victory of our country, the United States of America.

These efforts finally contributed to the formation of the War Refugee Board. It was established on January 22, 1944, by Roosevelt, as a United States government special agency for rescue of and aid to the war victims. It consisted of the secretaries of state, treasury, and defense. Its representatives, stationed in pivotal neutral cities throughout the world, devoted themselves with zeal and daring to rescue work despite the lateness of the hour. They succeeded in saving some thousands of Jews in Rumania and Hungary.

Silver's cooperation with the Revisionists was the beginning of collaboration between them which continued throughout the *Berihah* period. This was the name of an organized underground movement which guided Jews through Europe toward illegal immigration to Eretz Israel between 1944 and 1948. The Revisionists were active in the *Berihah* and Silver aided their efforts. Their activism and militancy struck a responsive chord in his heart as he wrote:

We are ready to pay ransom for Jews and deliver them from concentration camps with the help of forged passports. For this purpose we do not hesitate to deal with counterfeiters and passport thieves! We are ready to smuggle Jewish children over the borders, and to engage expert smugglers for this purpose, rogues whose profession this is! We are ready to smuggle money illegally into enemy territory in order to bribe as many as necessary of the killers of the Jewish people, those dregs of humanity![6]

There was also another factor to their kinship. Silver once declared that Orthodoxy has empathy with the Revisionists because they share a common fate. Both are constantly pushed around by the Establishment.[7]

Silver did not hesitate to call upon the Vatican to intervene in a forceful fashion for the rescue of European Jewry. When he learned that Chief Rabbi Herzog was considering a trip to the Vatican, Silver proposed that the Pope excommunicate all those aiding Hitler's genocide policy. In a July 7, 1944, telegram to Herzog, Silver and his colleagues stated:

In conjunction your proposed personal journey to Vatican to intervene for rescue of European Jewry our opinion present situation makes imperative drastic action suggest Vatican be strongly requested impose excommunication on all future participants in whatever way in murders of European Jews and their deportations STOP Likewise Papal blessing to be conferred on all aiding in rescue of innocent victims STOP This to be made known in all churches and gathering places STOP We are endeavoring governments make like intervention through diplomatic channels.[8]

These demands became all the more urgent as the Hungarian Jewish situation worsened following the German occupation of Hungary on March 19, 1944. Eichmann now began to set up a Special Task Force to direct the liquidation of Hungarian Jewry. Ghettoization and deportation soon were carried out, and by June only the Budapest Ghetto still contained a sizeable Jewish population. By then the Swiss press, and subsequently those of other neutral and Allied countries, published details about the dire circumstances of Hungarian Jewry. Silver and the *Vaad* immediately contacted Morgenthau to demand that the War Refugee Board alleviate the "tragic plight of the Jews in Hungary." They later telegraphed Herzog and urged that he also take up this problem with the Vatican. On August 29, 1944, Silver and the *Vaad* wired Herzog: "Respectfully urge you obtain air passage to Vatican and beseech . . . rescue remainder Hungarian Jewry." The Chief Rabbi did travel to Cairo afterwards to meet with the Papal Nuncio to the Middle East in a vain endeavor to gain a more active Papal stand in these crucial matters.[9]

Whenever information was obtained which indicated a possibility of saving some lives, the *Vaad* immediately acted. Later that year, Silver learned that the internees of the Polish Oswiecin Concentration Camp were in imminent danger of extermination. He telegraphed President Roosevelt on September 26, 1944:

We respectfully call to your excellency's attention information

received that Polish underground sent urgent heartrending
SOS to Polish Government stating that forty five thousand
civilian prisoners in Oswiecin Concentration Camp in Poland
in imminent danger of extermination among these prisoners
are citizens of Poland France Czechoslovakia and other
countries STOP Only strong warning to Germany and German
people can save these unfortunates STOP On eve of holiest day
for Jewish people [Yom Kippur] we appeal to you to exhaust
every effort to save these forty five thousand innocent souls as
well as the many others in various concentration camps
similarly in danger every moment is vital STOP From the
depths of bereaved hearts we pray for your deep concern in
this grave problem and for the action which must follow to
rescue these unfortunates.

The warnings of the Allies and particularly their victories on
the battlefield did alter the Nazi operation. The notorious death
camp in Oswiecin, more popularly known by its German name
Auschwitz, was partially closed down. On November 26, 1944,
Himmler ordered the destruction of the gas chambers and
crematoria so that the advancing Allies would find no evidence of
the mass murders.

Silver and his co-workers did not hesitate to appeal to Stalin
in a similar fashion. On October 19, 1944, they telegrammed
Marshal Joseph Stalin in Moscow:

Shadow fast falling on pitiful remnant Jews in concentration
and labor camps and in Hungary STOP Substantiated reports
Himmlers murderers commenced their extermination in advance of the victorious Russian armies STOP We respectfully
appeal for your intervention to issue warning to Germans that
strongest retaliation will meet every murderous act STOP We
appeal also that all steps within your power be taken in their
rescue STOP History will record your humane action to save
these unfortunates.

Despite the advanced stage of the war, Silver did not know

the full depth of the tragedy. He still nurtured the hope that some of the leading European *roshei yeshivah* were alive. Although Rabbis Elchanan Wasserman of Baranowicze, and Abraham Grodzinski, spiritual director of the Slobodka Yeshivah, had already been murdered, Silver sought to save them. On October 26, 1944, the following telegram was sent to Adolf Berle Jr., the Assistant Secretary of State:

> We must appeal in last moments for European Jewry and respectfully request your most urgent and desperately needed intercession latest cables report Germans leaving Kaunas took to Germany sixteen thousand Jews among them great Rabbis Wasserman Grodzinski. . . . we appeal that all possible rescue means be exhausted we respectfully suggest that inasmuch as shadow fast falling that State Department intervene with all neutral lands such as Spain Sweden Switzerland Ireland and others that these neutrals appeal in name of humanity and civilization to Germany to forever cease the wilful merciless destruction of Jews.

With the continuous forward thrust of the Allies in 1945 the entire ghastly reality was rapidly revealed. The full impact of what was then thought to be a total of five million murdered Jews stunned their surviving brethren. In the midst of his sorrow, Silver was already planning for the reconstruction. At a Southwest regional meeting of the *Agudat Harabanim* convened even before the German surrender on May 8th, Silver declared:

> We have now reached the chapter of "After the Death" [Leviticus 16:1]. We have been informed of the dreadful fact that more than five million Jews have been slaughtered. We anxiously await the return of peaceful conditions to the lands saturated with blood so the exact count of the victims can be ascertained. We will then also know the census of the remnant that survived. We must now actively help these refugees by making their rehabilitation possible. We must be prepared to

sacrifice our time and wealth so that we will remain a united people. . . .

Messengers must be sent to uncover what actually transpired. The survivors must be encouraged to once again live in accordance with the dictates of Torah. *Rabanim*, teachers and *shohatim* must be appointed for them. Comfort and aid must be generously extended since all is destroyed and uprooted. Even the cemeteries were not left intact.

We must also redeem those Jewish children who sought refuge in Christian institutions. We must prepare to extend remuneration, pray for success, and even be ready to fight for our rights.[10]

The name of the *Vaad* was now changed to *Vaad Hatzala and Rehabilitation*. Four of its representatives were soon sent to Europe. These included Rabbi Isaac Lewin, the son of the *rav* of Rzeszow, Poland, who was murdered by the Nazis; Rabbi Solomon P. Wohlgelernter of Seattle, Washington; Samuel Schmidt, and Zerah Warhaftig. The latter, a Lithuanian scholar, was among the group which arrived directly in the United States from Japan. A leader of the Mizrachi movement, Warhaftig later emigrated to Eretz Israel where he served as Minister of Religious Affairs in the Israeli government. Schmidt regularly wired Silver of the formidable difficulties which confronted the survivors. While the millions of gentile Displaced Persons were rapidly being returned to their home countries, the Jewish refugees refused to go back. They realized that they had no place to return to since their communities had been destroyed and their families were no longer alive. Those that did return to Poland from distant regions in Russia's interior were soon made to feel unwanted by the intense local anti-Semitism. Many survivors only thought in terms of *aliyah*, but the gates to Eretz Israel were still tightly sealed by the British government. American consular representatives were generally insistent upon all kinds of legal technicalities before finally granting immigration visas. Many were spiritually confused after the horrors of the Nazi inferno. Dismay, puzzlement, and hopelessness prevailed among those who somehow lived through the Satanic ordeal. Schmidt arranged for kosher kitchens in some of the D.P. camps and sought out *shohatim*. On his return, at a reception of the *Agudat Harabanim*, he described the eighty orphaned children in a French camp who pleaded for Talmudic and other rabbinic volumes. In Cincinnati, Schmidt published an open letter on the first page of the October 19, 1945, issue of *Every Friday*. It read:

> I am grateful to Rabbi Eliezer Silver who was primarily responsible for my mission to Europe and I am most grateful to the Almighty who has endowed me with strength to share in the anguish of our people.
>
> I am grateful to have been able to render a measure of help to a portion of the distressed survivors of the Nazi concentration camp, in a spirit of humility.[11]

Silver was agitated by the reports and descriptions of the survivors. The tales of their physical and spiritual needs left him restless. Despite his American activities, he felt that his place was on the other side among the remnant of Israel in Europe. However, Silver only wanted to go if he had the wherewithal to really help. He did not wish to be simply another investigator reporting on conditions. He insisted upon having one hundred thousand dollars placed at his disposal. In an October 8, 1945, letter to Rosenberg, Silver wrote:

> I am thinking of traveling to Europe to visit with the survivors. I will try to save, aid and reconstruct that which I can. I am also prepared to visit Eretz Israel if I find it necessary. I will undertake all this as a representative of the *Agudat Harabanim* and the *Vaad Hatzala*. However, only on condition that I will have ample funds available to distribute at my discretion. . . . After all, I am a member of the

presidiums both of the *Agudat Harabanim* and the *Vaad Hatzala*, and founder of the latter organization. I, therefore, do not wish to be subject to the decisions of others regarding what is to be accomplished. The minimum sum in my hands should be one hundred thousand dollars for the refugees and their rehabilitation.

The next months were spent in arranging the trip and raising the necessary funds. The American government agreed to Silver's wearing an Army uniform so its insignias would add to his protection in areas where anti-Semitism was still rife. Permission also had to be obtained from the United Nations Relief and Rehabilitation Administration (UNRRA) to visit the special camps under their jurisdiction. Silver also obtained letters of introduction from Senators Taft and Alben Barkley of Kentucky. In the midst of these preparations, Silver received his first mail from a Lithuanian *rav* since the war had cut off formal communications between this country and the United States. The correspondent was Rabbi Ephraim Oshry, then in Kovno, who later settled in America where he published his Holocaust responsa entitled *Mi-Ma'amakim*. Silver immediately wrote back to Oshry, expressing his great joy at once again hearing from a Lithuanian scholar. He also detailed the plans for his forthcoming journey and sought guidance regarding the overseas situation. The December 17, 1945, letter stated:

> I read your letter in both joy and sorrow. It is the first communication I received from blood soaked Lithuania, a country which is so dear and precious to me. I do not as yet know anything about which of my Lithuanian acquaintances, colleagues and family are still alive. We have tried to contact the survivors there with no success. There has been no response to the care packages we sent. Even worse, we fear that the Lithuanian Jews will feel that we have forgotten them. . . . I am now planning a trip to see for myself why we cannot do more for the survivors. Arrangements are now being

made so I will have all the necessary documents and funds. . . .

It is with deep happiness that I am writing to you since you were privileged to survive as a *rav* in Lithuania. You are now the spiritual leader of the remnant in Kovno, the spiritual heirs of our people. Please let me know how we can help our Lithuanian brethren. Also inform us how to rescue the orphaned children who were left with gentiles and in Church orphanages. Daily, our people in Sweden and other countries, plead with us to save their children and the orphans scattered among the non-Jews. We do not know how to proceed in this crucial matter.

Through the arrangements made for Silver, the *Vaad Hatzala* also gained the official recognition of UNRRA. The *Vaad* was now permitted to send aid and to establish schools in the camps under UN jurisdiction. The United States Immigration Department agreed to accept group affidavits from the *Vaad*, pledging financial support for those refugees without American relatives. Silver's departure date was set for June 12, 1946. He arranged for his son, Rabbi David Silver of Harrisburg, and his colleague, Rabbi Samuel Katz of Indianapolis, to assume some of his local responsibilities. The mundane matters in his community had to be arranged before the major problems overseas could be tackled. In a farewell message, published in *Every Friday* of May 31, 1946, Silver stated:

I express my ardent hope and wish that my people and the leaders of the synagogues and the *shohatim* and kosher butchers will continue in their loyalty to me as if I were here. I expect the same of the management of the kosher restaurant and all institutions that come under my jurisdiction.

In Europe great and difficult tasks await me, to organize and coordinate the work of rescue and rehabilitation among our Torah-true Jews and the rescue of our children and the establishment of homes for these children, in the name of the

Union of Orthodox Rabbis, the *Vaad Hatzala*, and Ezras Torah.

The day before his departure the Agudat Israel hosted a farewell reception for Silver in New York. The next day he flew overseas for the first time in his life. After a seventeen hour flight, Silver arrived in Amsterdam. Here he was greeted by a decimated community which was reconstituting itself. Over one hundred thousand Dutch Jews perished; seventy-five percent of the Netherlands Jewish population. In Amsterdam, Silver met Chief Rabbi Herzog who was there on a similar mission. Herzog was accompanied by his son, Jacob David, and Rabbi Zev Gold, a prominent Mizrachi leader. Herzog and Silver jointly planned their European visits so they could supplement each other's efforts. Despite the cordiality of their relationship, Silver asserted that the Chief Rabbi was not correct in traveling with a Mizrachi official. He should rather appear in his capacity as a rabbinical leader for all Jews, accompanied only by his son. Silver stressed that he refused to undertake this journey as an Agudat Israel representative in order not to introduce partisan politics into rescue work. He therefore only came as the spokesman of the American rabbinical and relief organizations.[12]

Silver was received by Queen Wilhemina who had been the symbol of the resistance movement in the Netherlands during the war. The Queen expressed her anguish and bitterness at the mass-killings perpetrated by the Nazi conquerors against the Jews of her realm. Sensing that her reputation as a friend of the Jews was correct, Silver raised the basic issue of returning the children of his people. He stated:

> Your Majesty, we mourn the death of millions of Jews, and every Jewish child that has been saved from the great conflagration is more precious to us than gold. I therefore beseech you, Queen of Holland and Mother of the people of the Netherlands, in the name of America's Rabbis, to issue a

decree to all Christian citizens of Holland to return immediately to their people all Jewish children unlawfully kept in monasteries and in Christian families.[13]

Silver's plea evoked only a diplomatic response from the throne and no such official proclamation was issued. Searching for these children remained the task of the *Vaad* representatives and other motivated individuals. It was never abetted in any country by official government policy and pressure.

From Holland, Silver next visited Belgium. Here forty thousand Jews were annihilated, some sixty percent of the Jewish population. Among the survivors there were also many refugees from neighboring countries. In Antwerp, Silver found a vibrant Orthodox community. The refugees themselves already established educational facilities, including an advanced yeshivah. An orphanage, supported by the *Vaad Hatzala*, also functioned. Among its children were many who were previously discovered in gentile environs. From Antwerp, Silver went to Brussels where the country's largest Jewish community resided. Here he was shocked at the secularization of the survivors. They were mainly concerned with their economic reorganization and scant attention was devoted to Jewish education.

Silver's next stop was Paris, which was teeming with foreign-born emigrants. Here, about ninety-thousand Jews perished due to the cooperation between the Vichy and German military governments. Most of these were not French born, and the victims were about a quarter of the total Jewish population. Here too, Silver found the Orthodox refugees busily opening Torah institutions. These included an advanced yeshivah for the Polish students who reached Paris. Named Yeshivat *Hakhme Tzorfat*, it suggested the period in which France excelled in Talmudic scholarship when Rashi, Rabbenu Tam, and other *Tosafot* authors resided there. There were also elementary schools and an orphanage founded by the *Vaad*. Silver, however, was upset by the constant controversy between the Orthodox survivors. Even their *rabanim* were bickering over their future course of action. From France, Silver went on to Czechoslovakia. Comprised of Slovakia and the Protectorate of Bohemia and Moravia, over one hundred and fifty thousand Jews perished in this area. This was more than eighty-five percent of the pre-war Jewish population. Silver first visited Prague which was filled with local survivors and those escaping from the areas which had fallen under Soviet influence. Despair was widespread as many vainly searched for their spouses and children. Others were fearful lest they be returned to the areas already annexed by Russia. Silver attempted to raise their flagging spirits both through individual contact and public sermons. The latter were delivered in Prague's various synagogues, including the ancient Altneuschul which was constructed in 1270. Those with relatives in the States were guided by Silver in contacting them so that aid and emigration could be abetted. Silver came across a nucleus of Telz yeshivah students in Prague. He immediately contacted their teacher, Rabbi Elijah Bloch, who had reopened the school in Cleveland. Bloch was informed that among the survivors was Rabbi Hayyim Stein, a leading Telz graduate who later became the spiritual director of its American branch. Silver arranged for these students to continue their studies together. The local *Vaad* office later telegraphed Bloch:

> Rabbi Silver Organisierte Studenten Telser Jeschivot And Laut Ihren · Instructionen Jedem Unterstuetzung Gegeben PUNKT 16 Sind Prag Weitere 30-40 Sollen Noch Ankommen
> [Rabbi Silver organized Telzer Yeshivah students and as per your instructions all help is given STOP 16 are already in Prague and another 30-40 will yet come][14]

Silver also visited Carlsbad which had been a popular resort and convention center for the Jews of Eastern Europe. Here he aided in building a *mikveh* and kosher public kitchen.

Throughout his visits, however, Silver anxiously looked ahead to his trip to Poland. This country had been the center of Torah learning and the hassidic lifestyle. It was also the region which suffered the greatest devastation. With the cessation of hostilities, around sixty thousand surviving Polish Jews were found in Poland and in camps in Germany. About one hundred and eighty thousand were later repatriated from the Soviet Union. Over three million Polish Jews had been murdered, ninety percent of the pre-"Final Solution" Jewish population. Many advised Silver against this journey even with his American letters of introduction and military uniform. There was rioting and unrest in Poland at this time since some political groups opposed to the Soviet controlled government had taken up arms. During these disturbances, murderous attacks upon Jews took place on public thoroughfares, buses and railroads. At times these assaults assumed mass proportions and resulted in full fledged pogroms in towns and cities. This wave of anti-Jewish excesses continued well into 1946, reaching its climax in a massive pogrom at Kielce, the capital of Kielce province, in Southeast Poland. On July 4th, while Silver was in Poland, an armed horde of Polish nationalists, joined by a few Communists, fell upon Kielce, murdering forty-two Jews and wounding many others. This pogrom convinced most of the Jewish survivors, including those who had returned from the Soviet Union, that there was no future for them in Poland.

Despite these precarious conditions, Silver insisted upon his visit. His first stop was Warsaw which was almost completely destroyed and desolate. Many of the buildings which remained standing could not be entered due to fear of imminent collapse. Only a single *minyan*, assembling at an old age home, still functioned. In the Warsaw suburb of Praga, the home of the martyred Rabbi Zemba, Silver came upon a larger community of survivors. The heads of the local Mizrachi group warmly welcomed him and volunteered to provide an escort for his safety. Silver, however, chose to rely upon his American military uniform, and only accepted a guide from his hosts. As he walked through the streets, Silver was approached time and again by refugees pleading for charity. Besides aiding these individuals, he also provided the funds to complete a *mikveh* and public kitchen. The sight of scholars pleading for sustenance in the area that was previously the heart of Polish Jewry greatly grieved Silver. He expressed his feelings in a communication with his colleague Rabbi Rosenberg. Evidently not trusting the reliability of the Polish facilities, Silver sent out the exact same message both through a Western Union Cablegram and an RCA Radiogram. It read:

> Visited Holland Belgium France Czechoslovakia and poor Poland STOP Found terrible situations *Talmidei Hakhamim* lying in streets and living in unsanitary conditions most of them came from Russia with patriarch beards from great jiches [families] STOP Gave great sums to individuals widows children *Roshei Yeshivot* bachurim and institutions STOP Everybody naked poor and heartbroken discouraged STOP Borrowed already money STOP Going back Poland today to poorest part Stettin Silesia STOP Need immediately at least more 5000 Ezras Torah 25000 *Vaad Hatzala* and 5000 *Vaad Roshei Yeshivot* STOP Sternbuchs desperate because no money they do marvellous work STOP Romanian Hungarian Karpato Russia Jews need also help STOP Great work must be done immediately to help Jews Poland and other countries and bring youth back to Torah STOP If you do not send help me and Sternbuch immediately whole rescue work will break down STOP I will borrow great sums your account because cannot see Jews dying before our eyes.

Silver met with the local American Consul and demanded that American visas be granted more freely to the refugees. He also requested the Consul's aid in arranging meetings with the political heads of Poland. While still in the Warsaw area, rep-

Rabbi Eliezer Silver during his 1946 European trip. *Top*: In Warsaw. *Bottom*: With Jan Masaryk, the foreign minister of Czechoslovakia

A delegation of Orthodox leaders, headed by Rabbis Eliezer Silver and Wolf Gold, meeting with Vice President Henry A. Wallace in Washington, D.C. in 1943, to petition for aid to save the Jews from Nazism

Several post-war Jewish world leaders. *Above left*: Rabbi Abraham Mordecai Alter of Gur. *Above right*: Rabbi Yitzhak Zev Soloveitchik of Brisk and Jerusalem. *Below left*: Rabbi Isaac ha-Levi Herzog. *Below right*: Rabbi Moshe Feinstein

resentatives of various Jewish communities invited Silver to visit with them. He chose to go to Lodz in central Poland which had become the largest reconstructed Jewish community in Poland. Over fifty thousand Jews resided there by the end of 1946. On the way to Lodz, Silver traveled through communities such as Sochaczew and Tyszowce, once vibrant centers of Jewish life. Silver now met only a handful of Jewish refugees in these areas. By nightfall he reached Lodz where the refugees turned out en masse to greet him. Many had been aided by the *Vaad* and they now wanted to publicly express their gratitude. This was the first visit of an American *rav*, the founder of the *Vaad*, whom they knew to be an able Torah scholar. Silver's wearing a United States Army uniform added to his charisma in the eyes of the survivors of the Nazi inferno. Thousands of his brethren, both young and old, lined the streets to cheer his arrival. When he alighted, the crowd surged forward to shake his hand and exchange greetings. Silver's eyes brimmed with tears as he responded to the warmth of the crowd. He was particularly moved by the many teen-agers and youngsters who turned out to greet him. Silver kept on grasping their hands while blessing and encouraging them. He then addressed the assembled throng from a balcony, urging them to continue their lives as dedicated Jews holding the torch of Torah study aloft.

Silver subsequently met with the *rabanim* and the yeshivah heads and their students who were in Lodz. He delivered lengthy Talmudic discourses before these groups and engaged in animated scholarly give and take with the yeshivah students. He also lectured at the Lubavitcher Yeshivah which had been established in Lodz, bringing the *Hassidim* special greetings from their *rebbe*. On the Sabbath, the main synagogue where Silver prayed was filled beyond capacity. Here too Silver delivered a rabbinic discourse based upon Talmudical and Maimonidean sources. He declared his intentions of refreshing their memories and rekindling in his listeners the desire to return to intense

Talmudic study. Silver wanted them to realize that even the ordeals of the concentration camps did not erase their knowledge of Jewish lore and their basic love for learning.

While in Lodz, Silver was informed that the Polish premier would receive him. Silver returned to Warsaw to meet with the premier, Edward Osobka-Morawski, a left-wing Socialist. At their conference, Silver vehemently complained that the Polish government had not yet repealed the laws enacted because of anti-Semitic influence. He particularly demanded that the prohibition against *shehitah* be rescinded. The premier responded that while his guest was concerned with the slaughter of cattle, he was more concerned with the slaughter of Jews and stopping the anti-Jewish excesses. To this Silver responded, "Those who interfere with the kosher slaughtering of cattle will later murder Jews. The anti-Semitic passions which are the basis of anti-*shehitah* laws ultimately engender all levels of anti-Jewish acts." Their meeting ended with Silver being asked for a detailed list of his requests. He later submitted it, particularly stressing that the emigration of the survivors be permitted at their request.

Silver next visited Cracow, once one of the most erudite and successful European Jewish communities. By the end of the hostilities, only a few Jews who had been in hiding were saved in Cracow. They were later joined by thousands of their brethren returning from Russia. Here too Silver was warmly greeted by the *roshei yeshivah* and their students then in Cracow. He visited the ancient cemetery where leading rabbinical scholars of the sixteenth and seventeenth centuries were interred. Finding the hallowed ground in a state of total neglect and destruction, Silver arranged for protective fences around the graves of the rabbis. Among those now guarded were the final resting places of Rabbis Moses Isserles (1525-1572), Yom Tov Lipmann Heller (1579-1654), Joel Sirkes (1561-1640), and Nathan Nata Shapiro (1585-1633). This entire historic cemetery was later renewed as a result of contributions from American and Canadian Jews.

Silver next visited the community of Sosnowiec in nearby Katowice Province. Some seven hundred Jews had resettled here, almost all of whom emigrated shortly afterwards. His visit was cut short when he was called back to Warsaw for a meeting concerning his requests for emigration permits. Silver reserved a seat in the first class compartment of the train from Sosnowiec to Warsaw. On his way to the railroad he encountered a ranting Polish mob. Despite his American military uniform, they sensed he was Jewish due to his beard. They soon gathered around him, shouting in Polish and exchanging threatening glances. Silver kept his cool and responded with English phrases of denunciation and malediction. The crowd was now puzzled by his English speech and proud deportment. Silver quickly continued on his way and was soon safely in his train compartment. He later learned that the Kielce pogrom took place that very evening. In addition, some hundred and fifty Russian soldiers were murdered by rampaging nationalistic mobs.

The next day, Friday, July 5th, Silver arrived at the ministry at the appointed hour. It was only then that Silver became aware of the riots and widespread tension as his appointment was delayed to Saturday. Enjoined from carrying on the Sabbath, Silver left his documents at the ministry in anticipation of the meeting. He spent the Sabbath among his brethren, worshipping in the only synagogue still standing among the ruins of Warsaw. In honor of the holy day, Silver wore his usual rabbinic garb.

At midday, he once again changed into his military uniform for his governmental meeting. Silver was joined by Mrs. Recha Sternbuch, the prime mover behind the Swiss branch of the *Vaad*, for this appointment. This time, Silver not only pleaded for permission for the refugees to emigrate to the United States and Eretz Israel in accordance with their choice, but also stressed the current riots. He demanded that the government protect both the lives and property of the Jewish Holocaust survivors. Silver was promised a favorable response to his requests by the Polish officials although they also stressed that the Jews would be able to reconstruct their communities in Poland. Silver was also encouraged to seek an audience with the country's president. On July 10, 1946, Silver was received by Boleslaw Bierut, the president of the new Polish government. Later Silver wrote that he told Bierut:

> I am a Rabbi and I have nothing to do with diplomacy. Yet I know how eager the Polish leftists are for recognition of their new regime by the outside world. Consider now, how will you be able to prove your authority to the world if you show yourselves incapable of controlling the groups of plunderers, pogromists in your midst?
>
> I am a Rabbi and not a diplomat; therefore take my sincere advice: it is better for you, the Poles, to rid yourselves of these bothersome and stubborn Jews once and for all. My advice is: "Let my people go." Issue passports and exit permits to all the Jews remaining in your land, and try to solve at the same time the problem of Polish citizens who were exiled to Siberia. My advice is that these exiles be returned to Poland on condition that they leave here as soon as possible. I promise you that the Czechoslovakian government will open their border to the Polish Jews and allow them to pass through on the way to Palestine.[15]

Silver also stressed that the remaining Jews would be loyal citizens to a leftist regime such as the new Polish government. Their main concern was to attain justice and peace from the ruling body. Once the government is guided by equitable principles, then Jewish law decrees that "the law of the land is law." The president assured Silver that the government recognized its grave responsibility to put down the riots and maintain law and order. Bierut also claimed that the Jewish method of slaughter was not prohibited, rather it must be adapted to the governmental hygienic regulations. When Silver asked whether he could quote him, the president responded: "Without any hesitancy."[16] The minister in charge also promised Silver ten thousand exit visas to be issued to rabbis and yeshivah students who were particularly ill at ease under the leftist regime.

At the conclusion of the audience, Silver blessed the president and his ministers, expressing his confidence that their promises would soon be fulfilled. He spent another few days in Warsaw among the refugees, guiding and encouraging their plans to emigrate and start life over again. From Warsaw he returned to Prague where he also conferred with governmental leaders. He particularly found an attentive and sympathetic individual in Jan Masaryk, the Foreign Minister. The son of Thómas G. Masaryk, Czechoslovak patriot and first president of its republic, Jan was greatly influenced by his father's Zionist commitment and major efforts against anti-Semitism. Jan Masaryk was termed by Silver "one of the few righteous gentiles of this generation." He faithfully promised Silver all the aid possible, illustrating that it would simply be an intensification of already existing government policy. Two years later Masaryk was found dead after the Communist *coup d'etat* in early 1948.

Silver then went on to the Slovakian region which was formerly a part of Hungary. He visited Pressburg, known in Czechoslovakian as Bratislava, one of the most ancient and important Jewish centers in the Danube area. The home of the *Hatam Sofer*, Rabbi Moses Sofer (1763-1839), Pressburg had been a vibrant center of Orthodoxy. It was now filled with survivors and refugees who warmly welcomed Silver. Here he felt intense anti-Semitism as he walked through the streets. Once he was accosted by a non-Jew for speaking Yiddish with local *rabanim* in the streets of Bratislava. The anti-Semite called a policeman to arrest them for speaking a foreign language. Silver threatened to contact the American Consul and the policeman dropped the charge. The non-Jew avenged himself against the Jews by beating up a few refugees. This incident greatly frightened the local community which feared that a pogrom would soon break out. After this incident quieted down, Silver continued his journey, visiting numerous smaller communities in the Slovakian area. He later returned to Prague where yeshivah students were already arriving from Poland as a result of his efforts. Silver arranged lodging for them, obtained clothes, and constantly discussed Talmudic topics with the young men.

Toward the end of his stay in Eastern Europe, Silver had to contend with rumors which were constantly spreading through the refugee community. The latest declared that the *Vaad Hatzala* was closing down. Silver assured his listeners wherever he spoke that the *Vaad* would continue its activities. On July 25, 1946, he cabled Rabbis Rosenberg and Kotler:

> Rumors circulating in Poland and other European countries that *Vaad Hatzala* near dissolution STOP Sternbuchs who doing excellent work in desperate situation panicky because above rumors STOP Became stilled due my personal guarantees and assurances that *Vaad Hatzala* continues and will attend near future as before STOP Wherever I was found *Vaad Hatzala* doing utmost achieved maximum had greatest recognition until last Passover STOP With my broad distributions helped regain good name of Agudat Harabanim *Vaad Hatzala* and Ezras Torah STOP Yeshivah bachurim with roshim on way to Paris and Munich we expect also near thousand orphans leaving Poland although situation there improved STOP Am leaving for Germany and Austria.

Silver next entered the American zone of occupied Germany where the tragedy of the Holocaust was most real and tangible. The small remnant of German Jewry which survived the war in Germany was joined by displaced persons who sought temporary refuge there. By the end of 1946, there was a record number of 160,000 Jewish Displaced Persons in Germany, mainly in the American zone. Silver found the refugees completely dependent upon the good offices of the UNRRA and the local military authorities. At times their relationships were strained and the D.P.s were caught between the two administrative groups. Silver related an incident he witnessed soon after his arrival. A groom was given a bottle of wine by UNRRA in order to celebrate his *Sheva Berakhot* (the six marriage benedictions recited with the blessing over wine). He was shortly afterwards arrested by an American soldier for possessing liquor. The wedding was cancelled as the would-be groom was sentenced to six months detention despite the testimony of UNRRA officials that they sold him the wine. Silver later aided the unfortunate victim by appealing to the American general in charge of this area. The groom was soon released, and the marriage took place.[17]

In another refugee camp in the American zone, Silver came upon a group of Jews who were simply starving. He saw them getting small portions of bread and witnessed Jewish children gathering crumbs from the floor. Shocked, he hurriedly sought out the officer responsible for this camp. Silver admonished him saying:

I, as an American citizen, was deeply ashamed to see the suffering and the want of the unhappy refugees in this camp. I am all the more ashamed since hearing of the outpouring of pity on the German people by the American occupation authorities.[18]

All Silver received in reply were excuses and evasive answers. He was all the more upset by the comfortable status of the local German community. Many resided in homes that were confiscated from Jews and utilized Jewish possessions and wealth. Despite these frustrations, Silver continued visiting the various camps, lecturing and encouraging the survivors. He also attempted to minimize the different viewpoints which were being espoused by the Orthodox groups in the camps. He appealed to the Mizrachi, Agudat Israel, and the Agudah faction dominated by the Klausenburger *Rebbe*, Rabbi Yekutiel Halberstam, to submit their questions to the central rabbinical authority. This body had been established by the refugee rabbis in the various camps. Known officially as the "Rabbinical Representative in the U.S. Zone," it was headed by Rabbi Samuel Abba Snieg, and functioned out of Munich. However, Silver's pleas in this area met with little success.

Silver finally reached Frankfort on the Main where Rabbi Emanuel Rackman was stationed as a chaplain in the American Air Force. The latter, a graduate of the Rabbi Isaac Elchanan Theological Seminary, who became the rabbi of Manhattan's Fifth Avenue Synagogue, thus described Silver's mode of travel and activity in a letter to Rabbi David Silver dated August 8, 1946:

> Your father arrived here Monday and left last night. I did all I could to make him comfortable. But how your mother couldn't force him to stay in the States is beyond me. He is living on Torah — not food — and he is lecturing beyond the capacity of any five humans half his age. He did say he fared better at Zeilsheim than any other camp he visited but as luck would have it, half the time he was there he fasted. The few little things I was able to do for him made me very happy but I was worried — as well as inspired — by his enterprise and locomotion.
>
> He may come via Frankfort again in a week but I pray that he doesn't get to Palestine and goes home instead for a rest.

Silver continued his journey and also visited with survivors in the British and Russian zones. From Germany he went on to Austria where he toured Vienna and some smaller Jewish settlements. Here too Silver found widespread malnutrition among the refugees. He demanded improvements in their food allowances from the military authorities and also arranged for the baking of additional bread with *Vaad* funds. From Austria, Silver crossed through Switzerland into Italy. Here he visited

Milan and Rome and was more favorably impressed with the efforts of the Joint and UNRRA. In Rome he lectured before the East European refugees who had organized the *Meor Hagolah* Yeshivah. In all the places he visited, Silver profusely distributed funds to both institutions and individuals. However, the main succor the refugees received from his visits was not the financial aid, but rather the spiritual encouragement. Before the eyes of the weary survivors appeared an erudite *rav*, preaching in Yiddish, and clad in the uniform of the United States Army. Rabbi Ephraim Oshry, then in Italy, described Silver's visit in the *Meor Hagolah* Yeshivah which the former had organized. Silver kissed every young pupil as if kissing a Torah scroll. He announced a prize of fifty dollars for every student who had mastered twenty-five folio pages of the Talmud. One youngster told the guest that he did not yet study Talmud, but he did know twenty-five chapters of the Psalms. He also was granted the full sum by Rabbi Silver.[19]

Simon Wiesenthal, who later became a persevering Nazi hunter, described his encounter with Silver in a D.P. Camp. Previously, during April of 1945, a train from Hungary arrived at the Mauthausen death camp. One of the newcomers succeeded in smuggling in a small prayer book. Wiesenthal at first greatly admired this individual for his courage since he must have known the strict regulations against bringing anything into the camp. This admiration soon turned to dismay when Wiesenthal observed the man lending his prayer book to other inmates for fifteen minutes apiece in return for a quarter of each person's daily soup ration. When Silver arrived in Wiesenthal's D.P. camp with a Torah scroll brought from America, Wiesenthal refused to attend the services of dedication. He told his friend he could never forget the greedy man who had bartered faith for food. Wiesenthal later related:

That night Rabbi Silver came to see me. He was a small man

who wore an American army uniform without insignia. He had
a small white beard, and his bright eyes shone with great
kindness. He must have been at least seventy-five, but his
mind was sharp and his voice was youthful. He told me he'd
been born in the Ukraine, the country of pogroms, and had
emigrated as a boy to America, the country of hope.

He put his hand on my shoulder. "So they tell me you're
angry with God?" he said in Yiddish, and he smiled at me.

I said not with God, but with one of His servants, and told
him what had happened.

He kept smiling. "And that's all you have to tell me?"

"Isn't that enough, Rabbi?" I asked.

"*Du Dummer* [you silly man]," he said. "So you look only
at the bad man who took something from the good ones. Why
don't you look instead at the good men who gave something to
the bad one?" He touched me with his outstretched palm and
left.

I went to the service the next day. Ever since I have tried
to remember that there are two sides to every problem,
although sometimes it is as difficult to see as the other side of
the moon.[20]

Another survivor detailed his encounter with Silver in a
German D.P. camp. Although not a former yeshivah student or
learned Jew, he still approached Silver and requested his aid in
gaining entry to the United States. Silver promised to help on
condition that he marry again while still in Germany with a
Holocaust survivor. The supplicant replied that he was not
prepared to even think of remarrying after having lost his first
wife and all his children. To this Silver responded that a holy
obligation rested upon the surviving remnant to once again
establish Jewish families. Everyone had to do his share in
replenishing the one million children murdered by the Nazis.
After Silver's response the survivor did remarry. Silver later
arranged for the couple to emigrate to the United States where
he helped them get started. Silver was the *sandek* at the

circumcision of their eldest son and thirteen years later joined the family for the son's *bar mitzvah*. This particular household was but one of many such families with whom Silver kept in touch after their American arrival.[21]

In Italy Silver decided to continue on to Eretz Israel. He arranged to go to Egypt first when he learned that a group of Shanghai refugee yeshivah students were experiencing difficulty with the local authorities. From Rome he flew to Cairo. Here he also visited local Jewish institutions and was particularly impressed by the educational institutions which were staffed by teachers trained in Eretz Israel. Silver succeeded in arranging for the *aliyah* of the Shanghai yeshivah students. He also toured parts of Egypt, posing for the traditional picture in front of the Pyramids with a camel and Arab guide.

From Cairo Silver flew on to Lod, arriving in the Holy Land on Friday, August 30, 1946. He immediately went to Jerusalem where the large Orthodox community had plastered the streets with signs welcoming the guest. That afternoon Silver visited Rabbi Alter of Gur, and Rabbi Joseph Tzvi Duschinsky, the spiritual leader of Jerusalem's separatist Orthodox community. Friday evening Silver prayed at the Western Wall, and was the guest of Rabbi Yitzhak Zev Soloveitchik of Brisk for the Sabbath meal. On the Sabbath day Silver was visited by many of the rabbis and communal leaders of the Holy City. On Sunday he visited the local yeshivot and the two Orthodox hospitals, Bikkur Holim and Sha'arei Zedek. That evening Silver lectured before the student body of the Hebron Yeshivah in Jerusalem, the country's leading Talmudic academy. After the lecture, Silver was feted at a repast sponsored by all the organizations associated with Agudat Israel.

Later that week Silver visited with the *Hazon Ish* in Bene-Berak where he also toured the newly established Ponevezh Yeshivah. Silver also was the guest of Rabbi Reuven Katz in Petah Tikvah. There Silver participated in ground breaking ceremonies for a new Beth Jacob school building. He was honored with officially opening a new street named "The Ninety-Three" in memory of the martyred Cracow Beth Jacob girls. After his return to Jerusalem, Silver was received by Sir Alan Cunningham, the British High Commissioner for Palestine. Silver impassionedly pleaded for the abrogation of the 1939 White Paper. Silver vividly described the sufferings of the Displaced Persons, most of whom wished to come on *aliyah*. He claimed that the majority were Orthodox Jews who would not sanction terrorist activities against the British. They would rather busy themselves with building religious institutions and schools. Their active participation in the country would influence the youth to desist from irresponsible acts which only injure innocent bystanders. Silver also stressed the importance of the *mitzvah* of settling in the Holy Land for the Torah Jew and detailed the many commandments which could only be observed there. He therefore appealed to Cunningham to open the gates of Palestine to his brethren.

A reception for Silver was also tendered by the *Vaad ha-Yeshivot* which had become a vibrant organization on the local Torah scene. All the *roshei yeshivah* attended and warm words of thanks were expressed to Silver for his aid over the years. Among those who spoke were Rabbis Tykocinski and Meltzer of the Etz Hayyim Yeshivah and Rabbi Sarna of the Hebron Yeshivah. In response Silver declared that his only consolation after experiencing the full depth of the European tragedy was the existence of so many first-rate yeshivot in the Holy Land. Silver concluded by comparing these institutions of learning to the historic school in Yabneh which was salvaged by Rabban Yohanan Ben Zakkai after the fall of the Second Temple.

After ten days in the Holy Land, Silver started on his return trip. Following brief stopovers once again in Rome and Paris, he returned to the States in time for Rosh Hashanah. The final lap of the journey was made in a military plane which landed in

Springfield, Massachusetts, on September 16, 1946. When he reached Cincinnati the local newspaper commented not only on the importance of his mission but also on his haggard appearance — Silver had lost thirty-five pounds while overseas.[22] Of all the countries he visited only one acknowledged his return. Rudolph Kuraz, the Czechoslovakian Consul General in New York, wrote to Silver on September 12, 1946:

> Permit me, first of all, to welcome you on your return from a great mission in the cause of help and reconstruction in Europe. We followed this journey with great interest and were glad to hear of your successes, especially with the Czechoslovakian authorities. And I have the honor to inform you that we will continue this traditional Masaryk-Benes [second president of the Czechoslovakian Republic] line.

Silver soon intensified the *Vaad*'s activities. Schmidt returned to Europe where he remained for the next eight months. However, with the continued resettlement of displaced persons, the *Vaad* was soon caught up in constant infighting and bickering. Dormant rivalries such as those between Mizrachi and Agudah partisans surfaced once again. There was also some tension between the *roshei yeshivah*, who were becoming a prime force in American Orthodoxy, and the *rabanim*. There were others who claimed that the *Vaad* had fulfilled its basic goals and could now leave the tasks at hand to the other organizations. An editorial in *Hapardes* defended the *Vaad* and Silver against the Mizrachi's allegations:

> When the *Vaad* aids the emigration of orphans, yeshivah students, and scholars, their political affiliation is not probed. No one asks whether they belong to the Mizrachi, Agudah, or are simply Jews without party membership. The truth is that there are not enough funds to go around. The Agudah leaders complain just like the Mizrachi people do. . . .
> The last outcry came about because a Mizrachi leader visiting Europe requested five-thousand dollars for *hatzala*

activities. The *Vaad* did not honor this request immediately. However, even when its founder and presidium member [Rabbi Silver] was in Europe, his requests were not answered either. The funds he brought with him did not suffice to meet the overwhelming needs he encountered. His telegraphs for urgent aid were not heeded. He realized that the treasury of the *Vaad* was empty, and instead borrowed incessantly to meet the demands of the hour. Many of these loans have yet to be repaid.[23]

As *aliyah* increased, Silver shifted the attentions of the *Vaad* to aiding the refugees reaching Israel. On June 22, 1948, Silver wrote to his colleagues, requesting their attendance at a *Vaad* meeting to plan "activities to strengthen the situation of the refugees in the Holy Land, particularly the scholars and Torah students. The time has come to undertake formal tasks there."

During the tenth anniversary year of the *Vaad*, Silver continued to stress the needs of these refugees reaching the nascent State of Israel. On February 17, 1949, he wrote:

This is now the tenth year since the *Vaad Hatzala* was established. During this time we were privileged to aid tens of thousands of victims, among them great scholars and *geonim*. . . .

During the last period we have decided to concentrate on the refugees reaching Israel. There it is not like the United States. There is no united service to sustain the scholars arriving like those which function here. We must instead undertake this task in the Holy Land. . . .

The tenth year must be sacred to the Lord. We must aid the devotees of the Torah and its students to successfully establish themselves in Israel.

Despite Silver's efforts, the *Vaad* never regained its former level of activity. Silver remained its head, but with the termination of the Holocaust and the initial restitution of the survivors the *Vaad*'s most fruitful years had ended.

Notes

1. *Hapardes*, January 1943, p. 6. For the last will and testament of these girls see *Ani Ma'amin*, ed. Mordecai Eliav (Jerusalem: Mossad Harav Kook, 1965), pp. 51-52. Dr. Hillel Seidman of New York, in a May 9, 1977 letter to the author, claimed that this event did not actually take place.

2. Zuroff, "Rabbis, Relief, and Rescue," pp. 95, 108; Interview with Rabbi David Silver, October 4, 1972; and *Divrei Yemei Vaad Hatzala*, p. 31 ff.

3. *Divrei Yemei Vaad Hatzala*, p. 32.

4. *Divrei Yemei Vaad Hatzala*, p. 34. Also the letter from Peter H. Bergson-Kook to the author, February 22, 1971; and the interview with Rabbi David Silver, October 4, 1972.

5. Rosenman's response cited by Hillel Seidman in "Moynihan At The Start of His Career and Not the End" in *Hatzofe*, February 13, 1976. For Rosenman's relationship with Roosevelt see Samuel I. Rosenman, *Working With Roosevelt* (New York: Harper and Brothers, 1952).

6. *Divrei Yemei Vaad Hatzala*, p. 38f.

7. MS by Rabbi David L. Silver, p. 23, clarified in his interview of October 4, 1972; and Zuroff, "Rabbis, Relief, and Rescue," p. 112.

8. The telegram, located in the *Vaad Hatzala* Archives, was signed by Union of Orthodox Rabbis, Rabbis Israel Rosenberg, E. Silver, *Vaad Hatzala* Emergency Committee Rabbis Aaron Kotler, Reuven Grosowski, Abraham Kalmanowitz.

Acknowledgment is extended to Mr. Zuroff for making copies of these documents available to the author. The next few telegrams cited in this chapter were also signed in this fashion.

9. Geulah Bat-Yehuda, "Yitzhak Eizik Halevi Herzog," *Men of The Spirit*, ed. Leo Jung (New York: Kymson Publishing Company, 1964), p. 130.

10. *Hapardes*, May 1945, pp. 8-9. The convention was held on April 16-17, 1945.

11. For details of the Schmidt trip see *Hapardes* October 1945, p. 5, and November 1945, p. 2. The *Agudat Harabanim* reception for Schmidt was held on October 23, 1945.

12. Glickman-Porush, *Ish Ha-Halakhah Veha-Maaseh*, pp. 68-69. Also see Chief Rabbi Herzog's *Massa Hatzalah* (Jerusalem, 1947), p. 43.

Details of Silver's European trip are from the above sources; *Divrei Yemei Vaad Hatzala*, pp. 39-47; and the pamphlet by Rabbi Silver, "Report on a Mission to the Remnants of Jewry in 16 Countries and a Visit to the Holy Land," ed. Tzvi H. Wachsman (Toronto, 1947), 28 pp. Details of the fate of the Jews in Hitler's Europe are from Lucy Davidowicz, *The War Against the Jews 1933-1945* (New York: Holt, Rinehart and Winston, 1975), pp. 357-401.

13. *Divrei Yemei Vaad Hatzala*, p. 43.

14. *Hapardes*, August 1946, p. 26.

15. *Divrei Yemei Vaad Hatzala* p. 44.

16. Glickman-Porush, *Ish Ha-Halakhah Veha-Maaseh*, p. 89.

17. *Ibid.*, p. 91.

18. *Divrei Yemei Vaad Hatzala*, p. 43.

19. Minutes of the memorial meeting held at the *Agudat Harabanim* office on the fifth anniversary of Silver's death, January 11, 1973 (Shevat ninth), citing the eulogy of Rabbi Oshry.

20. Simon Wiesenthal, *The Murderers Among Us* (London: Heinemann Publishers, 1967), p. 250. Silver's country of birth was Lithuania and not the Ukraine.

21. Dr. A. Klarman, "An Example of a Man of Righteousness," *The Day-Jewish Journal*, March 28, 1968.

22. *Every Friday* of September 27, 1946 stated that Silver weighed 165 pounds when he left, and returned weighing 130.

23. *Hapardes*, March 1947, p. 2f.

For additional indication of the tensions around the *Vaad*'s activities see the letter to Rabbi Silver from Rabbi Samuel Greineman of Mesivta Tifereth Jerusalem, January 16, 1947; and the letters to Rabbi Rosenberg from Silver, January 24, 1947 and February 16, 1947.

Details were also gained in an interview with Rabbi Simcha Teitelbaum, July 30, 1974. The latter had access to the inner workings of the *Vaad* since his father, Rabbi Aaron, was active in its operations.

9

The Man and His Ideals

✡☆✡☆✡☆✡☆✡☆✡☆✡☆✡☆✡☆✡☆✡☆✡☆✡☆✡

Silver's activities as the head of the *Vaad Hatzala* were probably the most rewarding of his life. They gave full vent to his endless energy, restlessness, and volatile personality. Never having lost the spirit of idealism and youthful enthusiasm, Silver remained the dedicated yeshivah student throughout his life. By nature an ardent fighter, he was no bitter-ender. Though he could and did kick up plenty of storms, he knew when and how to "call it quits." Simultaneously he was full of mellowness and generosity. Very often the individual who was the object of his anger benefited the most from his magnanimity. Rabbi Benjamin Zev Jacobson, an Agudah leader, described his first encounter with Silver when he sought additional aid from the *Vaad*. Jacobson was then a spiritual leader in Sweden, where many Holocaust victims sought refuge. To aid them, Jacobson journeyed to the United States to raise additional funds. When he met with Silver the latter rebuked him in anger, saying, "The *Vaad* is doing all it possibly can. There are endless demands made upon it, and there is no possibility of increasing the sum allotted for Swedish Jewry."

When Jacobson left Silver, he was upset and depressed. He felt that if the *Vaad*'s president reacted in this negative fashion there was no hope that his mission would be successful. His acquaintances, however, assured him that if he had provoked Silver to such anger he would attain his goals. The next day Silver presented him with a check for ten thousand dollars and also promised to raise additional funds for the Swedish *Vaad* branch.[1]

On another occasion a prominent European rabbinical leader visited the United States on a fund raising mission. At a welcoming banquet sponsored by the *Agudat Harabanim*, the guest rabbi spoke in a fashion which Silver deemed offensive. The speaker implied that the truly great *rabanim* were overseas and not in the United States. Silver walked out in a huff. The guest was upset and mentioned to Rabbi Menahem Kasher who was present that he would now be unsuccessful. Kasher retorted, "You will totally achieve your goals. Rabbi Silver will be your best friend." Silver later raised thousands of dollars for this cause and exerted all his influence to guarantee the success of the mission.[2]

At crucial meetings of the *Vaad*, when life and death decisions had to be made, there was often shouting among the participants. The key *rabanim* such as Silver and Rosenberg and the *roshei yeshiva* such as Kotler and Kalmanowitz were all strong willed individuals. Yet at a certain point, Silver was influential in ending the argumentation and shouting, and making the salient decision.[3]

Many times Silver was so moved by the causes he was called upon to aid that he himself contributed beyond his means. When he did not have funds available, Silver borrowed from his bank. His life insurance was constantly mortgaged as collateral for such loans. When the Cincinnati community presented Silver with a cash gift at a dinner in his honor, the money was intentionally placed in trust with an officer of his synagogue. The lay leaders were apprehensive lest their rabbi distribute the sum to charitable appeals before his family could benefit from their generosity.[4]

Silver's most impetuous act of borrowing was to aid Rabbi Joseph Kahaneman of Ponovezh. The latter was just beginning the construction of Kiryat Ponovezh in Bene-Berak as a memorial to Lithuanian Jewry. After the war ended, Kahaneman visited America to raise funds for this project. Silver was so enthralled with the man and his dream that he used his contacts to borrow fifty thousand dollars for his guest. The sum was never totally repaid by funds subsequently collected, and Silver had to personally cover a substantial portion. Nevertheless, this financial aid helped the nascent Ponovezh complex. Rabbi Kahaneman later referred to Silver as one of the "three American angels" who helped turn his dream into reality. The other two were wealthy businessmen.[5]

Once Silver's personal generosity and fund raising ability became known, he constantly received requests for aid. Some of these entreaties concerned basic institutions and fundamental problems facing the Jewish people. These requests kept Silver well informed of developments in the Jewish world. When Chief Rabbi Abraham Isaac Kook established an advanced yeshivah in Jerusalem, which later became known as Merkaz ha-Rav Kook, he appealed to Silver. In a letter dated July 24, 1929, he described the subjects planned for the school. Unlike the curriculum at other yeshivot which stressed solely the *halakhic* sections of the Babylonian Talmud, it was to be more inclusive. Rabbi Kook wrote:

Our goal is to have various departments of scholarship. The basic studies will be Talmud and the Codes. The Babylonian and Jerusalem divisions of the Talmud will be covered, including both the *halakhic* and *aggadic* sections. Scientific Jewish scholarship will also be pursued with an approach of sanctity and knowledge of the Lord.

Later that year, Silver's aid was requested by Rabbi Joseph Isaac Schneersohn of Lubavitch. In a moving letter, he described the tribulations of religious Jewry under Communist dominion. Dated October 30, 1929, it read:

It is terrifying to even think about the current tragic state of

Russian Jewry. The Yevsektsiya is stronger than ever and determined to completely estrange the youth from Torah. They have declared total war against observant parents in the expectations that they will certainly conquer the children. The government aids them in every way and all the funds necessary are at their disposal. Many Jewish schools have been opened under their auspices and youth groups are sponsored for children between the ages of three and fifteen. Observant Jewry vainly attempts to oppose them. However, its great poverty hampers its efforts. The depressed and desolate state of Torah Jewry defies the imagination. It totally lacks the wherewithal to combat the aims of the Yevsektsiya.

. . . The greatest problem we face is the lack of *mikvaot*. We must act immediately to save this *mitzvah* while a remnant of the previous generation which knows about its importance is still with us. The heart breaks to witness the widespread negligence of the laws of Family Purity, one of the basic precepts of our Holy Torah. There are cities with large Jewish populations without a *mikveh*. The local community is too poor to repair the old one or to construct a new one.

The Yevsektsiya is constantly agitating for the closing of the few *mikvaot* which are still open. Often they claim that the *mikveh* is located in the business area and must be relocated. Other times they charge that the *mikveh*, a religious institution, is located in a public bathhouse. It is forbidden by the law of the.land to include a religious function in a public building. Owing to this approach the few remaining *mikvaot* are being closed down.

The Reform spiritual leader and president of the Zionist Organization of America, Stephen S. Wise, also appealed to Silver. In a letter dated April 1, 1936, Wise requested aid towards the resettlement of Jews in Palestine. He wrote:

But we ought to face this situation with an eye to the future. No matter how much relief we furnish we cannot thereby eradicate the anti-Semitism which is crushing the Jews there, whether in Germany, Poland or elsewhere. We are trying to do what we can to fight for the inalienable rights of Jews wherever they are. But if we are realists we must recognize that as long as civilization is as backward as it is in those lands, Jews will be marked out for oppression and destruction. But aside from the long-range view of the situation, there is the immediate problem of getting out of Germany and Poland a maximum number of those who are condemned to a living death.

You have undoubtedly observed the preeminent part played by Palestine in absorbing such homeless Jews. . . . But what I must emphasize again is that Palestine alone, of all countries, is prepared and able to accept tens of thousands of additional Jews. We must save as many as we can from misery and despair in Germany and Poland. . . . I would be deeply grateful for a Passover message from you that you are contributing to the historic work which we are doing: enabling Jews to get out of the dark lands of intolerance into the bright haven of freedom in Palestine.

A few years later the difficult plight of the refugee *rabanim* in Eretz Israel was described to Silver by Rabbi Samuel Kipnis, the chairman of the Relief Committee for Refugee Rabbis. In a letter dated February 29, 1940, Kipnis wrote:

The financial status of the refugee rabbis is tragic. Most sources of financial help have been cut off by international conditions. *Rabanim* and *geonim* who headed large Jewish communities overseas are now impoverished and lack even the basic necessities of life. In the past, these great men supported others out of their income, and now they are themselves charity wards.

In addition to requests for communal projects, Silver also received numerous appeals from rabbinic scholars to enable the publication of their research and studies. Rabbi Kasher often requested funds for his monumental *Torah Shelemah*. Its numerous volumes were an encyclopedia of Biblical exegesis and explanations in the Talmud and Midrash. All the relevant material, both published and in manuscript, was arranged according to the Scriptural verse to which it applied, together with notes, expositions and supplements. Silver was enthused with Kasher's project and through the years raised substantial sums for its publication.[6]

Rabbi Abraham Dovber Kahane Shapiro, the far-famed spiritual leader of Kovno, also turned to Silver for aid. The first two volumes of his *Devar Avraham*, consisting of responsa and Talmudic novellae and elucidations, widely circulated among rabbinic scholars. There was much demand for their republication, and the "Kovner Rav" also had additional manuscripts ready for print. In a letter to Silver, dated September 13, 1929, he wrote:

> The costs are way above the means at my disposal here. The first volume with my revisions and emendations will take up around one hundred and fifty folio pages. Nevertheless, I feel I must listen to your exhortations to publish my writings. The manuscript itself seems to plead with me: "Do not conceal me; allow me to enter the world of Torah scholarship." These entreaties have convinced me that I have but one course of action. I will print what is ready, come what may.

Silver aided the rabbi of Kovno, and the revised edition of the first volume of the *Devar Avraham* appeared in 1930. However, his other writings were only to be published posthumously by his son in New York following the conclusion of World War II.

Rabbi Selig Reuben Bengis, the head of the *Bet Din*, and later the rabbi of the separatist Orthodox community *ha-Edah ha-Haredit* of Jerusalem, also turned to Silver for help. Bengis was himself a graduate of Volozhin where he studied under Rabbis Naftali Tzvi Yehudah Berlin and Hayyim Soloveitchik.

After serving as the rabbi of Kalvarija, Lithuania, Bengis came on *aliyah* in 1938. He published seven volumes of his *Li-Felagot Re'uven*, consisting mainly of discourses delivered on completing the study of a Talmudic tractate, interwoven with his novellae. In his letter, dated June 2, 1939, requesting help for the printing of his sixth volume, Bengis described the difficult circumstances in which he was attempting to publish:

> I fear that the present trying conditions will delay publication. You are fully aware of the harshness of these times. This has caused all the more poverty in Jerusalem and the Holy Land. . . . I trust that those who valued my earlier books will aid me once again.

Silver did extend support and the book appeared during 1940. Bengis even managed to raise the necessary funds to reprint earlier volumes of his writings during the ensuing war years.

Many authors also turned to Silver for his approbation for their publications. Since the invention of printing and the proliferation of books, approbations became the norm in rabbinic literature. They served both to protect the author's rights to his publication and to assure the readers that the work was in accordance with Jewish tradition. The former reason for approval became particularly needed during Silver's lifetime due to developments in printing technique which enabled the photographing of earlier editions. A publisher investing in reprinting a volume in this fashion had to be confident that others would not likewise republish the work. When a classic volume on the Laws of Family Purity entitled *Taharat Yisrael*, by Rabbi Yisrael Yitzhak Yanovsky, was reprinted in the United States in 1952, Silver wrote in his approbation:

> This volume, which was so highly regarded by the previous generation's rabbinic luminaries, does not need my approval. On behalf of the *Agudat Harabanim*, I only wish to exhort all

interested parties that it is forbidden to reprint this book for the next five years or until all the copies being published are sold. We must protect the rabbi who is now investing in its republication.

Silver was called upon to extol the contents of new works and to introduce the authors to the readers. One such fledgling author aided by Rabbi Silver was Chaim Noble in 1962. The latter, then in his early twenties, was a student in Brooklyn's Mirer Yeshiva Central Institute which had been organized by Rabbi Kalmanowitz. While others discouraged the young Torah student from publishing his Talmudic novellae at such a relatively early age, Silver warmly approved. In the approbation granted to Noble, Silver clearly indicated his familiarity with the new treatise entitled *Devar Chaim*:

> I must truthfully state that your book enlightened my eyes and brought me great joy. I found most of your novellae and elucidations to be profound and in the tradition of excellent rabbinic scholarship. I was amazed that someone as young as yourself was able to display such sound understanding and perception. Your insight is like that possessed by the outstanding rabbinic authorities. I particularly was impressed with your elucidations of the following topics. . . . I have written all this so you should know that I studied the entire volume. It is truly worthy of being circulated among the Torah luminaries who will greatly appreciate its contents.

Despite all the demands made upon him, Silver still continued his own studies and writings. His learning was done mainly in the early hours of the morning and late into the night. It was not uncommon for Silver to retire at two a.m. and to rise at six. His physical appearance was slight, yet he possessed boundless energy and rarely was fatigued. Silver's height was five feet five inches and his build average, his hair dark and beard brunette red until it turned gray. While engaged in his studies, Silver constantly recorded his new interpretations and explanations.

He published articles in rabbinic journals such as *Hapardes* and *Degel ha-Torah*, but he did not have the time to properly edit all his writings for publication.[7] Finally, in the last decade of his life, after the urgings of his family and colleagues, Silver's first volume appeared. Entitled *Anfei Erez*, it was published in 1960. Consisting of his Talmudic novellae, the volume was unique for a rabbinic tome of this type in that it was organized according to the Hebrew alphabet. Only the first two letters were covered in over five-hundred pages. Most of the new interpretations and insights were on four of the six sections of the Talmud: *Zeraim* ("Seeds"), *Mo'ed* ("Festivals"), *Kodashim* ("Holy Things"), and *Tohorot* ("Purities"). A second and third division of the *Anfei Erez* were printed in one volume in 1965. The second part covered the letters *gimmel* through *zayin*, while the third included all the remaining letters of the alphabet.

Following Silver's demise, thirty notebooks were discovered in his desk. They were filled with rabbinic elucidations in his handwriting and that of his father, Rabbi Bunim Tzemah Silver. These were later edited and published in 1975 under the joint authorship of Rabbi Eliezer Silver and his father and entitled *Tzemah Erez*. Silver's emendations to the writings of leading rabbis of the previous generation were also published. The 1946 edition of the *Nefesh Hayyah* of Rabbi Hayyim Eleazar Waks of Kalisz contained an addendum of Silver's comments. Likewise, his additions were incorporated into the *Hosen Yosef* of Rabbi Joseph Engel of Cracow which was published in 1945.

Silver's memory was phenomenal; he instantly recalled almost anything he ever studied or wrote. Once, learning with a young man he later ordained, Avraham Weiner, Silver requested that the student take out a volume from his library. Silver mentioned that some thirty years earlier he had written novellae in the column of a certain page. Sure enough, the new interpretation was there although Weiner was certain that Silver had not looked at the note since he wrote it down.

Silver's sense of humor and youthful vivacity remained with him even after he passed middle age into old age. He could stay up at conventions until the early morning hours. After a few hours of sleep Silver would be the first to an early *minyan*. He would then spend the day in endless rounds of appointments and meetings. Silver also traveled incessantly, rapidly moving from place to place. In one location he settled a dispute, in another he delivered a Talmudic discourse, while elsewhere he raised funds for a charitable cause. A Lakewood Yeshivah student related his experiences while journeying with Rabbi Silver to raise funds for the school. Stranded in Canada due to a heavy snowstorm, they stayed overnight in a motel. Silver studied Talmud with his young companion until two a.m. He then insisted that they go sleigh riding on the fresh snow. By six the next morning, Silver was learning once again. That day they flew to New York where Silver was met at the airport. He went on to his next mission while the yeshivah student collapsed from physical exhaustion for the next few days.[8]

Despite his extensive travels, Silver insisted on only eating food which was prepared by his wife or manufactured under his supervision in Cincinnati. His wife prepared sandwiches and canned goods which were marked for each day of his journey. At the most elegant of hotels and banquet halls, Silver did not hesitate to spread a napkin on the table upon which he placed his private repast. Even in the Holy Land, Silver only ate dairy and fish products wherever he stayed. On the Sabbath he utilized cans of chicken he brought from Cincinnati. The only exception was at the home of Rabbi Soloveitchik of Brisk where the guest ate all that he was served.[9] Silver was also careful not to accept hospitality from those who would soon be litigants before him, awaiting his decision. Silver was concerned lest their graciousness influence his judgment. In 1961 he was called upon to adjudicate a dispute between the rabbis supervising the slaughterhouse in Philadelphia. When Silver arrived, his colleagues insisted that he stay at their homes. Silver, instead, booked into a hotel, so that he could fairly assess the local situation in his inquiry.[10]

Silver was fluent in the English language and developed an understanding of the American milieu. In early 1964, the graduates of the Lomza Yeshivah sponsored an affair in New York honoring Norman B. Abrams, the registrar of the Rabbi Isaac Elchanan Theological Seminary. Abrams had studied at Lomza where his father served on the faculty.[11] The goal of the evening was to raise funds for their alma mater which was now located in Petah Tikvah. Rabbi Emanuel Rackman spoke in English when called upon to greet the gathering. When Silver rose to deliver the evening's main address, he turned to Rackman. Speaking in accented English, Silver twitted him for having neglected the Yiddish tongue. Silver then declared that he too could pour forth in English. To a surprised audience, Silver went on to deliver an intricate Talmudic discourse in that language.[12]

On another occasion, at an Agudah convention, one of the youth leaders was introduced as Fabian, the name he regularly used. An old-timer shouted from the audience that it was disgraceful that an Agudah leader should bear such a non-Jewish name. To this Rabbi Silver quickly rose and retorted, "If one of the authors of *Tosafot* was known as Rabbenu Peter, then our young colleague can be called Fabian."[13]

Silver's witticisms often extricated him from difficult situations. During his 1946 overseas journey, Silver met with Fiorello Henry La Guardia. The latter, a former congressman and mayor of New York City, was then the director general of the UN Relief and Rehabilitation Administration. La Guardia, born to a Jewish mother and Italian father, was raised as a Protestant. Nevertheless, he knew Yiddish well, and was warmly supported by the massive local Jewish community. When Silver called upon La Guardia, he showed him a letter of introduction from Senator Taft. La Guardia remarked that the Cincinnati Senator, whom he considered a reactionary on account of his conservative politics, was like the Nazis. Silver retorted that "Taft is neither a Nazi nor a Mussolini," in an obvious reference to La Guardia's Italian origin. Silver's escorts were shocked at his insult to the man whose aid they needed. Silver quickly retorted in Yiddish, "La Guardia is Jewish since his mother was. To him I can speak as one of us." The tension was broken and their meeting continued in an amiable fashion.[14]

Another time Silver was in a quandary within himself and with his associates regarding a Bonds for Israel dinner in his city. Every year Silver publicly supported this event and attended the dinner. In 1964 the guest of honor was to be Nelson Glueck, the president of the Hebrew Union College. Many Orthodox Jews felt that Silver should not be present at an affair honoring such a prominent Reform Jewish personality. Nevertheless, Silver did attend, since his concern for the cause and feeling of communal responsibilities won out. At the affair, when questioned about his presence, Silver declared, "How could I stay away from a dinner aiding the State of Israel? Regarding the guest of honor, he is, after all, the grandson of the eminent *rav* of Pren, Lithuania."

Silver's response stressed that he was not showing courtesy to the guest as the leader of Reform Judaism, but rather as the grandson of Rabbi Nahum Shraga Finkel-Revel. This retort settled the argument.[15]

Silver was loyal to his followers and congregants. He attended a *bar-mitzvah* in Hartford, Connecticut, of a congregant's grandson. The boy's father questioned why Silver had left Cincinnati to spend the Sabbath in the distant town of Hartford. Silver explained that the youngster's grandmother, a Cincinnati resident, had come to him for a blessing when the child was about to undergo a serious operation. He had told her not to worry and promised to attend the boy's *bar mitzvah*. Years later, Silver kept his word.[16]

Rabbi Hersh Livazer made the acquaintance of Silver at the

initial Agudat Israel conventions. After the former became a United States Army chaplain in 1943, he was constantly encouraged and aided by Silver. When planning for the army a Passover *seder* in consonance with *halakhah*, Livazer sought out Silver. He was immediately given the necessary *matzah*, wine, and money to purchase the other essentials. On another occasion, Silver needed Livazer's help in raising funds for the Beth Jacob School and Poalei Agudat Israel movements. Livazer respectfully explained that he was an Army officer and could not absent himself at will. A few weeks later the base commander paged Livazer to inform him that a general ordered his release. He was to travel to Cincinnati to aid Rabbi Silver. Only after the completion of this mission was Livazer to rejoin his military unit.[17]

Silver guided and aided the yeshivot which increased and gained strength on the American scene during his most active years. He was particularly close to the Rabbi Isaac Elchanan Theological Seminary and its head, Bernard Revel. Silver's own sons and elder son-in-law studied at the Yeshiva. In a June 10, 1930, letter to Revel, Silver expressed his gratitude, stating:

> I am doubly thankful to you for all the beneficial guidance which my sons gained within the walls of your *bet medrash*, the sacred Yeshiva. . . . They are filled with the spirit of Torah and authentic Judaism. I will never forget that all this was possible because of your influence and that of your house of study.

Years later, when inviting Revel to his daughter's wedding, Silver thus described the groom in a June 12, 1938, letter:

> He previously studied in our Yeshiva, the Rabbi Isaac Elchanan Theological Seminary. I rejoice in him because the influence of the Yeshiva still inspires him.

Silver's relationship with the Yeshiva went beyond the personal level. He also constantly served as a member of its Rabbinical Advisory Board which was appointed by the *Agudat Harabanim*. During Revel's lifetime, this organization strove for a close relationship with the school since it was practically the sole advanced yeshivah in the United States. The *Agudat Harabanim* considered itself the "spiritual guardian" of the Yeshiva. Until 1936, rabbinic ordination was granted by a joint ordination board. Serving on this board were representatives of the *Agudat Harabanim* and Yeshiva faculty members who were also members of this rabbinic group.[18]

After the Yeshiva opened its advanced secular department, the Yeshiva College, in 1928, there was some discord between the two groups. The *Agudat Harabanim* was composed primarily of European-trained men who had not received a secular education. They were not attuned to the innovations engendered by a liberal arts college. At times they were fearful lest the traditional yeshivah atmosphere be compromised. They also felt that those directors of the school who were not totally observant could not be depended upon to further the Yeshiva's ideals. To allay these misgivings, Silver and the *Agudat Harabanim* attempted to gain greater control over the Yeshiva following the demise of its principal leaders. Revel died on December 2, 1940, while Rabbi Moses Soloveitchik, the school's senior *rosh yeshivah*, passed away on January 31, 1941.

Rabbi Silver joined his other colleagues on the *Agudat Harabanim* presidium, Rabbis Rosenberg and Levinthal, in sending a telegram to the Yeshiva. In it they claimed the supervision of the school until a successor to Revel was chosen. Addressed to Samuel Levy, the borough president of Manhattan, who was then the chairman of Yeshiva's Board of Directors, and dated December 3, 1940, the telegram stated:

At a special meeting of Administrative Committee of *Agudat Harabanim* at which all officers participated we the presidium and the permanent Yeshiva advisory board of the *Agudat Harabanim* were instructed to supervise and conduct the affairs of the Yeshiva until such time that a worthy successor to the late Doctor Revel is chosen with the approval of the *Agudat Harabanim.*

In his response to Silver and his colleagues, Levy stressed the independence of the Yeshiva. Levy's telegram, dated December 4th, declared:

> May I express my amazement STOP It has always been my opinion that the affairs of the institution were managed by its Board of Directors and not by any outside agency STOP Arrangements for temporary supervision of Talmudic department being made by Board of Directors STOP Our sense of grief and loss and our reverence for Doctor Revel forbid any immediate consideration for successor STOP When a successor will be contemplated we shall be glad to consult with you.

Following Levy's answer, the leaders of the *Agudat Harabanim* once again met. Following their deliberations, a Hebrew letter was sent to Levy restating their feelings. A literal English translation was prepared for those members of the Yeshiva's directorate who were not fluent in rabbinic Hebrew:

> Behold the pain has not ceased yet, and we are still filled with sorrow at the loss of our great colleague, Rabbi Dov Revel, of blessed memory, and for the Yeshiva Rabbi Isaac Elchanan, which lost its head and captain. In a bitter day, at a time of sudden confusion, confusion of mind from the great double misfortune, terrifying news reached our ears affecting the spiritual position and the future of the Yeshiva. We could not at that time control ourselves and we decided to send you a telegram to inform you regarding our decision about our duties and interest in the Yeshiva. It seems that the telegram written in English has not conveyed the meaning of our resolution and assumed a more poignant form.
>
> And behold since we recognize the great value of the Yeshiva, the high, lofty position it occupies for Torah, imparting a spirit of sanctity to the students who shall be fit,

with their studies, with their conduct, to be Rabbis and leaders in Israel, and because we feel the great responsibility which rests upon us, the Rabbinate of this country, to strive with all our might, with the help of God, to continue the existence of the Yeshiva and to augment its light, therefore, now when time has passed and many things from both sides have been more clarified . . . it was decided to choose ten rabbis of the Union of Orthodox Rabbis. Five of them shall join the Directorate of the Yeshiva and five of them, together with five *roshei yeshivah*, shall constitute an advisory board which shall look after the spiritual end of the Institution; it shall not be defective, but be filled with the blessings of God.

Chosen along with Silver to serve as directors were Rabbis Rosenberg, Levinthal, Konvitz, and Joseph Dov Soloveitchik. Selected for the Advisory Board were Rabbis Hayyim Bloch, Judah Seltzer, Jacob Levinson, and Israel Dushowitz and Chaim Ben-Zion Notelevitz of Brooklyn. The Yeshiva, however, did not acquiesce to the demands of the *Agudat Harabanim*. These requests only exacerbated the tensions between them, with the student body becoming particularly resentful of the *Agudat Harabanim*'s involvement. The Yeshiva's students had long harbored misgivings about the *rabanim*'s commitment to the secular study programs inaugurated by Revel. Hyman Chanover, the president of the Yeshiva College Student Council, conveyed these feelings to Levy in a December 20th letter:

> We, however, cannot view but with apprehension the activity of groups outside the walls of the Yeshiva who we wish to believe, are motivated by a sincere interest in Yeshiva and in American Jewry. The ideal of Yeshiva and Yeshiva College, which places its emphasis first and foremost upon Yeshiva, on Torah, and then upon the harmonious blending with the secular training, as envisaged by Dr. Revel, has at times been severely criticized by these very same groups. That ideal must be our guiding force. We must recognize the fact that Yeshiva

and Yeshiva College are one integrated unit and not two independent ones where the interests of one conflict with the purpose of the other.

While the issue of a successor to Revel raged, the Yeshiva scene was further complicated by the sudden death of Rav Moshe Soloveitchik. The latter had served as the school's leading Talmudic instructor since his arrival in America in 1929. During this period he successfully introduced his father's (Rav Hayyim) unique method of Talmudic analysis and exposition into the Yeshiva. The students revered Rav Moshe and his death was greatly lamented. An editorial in the February 7, 1941, issue of *The Commentator*, the undergraduate newspaper of Yeshiva College, stated:

> We were just beginning to regain our senses from the stunning shock following the demise of the late Dr. Bernard Revel, of sainted memory, when another stupefying jolt jarred us upon the news of the death of Rabbi Moses Soloveitchik.
> For Rabbi Soloveitchik — or as all Jewry was wont to call him, Rav Moshe — represented the ideal goal in Jewish learning and sanctity as the Yeshiva strives to implant them in its students. Himself the scion of a long standing aristocracy of brilliant scholarship and superlative spirituality, he was the living incarnation of the long chain of Jewish tradition and of the Jewish spirit.

Soon after Rav Moshe's death, Rabbi Silver and his colleagues on the *Agudat Harabanim*'s executive committee met to discuss the Yeshiva's plight. They unanimously felt that Rav Moshe's son, Rabbi Joseph Dov Soloveitchik of Boston, should be selected as his father's successor. Once again they wrote to Levy to express their viewpoint. Their February 19th letter stated:

> At a meeting of the Executive Committee of the Union of Orthodox Rabbis of the United States and Canada, it was

moved to express to you, as Chairman of the Board of Directors of Yeshiva College, our condolence and deepest sympathy upon the passing of the great *gaon*, the *Rosh Yeshiva* of Yeshivath Rabbi Isaac Elchanan, Rabbi Moses Soloveitchik. . . .

We also wish to take this opportunity of informing you that it was the unanimous opinion of all rabbis present that in accordance with the established Jewish law and tradition Rabbi Dr. J. D. Soloveitchik is to succeed his great father as *Rosh Yeshiva*. Needless to say that Rabbi Dr. Soloveitchik, who is a Talmudical genius and a world-recognized rabbinic authority, is superbly qualified to fill his father's position.

Levy responded that the *Agudat Harabanim*'s suggestion would be presented to the Yeshiva's directorate. Silver and his associates immediately made it clear that their viewpoint was binding. On March 6th, they wrote to Levy:

We wish to call your attention that our letter was misunderstood by you and your board of directors. We did not intend to make any suggestions in the matter of the appointment of Rabbi Joseph Baer Soloveitchik to succeed his great saintly father for you to bring up before the board for discussion. We, as the *Agudat Harabanim*, the only authority on Torah Judaism in this country, merely stated the established law of the *Choshen Mishpat* — that Rabbi Soloveitchik is the lawful heir to his father's position. We felt as we do now that the Yeshiva, whose prime purpose is to educate rabbis to carry the banner of the Torah, cannot possibly overlook the undebatable and unquestionable decision of the law, clearly stated in the *Choshen Mishpat* without a single opinion to the contrary.

However, since our previous letter was misunderstood, we wish to clarify the point of the law again and ask of you that this matter shall not be kept in abeyance and should be disposed of in the course of the next ten days.

We expect a confirmation of the appointment of Rabbi

Joseph Baer Soloveitchik, to succeed the position of his father, within the said period.

While the rabbinic organization was demanding a rapid resolution of this succession problem, the opposition of some students to the *Agudat Harabanim* flared into the open. The cleavage which had developed between the American trained Orthodox students and the European *rabanim* was vividly displayed by an editorial in *The Commentator*. In it Rabbi Soloveitchik was opposed since he was the candidate of the *Agudat Harabanim*. The March 19, 1941, editorial declared:

> The intensity of the pressure that has been exerted to force the appointment of Rabbi Joseph B. Soloveitchik to the position of *Rosh Yeshiva* defies the imagination. . . .
>
> That the driving force in this tragic affair is the leadership of the *Agudat Harabanim* is no surprise. The record of anarchy in *Kashrut*, and the dire danger of a barren future to Torah-true Judaism are eloquent testimony to the hegemony of the *Agudat Harabanim* in American Orthodox life.
>
> Its driving arrogance has rendered impotent every budding and creative force in traditional Judaism, which it has managed to control.
>
> For twenty-five years, Dr. Revel, of sainted memory, fought to the full extent of his limited and precious strength to protect Yeshiva from the suicidal embrace of the leadership of the *Agudat Harabanim*. To prevent Yeshiva from becoming the political tool of this leadership required the constant attention of a sainted leader who could have been spending those efforts in the creative realms of Yeshiva life, which American Jewry vitally needed.
>
> The diabolical recognition of the first opportunity in twenty-five years to penetrate the Yeshiva organism should have been expected of this leadership.

There was, however, widespread support for Rabbi Soloveitchik among the Yeshiva faculty and senior rabbinic students. They, likewise, petitioned Levy for Soloveitchik's appointment. The students' petition read:

In this, the hour of our bereavement, we are comforted by his spirit which remains with us. For Rabbi Moshe left a son like himself, noble scion of the most distinguished contemporary rabbinic family, who follows faithfully in the path of his great forbears. We have had the privilege of listening to his lectures during the lifetime of his sainted father, and we were deeply impressed by his profound scholarship. One of the outstanding scholars of our generation, Chief Rabbi Shapiro of Kovna, has testified to the effect that Rabbi Dr. Joseph B. Soloveitchik possesses the depth and range in Talmudic studies of his immortal grandfather, Reb Chaim. Other equally prominent rabbis have proclaimed him the Talmudic marvel of our day. He is the sole successor to his father, and the true heir to the traditions of Wolozhin.

Therefore, we the undersigned, pupils of Rabbi Moshe Soloveitchik, senior students of Yeshiva, respectfully recommend the name of Rabbi Dr. Joseph B. Soloveitchik to your distinguished body as the successor to his sainted father.

Other letters of support for Rabbi Soloveitchik arrived, including an epistle from Rabbi Joseph Isaac Schneersohn of Lubavitch. The *Rebbe* wrote:

It is my hope that the great, excellent, and renowned *gaon*, Rabbi Joseph Dov Soloveitchik, will be selected to sit on his father's chair as the *rosh yeshivah* of the Rabbi Isaac Elchanan Theological Seminary. It is only fitting and proper that he inherit this position. He will bring abundant blessings to the Yeshiva after the recent loss of its two heads. The eminent *gaon* has the ability to restore the school's former glory and through him solace will be attained.

The move for Soloveitchik's appointment, begun by Silver and the *Agudat Harabanim*, finally bore fruit. Within a few months Rabbi Joseph Dov Soloveitchik was officially selected to inherit his father's position. On May 13, 1941, he delivered his first lecture in his new capacity in the Yeshiva's *bet medrash*. Many of the local *rabanim* and erudite laymen were present for the event. The new *Rosh Yeshivah* brilliantly analyzed the Talmudic discussion of "a buyer acquiring the right to the debt as soon as the bond is delivered to him." Thus began a new epoch in the Yeshiva's history in which Rabbi Soloveitchik was to become the focal sage and mentor.[19]

However, Silver and his colleagues did not succeed in swaying the Yeshiva's directorate in the selection of a new president. It was only in June of 1943 that Rabbi Samuel Belkin, the recipient of a Ph.D. degree from Brown University, was chosen the school's second president. Although Silver remained on good personal terms with Belkin, the *Agudat Harabanim* was gradually excluded from any official role in the Yeshiva. During the Belkin administration, the institution gained university status and expanded into a multi-faceted educational complex of both Jewish and secular studies. This growth was at times not totally approved of by the *rabanim*, and their influence in the school became peripheral as a result of this ever widening gap.[20]

Silver also was intimately involved with the other yeshivot. He supported the opening of the New Haven College of Talmud which later developed into the Ner Israel Rabbinical College. When this school was transferred to Cleveland in 1929, Silver recommended the young Belkin as a lecturer in Talmud for its faculty. Having just arrived in the United States, Belkin had previously studied at the European yeshivot of Radin and Mir. Silver was impressed with Belkin's erudition, and the latter began his American activities as an instructor at this school during the academic year of 1929-30.[21]

Silver was likewise a supporter of Mesivta Torah Vodaath which opened in 1925 in the Williamsburg section of Brooklyn. Under the guidance of its principal, Shraga Feivel Mendlowitz, the Mesivta developed into an advanced yeshiva which rivaled the viewpoint espoused by the Rabbi Isaac Elchanan Theological Seminary. The Mesivta did not introduce advanced secular studies and it took on a hassidic tinge. Mendlowitz was constantly concerned that the hassidic warmth and other distinguishing features of Torah Vodaath remain intact. During his final illness, he told his son-in-law: "Please see to it that the small flame of *Hassidut* is always present within the walls of our yeshivah."[22]

During the Depression years, the Mesivta's faculty often appealed to Silver for aid in raising funds. One such letter, dated March 25, 1931, described the difficulties of the school which did not have the necessary funds to pay its teachers:

> Conditions are at a new low. The elementary and high school teachers of our holy yeshivah are on strike. There is no money to pay their salaries. With our present financial difficulties, we all feel that only public appeals in synagogues throughout the country can save the school. We request that you head this national campaign for our institution.

Silver did assist the Mesivta during its critical years. Toward the end of this decade the position of the Mesivta was strengthened by the influx of refugees who identified with its viewpoint. Silver also intensified his connections with the Mesivta when he activated the Agudat Israel on the American scene. Much of its support came from Torah Vodaath faculty and students. At the Agudah's 1940 convention, Silver placed the Mesivta at the head of the list of yeshivot which the organization should support. He claimed that "Yeshiva and Mesivta Torah Vodaath are entirely ours" while the Rabbi Isaac Elchanan Theological Seminary was placed second.[23]

The Mesivta point of view was given additional credence by the attitude of some European rabbinic leaders. Even when the Nazi threat was near at hand, Rabbi Elhanan Wasserman felt

Rabbi Hayyim Mordecai Katz

Rabbi Elijah Meyer Bloch

Rabbis David Lifshitz and Joseph Dov Soloveitchik, 1977

Rabbi Eliezer Silver delivering a guest lecture at the Sephardic Yeshivat Porat Yoseph of Jerusalem in 1964. Seated to the right of Rabbi Silver is the *rosh ha-yeshivah*, Rabbi Ezra Atiyah

Rabbi Eliezer Silver delivering the first lecture in the new building of Yeshivat Mercaz ha-Rav of Jerusalem in 1964. To the left of Rabbi Silver is the *rosh ha-yeshivah*, Rabbi Nathan Ra'anan-Kook

that a yeshivah student should only save himself through the Mesivta and not the Yeshiva. On June 6, 1941, Wasserman wrote:

> I received your letter. However, I did not act as you requested. The yeshivot in America which can bring in students are those of Dr. Revel in New York and the Hebrew Theological College of Chicago. Both institutions are permeated with spiritual dangers since their fundamental principles are contrary to the Torah. What good will result if you escape from physical danger only to encounter spiritual peril. I therefore sent your letter to the *gaon*, Rabbi Shlomo Heiman, of the Mesivta Torah Vodaath in Brooklyn.[24]

Additional yeshivot conducted in the traditional fashion were also opened by those who reached the American shores. Some, begun as branches of European institutions, later became the sole continuation of these yeshivot. One of the latter was the Telz Yeshivah. Its branch was opened in Cleveland by Rabbis Elijah Meyer Bloch and Hayyim Mordecai Katz in 1941. Under their tutelage, the school retained the singular "Telz method" of Talmudic analysis which stressed precise inductive reasoning. Silver was soon traveling to raise funds for Telz and occasionally lecturing before its senior students. At times he arranged substantial loans for the school which enabled its maintenance during difficult financial periods.[25] After a 1946 visit in the Telz Yeshivah, Silver published the following statement of support:

> My soul rejoices and my heart is elated every time I visit the holy Telz Yeshivah in Cleveland. It is rapidly becoming one of the leading American yeshivot, by virtue of both its large student body and the high level of its curriculum. The illustrious name of Telz has been restored on these shores. From day to day the school grows stronger to the joy of all those who esteem Torah and "fear of the Lord."

> All this has come about because of the dedicated efforts of the true *geonim* Rabbis Elijah Meyer Bloch and Hayyim

Mordecai Katz. . . . They have already succeeded in raising students who are a credit to the traditional Telz standards. They are filled with Torah knowledge, superior religious deportment, and admirable character traits.

Silver also supported the efforts of the Lubavitcher movement to reestablish its network of yeshivot in the United States. On the occasion of a national campaign for these schools in 1943, Silver issued a declaration which stated:

All the world's Torah leaders know of the successful efforts of the Lubavitcher *Rebbe'im* in teaching Torah and the fear of God under the most difficult circumstances. They literally endangered their lives to spread these ideals in Russia and other countries. Only due to their unrelenting self-will did they succeed, thereby earning the gratitude of all rabbinic scholars.

Here too, in the United States and Canada, the Lubavitcher *Rebbe* has once again established schools in both large and small cities. These institutions will bring widespread blessings to the Jewish people. I have met their eldest students and found them to be outstanding in knowledge, ability, and diligence.[26]

Silver also exerted his influence in the determination of Agudat Israel and *Agudat Harabanim* policy towards the formation of the Jewish State. Silver himself had always been in favor of such a state, despite his Agudat Israel ties. Following the Balfour Declaration in 1917, Silver marched in a New York Zionist parade in its support. When Chief Rabbi Abraham Kook visited the United States in 1924, the *Agudat Harabanim* invited him to address its convention. Silver was in the chair when the Chief Rabbi spoke. In the middle of his address, an Agudist *rav* from the Midwest attempted to interfere with the guest. Silver immediately silenced the interrupter, demanding that the proper respect be shown to the distinguished visitor.[27]

The Holocaust mitigated the Agudat Israel's previous

opposition to the revival of Jewish nationhood through human agency. The plight of the refugees and survivors influenced even the most extreme Agudists to back the concept of a Jewish State. Silver sent a telegram supporting the Jewish Commonwealth to Congressman Sol Bloom, the chairman of the Foreign Affairs Committee. Dated March 3, 1944, it read:

> As President of Agudat Israel of America and as member of Presidium of Union Orthodox Rabbis of United States and Canada both organizations devoted to traditional Torah Judaism I wish to go on record with your committee as follows STOP There are specific precepts in our Torah for the reconstruction of Palestine as a Jewish Commonwealth which is the basic faith of all Torah true Jews STOP Therefore I strongly support House resolution including the ultimate establishment of Palestine as a Jewish Commonwealth in accordance with the precepts of our Torah and laws of Talmud.

After his return from Europe and Palestine, Silver was enthused with the love for Eretz Israel he uncovered among the refugees. In an address before the *Agudat Harabanim*'s annual convention on May 13, 1947, Silver said:

> If you wish to experience the holiness of Eretz Israel you will find it spreading among all the European countries. The soul of the Holy Land is already felt by the refugees in Poland, Germany, Austria, Italy and Slovakia. These areas have become a corridor to Israel since all the survivors are sustained by the hopes of reaching it. I saw simple people so inspired by Israel that they resembled ladders set on earth whose top reached the heavens.
>
> I finally reached the Holy Land myself and I saw many of its inhabitants basking in the Divine Presence. There is no end to the gracious spirit of the Eretz Israeli Jews. There are no words which do justice to the sanctity and spiritual joy I observed in Jerusalem.[28]

Silver advised his colleagues to actively work against the

British quota system which limited immigration. They should particularly strive to encourage the *aliyah* of rabbis, yeshivah students, and observant Jews. Only through their entry would the religious element succeed in diminishing the secular influences in the Holy Land.

Silver greeted the Partition Resolution of the General Assembly of the United Nations on November 29, 1947, with mixed emotions. He was saddened by the small portion of the Biblical boundaries of the Land of Israel which the UN awarded the Jewish people. Silver was particularly grieved by the loss of Jerusalem which was designated to be under a special international regime. In a statement issued after the UN action, Silver declared:

> There is no disagreement among Torah observant Jews regarding the boundaries of the Holy Land. The portion assigned to us by the United Nations is only about fifteen percent of our original land. The eastern part was already taken from us in 1921 with the formation of the Emirate of Transjordan.
>
> The area east of the Jordan River is an integral part of the Holyland boundaries as designated by the Torah. Let it be known that we will never revoke our rights to this territory. There is also the additional factor that the entire historic boundaries of Eretz Israel are only one seventieth of the lands under Arab dominion. Let the world take cognizance of this fact and judge accordingly.
>
> Likewise we cannot agree to the resolution which will not include our Holy City Jerusalem within the Jewish boundaries. This partition may be compared to a mother who must sacrifice some children in order to save one. Her joy is then mingled with much sadness and sorrow. Likewise our happiness is today mixed with grief. We will never be comforted until we redeem the entire Land of Israel in accordance with the Almighty's promise.
>
> Despite these manifold reservations, we must still

consider the present realities. The persecuted and dispersed
Jewish people are about to receive sovereignty over a portion
of their land. . . . We must therefore not despair. We should
rather immediately begin constructive tasks and pray that the
Almighty bless our efforts. . . .[29]

Following the actual declaration of the State of Israel, Silver
stressed his joy at this event. Addressing the annual convention
of the *Agudat Harabanim* on January 24, 1949, he stated:

It is a time of joy for the entire Jewish nation. These feelings
must now take the place of the great pain we have felt since
the unparalleled tragedies of the Holocaust which ended only
a few years ago. Nevertheless, we must now all rejoice in pride
as the Jewish people establishes its dominion over the Holy
Land. Even those of us who live afar are constantly concerned
with the happenings of our brethren in Israel. Their joy,
holidays, and worry are ours. We will "rejoice with trembling"
as we have been accustomed to do in the past.[30]

Later that year, Chief Rabbi Herzog once again visited the
United States. Silver arranged for the guest to come to Cincinnati. There he was greeted by several hundred Hebrew School
children assembled in front of the building which housed the
Orthodox Hebrew Board of Education. Silver was instrumental
in helping Herzog raise heretofore unsurpassed sums for the
United Jewish Appeal. In a greeting to the Chief Rabbi
published in *Every Friday* of May 20, 1949, Silver was quoted:

Together with all of our brethren in Cincinnati I welcome you
lovingly and respectfully, as befits a Prince. We are all
anxious for your complete success in your efforts for the good
of Torah, our people and our Holy Land. May we be deserving
of returning to our sacred shrine, that we may be privileged to
embrace its historic and precious stones, and united, may we
build there a strong citadel for the children of Israel. Let us
plant there vineyards and forests — trees of knowledge and

trees of life — and thus become worthy of true redemption and the reestablishment of our Holy Temple.

In 1951, Rabbi Judah Leib Maimon, Israel's first Minister of Religions, visited Cincinnati. Himself a prominent Mizrachi leader, Maimon was accompanied by Rabbi Mordecai Kirshblum who was soon to become president of the American branch of the movement. Arriving at the local airport in the wee hours of a Sunday morning, they hardly expected to be welcomed by an *Agudah* leader. Much to their surprise, Silver was at the airport along with a select group of his followers who joyfully greeted the veteran Zionist leader.[31]

Silver visited the State of Israel several times. In 1954 he attended the *Kenesiyyah ha-Gedolah* convened by the Agudat Israel in Jerusalem. This was the first international Agudah convention held since the Holocaust. Sadness tinged the atmosphere due to the void left by the many rabbinic leaders who perished during the war. The United States delegation discharged a key role in the *Kenesiyyah*. Rabbi Kotler was elected chairman of the American *Moetzet Gedolei ha-Torah*, while Rabbi Silver addressed a focal session.

In his talk Silver stressed the differences between this *Kenesiyyah* and the previous one. He stated:

Seventeen years ago at Marienbad I brought the message of Rav Hayyim Ozer to the *Kenesiyyah*. Then it was a gathering at the time "when the Ark set forward." The meeting was filled with numerous Arks of living Torah scrolls from all over the Jewish world. Sanctity was tangible in every corner.

Today, in this *Kenesiyyah*, we no longer have these *geonim* and saints with us. Instead we have the sanctity of the Holy Land and Jerusalem. In such a consecrated area we must be meticulous in our deportment. . . .[32]

In 1962 Silver briefly visited Israel for the groundbreaking ceremonies for the construction of a new campus for Jerusalem's

Hebron Yeshivah. Its *Rosh Yeshivah*, Rabbi Ezekiel Sarna, earlier called Silver from the Holy City requesting that he attend. Silver planned a short stay since he had to return for an affair in his own community. When Silver arrived at the New York airport, he discerned that he had left his passport at home. It took another day until it was brought to him. When he finally arrived at Lydda airport, he realized that a taxi would not bring him to the ceremonies in time. He then hired a helicopter. It soon landed in front of a startled throng in the Givat Mordecai section of Jerusalem in the midst of the festivities. "Rabbosai" (gentlemen), he announced, "I am here!" Sixteen hours later, Silver was back at the airport for the return flight to the United States.[33]

Silver returned to Israel for the next *Kenesiyyah ha-Gedolah* in 1964. During his stay in Jerusalem, the *Vaad ha-Yeshivot* tendered a public reception in his honor. Among the yeshivot he visited on this trip was Merkaz ha-Rav Kook. It had just moved to its new campus in the Kiryat Moshe section of the Holy City. Silver became the school's first guest lecturer in its new home when he delivered a Talmudic discourse before its student body. Together with Rabbi Moshe Feinstein, the acknowledged leading American respondent, Silver also visited Kefar Habad, founded by Lubavitcher *Hassidim* in 1949 in central Israel. The guests were warmly received by the thriving community. First they delivered guest lectures in the local *Tomkhei Temimim* Yeshivah. Afterwards they were feted at a public banquet attended by the residents and supporters of the village. This event was very moving for Silver for he was greeted by many *Hassidim* whom he had previously met in the D.P. Camps.[34]

Silver's final visit to the Holy Land was in 1966. This time, when met at the airport by Rabbi Abraham Sher, the director of the *Vaad ha-Yeshivot*, Silver declared, "This visit I am not interested in seeing institutions but rather in touring the Land." Silver stayed at the Sher residence in the *Geulah* section of

Jerusalem. Together with his host, he journeyed through the length and breadth of the country. Jerusalem served as their base, and each day they set out in a different direction. They even reached Elath, leaving by taxi early in the morning. That night they once again returned to the Holy City. Throughout their travels, Silver always checked the amount of the gratuities Sher intended to leave for service rendered on their behalf. Silver always insisted that he triple the sum.[35]

A year later Silver's health began to deteriorate. Rabbi Mordecai Gifter, *Rosh Yeshivah* of the Telz Yeshivah in Cleveland, visited with the ailing Silver. The Six-Day War had just ended, and Gifter referred to the Israeli victories as miracles. Silver interrupted his guest and stated:

I do not consider these victories to be miracles. The term miracle can only be utilized to describe a supernatural event. It is totally natural, however, when the Army of Israel triumphs in the Land of Israel over the enemies of Israel. The Natural Law inherent in the Almighty's creation calls for such victories and we need not attribute them to miracles.[36]

Notes

1. Benjamin Zev Jacobson, *Esah De'i LeMerahok* (Bene-Berak: Netzah, 1967), p. 64. Cf. Chaim Karlinsky, "The Fighting Rabbi," *Hatzofe*, February 5, 1971.

2. Related to the author by Rabbi Menahem Kasher in an August 7, 1974 interview.

3. *Vaad* meetings were thus described in an interview with Herman Hollander, a member of the *Vaad Hatzala*, on December 18, 1973. Mr. Hollander was interviewed by Mr. Ephraim Zuroff.

4. Silver's generosity was described in a letter to the author from Herman Landau, a member of the European Executive Committee of the *Vaad* in Switzerland, August 19, 1973; an interview with Mrs. Bessie Gershuni, Rabbi Silver's daughter, on December 27, 1971; and an interview with Rabbi Abraham Sher, October 25, 1970.

5. Interview with Rabbi David Silver, October 4, 1972; and the journal entitled "The Visionary at the Mountain: Rabbi Joseph Kahaneman," published by American Friends of Ponevezh Yeshiva in Israel for its Sixth Annual Dinner, May 17, 1960, p. 76. The businessmen were Sol Satinsky of Philadelphia, the president of Frankford Woolen Mills, and William Jaffe of Dayton, Ohio. The former's parents came from Ponevezh and the latter studied together with Rabbi Kahaneman in the same yeshivot in Lithuania.

6. Interview with Rabbi Menahem Kasher, August 7, 1974. Also see the letter from Kasher to Silver, May 6, 1925; Silver's letters to his colleagues of June 22, 1928 and 1932 (there is no exact date); and Kasher's letter to Silver, February 7, 1939.

Silver's scholarship is quoted in *Torah Shelemah* 1:147, n. 696.

7. For a complete listing of Rabbi Silver's publications see his bibliography *infra*, in the appendix. Still unpublished are many responsa on contemporary *halakhic* problems, and correspondence on rabbinic topics with both colleagues and yeshivah students.

8. Related by Rabbi Yitzhak Sladowsky, February 22, 1975.

9. Related to the author by Rabbi Abraham Sher, the director of the Israeli *Vaad ha-Yeshivot*, October 25, 1970.

10. The author, then the spiritual leader of the Lower Merion Synagogue in Bala Cynwyd, a suburb of Philadelphia, was a witness to this event.

11. See Dov Katz, *Tenuat ha-Mussar* (Tel Aviv: Abraham Zioni, (1958), 2:334. Abrams' father's name was Rabbi Avraham Pacher, his son having changed the surname in the United States.

12. The author, then a member of the faculty of the Rabbi Isaac Elchanan Theological Seminary, was present at this event.

13. The *Tzeirei* Agudat Israel youth leader was Fabian Schonfeld, later to become the president of the Rabbinical Council of America. This story was related to the author by Rabbi David Silver, in an October 4, 1972 interview. Cf. *Hapardes*, January 1961, p. 42 for a similar debate at an *Agudat Harabanim* convention.

Silver's reference to Rabbenu Peter was to a leading disciple of Rabbenu Tam who was known by this name. See Ephraim E. Urbach, *Ba'alei ha-Tosafot* (Jerusalem: Bialik Institute, 1955), pp. 191-193.

14. Related to the author by Rabbi David Silver in an October 4, 1972 interview.

15. *Ibid.* Cf. *Every Friday*, February 21, 1964. For a description of Glueck's family and his relationship to Bernard Revel, see the author's *Bernard Revel: Builder of American Jewish Orthodoxy*, p. 27.

16. Letter from Charles Batt of West Hartford to Rabbi David Silver, August 27, 1976.

17. Hersh Livazer, *Birkhato Shel ha-Rebbe* (Jerusalem, 1976), pp. 12, 19, 23-25.

18. For more complete details of the relationship between the *Agudat Harabanim* and the Yeshiva during Revel's lifetime see the author's *Bernard Revel*, pp. 135-57, and s.v. index. The term "spiritual guardian" was used in a discussion between Rabbi Judah Seltzer, executive secretary of the *Agudat Harabanim*, and Mendel Gottesman of the Yeshiva's directorate. See the letter from Gottesman to Samuel Levy, chairman of the Yeshiva's Board of Directors, February 28, 1941. Cf. *Hapardes*, May 1941, pp. 6-7.

19. The topic of Rabbi Soloveitchik's first lecture is from Baba Bathra, 75b-76a. The event is described in *Hapardes*, June 1941, p. 11.

20. For more details of this period in the Yeshiva's history and its relationship with the *Agudat Harabanim* see Gilbert Klaperman, *The Story of Yeshiva University: The First Jewish University in America* (London: The Macmillan Company, 1969), pp. 171-184.

21. For additional details of Silver's relationship with this school, see *supra*, at the end of chapter four. Belkin's association with it is detailed in *The Inauguration of Samuel Belkin: May 23, 1944* (New York: Rabbi Isaac Elchanan Theological Seminary and Yeshiva College, 1945), p. 7. Rabbi Silver's role in this appointment was related by his son Rabbi David Silver, in a July 14, 1976 interview with the author. Cf. letter from Rabbi J. Levenberg to Rabbi E. Silver, January 6, 1930.

22. Alexander Gross and Joseph Kaminetsky, "Shraga Feivel Mendlowitz," *Men of the Spirit*, ed. Leo Jung (New York: Kymson Publishing Co. 1964), p. 565. For the full details of Mendlowitz's life see Hillel Seidman, *Reb Shraga Feivel Mendlowitz* (New York: Shengold Publishers, 1976).

For the details of the Mesivta's relationship with the Yeshiva and Yeshiva College see the author's *Bernard Revel*, pp. 147-155.

23. *Hapardes*, September 1940, p. 15. Cf. letter Levinthal wrote to Rosenberg, October 27, 1940, complaining of Silver's praise of the Mesivta to the exclusion of the Yeshiva.

24. There is no salutation in the letter so the addressee could not be ascertained. A photographed copy of the letter is in the author's possession. The Hebrew original was printed in a pamphlet entitled *Kovetz Le-Hoshvei Shemo* (Bene-Berak), Ellul 5733, p. 7.

25. Details of Rabbi Eliezer Silver's relationship with the Telz Yeshivah were described by Rabbi Mordecai Gifter, the present Telz *rosh yeshivah*, in a letter to Rabbi David Silver, n.d. Cf. *Hapardes*, December 1942, p. 11; January 1945, p. 14; and September 1951, p. 21. The statement of support is cited from *Hapardes*, May 1946, p. 17.

For a general description of the Torah atmosphere in Telz and other post-World War Two Yeshivot see David Singer, "The Yeshivah World," *Commentary*, October 1976, pp. 70-73.

26. *Hapardes*, December 1943, p. 15. For a letter of support issued by Rabbi Silver for the Ner Israel Yeshivah in Baltimore see *Hapardes*, September 1951, p. 21.

27. These incidents were related to the author by Rabbi David Silver in an October 4, 1972 interview. Also see *Sefer Ha-Yovel Shel Agudat Harabanim*, pp. 62, 103. For a description of the 1917 march see Bernard Drachman, *The Unfailing Light* (New York: The Rabbinical Council of America, 1948), pp. 381-382. For details of Rabbi Kook's 1924 visit see the author's "The 1924 Rabbinical Delegation Visit," *Jewish Life*, November-December 1963, pp. 56-61.

28. *Hapardes*, June 1947, p. 6.

29. *Hapardes*, December 1947, pp. 3-4.

30. *Hapardes*, February 1949, p. 4; quotation is from Psalms 2:11.

31. Interview with Rabbi Mordecai Kirshblum, October 2, 1972. Cf. *Every Friday*, February 2, 1951.

32. *Hapardes*, October 1954, p. 35 and *Das Yiddishe Vort*, Tammuz-Av 1954, p. 12.

33. Interview with Rabbi Abraham Sher, October 25, 1970. Cf. the press clipping, n.d., in the Silver Archives.

34. *Hapardes*, September 1964, p. 40; and interview with Rabbi Sher, *ibid*.

35. Interview with Rabbi Sher, *ibid*.

36. Chaim Karlinsky, "Ha-Gaon Rebbe Eliezer Silver Zal," *Shanah be-Shanah*, ed. Aaron Pechenik (Jerusalem: Hechal Shlomo, 1968), p. 371.

10

Orthodoxy After World War II

☆☆☆☆☆☆☆☆☆☆☆☆☆☆☆☆☆☆☆☆☆☆☆☆☆☆☆☆

Following the conclusion of the War, Silver intensified his local activities in addition to continuing his many world-wide involvements. In 1947 he was the guiding spirit behind the organization of the Chofetz Chaim Day School, the first such institution in Cincinnati. After it opened, Silver published the following letter of support:

> I am happy to congratulate the new trend in our community for an intensified Jewish education. With the help of God we already have the first grade of the new Jewish Day School in operation. Here, the regular school subjects as well as the necessary Jewish curriculum, are being taught by the best teachers of the Beth Jacob Seminary and Public School teachers. Thank God, a very successful beginning has been made in this direction. Next year, with the Almighty's help, we shall inaugurate a second grade group and continue to enlarge until a complete eight grade Jewish Day School is established.[1]

A decade later, after having observed scores of youngsters receiving an intensified Jewish education at the school, Silver declared:

> Chofetz Chaim Day School is the dearest institution to me and closest to my heart. I consider it the most outstanding institution I organized in Cincinnati for the teaching and learning of Torah and genuine Judaism.

Silver was active on behalf of the community's Orthodox Jewish Home for the Aged. He spearheaded a drive for over one and a half million dollars for the construction of new facilities for the senior citizens. In 1963, the new Home was dedicated at Towne Avenue and the corner of Paddock Road. Silver marched at the head of a procession bearing Torah scrolls to the synagogue in the new building.[2] Silver also constructed new *mikveh* facilities in 1965 in the Roselawn area which was now the center of the Jewish population.[3]

Silver continued to uphold Orthodoxy in the community at large. In 1950 the spiritual leader of Chicago's Anshe Emet Synagogue, Solomon Goldman, was invited to address the Silver Jubilee celebration of the Cincinnati Bureau of Jewish Education. On the past *Yom Kippur*, Goldman had delivered a sermon which the Chicago Orthodox rabbinate considered offensive. They then issued a public protest against Goldman. Silver republished their statement and added his own censure of the guest speaker:

> I am reprinting the above protest of the Orthodox Rabbis of Chicago which was also endorsed by the Union of Orthodox Rabbis of the United States and Canada, because I feel the appearance of Solomon Goldman as speaker at the Silver Jubilee of the Cincinnati Bureau of Jewish Education must not remain unchallenged as an act unfriendly to Torah Judaism.
>
> I wish to add that this is not the first time that Dr. Solomon Goldman had digressed from the path of traditional Judaism. I recall that more than twenty years ago Dr. Goldman attempted to force his Orthodox congregation in Cleveland to digress from the *Shulhan Arukh*. He even appeared in court to defend his action. The court decided against him at the time after hearing a group of expert witnesses which I headed.[4]

In 1953 Silver rebuked the local B'nai Brith lodge and the

Community Center for weekly sending the *American Israelite* to their members. In its issue of July 10th, the *Israelite* featured a report of a wedding at a Cincinnati church at which a Reform spiritual leader officiated jointly with the pastor. Silver published the following open letter in the next edition of *Every Friday*:

> I wish to express my strong feeling about a distasteful incident on the part of a rabbi who recently performed the marriage of a Jewish young man who happens to be a *kohen*, to a Christian girl in a local church. This marriage was given front page publicity in a local Anglo-Jewish weekly.
>
> I am not peeved so much at the "Rabbi" who officiated since he belongs to a group that has completely severed relationship with traditional Jewish laws. Such "Rabbis" we may regard as ministers of another religion. Nor can I find fault with the local paper whose policy is apparently to support mixed marriages and other things that are contrary to traditional Judaism. The thing that I am concerned with most deeply, is the unfortunate fact that this paper has brought the "Rabbi" with his shameful action as missionary propaganda into the homes of pious traditionally minded Jews.
>
> I therefore abhor and condemn most vigorously the leadership of the local B'nai B'rith and the leadership of our Jewish Community Center because they send this paper to all their members. In this way they assist in the dissemination of missionary propaganda among the traditional Jewish homes, teaching our sons and daughters that mixed marriages are not contrary to Jewish principles, since a rabbi is performing such marriages and will continue to do so in the future. Continuous propaganda of this type encourages our children to emulate his example and to visit churches for the purpose of bringing into our homes the laws and customs of a strange religion.
>
> That is why I protest vehemently against the leadership of the local B'nai B'rith, an organization of which I am a member and which has many members, perhaps a majority of

them traditionally minded Jews. The same protest I make against our Jewish Community Center, which by means of our financial support, helps spread this kind of missionary propaganda.

This protest was soon picked up by *The National Jewish Post* and re-echoed throughout the American Jewish community. Silver was by now a permanent figure on the Cincinnati scene. His devotees affectionately referred to him as "Quicksilver" in testimony of his constant activity. A reporter visiting his home later wrote:

Quicksilver. That is the word which sticks to my mind when I think of him. What is accomplished in Rabbi Silver's home in one day, is achieved by large Jewish organizations only in weeks, and sometimes in months. And this is no exaggeration. Rabbi Silver has no secretary. His wife gives him some help and when his daughter pays him a visit, she is put immediately to work. Little details may be undertaken by admirers and partisans, but the great outline of the multiple tasks are conceived by himself, with every nerve and organ brought into play. He can keep no specific office hours because 24 hours a day are simply inadequate for the complete performance of all his duties.[5]

Silver's anniversaries were publicly celebrated by the community. In 1956 his seventy-fifth birthday was observed at a public dinner in the Chofetz Chaim Day School building. In 1961 Silver was honored on his eightieth birthday at a testimonial dinner in the Jewish Community Center. Rabbi David Silver, delivering the main address of the evening, emphasized his father's strength of character by alluding to the high hat which he wore on formal occasions:

Of the clothes that Father wears, there is one garment that invariably draws people's attention. It is his high hat — his silk topper — that he wears on Shabbos and Yom Tov and special occasions. Wherein does a high hat differ from the felt hats most of us wear? The felt hats are usually flexible and can be turned into a variety of shapes. The high hat has a definite, unyielding shape that is surely true of Father. He is positive, definite, unyielding in his convictions and in his views. More contents can also be placed within such a high hat than into any other type of hat.

Jewish Orthodoxy has in him its most ardent champion and consistent leader. Yet he is fully broad minded. Within his heart is love for all his people. In his mind is concern for their common welfare and well being. . . . Above all, as a man of conviction, his aim has never been simply to find grace in the eyes of the public. He aims to say and do what he deems to be right — even if it displeases.[6]

While Silver continued to guide his own community, he was also caught up in the maelstrom of Orthodoxy on the American postwar scene. The yeshivah educated and Agudat Israel Orthodoxy which Silver helped establish in the States was gradually asserting itself. Unlike previous newcomers who chose the New World, these immigrants arrived solely to seek refuge from the horrors of Hitler. Many were resolute in their determination to retain their previous Torah *Weltanschauung*. One such new arrival later declared:

Frankly speaking, I did not come without apprehensions. My uncle had frequently before sent papers to my father for our family, but we would never have thought of going to the *trefa* land, where, we heard, it was almost impossible to live as a good Jew. . . . Here, perhaps, I think, lies the great mistake of many of the earlier immigrant groups who thought that they had to discard their religion and customs when they entered the harbor of New York. People like I, from a good hassidic background, who came to the United States because Europe after the war had turned into a living hell, were determined to do what they could not to yield an iota of their faith. I had succeeded even during the harrowing years of the camps in never letting a day go by without putting on *tefillin*. They were the only thing I did not permit to be taken away from me. And I had never cut my beard or *peyes*. I had no intention of acting differently in the United States.[7]

Rabbi Aaron Kotler was soon recognized as the leading spokesman for this element. When his initial work with the *Vaad Hatzala* was concluded, Rav Aharon reopened the Kletsk Yeshivah in 1943, choosing the quiescent location of Lakewood, New Jersey. The school began with fifteen students. A charismatic leader, Rabbi Kotler soon attracted scores of American youngsters. To them he was known simply as "the Rosh Yeshivah" par excellence. Totally committed to the Lithuanian tradition of Talmudic study exclusively, the "Rosh Yeshivah" refused to allow his disciples to pursue collegiate studies. His influence rapidly spread beyond Lakewood, and students in many American yeshivot considered Rav Aharon their mentor. Both his erudition and ethical perfection were widely admired. It was known that on the highway to Lakewood, he would direct the driver away from the automatic toll booth to a manned one, stating, "It is not respectful of humanity to pass up a man for a machine — as though the man is unnecessary."[8]

Rav Aharon was not only active in his own yeshivah, but also asserted his leadership in other organizations such as the *Agudat Harabanim* and Agudat Israel. Many now turned to Rabbi Kotler and the other yeshivah heads as the ultimate Torah authorities. The *roshei yeshivah* began to supplant the elder *rabanim* as the prestigious leaders of American Orthodoxy.

This transition was not without its whimsical results as well. A few novice students soon considered themselves even more pious than their own teachers. A student visiting with Rav Aharon asked his wife at which bakery the cake she served had been purchased. On another occasion the "Rosh Yeshivah" was rebuked by a student in Lakewood for turning around after the *kedushah* and not waiting for the cantor to complete the blessing.[9] Even Rabbi Joel Teitelbaum of Satmar, who successfully reestablished his court in the Williamsburg section of Brooklyn, was not spared from such indignities. A mirror in his home was broken by his *Hassidim* who felt it improper for his wife to use such a profane contrivance.

Rabbi Silver soon discovered that there were basic differences between his outlook and that of the *roshei yeshivah* and their followers. The original standpoint of the *Agudat Harabanim* consented to the utilization of the English language as the secondary tongue in the education of children. Silver upheld this position, and never insisted that instruction be solely in Yiddish. Rav Aharon, on the other hand, constantly stressed the primacy of Yiddish. Addressing a convention of Torah Umesorah-National Society of Hebrew Day Schools in 1947, Rabbi Kotler declared:

> It is essential that the language of instruction be Yiddish. This is the tongue that has been sanctified by our fathers and forefathers during the past generations. This has enabled the survival of Torah and Judaism during the recent past. Mass assimilation among the gentiles will result if we utilize the language of the land. Our Jewish children will then emulate non-Jewish practices.[10]

Silver also decided to exclude himself from endorsing the issuance of a ban which reflected a major standpoint articulated by the *roshei yeshivah*. Many Orthodox rabbis, particularly those belonging to the Rabbinical Council of America, likewise joined local rabbinical boards which included Reform and Conservative spiritual leaders. Trained in the United States, these rabbis felt at ease with their non-Orthodox colleagues. They considered themselves perfectly free to cooperate with them on non-*halakhic* matters which affected the general welfare of the Jewish community. The recently arrived *roshei yeshivah*, however, espoused a policy of separation. They held that participation in mixed boards of rabbis implied recognition and legitimization of the Reform and Conservative movements. They similarly opposed synagogues belonging to the Synagogue Council of America, a group which acted as the overall Jewish religious representative body in relations with Catholic and Protestant national religious agencies, the United States government, and the United Nations.

The position of the *roshei yeshivah* was further fortified by those yeshivot whose graduates were competing with Yeshiva University alumni for Orthodox rabbinical positions. Most of these other schools followed the teachings of the *roshei yeshivah* and were anxious to illustrate that their rabbis were faithfully Orthodox. This was in contrast to those of Yeshiva University who generally joined mixed groups. The leader of the separatist yeshivot was Mesivta Torah Vodaath whose student body was second in size only to that of Yeshiva University. On February 1, 1956, eleven leading *roshei yeshivah* issued a public ruling which prohibited the membership of rabbis and synagogues in mixed groups. The yeshivah heads declared:

We have been asked by a number of rabbis in the country and by alumni and rabbinical graduates of the yeshivot, if it is permissible to participate with and be a member of the New York Board of Rabbis and similar groups in other communities, which are composed of Reform and Conservative "rabbis."

Having gathered together to clarify this matter, it has been ruled by the undersigned that it is forbidden by the law of our sacred Torah to be a member of and to participate in such an organization.

We have also been asked if it is permissible to participate with and to be a member of the Synagogue Council of America, which is also composed of Reform and Conservative organizations.

We have ruled that it is forbidden by the law of of our

sacred Torah to participate with them either as an individual or as an organized communal body.

May the Almighty have mercy on His people, and close the breaches [in Torah life] and may we be worthy of the elevation of the glory of our sacred Torah and our people Israel.[11]

Among the signatories of the ruling were Rabbis Feinstein, Kalmanowitz, Kotler, and Ruderman. Representing Mesivta Torah Vodaath were its *roshei yeshivah*, Rabbis Yaakov Kamenetzky and Gedalya Schorr. Two prominent European-trained Yeshiva University faculty members, Rabbis David Lifshitz and Mendel Zaks, likewise signed the prohibition. On the other hand, the school's senior *rosh yeshivah*, Rabbi Soloveitchik, did not set his hand to the pronouncement. Although not a *rosh yeshivah*, Rabbi Silver was also asked to sign the ruling. In principle he agreed with this viewpoint but refused to sign the prohibition. He felt that it was partially motivated by anti-Yeshiva University sentiments. Silver feared that an inflexible stand would only exacerbate these tensions and not really solve the problem of mixed groups.

Silver earlier sensed the eclipse and decline of the *Agudat Harabanim* as an organization of practicing rabbis. The lay leadership of Orthodox synagogues was now in the hands of second and third generation Americans. They generally turned to graduates of Yeshiva University and Chicago's Hebrew Theological College for their spiritual leadership. Invariably they preferred members of the Rabbinical Council of America over those of the *Agudat Harabanim*. The new element that strengthened American Orthodoxy after World War II turned to the *roshei yeshivah* rather than to the *rabanim*. At the 1952 Convention of the *Agudat Harabanim*, Silver attempted to resign the presidency and urged that steps be taken to revitalize the organization through its younger members. Silver stated:

This week we read the Torah portion of *Va-Yishlah* ("And he sent forth"); between the portions of *Va-Yetzeh* ("And he went out") and *Va-Yeshev* ("And he dwelt"). I have been sent forth by you these past thirty-five years as your treasurer, president and presidium member. In your name I traveled to Europe to save that which could be salvaged after the Holocaust. I aided in planting and tending the vineyard of Judaism here. Now the time has come for me to read the chapter of *Va-Yetzeh*. I must go forth to rest and prepare my manuscripts for publication. . .

Now that I am about to leave, I wish to stress that all we accomplished was not just for ourselves. It was also to enable the next generation to continue our work. Thank God, we are now privileged to have many fine young rabbis throughout the country.

I feel that our organization will only survive if we undertake the following proposals:

We should build bridges of cooperation with our young sons in the rabbinate in order to include them in our holy work. . . .

We must open a special office which will be devoted to seeking rabbinical positions for our members. Rabbinical visits should be arranged throughout the land in order to improve Torah standards.[12]

Rosenberg also joined Silver in declining to stand for reelection. Nevertheless, the *Agudat Harabanim* membership insisted on once again selecting them for the presidium. Elected in place of the late Rabbi Levinthal was Rabbi Moses Rosen, an erudite Brooklyn *rav* and author of many rabbinic volumes.

The first real basic change in the *Agudat Harabanim* leadership finally did come about in 1956. Before the election session, intense efforts were made to call the membership to arms by the various factions. Consequently many yeshivah faculty members came out for the crucial session. The slate proposed by the nominating committee was rejected by the assembled *rabanim*. After an all night session which resulted in a secret ballot, a new presidium was chosen. Only Silver retained his position. This time he was selected as its chairman in place of Rosenberg who had passed away earlier that year. Elected as the other members of the presidium were Rabbis Pinchas Teitz and David Lifshitz. The former, a younger *rav*, had successfully developed a model Orthodox community in Elizabeth, New Jersey. On the other hand, Lifshitz was no longer the head of a congregation in the United States. In Europe, he had served as the *rav* of Suwalki and now was a *rosh yeshivah* at Yeshiva University. Another non-practicing rabbi, Simcha Elberg, was chosen chairman of the administrative committee. Elberg, remaining in this position for the ensuing decades, became a prime mover on the new *Agudat Harabanim* scene. Four years later, the presidium was enlarged to five with the addition of the two most prestigious leaders of the yeshivah world, Rabbis Kotler and Feinstein. The *roshei yeshivah* now constituted a majority of the organization's leadership. Following Rav Aharon's death in 1962, his position was filled by Rabbi Kamenetzky of Torah Vodaath.[13]

The new leadership intensified the opposition to the Rabbinical Council of America since many of its members continued to belong to mixed boards. Silver, however, persisted in urging cooperation between the two main rabbinic groups. He stated at the 1958 *Agudat Harabanim* convention:

> We have come to appreciate the achievements of the young rabbis who are not our members. After all, they are our children and grandchildren. In the past we have never spurned them and always worked together in mutual respect. There was never enmity or rancor between us. . . . Such have been our deeds in the past. I trust we will continue to unite with all the scholars in our generation. Together we will construct the parapet around the Torah. We will stand guard in unison with all our brethren to whom Torah is dear.[14]

Instead, the 1960 convention of the *Agudat Harabanim*

adopted a resolution strongly forbidding membership in mixed organizations. The resolution declared:

> 1) The Convention of the *Agudat Harabanim* declares as an authoritative Torah doctrine that it is strictly forbidden to belong to the [New York] Board of Rabbis or to the Synagogue Council [of America].
>
> 2) Any *rav* belonging to these groups will forfeit his *Agudat Harabanim* membership unless he resigns from the forbidden organization within thirty days.
>
> 3) The convention demands that the Union of Orthodox Jewish Congregations leave the Synagogue Council. All Orthodox rabbis must also resign from the Board of Rabbis.[15]

Opposition to the Reform and Conservative rabbinate was also intensified by the latter's amending the traditional *ketubah* text. In 1954, the Conference on Jewish Law, a joint body created by the Jewish Theological Seminary and the Rabbinical Assembly, promulgated a change by the addition of a paragraph to the traditional marriage contract. It authorized the religious court of the Seminary and the Assembly to impose financial obligations on either spouse under given conditions. The purpose of the change was to provide a practical device for ensuring that husbands civilly divorced also grant a *get*, or religious divorce, so that the woman could re-marry under Jewish law. There was widespread opposition to this change by the Orthodox rabbinate. It was held that tampering with the *ketubah* text was improper. They also considered the Conservative rabbinate unqualified to deal with such intricate *halakhic* questions. The *Agudat Harabanim* emphatically negated this innovation. As the new *ketubah* gained acceptance in marriages performed by Conservative rabbis, the *Agudat Harabanim* intensified its opposition. In 1957 they sponsored a public assembly against the Conservative *ketubah*. In accordance with the new trend, the main addresses were delivered by *roshei yeshivah* although the

practicing rabbis were equally opposed. The paramount speech
was that of Rabbi Kotler:

> To our sorrow there is widespread misunderstanding about
> Judaism. Many think that just as there are differences
> between Ashkenazic and Sephardic Jews there are likewise
> divergencies between Conservative and Reform. In truth there
> is no such comparison. There is no difference between Reform
> and Conservative since both deny the Divine Revelation of
> Torah. They, therefore, both annul Torah precepts and the
> basis of our religion. Their spiritual leaders constantly lead
> our people astray. One is not permitted to aid them nor to
> justify their actions in any way.[16]

Rabbi Judah Leib Maimon, with whom Silver had
established a warm relationship, also was censured severely by
the American *roshei yeshivah*. Israel's first Minister of Religions
had come into conflict with Rabbi Yitzhak Zev Soloveitchik of
Brisk. Their controversy centered around the construction of the
Heikhal Shlomo building in Jerusalem as the center of the Chief
Rabbinate. Soloveitchik feared lest this religious center engender
a formal rabbinic body which would modify Jewish law.
Maimon criticized this position in an article in the popular
afternoon newspaper, *Maariv*. There was widespread chagrin in
Israeli yeshivah circles that Maimon dared to publicly challenge
the revered *rav* of Brisk. The American *roshei yeshiva* sponsored
a public assembly on June 1, 1958, in support of Soloveitchik.
Once again, the main address was delivered by Rav Aharon.
Despite these developments and his close relationship with the
Brisker *Rav*, Silver remained on good terms with Maimon.
During his brief 1962 stopover for the Hebron Yeshivah
festivities, Silver also managed a quick visit to Maimon's
bedside in a Jerusalem hospital where he suffered his final
illness.[17]

Celebrations of Silver's eightieth birthday also accentuated
the new trends in American Orthodoxy. On January 27, 1960, the

Rabbi Eliezer Silver with his grandchildren. In the background is Mrs. Fannie Eisenberg, the mother of Mrs. David Silver

Rabbi Eliezer Silver participating at wedding in 1960. *Left to right:* Rabbis Moshe Feinstein; Eliezer Silver; Samuel Belkin

Rabbi Eliezer Silver dancing at a wedding in 1960

Rabbi Eliezer Silver speaking at an Agudat Israel of America dinner. Seated beside Rabbi Silver (*right to left*) are Rabbis Aaron Kotler, Yaakov Kamenetsky, and Jacob Ruderman

Rabbinical Council of America's luncheon celebrating Rabbi Eliezer Silver's eightieth birthday (1961). *Front row, left to right:* Rabbis Abraham AvRutick; Theodore Adams; Joseph D. Soloveitchik; Eliezer Silver; Pesach Levovitz. *Back row, left to right:* Sidney Applbaum; Yehuda Gershuni; David Silver; Emanuel Rackman; Charles Weinberg; Louis Bernstein

Agudat Harabanim had honored Silver on his entering his eightieth year at a banquet in Rockaway's Park Inn Hotel. Among those who greeted the guest of honor were Rabbis Kotler, Feinstein, and Kamenetzky. The Rabbinical Council of America celebrated Silver's eightieth birthday at a festive luncheon on February 18, 1961. Besides the active pulpit rabbis in attendance, Rabbi Joseph Dov Soloveitchik also participated. In response to the testimonials of the American trained rabbis, Silver wittily referred to the new direction of the *Agudat Harabanim*. Before an amused audience he stated:

> In Europe there were always a few zealots in each community. But in the *Agudat Harabanim* there is now a new situation — an organization comprised almost entirely of zealots.
>
> Zealotry has its place in life, but it is not appropriate at all times. Had Pinhas constantly acted in this fashion, he would never have been blessed with God's convenant of peace.[18]

The enhanced status of the *roshei yeshivah* resulted in a lessening of the respect accorded to the rabbinate by some yeshivah students. They turned to their teachers for guidance in *halakhic* questions and not to the *rabanim*. Elberg, in a signed editorial in *Hapardes*, decried this new situation. He stressed that among the *rabanim* there were first-rate scholars such as Rabbi Silver:

> Recent years have seen a marked increase in the number of advanced yeshivah students. However, their attitude to *rabanim* is entirely negative. They are not at all respectful to the *rabanim*. When even the most erudite *rav* delivers a lecture on the Sabbath before Passover or *Yom Kippur*, the yeshivah students do not attend. At times their attitude is one of mockery and sarcasm even towards veteran *rabanim* who are one thousand times more learned than they.
>
> This situation is sad. We are obligated to do all in our

power to return the rabbinate to its previous prestige. The only method to accomplish this is through the study of Torah. *Rabanim* must indicate that ceaseless Torah study is the basis of our life and existence. There are still glittering examples of such dedication in our generation. The late *gaon*, Rabbi Moses Rosen, studied all his life, including the more than forty years spent in the United States. Even now there is the *gaon*, Rabbi Eliezer Silver, among us. For many decades study has not ceased from his lips.[19]

This attitude of many yeshivah students was exemplified at the funeral of Rabbi Kotler who passed away on November 29, 1962. The death of the *Rosh Yeshivah* evoked widespread grief in the Torah world. Before his body was flown to Israel for burial, a funeral service was held in New York. The Kalwarier Synagogue on the Lower East Side was selected for the rite because of its open square in front. The event became a demonstration of the strength of rejuvenated American Orthodoxy with a crowd of mourners at the funeral estimated at twenty-five thousand by the New York police. In Israel, over twenty thousand persons later accompanied the bier to the Har ha-Menuhot cemetery on the outskirts of Jerusalem.

The *Agudat Harabanim* was not consulted in the planning of the funeral. The details were rather worked out by those *roshei yeshivah* who came to Lakewood and the students. *Roshei yeshivah*, Agudat Israel leaders, and the Satmar Rebbe delivered the eulogies in the Kalwarier Synagogue. Rabbi Silver was the sole speaker at Idlewild Airport. Standing on a police car in order to be heard, Silver recalled the tense days of joint efforts with Rav Aharon in the *Vaad Hatzala*:

During the Holocaust, we accomplished much through the *Vaad Hatzala*. I wish to testify that the maximum was attained when we followed the viewpoint of the *gaon*, Rabbi

Aaron Kotler. He was the dynamic spirit behind all our endeavors.[20]

At the funeral the students of the deceased took charge of the order of the service. They neglected to request that Rabbi Elijah Henkin speak although the latter had been a devoted disciple of Kotler's father-in-law, Rabbi Isser Zalman Meltzer. While Henkin was not a *rosh yeshivah*, a prominent yeshivah head, Rabbi Joseph Dov Soloveitchik was also overlooked. Although he identified with the Mizrachi movement since the conclusion of World War II, Soloveitchik constantly aided Kotler in raising funds for the Agudah's independent Israeli school system. During Rav Aharon's final illness, Soloveitchik was also instrumental in helping the Lakewood Yeshivah meet its budget. Nevertheless, the students chose to pass over him to display their antipathy for Yeshiva University Orthodoxy. When the seating capacity of the Kalwarier Synagogue was partially full, it was reported that students instructed its lay leaders not to allow any more rabbis in. They were rather to only permit "*benei Torah*" or proper yeshivah students to enter. Once again, the *Hapardes* rabbinical journal protested these happenings. An article headlined "Desecration of the Honor of the Rabbinate" stated:

> Why didn't the yeshivah students consult with the *Agudat Harabanim* concerning the funeral arrangements and the eulogizers? If the rabbinic organization had been involved in these matters, then a *gaon* and saint like Rav Henkin would not have been passed over. Likewise, another great rabbinic personality and *gaon* [Rabbi Soloveitchik] would not have been snubbed. If they had only consulted with the *Agudat Harabanim*, then the doors of the Synagogue would not have been closed to many important *rabanim*. What kind of yeshivah student could issue such a disgraceful order to only permit the entry of *benei Torah* and not *rabanim*? Is the honor due to the *rav* less than that which the yeshivah student deserves? Hundreds of *rabanim*, among them *geonim* and

giants of Torah, had to stand outside for hours. They were not allowed inside the Synagogue although there was room for another few hundred.

If Rav Aharon had been alive, he would have been upset and agitated by this desecration of the rabbinate.

The arrangements for the funeral of this great man should not have been left in the hands of a few yeshivah young men. It should rather have been left to the leading *rabanim* with whom Rav Aharon jointly worked for the strengthening of Torah and Judaism.[21]

This new trend in American Orthodoxy also resulted in some vigorous opposition to Zionism and the State of Israel. This viewpoint was strongly espoused by Rabbi Teitelbaum of Satmar. He considered the establishment of the State of Israel a violation of the oaths by which, as the Talmud teaches, the Jewish people are bound. These included neither retaking the Holy Land by force nor rebelling against the nations of the world.[22] According to Teitelbaum, the establishment of the State delayed the coming of the Messiah and the complete redemption. In 1953 he became the official spiritual leader of Jerusalem's *Neturei Karta* (Aramaic for "Guardians of the City") community, although continuing to reside in the United States. The *Neturei Karta* were also extreme anti-Zionists, having split with the Agudat Israel in 1935. The Satmar position was also adopted by some American yeshivah pupils who began making their position public before the entire American community. Their protests intensified when specific issues, such as the drafting of women into the Israeli Army, were debated in the Holy Land. Massive demonstrations were held in front of the Israeli Consul in New York. Announcements criticizing the Israeli government were posted on New York streets, and advertisements were even placed in the *New York Times*.

Silver penned an open letter to respond to these activities. He decried these appeals befoi the gentile world, declaring that such actions were not in consonance with the Torah. The letter, dated April 29, 1958, was sent to American Orthodox rabbis. In it Silver stated:

I am writing this letter as one who has been among the Orthodox rabbinic leaders in the New World for over fifty-one years. Before that I studied with the greatest European *geonim* for about ten years. Among those I served were the *geonim* of Brisk, Dvinsk, and Vilna. I was able to observe both their private and public deportment. As a responsible rabbinic leader, I today address this letter to my colleagues in knowledge, Torah, and meritorious deeds. I have always been ready to join with you in defending the Torah and Jewish life against its detractors. Whether those who leave its path are here or in Israel, I will oppose them. Nevertheless, my disagreement will be in the spirit of the Torah "whose ways are ways of pleasantness." I will conduct myself in the tradition of ancient Israel, neither lying nor speaking falsely. I will always be with you to strengthen Torah and religious life in a spirit of love for those who observe and study it.

Nevertheless, I must declare the unpleasant truth to you. The recent actions by some of the scholars and guardians of our religion have overstepped the traditional path of scholarship and fear of God. The "evil spirit" has compromised their true sanctity. Their recent actions have been totally incorrect. They have appealed to the gentile world in its language and newspapers. They have spoken evil against our sons and daughters, our people and land. It is as if they have taken the case before non-Jewish courts. They have slandered our daughters before our enemies, some of whom are still covered with the blood of Jewish children. Many of these non-Jews were part of the conspiracy to idly stand by while our European brethren were slain. The mouths of these gentiles were then filled with deceit and falsehood was their password. Before such individuals have righteous Jews now appealed by disgracing our modest daughters. They have also vilified our young men whom our sages declare are filled with

good deeds as a pomegranate with seeds [Erubin, 19a]. It
pains me that so called pious Jews stooped so low as to
demean Jewish daughters before such individuals. It is a
shame that I did not observe such total dedication on the part
of these Jews when I stood at the head of the *Vaad Hatzala*. I
wonder why they now display such consecrated efforts to
disgrace the honor of Israel before the gentile world. I am very
ashamed. Let me state the bitter truth. The sanctity of Torah
in the Holy Land could have been safeguarded in dignity and
honor. However, Satan and the "evil spirits" have attached
themselves to many of us and abated all constructive efforts. I
exhort my brethren to beware of Satan's power. Desist from
your present course of action. This was not the path charted
by my revered teachers, the *geonim* of the previous
generation. Forgive me, my brothers. However, only truth is
on my lips. I will continue to discharge my duties, and I bless
you in love and friendship.[23]

Silver's letter did not abate the course of action of the
Satmar element. It did, however, strengthen the more moderate
forces in American Orthodoxy. His viewpoint was widely cited
in Mizrachi circles. Silver later participated in a Mizrachi conference. Afterwards, at an Agudah conclave, there were those
who desired to disbar Silver. It was reported that Rabbi Kotler
opposed this request, stating:

People will say that we have pierced our Master — but which
Rabbi Silver do you wish to dispose? Is it the erudite Silver
who is renowned for his Torah knowledge? Or is it the Rabbi
Silver who is an undisciplined party member? Or is it the
Rabbi Silver who is a master politician? After all, there are
many different Silvers![24]

Silver did continue his activities for the Agudah,
particularly raising funds for its independent school system. He
likewise continued to support its labor movement, Poalei Agudat
Israel. In 1960 it contravened a decision of the *Mo'etzet Gedolei*

ha-Torah by joining the Israeli government. As a result many *roshei yeshivah* boycotted the organization. Silver nevertheless participated in Poalei Agudah's 1964 American convention celebrating its fortieth anniversary.[25] He also remained involved with the total complex of local communal activities. One such involvement embroiled Silver in national controversy. In 1961, The Cincinnati Jewish Community Center decided to open its facilities on Saturday afternoon. Rabbi Silver was consulted by the Center's leadership to help plan a program of activity which would be in consonance with the Sabbath. Under his guidance, the Center adopted fourteen regulations for their Saturday afternoon events. These included:

1. No program shall be scheduled Friday evening or Saturday prior to 1:30 p.m.
2. No parking of automobiles or bicycles.
3. No smoking, card playing or cooking.
4. No sale of any kind, whether by cash or tickets, including vending machines.
5. No music, including radio and television.
6. Lights may be turned on and off but by non-Jewish personnel only.
7. Loudspeakers may be operated but by non-Jewish personnel only.
8. Steam room may be operated but by non-Jewish personnel only.
9. If showers are used, hot water tanks must be pre-heated and temperatures kept at no higher than 75 degrees.
10. No writing or cutting, no arts and crafts, power tools or work tools or electric-power exercise machines.
11. Public telephones will be blocked.
12. Swimming is permitted but bathing suits may not be carried to or from the Center, or wrung out on the Sabbath. The Center will supply polyethelene bags in which wet suits can be deposited to be picked up after the Sabbath.

13. The Health club shall be bound by all the rules applicable to all other areas of the Center.
14. No staff member who conscientiously objects to working as a matter of religious principle shall be required to do so.

In a supplementary statement to these regulations, Silver stressed that there could be no carrying of articles from one part of the Center to the other. The Center called attention to the fact that it did not have an indoor swimming pool. Its outdoor pool, used only in the summer, was heated by the atmosphere. The innovations in Cincinnati were soon detailed in national Jewish publications. An interview with Silver regarding Sabbath programming appeared in the Jewish Welfare Board *Circle*.[26] Silver explained that he agreed to the Center's opening under these conditions so that children could spend Saturday afternoons in a Jewish environment:

> You see, for a long time I have been thinking that too many Jewish children spend Saturday afternoon in desecrating the Sabbath. They go to all kinds of commercial recreational places, movies, and other places which are bad for their morals and certainly violate Jewish tradition. It was therefore my thought, that if the Center could be open in accordance with Jewish tradition, our Jewish children could spend Saturday in a Jewish environment and, I had hoped, even get a taste of what the Sabbath really means. Of course, I was hoping that the leaders of the Jewish Community Center in Cincinnati would agree to create such an atmosphere in accordance with Jewish law and Jewish tradition.

Silver was also asked whether community centers in other cities should be opened on Saturday afternoons. In response, he stressed that only for Cincinnati could he accept this responsibility:

> I was glad to advise the Jewish Community Center of

Cincinnati on this matter. I would not presume to give advice to Jewish Community Centers in other cities. For one thing, I know the leaders of the Jewish Community Center in Cincinnati and I have confidence in their sincerity. I know they operate a kosher kitchen with adequate supervision. Besides, I live in Cincinnati and can "keep an eye" on what is happening here.

The Jewish Community Center leaders in other cities can consult with the rabbis in their communities and arrive at their own decisions. You may be aware that I am well known in the Orthodox Jewish community of America and that many rabbis in this country were my students and, in general, have confidence that my recommendations were based on a very sound knowledge and interpretation of the *halakhah*.

I would like to take this opportunity to emphasize at this time that in my opinion it is more important for the Center to be open on the Sabbath than on other days of the week. You see, on the weekdays Jewish people, adults as well as children, are busy and have many places to go for their leisure-time activities which are not harmful to them. However, on the afternoon of the Sabbath, the Jewish Community Center of Cincinnati will be the only place where I know with confidence they will be able to go and have a very positive experience in the spirit of Jewish tradition in a beautiful new Center building. I firmly believe that if this program is carried out properly it will help all of Jewish life in our community.

Controversy soon broke out as other communities desired to emulate the Cincinnati program. Their rabbis did not approve since they feared such functions would result in Sabbath desecration. When a Detroit Center opened its Health club facilities on the Sabbath, its Orthodox members vehemently contested the move. They declared themselves:

. . . amazed at the complete disregard and lack of respect in opening the Detroit Center's Health club facilities on Saturdays. We now publicly declare that we will continue unremittingly with our efforts to persuade the Center to revoke its recently adopted policy of Sabbath opening. . . . We will not desist from our determined effort to restore proper Sabbath observance in a Jewish communal institution.[27]

Silver was criticized for having publicized his local stand. While he could control the activities in his communal Center, other rabbis were not in such a strong position. Many *roshei yeshivah* and leaders of the *Agudat Harabanim* agreed with this viewpoint. Silver finally joined with his colleagues in issuing a ruling which prohibited the opening of Centers in other communities. In a June 23, 1961, letter sent to his rabbinic colleagues, Silver stated:

It is not correct that I have issued a general ruling which permits the opening of Centers on the Sabbath. My colleagues, the elder *rabanim*, inform me that this impression has resulted in religious transgressions. I therefore join with the other leading rabbis in prohibiting the opening of Centers on the Sabbath and Festivals. Every rabbi and teacher is obligated to stop this practice since it may result in massive Sabbath and Holy Day desecration. Please publicize my prohibition in this matter in conjunction with the similar stand of my distinguished colleagues.

Silver's role in the controversy was mitigated with the circulation of his letter. Nevertheless, the Sabbath activities of the Jewish Community Centers was to remain an open issue.

A few years later, Silver was once again defending the American trained rabbinate before his European colleagues. At the session devoted to *Kashrut* at the 1964 *Agudat Harabanim* convention, the validity of the supervision of the Union of Orthodox Congregations was questioned. This certification was conducted in cooperation with its rabbinical arm, the Rabbinical Council of America. Silver declared that this supervision was reliable, although it was important to ascertain exactly who was the rabbi responsible for each individual product.[28] Thus, during this period, Silver was constantly defending segments of Orthodoxy against detractors from within its own ranks. The days when he was constantly on the offensive had ended.

Notes

1. *Every Friday*, October 17, 1947. Also see the issues of July 4, 1947; December 22, 1950; and November 26, 1954. The next quotation is from the June 8, 1956 issue.

2. *Every Friday*, September 20, 1963. Also see the issues of April 20, 1956 and June 29, 1962.

After his death, the Board of Directors dedicated a monument in Rabbi Silver's memory on the grounds in front of the Home. On it was inscribed a poem which read:

He said unto his leaders,
"Go forth and build anew
A dwelling for our elders,
Mothers dear and Fathers true."
Though in their eyes was doubt indeed
before this awesome task,
He knew it was a holy plan
the Lord Himself would ask.
His spirit did their souls inspire;
his vigor fused their will;
Then soon the Home of Homes did rise
and did with aged fill.

Now, he has left us;
but has not truly gone,
For here, wherein our elders dwell,
forever he lives on.

3. *Every Friday*, February 19, 1965.

4. *Every Friday*, February 3, 1950. For Silver's role in the earlier Goldman controversy see *supra*, chapter four.

5. Dr. Z. H. Wachsman, *"Ha Rav D'Poh* — Rabbi Eliezer Silver," *Every Friday*, December 21, 1945, p. 5.

6. MS of Rabbi David Silver's address. Cf. *Every Friday*, March 3, 1961.

7. The life story of an Hungarian Jewish refugee as recorded in the appendix to George Kranzler, *Williamsburg: A Jewish Community in Transition* (New York: Philipp Feldheim, 1961), p. 232.

Cf. Liebman, "Orthodoxy in American Jewish Life," pp. 32-33, 67-69, and 87-88.

8. Cf. Shaul Kagan, "Reb Aharon Kotler: Ten Years After His Passing," *Jewish Observer*, May 1973, p. 7.

For Rabbi Kotler's biography see Aharon Ben-Zion Shurin, *Keshet Giborim* (Jerusalem: Mossad Harav Kook, 1964), pp. 244-248; and the pamphlet "When the World Mourned," published by the Rabbi Aaron Kotler Memorial Fund of Lakewood, New Jersey, following his death on November 29 (Kislev 2), 1962.

The Yeshivah in Lakewood was originally known as the Beth Medrash Govoha. After his death, it was renamed the Rabbi Aaron Kotler Institute for Advanced Learning.

9. The author heard about the former incident and witnessed the latter while studying in the Lakewood Yeshivah in 1954. The student evidently did not realize that it was only an individual opinion which required the congregation to remain standing still until after the blessing. See *Arukh Ha-Shulhan*, Orah Hayyim, 95:5, citing the *Eliyahu Rabbah*.

The breaking of the mirror in the home of the Satmar Rebbe is related by Liebman, "Orthodoxy in American Jewish Life," p. 84. For details of Satmar in the United States see Israel Rubin, *Satmar: An Island in the City* (New York: Quadrangle Books, 1972).

10. *Hapardes*, May 1947, p. 8.

Also see *She'eylot U'Teshuvot ha-Maor*, ed. Meir Amsel (New York, 1966), 1:554.

For the original *Agudat Harabanim* viewpoint see *supra*, chapter one. Silver's position is detailed in *Hapardes*, January 1961, p. 42.

11. *Hapardes*, June 1956, p. iii. The English translation is based upon that which appeared in *The Jewish Observer*, April 1975, p. 9. Also see Liebman, "Orthodoxy in American Jewish Life," pp. 51-52; David Rudavsky, *Modern Jewish Religious Movements: A History of Eman-*

cipation and Adjustment (New York: Behrman Paperback, 1967), pp. 386-387; Louis Bernstein, "The Emergence of the English Speaking Orthodox Rabbinate" (unpublished Ph.D. dissertation, Bernard Revel Graduate School of Yeshiva University, 1977), pp. 304 ff; and Ralph Pelcovitz, *Danger and Opportunity: Essays on Traditional Judaism in a Time of Crisis* (New York: Shengold Publishers Inc., 1976) pp. 32-37.

Rabbi David Silver explained his father's stand on this issue to the author in a July 10, 1974 interview. For an earlier instance of American controversy concerning mixed rabbinic groups in 1939 see the author's *Bernard Revel*, pp. 174-175.

This issue had also been a cause celebre in German Orthodoxy. See Hermann Schwab, *The History of Orthodox Jewry in Germany* (London: The Mitre Press, 1950), pp. 60-81.

12. *Hapardes*, January 1953, pp. 45-46.

13. *Hapardes*, January 1957, pp. 32-49; and Liebman, "Orthodoxy in American Jewish Life," pp. 33-34.

14. *Hapardes*, January 1959, p. 39.

For additional details of the relationship between these two rabbinic organizations also see Bernstein, "The Emergence of the English Speaking Orthodox Rabbinate," pp. 267-273.

15. *Hapardes*, January 1961, p. 43.

16. *Hapardes*, July 1957, p. 28.

For details of the Conservative *Ketubah* see United Synagogue Review, Vol. 8, No. 3 (December, 1954), p. 1. For some of the Orthodox opposition see A. Leo Levin and Meyer Kramer, "New Provisions in the Ketubah" (Community Service Division of Yeshiva University, 1955); and Norman Lamm, "Recent Additions to the Ketubah: A Halakhic Critique," *Tradition*, 2:1 (Fall 1959), pp. 93-118. Also see Eliezer Yehudah Waldenberg, *Tzitz Eliezer* (Jerusalem, 1957), Vol. 5, pp. 23-25; and Joseph Elijah Henkin, in *Noam* (Jerusalem, 1958), Vol. 1, pp. 283-286.

17. *Hapardes*, June 1958, p. 32 and July 1958, p. 39; and interview with Rabbi David Silver, October 4, 1972.

18. *Hapardes*, February 1960, pp. 33-34; and interview with Rabbi Charles Weinberg, August 19, 1975. Weinberg was president of the Rabbinical Council of America at the time of the luncheon honoring Silver. Also see the *Rabbinical Council Record*, April 1961, p. 1.

19. *Hapardes*, June 1962, p. 3. Also see Pelcovitz, *Danger and Opportunity*, pp. 45-50.

20. *Hapardes*, December 1962, p. 33. The New York funeral was described in *The New York Times* and *New York Herald Tribune* of December 3, 1962.

21. *Hapardes*, December 1962, p. 40. Also see Liebman, "Orthodoxy in American Jewish Life," p. 85.

22. The oaths are detailed in Ketubot, 111a. Rabbi Teitelbaum expounded his position in a number of volumes including *Al ha-Geulah va-Al ha-Temurah* (New York: Jerusalem Publishing, 1967). This book elicited a response by Rabbi Menahem Kasher, entitled *ha-Tekufah ha-Gedolah* (Jerusalem: Torah Shelemah Institute, 1968). Also see Norman Lamm, "The Ideology of the Neturei Karta: According to the Satmarer Version," *Tradition*, 13:1 (Fall, 1971), pp. 38-53.

23. The letter was later published in *Torah U-Melukhah*, ed. Simon Federbusch (Jerusalem: Mossad Harav Kook, 1961), pp. 99-100.

24. Hillel Seidman, "Ha-Rav ha-Kollel shel Yehudei Artzot ha-Brit," *Hatzofe*, February 23, 1968.

Rabbi Kotler's reference to "people will say that we have pierced our Master" is based upon Gittin, 56a.

25. Related to the author by Mr. Haim Zohar in a December 17, 1977 interview. Zohar also attended this event as a representative of the Israeli government.

26. *JWB Circle*, March 1961, p. 2. The regulations and supplementary statements cited above also appear in this newspaper.

27. *The National Jewish Post and Opinion*, July 21, 1961, p. 16. The documents on this controversy were supplied to the author by Mr. Emil Dere, who was then involved in a similar debate regarding the Jewish Community Center of Richmond, Virginia.

28. *Hapardes*, January 1965, p. 38. The convention was held on December 7-9, 1964.

11

The Final Years

Silver continued his activities despite his advanced years. In 1963, he underwent surgery. Upon his recovery, the *Agudat Harabanim* sponsored a repast of thanksgiving at the Washington Hotel in Belle Harbor, New York, on June 17, 1963. At this event the speakers were not only the *roshei yeshivah*, but also the practicing rabbis amidst the organization's membership. Among them were Rabbis Isaac Small of Chicago, Moshe Dan Sheinkopf of Springfield, and Joseph Dov Soloveitchik of Spring Valley. When Silver entered his eighty-fifth year, Elberg published an editorial of evaluation in *Hapardes*. Stressing Silver's unique achievements in both the fields of Torah knowledge and communal activities, Elberg considered him the prime representative of the authentic rabbinate on the American scene:

Rabbi Silver has exemplified the true rabbinate for over fifty years. In all his speeches and pronouncements there is the feeling that the authentic rabbinate is voicing its opinion. . . .

Let us now admit that not always did we "youngsters" properly understand him. Now we can first understand how far-reaching his insight was. He understood nuances of the situation which we did not. He warned us about developments which would harm the rabbinate. Let us admit that he was able to gauge the circumstances better than we.

We were entirely wrong in thinking that rabbinical leaders could be developed overnight. We fooled ourselves when we thought that Rabbi Silver's leadership could be replaced. Today we know there is no one like him. Years ago we considered him "old." Now we see that he is still among our youngest and most active members. . . .[1]

On *Rosh Hashanah* of 1966, Silver stumbled and fell while walking to the *Tashlikh* ceremony [symbolic casting of sins at a running stream]. Later it was learned that he had suffered a minor stroke at that time. Silver's energies slowly began to fail and he curtailed his activities. The Telz Yeshivah of Cleveland was particularly thoughtful towards Silver during this period. Once a month one of their *roshei yeshivah* came to Cincinnati to visit with him. Their social calls enlivened Silver since he could discuss Torah topics with them. In Israel Rabbi Sher prayed for him at the Western Wall. Finally, on February 7 (Ninth of Shevat), 1968, Silver passed away in Cincinnati, fourteen days short of his eighty-seventh birthday.[2] The next day he was interred locally after funeral services at his Knesseth Israel synagogue. Eulogizing Silver at the congregation were Rabbis Feinstein, Gifter, Lifshitz, Teitz, and Schneur Kotler of Lakewood. For Agudat Israel, Rabbi Morris Sherer, its executive vice-president, expressed his tribute. On behalf of the family, his son-in-law, Rabbi Yehuda Gershuni, spoke. In Jerusalem a public eulogy was held at the Hebron Yeshivah at the conclusion of the seven days of mourning. The *Agudat Harabanim* also sponsored a public memorial assembly in New York which was attended by hundreds of *rabanim* and yeshivah students. Once again, Elberg portrayed Silver in an insightful article regarding his leadership:

Rabbi Silver was the leader of all the Jewish people, and not just of any group or party. He was not one to limit his concern and outlook. He was the head of the *Agudat Harabanim*. Yet he also smiled at the Rabbinical Council of America. He was the founder of the Agudat Israel in the United States. Nevertheless, he did not consider the Mizrachi an ideological opponent. By nature he was a true Lithuanian *mitnagged*, born and bred in such surroundings. Still he was filled with hassidic fervor. He was in constant contact with the Lubavitcher Rebbe. When he visited Eretz Israel, his first deed was to call upon the Gerer *Rebbe.* . . .

His far reaching outlook was always attuned to all of the Jewish people. He refused to be provincial and shortsighted. All the contradictions which seemingly appeared in his deeds were in reality only a reflection of this broad perspective.[3]

On March 27th, the Rabbinical Council of America joined with Yeshiva University in conducting a memorial session. Here the main speaker was its senior *rosh yeshivah*, Rabbi Joseph Dov Soloveitchik. In his talk, he compared Silver to his grandfather by saying, "Since my grandfather, Rav Hayyim Brisker, no one has arisen to combine in himself such greatness in Torah and charitable deeds as Rabbi Eliezer Silver."

These words were indeed the most appropriate epitaph for Silver. He succeeded in remaining loyal to the ideals which nurtured him in Eastern Europe. Despite the many decades he spent in the United States, the spirit of his mentors constantly motivated and permeated the life of Rabbi Eliezer Silver.

Notes

1. *Hapardes*, March 1965, p. 3.

2. Details of Silver's final illness were related to the author by Rabbi David Silver in a July 24, 1974 interview. Also see the letters of Mrs. Eliezer Silver to Rabbi Sher of March 14, May 8, and September 4, 1967.

3. *Hapardes*, March 1968, p. 3.

APPENDIX 1

Constitution of the
United Orthodox Rabbis of America
ORGANIZED 24TH OF TAMUZ 5662 IN NEW YORK *

the association in formation

At a gathering of the heads of the nation, the rabbis of America, the enhancement of Torah and Judaism was discussed. Recently its status has drastically deteriorated in the United States due to various reasons. It was therefore decided to organize the United Orthodox Rabbis of America. Its goal will be to strengthen the weakened hands of the rabbinate and to remove stumbling blocks from the path of our nation. In unity we will repair the breaches in the House of Israel for the benefit of our religion and people.

the time of the meeting

The temporary committee appointed to arrange the meeting sent letters urging the rabbis to come to New York on Tuesday, the 24th of Tamuz, 5662. Many rabbis did indeed respond and rushed to New York even in advance of the date of the convention.

the death of the chief rabbi

It was the will of God that on the very day that the rabbis met, the lamp of the Lord was extinguished. The night before, the great sage and saint, Rabbi Jacob Joseph, the Chief Rabbi of New York, passed on to his eternal reward. The next morning the

---

*This constitution is discussed in chapter one.

315

rabbis gathered together with the city's lay leaders at the auditorium of the Machzikei Talmud Torah school at 227 East Broadway. With broken hearts and eyes filled with tears, they discussed where to bury the sage and the establishment of a fund to support the widow. On the next day, Wednesday, the 25th of Tamuz, the rabbis participated in his funeral, along with one hundred thousand of our brethren. May the memory of that sage and saint protect the Jewish nation which treasures his final resting place and awaits the Almighty's salvation.

the establishment of the organization

On Thursday, the 26th of Tamuz, the rabbis began the holy task of formulating the rules that would govern the members and the association. After much discussion, these were the final resolutions which were adopted for the good of our holy religion.

BYLAWS

I MEMBERSHIP

1. Only those rabbis ordained by the well-known scholars of Europe are eligible for membership. In addition, they must be the spiritual leaders of Orthodox congregations in the United States.

2. A new rabbi will only be considered if he is sponsored by a member as a qualified scholar worthy of joining the organization. The executive committee will then appoint a committee of three to check on the candidate's ordination and deportment. They will then report to the executive committee. If they unanimously agree, the rabbi will be accepted as a member. Otherwise, the final decision will be made at the organization's annual convention by majority vote.

II DUES

1. Each member will pay six dollars to defray the Association's expenses. Each half year half the sum will be due in accordance with the following schedule: in Tamuz three dollars, and in Tevet the remaining three dollars.

2. If a member will be in arrears for six months, the secretary will send him a letter requesting that he pay within a

week. At the annual convention, the secretary will read the names of those members still in debt. The majority will then decide whether they still can continue to be members of the Association.

III ACTIVITIES

1. At every annual convention, a chairman, recording secretary, corresponding secretary, treasurer, and six committees will be chosen. The committees will be: 1) An executive committee to guide all the organization's activities. 2) An education committee to supervise the studies in the Talmud Torahs and Hebrew schools. 3) A Yeshivah committee to supervise the existing yeshivot and to plan for the formation of new ones. 4) A Sabbath committee to strengthen its observance among our people. 5) A *Kashrut* committee to supervise those products requiring rabbinic approval. Members of this committee must function in various cities to guarantee that the products will be properly supervised and absolutely acceptable. 6) A committee on mutual well-being and aid. It will be responsible for amicable relations between the rabbis and the moral and economic support of members in need.

2. At the annual convention a committee of rabbis will be authorized to ordain those local scholars worthy of rabbinic certification.

IV THE ASSOCIATION'S GOALS

1. The strengthening of religious life.
2. Peace and unity.
3. Mutual aid.
4. Charity.

V THE STRENGTHENING OF RELIGIOUS LIFE

1. *Education*

1) The Association in general, and each individual member in particular, must strive to improve educational facilities. They must see to it that the principles of true faith and commitment envelop the existing and future schools.

2) The teachers are to translate into Yiddish, the native

language of the children's parents. When necessary for the clarification of the topic, the teachers may also utilize English. In areas where only English is spoken, it may be the basic tongue.

3) Those Talmud Torah and *hedarim* teachers desirous of *Agudat Harabanim* support must be tested by educational experts to ascertain whether they belong in this profession.

4) The teachers must be Godfearing and their deeds in accordance with the Torah.

5) Every teacher must receive a certificate of approbation from one member of the *Agudat Harabanim* and two pedagogues. They must testify to his religious dedication and teaching abilities.

6) The education committee must meet with educators to draw up a proper curriculum for the various levels of study. These guidelines must integrate the study of Hebrew with religious knowledge. All educational institutions associated with the *Agudat Harabanim* must follow this course of study. These important topics must no longer be left in the hands of individuals on an ad hoc basis. Only under such an organized system will the proper teachers succeed. The students will experience success in their studies, and the educational level of the schools will be constantly supervised.

7) The education committee, in consultation with the educators, will plan a graded system of study so that teachers will no longer have various levels of students in one class. This past practice suppressed the true abilities and progress of the students.

8) The *Agudat Harabanim* will attempt to influence laymen to establish evening schools for those youth who work or attend secular schools by day. This way they can continue the study of the Torah. At the very least, they will not forget that which they learned in their youth. The evening lectures should be devoted to Torah, ethical instruction, and the basic history of the Jewish people.

9) The yeshivot affiliated with the *Agudat Harabanim* should conduct both their curriculum and deportment in accordance with the dicta of the supervising committee. The rabbis must see that the study is properly organized so that the

yeshivah students will truly succeed in their dedicated endeavors.

10) The Yeshivah committee should also supervise the secular subjects taught in the yeshivot. Only necessary subjects should be taught by qualified instructors. The committee should be careful lest the students regard the yeshivah simply as a stopover before they pursue advanced secular studies. Such an attitude will impair their accomplishments in the yeshivah.

2. Sabbath observance

1) Ways must be discovered to strengthen Sabbath observance among the people. Wide publicity should be given to these ideas so that the masses will not pay attention to the claims that all hope is lost for Sabbath observance in this country.

2) The rabbis should not grant any certification of *Kashrut* to Sabbath desecrators. All those involved in the production of kosher meat, wine, Passover liquor and *matzot* should be observant of the Sabbath. However, once manufactured, a trustworthy agent can be supervised if he promises that these products will not be sold on the Sabbath.

3) The rabbis must warn the people not to buy bread from bakeries which bake on the Sabbath. Not only is purchasing such products considered aiding a sinner, but it is practically certain that there is also non-kosher oil and shortening in the baked products.

4) The *Agudat Harabanim* in general, and each rabbi in particular, must exert every effort to locate employment for workers desirous of observing the Sabbath. They should constantly try to influence the owners of factories to employ Sabbath observers. They should be enabled to rest the entire Sabbath in accordance with the Torah.

5) The *Agudat Harabanim* must constantly chart the activities of the unions. When there is a strike, the rabbis should influence the workers to include the right for Sabbath observance among their demands. In return for this, the organization will agree to support all the just demands of the workers. The rabbis will pressure the owners and employers to comply with the requests of the union.

6) The *Agudat Harabanim* will request all Jews who still value tradition to patronize only those business people who observe the Sabbath. It is well known how much these people suffer because of their religious principles. It is a meritorious act to sustain them.

7) The *Agudat Harabanim* will request that all Jewish charitable organizations set up divisions to seek employment for Sabbath observers. These people, committed with heart and soul to religious observance, plead for work which will permit Sabbath observance. The *Agudat Harabanim* will do everything possible to aid the charitable organizations in these endeavors.

3. *Kashrut supervision*

1) Attempts must be made to establish proper *Kashrut* supervision, particularly regarding the slaughter, inspection, and sale of kosher meat.

2) All aspects of *shehitah*, the inspection of meat, the supervision of *mikvaot*, the manufacture of *tefillin*, *mezuzot*, *tzitzit*, wine, Passover liquor, and *matzot* should be under the supervision of a member of the *Agudat Harabanim* who resides in the city of production. The rabbi should also supervise the manufacture of these products in the surrounding areas if there is no other rabbi nearby.

3) If a competent member of the *Agudat Harabanim* resides in a city, even though not officially its rabbi, he still should be responsible for *Kashrut* supervision. All the *shohatim*, butchers, and manufacturers of items requiring supervision should accept his rulings. This will result in the strengthening of *Kashrut* observance.

4) When a rabbi finds it necessary to publicly disqualify a butcher for violating the *Kashrut* laws, then no other rabbi may reinstate the butcher. Only when the original rabbi will agree can the butcher qualify once again. If the two rabbis continue to disagree, then a third rabbi should be consulted to resolve the dispute.

5) A rabbi of a city should not prohibit a *shohet* on his own, because this will increase controversy among Jews. The rabbi should rather bring the case before the organization's executive committee. With the consent of both parties, the committee will

send one or two rabbis to the location of the dispute. There the issue will be resolved in accordance with Torah law.

6) All rabbis are obligated to make every effort to see that two *shohatim* work together in every local slaughterhouse. This is an ancient ordinance to safeguard proper *shehitah* which is widely observed among all the Jews in their countries of dispersion. The organization will strongly support the rabbis in these efforts.

7) The rabbis must supervise the *mikvaot* in their cities and surrounding communities. These must be conducted on a high standard, both as far as *halakhic* and hygienic requirements are concerned.

8) The association must attempt to influence those localities without *mikvaot* to construct them. However, this must not be left in the hands of lay people since the slightest mistake can void the *mikveh*. The community should rather turn to the nearest rabbi to supervise its construction in accordance with the requirements of the Torah.

4. *Family laws*

1) All aspects of divorce, *halitzah*, marriage and conversion should be supervised by the *Agudat Harabanim*. Many irksome and difficult problems are caused by ignoramuses engaged in these areas. They interfere with the traditions of family purity which have been dear to the Jewish people throughout the generations.

2) The association must do everything in its power to insist that only proper rabbis conduct the above mentioned rituals. The public must be educated not to turn to just anyone in these areas. The *Agudat Harabanim* will not validate any ritual act supervised by unqualified individuals.

3) It is obligatory upon all members of the *Agudat Harabanim* not to accept a *get* or document of *halitzah* administered by individuals not known to be experts in these matters. They should also not send *gittin* for delivery by such unqualified people. The association must also publicize among rabbis in other countries that such individuals are not trustworthy.

4) The *Agudat Harabanim* must declare that only rabbis or

knowledgeable people may officiate at marriages. The latter must have authorization from a rabbinic authority and the permission of the local rabbi.

5) The *Agudat Harabanim* must appeal to the societies and synagogues in the country to be the leaders in these attempts to properly establish religious life here. They should insist that only a proper rabbi or someone worthy of the task be entrusted with officiating at marriages. Those not so learned can be honored with the recitation of the seven blessings after the actual marriage.

6) All members of the *Agudat Harabanim* should send the essential information regarding *gittin* they administer to the organization's central office. The secretary should record these details for future consultation.

7) No individual rabbi should decide on his own how to write the names of cities and rivers in areas where *gittin* were not previously written. He should rather consult with three expert rabbis. If they cannot reach a unanimous conclusion, then the question should be presented before the general membership of the organization.

8) A complaint brought before a member of the *Agudat Harabanim* regarding a divorce, marriage or *halitzah* should carefully be investigated by him. If he feels that he needs help from the organization, he should turn to the executive committee. They are obligated to do everything in their power to enhance the status of our holy religion.

VI PEACE AND UNITY

1) Unity in outlook and activity should be achieved for the welfare of our members and the organization, and for the enhancement of Torah and tradition.

2) A member of the *Agudah* called to a rabbinical position in a city where a colleague already resides must appear before the executive committee. Only after they have ascertained that there is no encroachment may the new rabbi move there.

3) If an unqualified person settles in a community and poses as a rabbi, the *Agudah* will attempt to quietly influence him to leave. If this is unsuccessful then the annual convention of the organization will determine the future of this imposter.

4) A rabbi receiving a question which may also affect the Jewish community at large can issue his decision based upon the traditional sources. Nevertheless, the rabbi must also present the problem and his solution before the entire organization. After all the rabbis analyze the problem, a decision will be taken in accordance with the will of the majority. This will then become the official position of the organization. In this fashion the honor of Torah will be safeguarded, and there will not be a situation where rabbis issue contradictory rulings.

5) Any rabbi taking part in discussions concerning these communal questions must give reasons for his opinion. He may elaborate or be brief, but his viewpoint must be explained.

6) A communal question is one that does not simply concern a local community but also involves all places where Jews reside. If every local rabbi will decide on his own there invariably will be controversy among them. Therefore such questions should be placed before the entire membership of the Association.

7) Those that ask and those that respond should officially inform the secretary of their viewpoints. He must publicize the essence of their opinions to the entire membership.

8) In order that there not be unnecessary arguments regarding the utilization of titles of honor for the rabbis, all official communications will address them simply as "rabbi and colleague."

9) To enhance peace and truth, all rabbis should exert their full influence so that their congregants will submit their disputes to rabbinical courts. It is a disgrace when Jews quarrel in non-Jewish courts. This is particularly so when the controversy concerns an internal Jewish community issue. The association must try to end such disputes in an amicable and well-disposed fashion.

VII MUTUAL AID

1) Each member should aid his colleagues in both spiritual and temporal matters.

2) The *Agudah* will not only support its own members but will also assist any competent European rabbinic arrival. He will be assisted in every way even if he does not enter the active

rabbinate. All that will concern the organization will be the newcomer's greatness in "Torah and fear of Heaven."

3) The *Agudah* will attempt to influence Jewish communities to engage bona fide rabbinical leadership to enable them and their children to walk in the path of Torah and tradition.

VIII CHARITY

1) Many different types of organized charity must be established in this country. Since the assembled rabbis could not remain in New York for a long period, it was decided to authorize the executive committee to deal with this topic. Its members will decide how to bring order to charity collections in an equable and upright fashion.

2) All charity collectors for various causes both in the United States and overseas must get a letter from a member of the executive committee testifying to the necessity of his endeavors. The rabbi must also certify that the collector is honest and reliable. Only in this fashion will the act of charity be complete.

Registry of the founding members
of the United Orthodox Rabbis of America

1. Rabbi A. Gordon, 183 East Broadway, New York
2. Rabbi A. A. Rosen, Lafayette St., New Haven, Conn.
3. Rabbi A. Ch. Levenson, 14 Front St., Baltimore, Md.
4. Rabbi A. E. Hirschowitz, 61 East Broadway, New York
5. Rabbi A. I. G. Lesser, 616 Carlisle Ave., Cincinnati, O.
6. Rabbi A. L. Alperstein, 262 East Broadway, New York
7. Rabbi A. M. Franklin, 259 Spring St., Buffalo, N.Y.
8. Rabbi A. M. Shereshewsky, 3 Davis St., Boston, Mass.
9. Rabbi B. Abramowitz, 73 Canal St., New York
10. Rabbi B. L. Leventhal, 716 Pine St., Philadelphia, Pa.
11. Rabbi B. S. Rabbiner, 24 Orchard St., New York
12. Rabbi Ch. Susizky, 22 Paliside Ave., Yonkers, N.Y.
13. Rabbi Ch. D. Bachrach, 17 Smith St., Providence, R.I.
14. Rabbi Ch. H. Papkin, 17 Lane St., New Bedford, Mass.
15. Rabbi Ch. J. Silver, 17 Ledge St., Worcester, Mass.
16. Rabbi Ch. M. Lasker, 7 Division St., Troy, N.Y.

17. Rabbi D. Ginsburg, 21 Harrison St., Rochester, N.Y.
18. Rabbi D. Radinsky, 1827 Pitkin Ave., Brooklyn, N.Y.
19. Rabbi E. Epstein, 223 W. 13 Street, Chicago, Ill.
20. Rabbi H. A. Sirk, Chelsea St., E. Boston, Mass.
21. Rabbi H. Berman, 25 S. High St., Baltimore, Md.
22. Rabbi H. Grodsinsky, 212 S. 13 St., Omaha, Neb.
23. Rabbi J. Feinberg, 335 Breck St., Scranton, Pa.
24. Rabbi J. J. Swerenowsky, 11 Rutgers Place, New York
25. Rabbi J. M. Shapiro, 80 Rutgers St., New York
26. Rabbi J. S. Hurwitz, 76 Pleasant St., Hartford, Conn.
27. Rabbi Jos. Grosman, 114 E. Chestnut St., Hazleton, Pa.
28. Rabbi Jos. Kamesarsky, 73 W. 13 St., Chicago, Ill.
29. Rabbi J. A. Fromer, 72 York St., New Haven, Conn.
30. Rabbi J. D. Bernstein, 1590 Madison Ave., New York
31. Rabbi I. F. Israelite, 29 Division St., Chelsea, Mass.
32. Rabbi I. L. Levin, 151 Division St., Detroit, Mich.
33. Rabbi I. I. Owshowitz, 2722 Myrtle Place, Denver, Colo.
34. Rabbi I. L. Seltzer, 102 Oak St., Bangor, Me.
35. Rabbi I. M. Feinstein, 34 Deer St., Portland, Me.
36. Rabbi L. Binkowitz, 186 Clinton St., New York
37. Rabbi L. J. Anixter, 461 Clark St., Chicago, Ill.
38. Rabbi M. L. Schwartz, 7 Jane St., Portchester, N.Y.
39. Rabbi M. L. Bernstein, 412 S. Park St., Elizabethport, N.J.
40. Rabbi M. M. Maharam, 226 Catharine St., Philadelphia, Pa.
41. Rabbi M. M. Motlin, 220 East 98 St., New York
42. Rabbi M. S. Margolius, 3 Baldwin Pl., Boston, Mass.
43. Rabbi M. S. Siwitz, 31 Federal St., Pittsburg, Pa.
44. Rabbi M. S. Silber, 412 N. Plymouth Ave., Minneapolis, Minn.
45. Rabbi O. L. Zarchy, Louisville, Ky.
46. Rabbi S. Englander, 323 Catharine St., Philadelphia, Pa.
47. Rabbi S. Israelson, 119 Agnes St., Toronto, Ont., Canada
48. Rabbi S. Lipshitz, 566 Carlisle Ave., Cincinnati, O.
49. Rabbi S. Rappaport, 32 Grays Ave., Springfield, Mass.
50. Rabbi S. Rosenberg, 54 Moore St., Brooklyn, N.Y.
51. Rabbi S. Sprintz, 13 Wercers St., Montreal, Canada
52. Rabbi S. E. Jaffe, 219 Henry St., New York
53. Rabbi S. H. Album, 264 W. 14 St., Chicago, Ill.
54. Rabbi S. J. Friederman, 116 Salem St., Boston, Mass.
55. Rabbi S. J. Rosenfeld, 1007 N. 10 St., St. Louis, Mo.
56. Rabbi W. Samuelson, 612 Hanover St., Baltimore, Md.
57. Rabbi W. L. Wittenstein, 7 Mercer St., Pittsburg, Pa.
58. Rabbi Y. E. Edelson, 2743 13 Ave., Denver, Colo.
59. Rabbi Z. Hoffenberg, 55 Pleasant St., Hartford, Conn.

Deposition of Rabbi Eliezer Silver,
November 3, 1927
at the hearing against Solomon Goldman,
spiritual leader of Cleveland's Jewish Center.*

Rabbi Eliezer Silver, of lawful age, being by me first duly sworn, as hereinafter certified, deposes and says as follows: *Sworn in by notary.*

Q. State your name, age, residence and occupation.

A. Eliezer Silver, 46 years old, 1563 Divide Street, Springfield, Massachusetts. I am a Rabbi.

Q. Rabbi of what congregation?

A. Of four congregations.

Q. In Springfield?

A. Yes.

Q. From what colleges or institutions have you graduated and when?

A. Zembrover, in the city of Dvinsk, Latvia, under Rabbi M. S. ha-Kohen, Rabbi Grodzenski's *kibbutz* in the city of Vilna, Poland, and under Rabbi Soloveitchik of Brisk, in Brisk, Poland.

Q. Are these secular or religious colleges?

A. Religious.

Q. What courses of study did you pursue in these institutions?

---

*This deposition is discussed in chapter four. It has been edited to correct errors in transcription.

A. I studied the Talmud and *Poskim.*

Q. And for what period of time?

A. Twelve years.

Q. Have you had any secular collegiate training?

A. Private.

Q. Covering what particular studies?

A. Russian language and the other secular studies.

Q. After leaving college what experience or training did you have in Judaism?

A. I was a rabbi since leaving. A rabbi in Harrisburg, Pennsylvania, for eighteen years and in Springfield, Massachusetts, three years, and instructor in Vilna, for one year.

Q. Instructor of what?

A. Instructor of Talmudical studies.

Q. After reaching this country, Rabbi, for what length of time have your pursued your studies in Judaism?

A. The whole time since I came twenty-one years ago I am studying.

Q. During that period, have you written any books or pamphlets and periodicals?

A. Yes.

Q. On Jewish subjects — on Judaism?

A. On *halakhah.*

Q. Are you a member of the presidium of Orthodox Rabbis of the United States and Canada?

A. Yes.

Q. What is the presidium of that organization?

A. There are five presidents and I am one of the five.

Q. How long have you occupied that position?

A. As a member of the presidium?

Q. Yes.

A. Four years.

Q. Did you ever have any talk with Solomon Goldman regarding his attitude towards Judaism?

A. No.

Q. Did you, as a member of that presidium, take up, on behalf of the Union, the attitude of Goldman toward Orthodox and Traditional Judaism at a convention at Lakewood, New Jersey?

A. Yes.

Q. What, if any, communications did you send to Goldman from the Union on that subject?

A. I wasn't at that meeting when they sent a communication.

Q. Did you see the communication?

A. No, I didn't, but I heard in the office about this.

Q. Do you know whether a protest against changes being made by Goldman was sent by the Union to Goldman?

A. Yes.

Q. Did you sign that protest on behalf of the Union or as one of the presidium?

A. I don't remember.

Q. I now hand you what purports to be a copy in Hebrew of a protest issued by the Union of Orthodox Rabbis of the United States and Canada to protesting members of the Jewish Center.

A. Yes. This was sent to him. This was given to the committee representing the protesting members.

Q. What was the occasion of this protest or document?

A. A committee had been formed in Cleveland to protest a man by the name of Goldman who makes changes in the Jewish Center congregation such as allowing men and women to sit together in the Center. We therefore decided to send this protest.

Q. And what you now have in your hand is a copy of that protest that was sent to this committee?

A. Yes.

Note: We offer in evidence a copy of the protest in question which may be marked "Plaintiff's Exhibit No. 1."

Q. Are you acquainted with the Jewish Theological Seminary of New York?

A. I was never inside of it.

Q. Are you a believer in and supporter of Orthodox Judaism?

A. Yes.

Q. What are the duties and privileges of a rabbi in Judaism?

A. He must take part in all that happens in Jewish life. He must attend to this — that is always the main thing. He must also decide the laws when questions come to him and teach the people — that is all.

Q. He is a judge of the law?

A. Yes, he is the judge of the law between man and man, and he must decide questions between man and God, too.

Q. What is Orthodox Judaism?

A. To believe and to keep all the traditional laws which are in the rabbinical literature since the Mosaic law, including the Talmud law and Code of Karo, and other rabbinical laws.

Q. What is Traditional Judaism?

A. Traditional Judaism is that which is based on the rabbinical literature.

Q. What is the difference, if any, between Orthodox and Traditional Judaism?

A. No difference.

Q. May a congregation devoted to the cause of Traditional Judaism properly describe itself as Orthodox?

A. Yes.

Q. What is the Traditional Law in Judaism?

A. Traditional Law is the same as Traditional Judaism — all the laws that are written in the Talmud and Code of Karo, and the other rabbinical literature. (Traditional Judaism is the same as Traditional Law.)

Q. What is Reform Judaism?

A. They deny the authority of the rabbis, rabbinical literature and some of the Code of Karo.

Q. Do they also deny the revelation at Sinai?

A. Most of them do.

Q. How is Reform Judaism distinguished from Orthodox or Traditional Judaism?

A. They run away from the model and customs of Orthodoxy.

Q. And also in the basic belief?

A. Yes.

Q. In the Mosaic Code are there what is known as the ceremonial laws?

A. Yes.

Q. If so, what is this law?

A. To construct the tabernacle, to bless the people by the priests, to bless God after meals, and other kinds — there are a couple of hundred ceremonial laws.

Q. Is the ceremonial law as binding and of equal authority as any other part of the Mosaic code?

A. Yes.

Q. What is Conservative Judaism?

A. The same as Reform because that is the first step of reform.

Q. How is it distinguished from Orthodox Judaism?

A. Because the rabbinical literature is not authoritative for them.

Q. How do the customs, ritual and practices in Conservative congregations differ from those of Orthodox congregations?

A. There are some differences — in their congregations men and women sit together and they permit other things which are against Orthodoxy and which Orthodox rabbis do not permit in their congregations.

Q. Are they essentials or non-essentials?

A. Essentials.

Q. What is the attitude of Conservative Judaism towards revealed religion and especially toward the Sinaitic origin of the Torah?

A. I believe that it is the same as Reform.

Q. Could an Orthodox Jew conscientiously worship in a Conservative synagogue?

A. No.

Q. Have Orthodox and Conservative congregations, ever, to your knowledge, worshipped in the same synagogue?

A. To my memory, never.

Q. What is the source and authority for the ritual and ceremonies that distinguish Orthodox Judaism?

A. First is the Talmud, and after the Talmud the Code of Karo, and the other commentaries written on Karo's code.

Q. Can you name some periodicals and books which discuss Orthodox, Reform and Conservative Judaism, and are regarded as authoritative in the Jewish world on these subjects?

A. Some of them are *Chasam Sofer, Yehudah Ya'aleh, Maharam Schick,* and the letters of Rabbi S. R. Hirsch, and others.

Q. Do these, that you have now named, discuss Conservative or Reform Judaism, or only Orthodox?

A. They discuss that he who is not Orthodox is Reform.

Q. Do you know Professor Kaplan?

A. I heard about him.

Q. Do you know what his position is with regard to Orthodox, Reform or Conservative Judaism?

A. In my view he is a Reform Jew.

Q. When did the word "Orthodox" first appear in Judaism, if at all?

A. When Reform began.

Q. You know of the United Synagogue of America?

A. Yes, I know about it.

Q. Do you know how its membership is made up?

A. I know that they have a couple of hundred congregations as members.

Q. Do you know whether these congregations are partly Orthodox and partly Conservative?

A. Partly Orthodox by mistake.

Q. What is the origin of the separation of the sexes during services in the Synagogue?

A. I wrote an article some years ago, and I can leave it with you or explain it.

Q. Explain it.

A. Firstly, because in the Temple in Jerusalem there were two sides — one a women's side called *Ezrat Nashim*. This means that women can be there as well as men, but when there was a religious event then there was a gallery for the women upstairs and for the men downstairs. This is in that place. Then there is the second place which is called *Ezrat Israel*. There it is said in the Talmud that no woman can be there unless she is there for some special ritual reason. Even then, only a woman, one or two can come, but women in general must not come there. Therefore, according to the Code of Karo and later rabbinical literature, the synagogues are holier than the *Ezrat Nashim*. They are the same as the second one, as the *Ezrat Israel*. But even in this *Ezrat Nashim* it is not permissible for men and women to be there together. There are two reasons for this separation: one given in the Talmud of Babylonia and that of Jerusalem is that men and women should not be together because of the evil inclination. This would be in accordance with the Mishnah in Sukkah, 51b-52a. According to this, when the men are inside and the women outside, or women are in another place or a little higher, it would be permitted as long as they are not together. However, according to Maimonides in his explanation to the Mishnah in Sukkah, the men are not even allowed to see the women during the time of prayers. Therefore, even when the women would be separate with the men down and the women just a little higher, it would not be permitted. Only when the women are in the gallery and the men downstairs would prayer be permitted, because then they cannot see one another.

In our congregations, because of these two reasons, the men and women are not together. Even when separated in the same room with women on one side and men on the other side — it is still not permitted because of the second reason. We therefore have the women upstairs and the men downstairs. This is one basic explanation which is found in the *Chasam Sofer* 19, *Maharam Schick* 77, *Torat Chesed* 37, and *Yehudah Ya'aleh* 38.

A second explanation is that no woman, even not together with men, can enter the *Ezrat Israel*, unless only one or two women for some special reason. This can be found in Kiddushin, 52b, and the commentary of Rashi there. In other places in rabbinical literature they say that this is part of the Mosaic Law — it is called *Mideoraitha*. It is stated in the Zohar that when a woman enters the Temple together with men it is the same as placing an idol of the pagans in the Temple. This is in the Zohar to *Bamidbar*, and in *Teshuvah Me-Ahavah* 229, division 10. The same is in the book *Har Tavor*.

There is another reason: Some women have their menstrual periods and at that time they cannot be in the congregation, even upstairs. There are some of the *Poskim* who do permit it, but even they say that the women cannot be downstairs. And this continues until they go to *mikveh*. Until that time they cannot be inside. This is in the Code of Karo to Orah Chayyim, 88; and to Yoreh De'ah, 195. It is also in the *Maharam Lublin*, 59, and the *Maharit*, 132. There it is also said that the place where the women go isn't as holy as the place where the men go to pray. Because the men pray more and the women need only pray a little bit at home; therefore the place where the men pray is holier than the place where the women go to pray.

Then it is said that the place where the men prayed cannot be changed from a holy place to a secular area. Therefore we cannot make the location where men pray a place for women as well. This would be prohibited by the concept of lessening the sanctity of a holy place.

Then there is another reason since it states in the Babylonian Talmud, Sotah 48a, that "When men sing and women join in it is licentiousness; when women sing and men join in it is like fire in tow." This certainly cannot be done in a holy place. Therefore the *Shoel U-Meshiv*, Book Six, says that in the Temple of Jerusalem they did not let the women inside even when they needed to go in when it was the time for singing, praying or *mikra bikkurim* (the reading of the portion of the first fruits).

Another reason is that in the Talmud there are advices. Those advices which the people of Israel accepted as customs have the authority of law. The Talmud of Pesahim, 111a, states that it is advisable that a man should not be between two women and a woman should not be between two men. Because we took their advice in the congregation, at least, this became a law.

Another reason is that every married woman, according to the Mosaic Law, must go with her head covered in public places, especially at the time of prayer. And there it is said that we cannot pray and look at a woman whose hair is not covered. Since some of the women come to the synagogue with uncovered heads, we cannot pray at the time when they are inside. For the source see the Talmud Kethubot, 72a.

There is also another law. When a custom has been in force for centuries and no rabbis were against it, then it has the authority of law. The rabbis who come afterwards cannot change this custom until they are more in number and greater in authority. Then they can change the custom only if there is some reason for the change. If the custom has its origin in the Talmud then the rabbis can never change it.

This is found in the *Maharam Schick* 77, and even one of the greatest Talmud scholars, who was known as Rav, could not change a custom. Sixteen hundred years ago — when he came into some place and found a custom there which was against his teachings, he could not destroy this custom since it had been observed for years and years. This is cited in the Talmud Ta'anit, 28b, and discussed in many rabbinical books.

In the *Pit-hei Hayyim* it is said that a synagogue is the same as the inside room of the Temple (as I explained, there are two parts). Even when the women must do some duties together with the men, as for instance, to read the chapter of *Zakhor* in the Torah, they are still not permitted to go inside the synagogue. Rather the man must come to them to read it. There is not one book in the whole rabbinical literature since the Talmud which permits men and women to sit together in the synagogue at the time of prayer. No one since the time of the Talmud up to now has permitted this.

Q. Why are women allowed to enter the synagogue to go to a wedding?

A. Even in the Temple of Jerusalem a woman was permitted to enter when the act could not be done without her. Therefore, in case of sacrifice which she brought which could not be brought without her — she could enter. Since a wedding could not be without a woman, therefore women can enter. But at the time of prayer it is not permitted because in the Temple it was not permitted. This is found in the Talmud Kiddushin, 52b and the commentary of Rashi there.

Q. Are mixed pews ever permitted in Orthodox Synagogues?

A. No.

Q. Are late Friday evening services ever permitted?

A. No. Kabbalat Shabbat (Sundown services, reception of the Sabbath) must be before sundown.

Q. What law was given by God to Moses at Sinai?

A. The Five Books of Moses and some laws which are now in the Talmud.

Q. Would you say that the written and oral laws were revealed to Moses at Sinai?

A. Yes.

Q. Are those laws changeable — are they subject to change?

A. No.

Q. Is that equally true of the written law, as well as the oral law?

A. It is equally true.

Q. This oral and written law is divided into two kinds, one

between God and man and the other between man and man?

A. Yes.

Q. What have you to say as to whether the law between God and man may be changed or amended?

A. It can not be changed, and if amended it can be only to strengthen the old law.

Q. Do you mean by that interpreted?

A. It can be explained or interpreted.

Q. Coming now to the law between man and man, may that law be changed?

A. No, it cannot be changed.

Q. May that law be interpreted or explained?

A. Yes, it can be if it is not against the Talmudic law or the old great Talmudical scholars' explanation.

Q. With respect to the law between man and man, can other laws be added that do not change the original law?

A. Yes.

Q. With respect to the right to amend or to change the law generally, what is the distinction between the law between man and man and the law between man and God?

A. The laws between man and God we can amend only to make the old laws stronger, but the laws between man and man we can make entirely new laws which are not connected with the old ones, but not against the old laws:

Q. But the new laws you make between man and man must not contradict or overthrow the old laws between man and man?

A. Yes, certainly.

Q. Is there anything in the *halakhah* that gives the right to a Jew or to any body of Jews to change the written or oral law?

A. No.

Q. Have you in mind at this time the statements that you have just made with respect to any amendment or with respect to a prohibition in the change of the law?

A. Yes, there is in the Talmud that no one can come to change even a custom of Israel. However, a new law made by some of the rabbis to strengthen the old one can be changed by other rabbis afterwards, provided they are more in number, wisdom and position. That is, the law made by old rabbis — but the laws that are in the Talmud can never be changed.

Q. The Talmud consists, as I understand it, of the Mishnah and the Gemora?

A. Yes, there are two Talmuds, Babylonian and Jerusalem.

Q. The Mishnah is the Oral Law and the Gemora is the interpretation of that Oral Law?

A. Yes.

Q. What work in Judaism did Maimonides accomplish?

A. He made a book in which he took all the laws of the Talmud and the *Geonim* and the other rabbinical literature and brought them together in one book, but he didn't make new laws.

Q. What was Maimonides?

A. A philosopher, a doctor and a great talmudical scholar.

Q. Did he in his book set out any philosophic explanation of the laws?

A. Yes.

Q. Do I understand, you, Rabbi, to say that the Talmud is the final authority to which Judaism has always gone for the purpose of learning what is the law in Judaism?

A. Yes.

Q. Has there ever been created, since the days of the Talmud, any body or organization of men that had the power to change the interpretation of the law as found in the Talmud?

A. No.

Q. What was the work accomplished by Joseph Karo?

A. He did the same as Maimonides. He took his laws and those in the books of the other rabbis after the Rambam, and put them together in a new book. This is called the Laws of Karo.

Q. The work of Karo, do I understand, was to codify the laws and interpretation of the laws as found in the Talmud so that the ordinary illiterate Jew or man without special scholarship could know what the law was?

A. Yes, that which was in the Talmud and rabbinical literature up to his time. He made his book for the plain people to understand.

Q. Was there a body or organization of Jewry subsequent to the Karo Code that undertook to change or modify that code?

A. No.

Q. Does Jewry recognize the right of a rabbi, for the purpose of the locality in which he lives, to establish laws or customs that are binding on that particular locality but are not binding on Jewry generally — is there such a custom as that in Jewry?

A. Yes — he can make new customs that are not against the old ones. But if they are against the old ones he cannot make them.

Q. What is the binding force, if any, of a Midrash?

A. If in the Midrash there is a law against the Talmud then we take the law from the Talmud but not from the Midrash — then we consider the Midrash a mistake; but when there is a law in the Midrash which isn't in the Talmud and in no other books of the Mishnah then we follow the Midrash.

Q. The Midrash, as I understand you, is a law that has been rejected by some rabbis, and was that law, in order to give it force, afterwards adopted by Jewry generally as the law and recognized?

A. The laws not against the Talmud are recognized.

Q. In order to become a law, a Midrash in its inception, in the beginning I mean, must be adopted by all Jewry before it can become a Midrash?

A. No. Take the Mishnah. One rabbi spoke with the others and after a convention of rabbis, they made the Mishnah. The Talmud was composed the same way, but not the

Midrash. The Midrash was compiled as follows: some rabbis took part of one rabbi's writings and part of another rabbi's writings and made an encyclopedic volume. In it are some commentaries on the Bible, some legends, and some letters. Therefore, when looking into the Midrash, one must also remember the Talmud. When looking in the Midrash alone, we cannot follow this law if we find in the Talmud otherwise. But when this law is a new law and is not in the Talmud, then we can and must go by the Midrash. And the same as the Midrash is the Zohar.

Q. How does Zohar differ from Midrash?

A. The same, but the Zohar is more cabalistic or mystical.

Q. Do you mean by that that it has its origin in some Oriental time?

A. Yes.

Q. Does it have the force of law?

A. When it isn't against the Talmud — the same as the Midrash.

Q. There is another body of laws or commentaries, as I understand it: is it called *Sofrim*?

A. It is the same as rabbinical literature. It is what a large number of writers have said on religious subjects — this is *Sofrim*.

Q. That is not of any force except as a commentary — if it is contrary to the Talmud it has no force at all?

A. No, nothing.

Q. In order to get at what the actual law is, the Rabbi must in all cases go right back to his Talmud?

A. Yes. If the origin is in the Talmud, it is a law.

Q. Assuming that proof establishes any of the following facts, I ask you whether such facts if so established are in accordance with or contrary to the doctrine, belief, ritual or practice of Orthodox or Traditional Judaism:

Q1. A public announcement in the Synagogue by the rabbi that the Pentateuch or Five Books of Moses were not inspired by God; were not written by Moses; and that the

Decalogue or Ten Commandments were not given or revealed by God to Moses at Sinai?

A. This is heresy and it is said in the Mishnah of Sanhedrin, 90a, that this man's soul will not survive in the other world.

Q1a. Suppose a Rabbi says from his pulpit to his congregation that the story of the flood is a myth, has no foundation in fact, and that a twelve-year-old boy would not believe it: Is that considered within or without?

A. I view this as heresy.

Q2. The seating of men and women together during services in the Synagogue?

A. It is contrary to all the sources in the Talmud.

Q2a. The failure of the rabbi to say grace after meals at congregational dinners.

A. This is contrary to Mosaic Law and Talmudic Law.

Q3. In connection with that which you say that it is contrary to the Mosaic Law — is there such a law found in the Pentateuch?

A. Yes.

Q3a. Commanding that grace be said after congregational dinner?

A. Yes.

Q3b. And it is explained in the Talmud too, that it is in the Five Books of Moses?

A. The place in the Talmud is Berakhot, 21a.

Q3c. Then it is not simply a custom but it is a law?

A. It is a law, unless a man is eating *trefah*, then he could not pray after the meal, which in itself is unlawful.

Q4. Permitting the rabbi to forbid the priests to pronounce the priestly blessing during the Holiday services.

A. This is contrary to the Talmud, which is originally in the Five Books.

Q4a. You say that it is a law, not a custom?

A. Yes, a law.

Q4b. Have you in mind at this moment the particular citation in the Talmud where the law is found, or in the Pentateuch?

A. Yes — in the Pentateuch in Nasso — in the Talmud in Sotah, Shabbat, Kethubot, and other places.

Q5. Is the rabbi permitted to forbid the ceremony of kneeling during the services on the Day of Atonement?

A. This is contrary to traditional customs and no custom can be changed. While this is not a law in respect to the synagogue, it was a law in respect to the Temple. In the Temple the law provided that kneeling should take place on the Day of Atonement, and that insofar as the synagogue is concerned, Jewry through the centuries have adopted the law as a custom found in the Temple — and therefore, insofar as the synagogue is concerned it has become a custom with the force of law. That at least the cantor and the rabbi shall kneel — and that no custom can be changed—and this is in *Chasam Sofer*, Yoreh De'ah, 107.

Q5a. What is the authority for the kneeling in the Temple on the Day of Atonement?

A. In the Talmud Yoma, Tamid and Midot — and this is in the Temple, and on the Day of Atonement the custom is in the commentaries and in the *Matteh Ephraim* and other codes.

Q5b. What do you say of the duty of the rabbi and the cantor to kneel upon certain occasions for instance, the Day of Atonement and New Year's?

A. On the Day of Atonement and New Year's they are permitted and must kneel, but not on other days. But they must kneel on these three days — and on these days, Atonement four times, on New Year's — once each day.

Q6. By permitting and authorizing the omission of the beginning of the hymn *El Adon* meaning "Almighty Master" in Sabbath morning services.

A. It isn't done by a rabbi, and if so he isn't following Traditional Judaism.

Q6a. There is no law for it?

A. No, custom is a law. It is a custom.

Q6b. What is the source or authority of this custom?

A. The authority for this is in the old prayer books — this prayer is found in the prayer books used in the Orthodox Synagogue.

Q6c. Made up when — what was its origin?

A. I cannot tell you the right date, but it is more than 600 years. Some prayers are 1600 years old, some 1800 years old — some go back further.

Q6d. The prayers that are contained in the prayer book, do you know from where those prayers were taken?

A. Some from the Talmud and some are taken from the Psalms of David — and some which are taken from time to time from the great rabbis since the Talmud.

Q6e. Does the prayerbook, which itself is 600 years old, contain prayers that are a good deal older?

A. Some of them are in the Psalms and some in the Talmud, as well as from the *Anshe Kneset Hagedolah* — which means members of the Great Assembly.

Q6f. When you say the "Great Assembly" do you mean at the time of Ezra, 444 B.C.E.?

A. Yes.

Q7. By permitting the rabbi in his sermons and in conversation to ridicule and belittle the great religious figures in Israel; that is the men who have been prominent in the history of Israel.

A. Contrary to the Talmud Sanhedrin 99b, and Baba Metzia 85b.

Q8. By forbidding the standing of the congregation when the Ark is opened.

A. This is contrary to the customs and the custom can be found in old Machzorim and in *Mateh Ephraim*.

Q8a. Was this a custom that was practiced in the Temple?

A. There was no opening of the Ark in the Temple, because the Ark was inside and the people were outside.

Q8b. How old is this custom that you speak of?

A. I believe it is a couple of hundred years old — about 1200 years. But the origin of this is in the Talmud that when the Ark is opened — then the people must stand. They must wait until they take the scrolls out and right after the opening they must stand — and therefore, it is the custom that at any time when the Ark is open the people stand. This is found in the Talmud Megillah.

Q8c. That custom you say finds its foundation in the Talmud?

A. Yes, and the Talmud explains this further regarding a verse in the Book of Ezra, and the Talmud has taken this custom from the Book of Ezra.

Q9. By forbidding the mourners in the congregation to say Kaddish individually in a voice audible to the congregation.

A. If they are saying the Kaddish together that is all right, but their voices should be heard by the people so that they may answer amen.

Q9a. Does this practice rest in custom, or does it rest in law?

A. In custom, but this custom is found in the Talmud also.

Q10. The omission to wash the hands before meals at congregational dinners.

A. This is contrary to the Talmudical law.

Q10a. Have you in mind the particular authority in the Talmud where that is found?

A. Yes — Chullin, 106a, and in the Code of Karo, Orah Hayyim, 160-162, etc.

Q11. The eating with uncovered heads at congregational dinners.

A. This is a custom which originated in the Talmud too, but afterwards some of the *Poskim* explained that at the time of prayers they could not be without hats. Even to say a prayer at the meals, they are not permitted without hats. This originated in the Talmud and in the Code of the *Birkhei Yoseph*, chapter two, and in other places. After that it was a custom that especially a rabbi should not go without a hat in general, and especially at meals.

Q12. [How do you view] the kissing of brides by the rabbi during marriage ceremonies?

A. It is said that when a man does this we cannot believe him even as a witness — this is according to Maimonides, *Hilkhos Sanhedrin* 19, and in *Shoel UMeshiv* book 4, part 3, chapter 132, and according to all the *Poskim* [his conduct] is contrary to the Mosaic law.

Q13. The omission of the seven blessings at the wedding table.

A. It is contrary to Karo's Code.

Q13a. Do you have in mind the particular authority?

A. It is in the Talmud Kethubot, 8a — and in *Karo, Even Haezer* 62.

Q14. The carrying of books by the rabbi openly through the streets on the Sabbath Day while on his way to service.

A. It is contrary to the Talmud Shabbat, and it originated from the Mosaic law.

Q15. What is the idea in back of that law about carrying books?

A. When the Jewish people were in the desert or wilderness there were two places, one place which was considered a private place, *Reshut Hayachid*, and the second place was the public place, called *Reshut Harabim* — and in the Mosaic law it is said that no work can be done on Saturday — and the work at that time was carrying from the private place to the public place and from the public place to the private place. Therefore, it was counted as work, and no work can be done on Saturday — and therefore even at this time nothing can be carried from the private places to the public places. (From the house to the streeet.) Especially is this so in cities where over 600,000 population reside.

Q16. The omission of that part of the Sabbath service beginning with *Pitum Haktoret* having reference to the composition of the incense.

A. Contrary to Jewish custom which is in the Talmud.

Q17. Omission to recite on most Holidays the poetry known as *Piyutim.*

A. This is said in some places — there are also some places that do not say these *Piyutim* — but in the places where the custom is that they should say it, no rabbi can omit it, as stated in Talmud Ta'anit, 28b.

Q18. By permitting the rabbi to be absent regularly from Friday evening services known as Kabbalat Shabbat (reception of the Sabbath).

A. Contrary to traditional laws.

Q18a. Have you any authority for that in the Talmud?

A. Maybe he is praying at home, but in the Talmud there are two sources which state that he must pray in the synagogue. This is mentioned in Baba Kamma 60b and in Berakhot 8a. The Talmud continues in Berakhot and declares, "Whosoever has a synagogue in his town and does not go there in order to pray is called an evil neighbor." In Avot of Rabbi Nathan, chapter 36, and *Derekh Eretz Rabba*, chapter 11, it says that such a man's soul does not survive after death. The Jerusalem Talmud Berakhot, chapter 5, says that he who does not enter the synagogue in this world will not be taken into the holy synagogue in the world to come.

Q19. Refusal of the rabbi and Board of Trustees to appear for trial on summons issued by the Union of Orthodox Rabbis of the United States and Canada.

A. It is contrary to traditional law, which is in Yoreh De'ah 334, and *Choshen Mishpat,* the laws of *dayanim,* and Talmud Baba Kamma, 113a.

Q20. By permitting the reading of the scrolls during services by facing the audience.

A. This is wrong, and it is in the Book *Mikrae Kodesh*, page 2, and has its origin in the Bible.

Q21. By abolishing daily study of the Mishnah and Talmud.

A. Contrary to a Rabbi's ethics and every rabbi must try to study daily.

Q22. Permitting the rabbi to close the main synagogue on Sabbath afternoons where previously 200 attended lectures.

A. This is nothing if there are other places.

Q23. By permitting slurs against Orthodox traditions.

A. This is contrary to Traditional Judaism.

Q24. By permitting the cantor and choir not to officiate at

Friday evening services known as Kabbalat Shabbat, but only at the late Friday evening services.

A. He has no right to do this. But once the cantor officiates at late Friday services, I would not allow him to officiate at any services in my synagogue. To attend late Friday evening services and not sundown services on Friday, is contrary to Orthodox practice and Traditional Judaism.

Q25. By permitting the rabbi to urge and advise the congregation from the pulpit on Rosh Hashanah to read and study the book known as the *Mind in the Making* by Dr. James Harvey Robinson, forbidden by certain colleges on account of its radical tendencies.

A. An Orthodox rabbi would not advise this.

Q26. By permitting the omission of the blessing before meals at congregational dinners.

A. This is contrary to the Talmud.

Q26a. Have you a particular authority in the Talmud?

A. It is in Berakhot, chapter 6.

Q27. By permitting the rabbi to be absent regularly from daily evening or morning services.

A. It is the same answer as Q.18a — that he is a bad neighbor and his soul will not be taken into the holy synagogue in the world to come.

Q28. By permitting the rabbi to insult from the pulpit and threaten the expulsion of members who dare to criticize the changes forced on the congregation by him.

A. Against the ethics of a rabbi.

Q29. By permitting the rabbi to partake of meals at public hotels and restaurants and at public affairs without enquiring concerning *Kashrut* known as the dietary laws of Moses.

A. This is contrary to Traditional law.

Q29a. Have you any particular authority?

A. Tosefta and Maimonides — that when there are a lot of restaurants that are not kosher he must inquire for one which is kosher. Tosefta Avodah Zarah, chapter two: and Jerusalem Talmud Avodah Zarah, chapter five;

Rambam, *Maachalot Assurot*, chapter 11; and Karo Code, Yoreh De'ah, 119.

Q30. By permitting the rabbi to hold graduation exercises and distribute prizes and diplomas to be carried home by graduates on a Friday night.

A. This is wrong because it is the same as if he was doing it when he makes others do wrong. This is in the Talmud too, in Niddah, 57a; Avodah Zarah 6a, 14a, 22a; and Pesahim 22b and other places.

Q31. By permitting the rabbi and Forum Committee to invite speakers on Sunday mornings who are widely known for their religious radical tendencies to address young men and women.

A. It only shows that he isn't going in the way of Traditional Judaism.

Q32. By omitting during the services the calling of one by his biblical name to the reading of the Torah.

A. In the places where it is the custom to call everyone by his biblical name it cannot be changed, and this is [stated] in the Karo codes, and [is] according to Ta'anit 28b [and] not changeable.

———————————

Signature of the Witness

APPENDIX **3**

Bibliographies

RABBI ELIEZER SILVER'S   רשימה של חידושי־תורה ודברי
PUBLISHED WRITINGS   *מחשבה של הרב אליעזר זילבר ז"ל

1) אייר תרע"ז: "קושיא בענין דיחוויי בעל חי" וגם "בדין מופלא הסמוך
לאיש" — **יגדיל תורה,** שנה שניה (להוסדו והופעתו בארה"ב),
קונטרס שני, סימן י"ד, עמודים ל"ט־מ"א.

2) תרפ"א: "כיבוס מטומאה" — **דגל התורה** בעריכת מנחם כשר, ורשא,
סימן נ"ו, דף מ"ב, עמוד ב'.

3) תרפ"ב: "מקדש בעגלה ערופה" — **דגל התורה** בעריכת מנחם כשר, סימן
א', דף ק, עמוד א'.

4) תרפ"ה: "בענין מנחה שנתערב בחולין" — **מגדל תורה** בעריכת משה
בנימין טאמאשאוו, נוא־יארק, עמודים מ"ד־מ"ז.

5) ניסן תרפ"ז: "קדשים־שלמים שנשחט לשם עולה" — **הפרדס,** שנה א',
חוברת א', סימן ד', עמודים ד'־ו.

6) תרפ"ז: הסכמה כוללת חידושי תורה לספר **קרנות המזבח** לאברהם
שמואל זילבערשטיין, לובלין, עמודים ח"י־ג.

7) אלול תרפ"ז־תשרי תרפ"ח: "נדרים ונדבות" — **הפרדס,** שנה א', חוברת
ו־ז, סימן ס', עמודים ג־ד.

8) תרפ"ט: חידושי תורה מצוטטים בספר **המאור** לאלעזר מאיר פרייל,
ירושלים, חלק ראשון, סימן ס"א, עמוד רע"ו; וסימן ס"ד, עמודים
רצ"ד־רצ"ה.

9) סיון תר"ץ: "חינוך כהונה" — **הפרדס,** שנה ד', חוברת ג', סימן א', עמודים
ו־ז.

10) טיון תרצ"א: "כוזן גדול בירושלים" — **הפרדס,** שנה ה', חוברת ג', סימן
כ"ג, עמודים ז־ח.

---

* נעזרתי בהכנת הרשימה הזאת במכתבו של הרב דוד איש־צמח (וקסמן) ז"ל מפתח
תקוה להרב דוד זילבר, ט"ו סיון תשל"ב.
לעיל בפרק התשיעי יש דיון על תורתו של הרב אליעזר זילבר.

348

11) סיון תרצ״ב: "בעניני מעילה בהקדש ומשלחן גבוה קזכו" — **הפרדס**, שנה ו', חוברת ג', סימן י״ד, עמודים ט״ו.

12) תרצ״ג: הסכמה כוללת חידושי תורה לספר **זכרון שלמה** לשלמה בעגלאייזען, לובלין, עמוד ג.

13) כסלו תרצ״ד: "הצטרפות הכוחות או עבודות וזמנים" — **הפרדס**, שנה ז', חוברת ט', סימן נ״ח, עמודים כ-כ״ג.

14) סיון תרצ״ד: "בענין נר המערבי" — **הפרדס**, שנה ח', חוברת ג', עמודים ד-ה.

15) אלול תרצ״ח: "פרקים מהדרן על סיום הש״ס" — **הפרדס**, שנה י״ב, חוברת ו', עמודים ה-ז.

16) תשרי-חשון ת״ש: הסכמה לאיסור על עופות הנשחטים מבלי סימני ועד הכשרות הכלל — **המסלה** (יוצא לאור ע״י ועד הרבנים דנוא-יארק רבתי), שנה ד', חוברת ט-י', עמוד י.

17) כסלו תש״ג: "מעילה" — **מתיבתא** (ירחון תורני של מתיבתא תורה ודעת, ברוקלין) שנה א' חוברת ב', עמודים ג-ד.

18) טבת תש״ג: "בעניני אגודת ישראל" — **ספר היובל לשנת השלושים של אגודת ישראל** בעריכת שבתי הלוי שנפפלד, לונדון, עמודים ז-ח.

19) תש״ג: "מכתב בעניני הכלל ואגוה״ר" — בספר **צבי חמד. קונטרס עונג וגם שמחה** לצבי הירש פריעדמאן, נוא-יארק, עמודים ע״ב-ע״ג.

20) אב תש״ד: "שיעור דף יומי-זבחים קי״ז בכנסיה של אגודת ישראל" — **הפרדס**, שנה י״ח, חוברת ה', עמודים כ״א-כ״ב.

21) תש״ה: הגהות על ספר **חוסן יוסף** של יוסף ענגיל (מוציא לאור אשר העתיק את הספר הנוכחי מאת כתב ידו של המחבר-יואל פינק), הוצאת ש.י. פעלדהיים, נוא-יארק.

22) תש״ו: "חידושי תורה וביאורים" על ספר **נפש חיה** לחיים אלעזר וואקס מקאליש, הוצאת האחים שולזינגר, נוא-יארק, עמודים א-ח בסוף.

23) תש״ט: "בענין קביעות סעודה על ידי קידוש" — **שערים מצויינים בהלכה** (על קיצור שולחן ערוך) לשלמה זלמן ברוין, נוא-יארק, חלק שני, עמוד פ״ו.

24) תש״ט: "בענין עוף טמא" — **תורה שלמה**, בעריכת מנחם כשר. חלק א' לבראשית א', עמוד קמ״ז בהערה.

25) תשי״א: "בענין הכנסת טומאה למקדש" — **ספר היובל הפרדס** בעריכת שמחה עלברג, נוא-יארק, עמודים ט״ו-י״ח.

26) תשי״ב: "בענין כהן בבית הקברות" — **כל בו על אבלות**, ליקותיאל יהודה גרינוואלד, נוא-יארק, חלק ג', עמוד ע״ה.

27) ניסן תשי״ב: "בדין נזירות בעבר" — **הפרדס**, שנה כ״ו, חוברת ז', עמודים א-ג.

28) תשרי תשי״ג: "הוראה ופסק הלכה למעשה בענין דזשעלאטיין" — **כרם** (ירחון להלכה ולמדע היהדות) בעריכת אהרן חיים צימערמאן, נוא-יארק, שנה ב', עמודים ה-ט.

29) תשי"ג: הסכמה כוללת חידושי תורה לספר **עבודת תמיד** למרדכי צבי שוַארץ, נוא-יַארק, עמוד י.

30) תשרי תשי"ד: "מאמר בענין קדשים" — **כרם**, עמודים כ"ז-כ"ח.

31) חשון-כסלו תשי"ד: "מאמר בענין טהרות" — **כרם**, עמודים א-ב.

32) כסלו תשי"ד: "החזון איש והערות על ספריו" — **הפרדס**, שנה כ"ח, חוברת ג', עמודים ג-ה.

33) אדר א' תשי"ד: "בדין אין שבות למקדש" — **הפרדס**, שנה כ"ח, חוברת ו', עמודים א-ב.

34) תשט"ו: חידושי תורה מצוטטים בספר **המאור** לאלעזר מאיר פרייל, ברוקלין, חלק שני, סימן י"ג, עמוד כ"ה; וסימן י"ד, עמוד כ"ו.

35) תשט"ז: סיפור אודות ר' חיים בריסקאר מצוטט בויקהל **משה** למשה גרדון, נוא-יַארק, חלק שני, עמוד ר"ל.

36) תשט"ז: "בענין מקואות, חלב עכו"ם, יחוד עם אשה בעלוויטַאר ובטקסי" — **טהרת יום טוב** לחנניא יום טוב ליפא דויטש, נוא יארק, חלק ז', עמודים מ"ח-מ"ט.

37) תמוז תשי"ז: "דין שרפה בבשר שנטמא באב ובולד הטומאה" — **הפרדס**, שנה ל"א, חוברת י, עמודים ה-ו.

38) תשי"ז: אגרות בעניני צניעות, מילה, שחיטה, ומשגיחי כשרות — **טהרת יום טוב** לחנניא יום טוב ליפא דויטש, נוא-יַארק, חלק ח', עמודים נ"ה-נ"ו, ס"א-ס"ב.

39) תשי"ז: דברי פתיחה וקונטרס דברי תורה — **דברי ימי ועד הצלה**, נוא-יַארק, עמודים א-ס"ב; ובחלק האנגלי עמודים ז-ס"ד.

40) תשי"ז: "שריפת פרים הנשרפים" — **פרי עץ חיים** (מוקדש לזכרונו של מרן הגאון ר' אליה מאיר בלוך ע"י הסתדרות תלמידי ישיבת טלז), קליוולַאנד, עמודים ע"א-ע"ד.

41) ניסן תשי"ח: "מאמר בענין כהן גדול בירושלים" — **כרם**, עמודים א-ב.

42) סיון תשי"ח: "גדר יחיד, ושותפין" — **הפרדס**, שנה ל"ב, חוברת ט', עמודים ז-ח, כ"ט.

43) חשון-כסלו תשי"ט: "פלפול לחנוכה באגוה"ר"—**המאור**, שנה י', חוברת ב', עמודים ג-ד.

44) טבת תשי"ט: "על חגיגת הבת מצוה, ועל השחיטה התלויה" וגם "דיר ישראל וחולבים עכו"ם" — **המאור**, שנה י', חוברת ג', עמודים כ"ו-כ"ז; ל"ד.

45) טבת תשי"ט: "שריפת קדשים בלשכות" — **הפרדס**, שנה ל"ג, חוברת ד', עמודים ה-ו.

46) תשרי תש"ך: "בדין חטאות העוף ועולת בהמה" — **המאור**, שנה י"א, חוברת א' עמודים ג-ד.

47) טבת תש"ך: "כל שבידו לא היה דיחוי" — **הפרדס**, שנה ל"ד, חוברת ד', עמודים ז-ט.

48) סיון תש״ך: ״איסור ניתוח מתים״ — **הפרדס**, שנה ל״ד, חוברת ט׳, עמודים ט״ו-ט״ז.

49) תש״ך: **ענפי אר״ז**, חלק ראשון, ערכי א׳-ב׳, ברוקלין, נוא-יארק.

50) תשכ״ב: ״בעניין ברכה על ענבים שעם גרעינים ובלי גרעינים״ — בספר **יסודי ישורון** לגדליה פעלדער, נוא-יארק, חלק ד׳, עמודים iii-iv.

51) תשכ״ג: ״בדין קדשים שנשחטו לשם חולין״ — **בספר היובל לרב ד״ר ישראל אלפנבין**, בעריכת י.ל. הכהן מימון, ירושלים, עמודים צ״ט-ק״א.

52) תשכ״ה: **ענפי אר״ז**, חלקים ב׳-ג׳, ערכי ג׳-ת׳, ברוקלין, נוא-יארק.

53) תשכ״ו: אגרות המצטטות את תורתו **בספר דברי יהושע** ליהושע קלעוואן, נוא-יארק, עמודים ק-ק״ח.

54) תשכ״ז: ״בדין שאשה אסורה להיכנס לבית הכנסת כשאין שם מחיצה כשרה המבדלת״ — **שו״ת המאור** בעריכת מאיר אמסעל, נוא-יארק, כרך א׳, עמוד מ׳.

55) תש״ל: ״בדיני פיגול״ — **אחיעזר. קובץ אגרות**, חליפת מכתבים עם ר׳ חיים עוזר בעריכת אהרן סורסקי, בני ברק, חלק א׳, עמודים ע״ט-פ״א.

56) תשל״ד: ״בדיני טרפות ובאיסור אבר מן החי״ — בספר **היכל צמח** לצמח האפענבערג, ירושלים, סימן מ״ו, עמודים קנ״ט-קס״א.

57) תשל״ה: **צמח אר״ז**, ברוקלין, נוא-יארק.

58) תשל״ט: ״על דברי הר״ן במגילה ובד׳ כוסות״ — **עם התורה** (חוברת תורנית של צעירי אגודת ישראל בארה״ב), חוברת י״א, עמודים ט-י״ג.

GENERAL BIBLIOGRAPHY

*English Books**

Adler, Cyrus, ed. *The American Jewish Yearbook: 5663 (1902-1903)*. Philadelphia: Jewish Publication Society of America, 1902

Avery, Edwina Austin, ed. *Laws Applicable to Immigration and Nationality*. Washington D.C., 1953

Berman, Jeremiah, J. *Shehitah*. New York: Bloch Publishing Co., 1941

Cahan, Abraham. *The Education of Abraham Cahan*. Translated by Leon Stein, Abraham P. Cohan, and Lynn Davison. Philadelphia: Jewish Publication Society of America, 1969

Cohen, Morris Raphael. *A Dreamer's Journey*. Boston: Beacon Press, 1949

Davidowicz, Lucy. *The War Against the Jews 1933-1945*. New York: Holt, Rinehart and Winston, 1975

Drachman, Bernard. *The Unfailing Light*. New York: Rabbinical Council of America, 1948

Eckman, Lester Samuel. *Revered by All*. New York: Shengold Publishers, 1974

Epstein, Louis. *Marriage Laws in the Bible and the Talmud*. Cambridge, Massachusetts: Harvard University Press, 1942

Friedenwald, Herbert, ed. *The American Jewish Yearbook: 5672 (1911-1912)*. Philadelphia: Jewish Publication Society of America, 1911

Gastwirt, Harold P. *Fraud, Corruption and Holiness*. New York: Kennikat Press, 1974

Goldman, Alex J. *Giants of Faith*. New York: Citadel Press, 1964

Gordon, Benjamin L. *Between Two Worlds*. New York, 1952

Grinstein, Hyman B. *The Rise of the Jewish Community of New York: 1654-1860*. Philadelphia: Jewish Publication Society of America, 1945

Gutstein, Morris A. *A Priceless Heritage*. New York: Bloch Publishing Co., 1953

---

*Abbreviations:

AJYB   *American Jewish Year Book*

PAJHS   *Publication of the American Jewish Historical Society*

Hapgood, Hutchins. *The Spirit of the Ghetto*. New York: Funk and Wagnalls Co., 1909

Howe, Irving. *World of Our Fathers*. New York: Harcourt, Brace, Jovanovich, 1976

Ibn Daud, Abraham. *Sefer Ha-Qabbalah: The Book of Tradition*. Translated by Gerson D. Cohen. Philadelphia: Jewish Publication Society of America, 1967

The Inauguration of Samuel Belkin: May 23, 1944. New York: Rabbi Isaac Elchanan Theological Seminary and Yeshiva College, 1945

The Jewish Communal Register: 1917-1918. New York: Kehillah, 1918

Joseph, Samuel. *Jewish Immigration to the United States from 1881 to 1910*. New York: Columbia University Press, 1914

Kehilath Jeshurun Year Book: 1946. New York, 1946

Kinot for the Ninth of Av. Transl. Abraham Rosenfeld. London, 1965

Klaperman, Gilbert. *The Story of Yeshiva University: The First Jewish University in America*. London: The Macmillan Company, 1969

Kranzler, David. *Japanese, Nazis and Jews*. New York; Yeshiva University Press, 1976

Kranzler, George. *Williamsburg: A Jewish Community in Transition*. New York: Philipp Feldheim, 1961

Liebman, Charles S. *The Ambivalent American Jew*. Philadelphia: Jewish Publication Society of America, 1973

Litvin, Baruch. *The Sanctity of the Synagogue*. New York: Spero Foundation, 1959

Pelcovitz, Ralph. *Danger and Opportunity: Essays on Traditional Judaism in a Time of Crisis*. New York: Shengold Publishers, 1976

Rischin, Moses. *The Promised City: New York's Jews, 1870-1914*. Cambridge, Mass.: Harvard University Press, 1962

Rosenman, Samuel I. *Working With Roosevelt*. New York: Harper and Brothers, 1952

Rothkoff, Aaron. *Bernard Revel: Builder of American Jewish Orthodoxy*. Philadelphia: Jewish Publication Society of America, 1972

Rubin, Israel. *Satmar: An Island in the City*. New York: Quadrangle Books, 1972

Rudavsky, David. *Modern Jewish Religious Movements: A History of Emancipation and Adjustment*. New York: Behrman Paperback, 1967

Sachs, A.S. *Worlds that Passed*. Philadelphia: Jewish Publication Society of America, 1928

Schiff, Alvin Irwin. *The Jewish Day School in America.* New York: Jewish Education Committee Press, 1966

Schniederman, Harry, ed. *The American Jewish Yearbook:5686 (1925-1926).* Philadelphia: Jewish Publication Society of America, 1925

———*The American Jewish Yearbook: 5692 (1931-1932).* Philadelphia: Jewish Publication Society of America, 1931

Schwab, Herman. *The History of Orthodox Jewry in Germany.* London: Mitre Press, 1950

Shimoff, Ephraim. *Rabbi Isaac Elchanan Spektor.* New York: Sura Institute and Yeshiva University, 1959

Simon, Solomon. *In the Thicket.* Philadelphia: Jewish Publication Society of America, 1963

Weinstein, Jacob J. *Solomon Goldman: A Rabbi's Rabbi.* New York: Ktav Publishing House, 1973

Wiernik, Peter. *History of the Jews in America.* New York: Jewish Press Publishing Co., 1912

Wiesenthal, Simon. *The Murderers Among Us.* London: Heinemann Publishers, 1967

Yaakov Rosenheim Memorial Anthology. New York: Orthodox Library, 1968

Hebrew Books

Album, Zvi Shimon, *Sefer Divre Emet.* 2 vols. Chicago, 1904 and 1912

Amsel, Meir, ed. *She'eylot u-Teshuvot ha-Maor.* New York, 1967

Braun, Solomon. *She'arim Metzuyanim be-Halakhah* on the *Kitzur Shulhan Arukh.* New York: Hadar Publishing Co., 1951

Constitution of the United Orthodox Rabbis of America. New York: Zim Publishing, 1902

Divrei Yemei Vaad Hatzala. New York: Vaad Hatzala, 1957

Eisenstadt, Ben-Zion. *Hakhmei Yisrael Be-America.* New York, 1903

Eisenstein, Judah David. *Otzar Zikhronothai.* New York, 1929

Eliav, Mordecai, ed. *Ani Ma'amin.* Jerusalem: Mossad Harav Kook, 1965

Epstein, Louis. *Hatza'ah Lema'an Takanat Agunot.* New York, 1930

———*Leshe'eylat ha-Agunah.* New York, 1940

Epstein, Yehiel Michal. *Arukh ha-Shulhan*

Federbusch, Simon, ed. *Torah u-Melukhah.* Jerusalem: Mossad Harav Kook, 1961

Freiman, Abraham Hayyim. *Seder Kiddushin ve-Nissuin.* Jerusalem: Mossad Harav Kook, 1945

Glickman-Porush, Menahem. *Ish ha-Halakhah veha-Maaseh.* Jerusalem, 1947

Gottlieb, Samuel. *Ohalei Shem.* Pinsk, 1912

Jacobson, Benjamin Zev. *Esah De'i le-Merahok.* Bene-Berak: Netzah, 1967

Kaplan, Zev. *Edut be-Yaakov.* Warsaw, 1904

Kasher, Menahem. *Ha-Tekufah ha-Gedolah.* Jerusalem: Torah Shelemah Institute, 1968

—— *Torah Shelemah,* Volume One. New York, 1949

Katz, Dov. *Tenuat ha-Mussar.* 5 vols. Tel Aviv: Abraham Zioni, 1958-63

ha-Kohen (Kagan), Israel Meir. *Niddehei Yisrael.* Warsaw, 1894

Konvitz, Joseph. *Divrei Joseph.* 2 vols. New York, 1947-48

K'vod Chachomim. Philadelphia: Jubilee Volume in Honor of Bernard Levinthal's Seventieth Birthday, 1935

Landau, Bezalel. *Ha-Gaon mi-Tshebin.* Jerusalem: Hotza'at Usha, 1967

Ledor Aharon. New York: Agudat Harabanim, 1937

Leoni, Eliezer, ed. *Wolozhin.* Tel Aviv: Wolozhin Landsleit Associations, 1970

Levy, Simcha. *Simhat ha-Levi.* New York: Shulsinger Bros. 1967

Lewin, Binyamin, M. *Otzar ha-Geonim* to Baba Kamma

Lipschitz, Jacob ha-Levi. *Toledot Yitzhak.* Warsaw, 1897

—— *Zikhron Ya'akov.* 3 vols. Kovno, 1924-30

Livazer, Hersh. *Birkhato Shel ha-Rebbe.* Jerusalem, 1976

Medini, Hayyim Hezekiah. *Sedei Hemed*

Paris, Norman, ed. *Brocho L'Menachem.* Saint Louis, 1955

Rackman, David. *Kiryat Hanah David.* New York: Shulsinger Brothers, 1967

Rand, Oscar Z., ed. *Eduth Le-Yisrael.* New York: Ezras Torah, n.d.

—— ed. *Toldot Anshe Shem.* New York, 1950

Rosing, Abraham Ephraim. *Yemei Shenotai: Madbeah Shel Abraham,* 1971

Rothstein, Shmuel. *Ahiezer.* Tel Aviv: Netzah, n.d.

Sefer ha-Yovel Shel Agudat Harabanim: 1902-1927. New York: Agudat Harabanim, 1928

Seidman, Hillel. *Reb Shraga Feivel Mendlowitz.* New York: Shengold Publishers, 1976

Shurin, Aharon Ben-Zion. *Keshet Giborim*. Jerusalem: Mossad Harav Kook, 1964

Silver, Eliezer. *Anfei Erez*. 2 vols. New York, 1960, 1965

Soloveitchik, Joseph Baer. *Beit ha-Levi*

Soloveitchik, Joseph B. *Be-Sod ha-Yahid ve-ha-Yahad*. Jerusalem, Orot, 1976

Stern, Joseph Zechariah. *Zekher Yehosof*

Sursky, Aaron. *Ahiezer*. 2 vols. Bene-Berak: Netzah, 1970

Teitelbaum, Joel. *Al ha-Geulah ve-al ha-Temurah*. New York: Jerusalem Publishers, 1967

Urbach, Ephraim E. *Ba'alei ha-Tosafot*. Jerusalem: Bialik Institute, 1955

Wachs, Hayyim Elazar. *Nefesh Hayah*. New York: Shulsinger Brothers, 1946

Waldenberg, Eliezer Yehudah. *Tzitz Eliezer*. Vol. 5. Jerusalem, 1957

Weinberger, Moshe. *Ha-Yehudim veha-Yahadut be-New York*. New York, 1887

Willowski-Ridbaz, Jacob David. *Nimukei Ridbaz al ha-Torah: Bereshit u-Shemot*. Chicago, 1904

Yehezkeli-Prager, Moshe. *Nes ha-Hatzalah Shel ha-Rebbe me-Gur*. Jerusalem: Yeshurun, 1959

Zevin, Shlomo Joseph. *Ishim ve-Shitot*. Tel Aviv: Bitan ha-Sefer, 1952

Articles

Bat-Yehuda, Geulah. "Yitzhak Eizik Halevi Herzog." In *Men of the Spirit*, ed. Leo Jung. New York: Kymson Publishing Co., 1964, pp. 123-138

Davis, Moshe. "Jewish Religious Life and Institutions in America." In *The Jews: Their History, Culture and Religion*, ed. Louis Finkelstein. Philadelphia: Jewish Publication Society of America, 1960, 1:539

Epstein, Joseph. "Yeshivat Mir." In *Mosdot ha-Torah be-Europa: be-Vinyanam uve-Hurbanam,* ed. Samuel K. Mirsky. New York: Ogen Publishing House of Histadruth Ivrith of America, 1956, pp. 116-132 (Hebrew)

Even, Isaac. "Chassidim in the New World." In *The Jewish Communal Register: 1917- 1918*. New York: Kehillah, 1918, pp. 341-346

Feinstein, Yehiel Michal. "Eulogy for Rabbi Eliezer Silver." In *Kovetz*

Rabbani Torani, ed. Hayyim Greenberg, Nisan-Ellul 5729-1969, pp. 3-4 (Hebrew)

Goldstein, Sidney. "Springfield." In *Encyclopedia Judaica*, ed. Cecil Roth and Geoffrey Wigoder. Jerusalem: Keter Publishing House, 1971, 15:318-19

Gottlieb, Moshe. "The First of April Boycott and the Reaction of the American Jewish Community." In *PAJHS*, 57, no. 4 (June 1968), pp. 516-556

———"In the Shadow of War: The American Anti-Nazi Boycott Movement in 1939-41." In *PAJHS* 62, no. 2 (December 1972), pp. 146-161

Grinstein, Hyman B. "The Efforts of East European Jewry to Organize its Own Community in the United States." In *PAJHS*, 49, no.2 (December 1959), pp. 73-76

Gross, Alexander and Kaminetsky, Joseph. "Shraga Feivel Mendlowitz." In *Men of the Spirit*, edited by Leo Jung. New York: Kymson Publishing Co., 1964

Herzog, Issac Halevy. *Massa Hatzalah*. Jerusalem, 1947 (Hebrew)

Isaacs, Judah M. "Abraham Jacob Gershon Lesser." In *Guardians of Our Heritage*, ed. Leo Jung. New York: Bloch Publishing Co., 1958, pp. 347-359

Kagan, Shaul. "Reb Aharon Kotler: Ten Years After His Passing." In *Jewish Observer*, May 1973, p. 7

Karlinsky, Chaim. "The Fighting Rabbi." In *Hatzofe*, February 5, 1971 (Hebrew)

———"Ha-Gaon Rebbe Eliezer Silver Zal." In *Shanah be-Shanah*, ed. Aaron Pechenik. Jerusalem: Hechal Shlomo, 1968, p. 371 (Hebrew)

Karp, Abraham J. "New York Chooses a Chief Rabbi." In *PAJHS*, 44, no. 3 (March 1955), pp. 129-198

Klarman, A. "An Example of a Man of Righteousness." In *The Day—Jewish Journal*, March 28, 1968 (Yiddish)

Kranzler, David. "How 18,000 Jews Survived the Holocaust While Europe Burned." In *Jewish Life*, Tishrei 5736, pp. 28-39

Kranzler, Gershon. "Setting the Record Straight." In *The Jewish Observer*, November 1971, pp. 9-14

Lamm, Norman. "The Ideology of the Neturei Karta: According to the Satmarer Version." In *Tradition*, 13:1 (Fall 1971), pp. 38-53

———"Recent Additions to the Ketubah: A Halakhic Critique." In *Tradition*, 2:1 (Fall 1959), pp. 93-118.

Levin, A. Leo and Kramer, Meyer. "New Provisions in the Ketubah." New York: Community Service Division of Yeshiva University, 1955

Liebman, Charles S. "Orthodoxy in American Jewish Life." In *AJYB: 1965*. Philadelphia: Jewish Publication Society of America, 1965, pp. 27-30

Lipsky, Louis. "Religious Activity: New York." In *The Russian Jew in the United States*, ed. Charles S. Bernheimer. Philadelphia: John C. Winston Co., 1905, pp. 148-56

Margolies, M.S. "The Union of Orthodox Rabbis of the United States and Canada." In *The Jewish Communal Register: 1917-1918*. New York: Kehillah, 1918, pp. 1180-81

Philipson, David. "Cincinnati." In *The Universal Jewish Encyclopedia*, ed. Isaac Landman. New York, 1943, 3:205-210

Pool, David de Sola. "Judaism and the Synagogue." In *The American Jew: A Composite Portrait*, ed. Oscar I. Janowsky. New York: Harper and Bros., 1942, pp. 37-41

Rakeffet-Rothkoff, Aaron. "Rabbi Meir Simchah Ha-Kohen of Dvinsk." In *Jewish Life*, January 1973-Shevat 5733, pp. 51-58

Rothkoff, Aaron. "The American Sojourns of Ridbaz; Religious Problems within the Immigrant Community." In *PAJHS*, 57, no. 4 (June 1968), pp. 557-72

———"Chaim Ozer Grodzenski." In *Jewish Life*, May-June 1967/ Sivan-Tammuz 5727, pp. 40-49

———"The Meitsheter Illui." In *Jewish Life*, November-December 1967/Kislev-Teveth 5728, pp. 29-35

———"The 1924 Rabbinical Delegation Visit." In *Jewish Life*, November-December 1963, pp. 56-61

Seidman, Hillel. "Moynihan at the Start of his Career and Not the End." In *Hatzofe*, February 13, 1976 (Hebrew)

———"Ha-Rav ha-Kollel Shel Yehudei Artzot ha-Brit." In *Hatzofe*, February 23, 1968 (Hebrew)

———"Yeshivat Etz Hayyim of Kletsk." In *Mosdot ha-Torah be-Europa: be-Vinyanam uve-Hurbanam*, ed. Samuel K. Mirsky. New York: Histadrut Ivrit of America, 1956 (Hebrew)

Shapiro, Chaim. "Escape from Europe: A Chronicle of Miracles." In the *Jewish Observer*, May 1973, pp. 20-23

Silber, Saul. "The Gaon of Rogatchov." In *Jewish Leaders*, edited Leo Jung. New York: Bloch Publishing Co., 1953, pp. 393-404

Silver, Eliezer. "Address Delivered by Rabbi Eliezer Silver at the

Opening of the Special Conference of Agudat Israel for the Strengthening of the Jewish Religion." New York: Agudat Israel, 1942

———"Report on a Mission to the Remnants of Jewry in 16 Countries and Visit to the Holy Land," ed. Zevi H. Wachsman. Toronto, 1947

———"They Fought for Our Cause: the Influential Taft Family and Their Attitude to Jewry," ed. Z.H. Wachsman. Toronto: Daily Hebrew Journal, 1946

Singer, David. "The Yeshivah World." In *Commentary*, October 1976, pp. 70-73

Singer, Shmuel. "His Title was 'Hillel Hakohen'." In the *Jewish Observer*, May 1975, p. 17

Sursky, Aaron. "Thirty Years Since the Establishment of a Torah City in the Shanghai Diaspora." In *Beth Jacob*, January 1972, pp. 10-13 (Hebrew)

Tabak, Israel. "Rabbi Abraham Rice of Baltimore: Pioneer of Orthodox Judaism in America." In *Tradition*, 7, no. 2 (Summer 1965), pp. 102-103

"The Visionary at the Mountain: Rabbi Joseph Kahaneman." Published by American Friends of Ponevez Yeshiva in Israel for its Sixth Annual Dinner, May 17, 1960

Wachsman, Z. H. "HaRav D'Poh-Rabbi El. Silver." In *Every Friday*, December 21, 1945, p. 5

Weiss-Rosmarin, Trude. "Kashruth and Conservative Rabbis." In *The Jewish Spectator*, September 1960, pp. 6-7

"When the World Mourned." Published by the Rabbi Aaron Kotler Memorial Fund of Lakewood, New Jersey, following his death on November 29 (Kislev 2), 1962

Wolpin, Nisson. "Never Again." In *The Jewish Observer*, May 1975, p. 7

"Yaldei Teheran Ma'ashimim." Jerusalem: Agudat Israel, 1943 (Hebrew)

Dissertations

Bernstein, Louis. "The Emergence of the English Speaking Orthodox Rabbinate." Ph.D. dissertation, Bernard Revel Graduate School of Yeshiva University, 1977

Kranzler, David. "The History of the Jewish Refugee Community of

Shanghai, 1938-1945." Ph.D. dissertation, Bernard Revel Graduate School of Yeshiva University, 1971

Zuroff, Ephraim. "Rabbis, Relief, and Rescue: American Vaad Hatzala, November 1939-April 1943." M.A. project, Hebrew University, 1975

Archives

Revel Archives of Rabbi Bernard Revel, the founder of Yeshiva College, at the home of Mrs. Bernard Revel, New York

Rosenberg Archives of Rabbi Israel Rosenberg, president of the Agudat Harabanim, at the Jewish Theological Seminary, New York

Silver Archives of Rabbi Eliezer Silver, at the home of Rabbi David L. Silver, Harrisburg, Pa.

Vaad Hatzala Archives, New York

Yeshiva University Archives, New York

Periodicals, Newspapers and Encyclopedias

The Brooklyn Jewish Center Review, October 1952.

Every Friday, May 8, 1931; March 9, 16, 1934; September 20, November 8, 1935; May 29, September 18, December 4, 1936; July 7, 1939; August 30, 1940; September 27, 1946; July 4, October 17, 1947; February 3, December 22, 1950; February 2, 1951; November 26, 1954; April 20, June 8, 1956; March 3, 1961; June 29, 1962; September 20, 1963; February 21, 1964; February 19, 1965

The Jewish Day, August 1, 1930

Jewish Encyclopedia, ed. Isidore Singer. 12 vols. New York; Funk and Wagnalls Company, 1904

Jewish Observer, April 1975

JWB Circle, March 1961

Kovetz le-Hoshvei Shemo, Ellul 5733

Kovetz Rabbani Torani, Nisan-Ellul 1969

The National Jewish Post and Opinion, July 21, 1961

New York Herald Tribune, December 3, 1962

Noam, vols. 1 and 17

Hapardes, August 1930; November 1931; June 1932; March, December 1933; October 1935; February, July 1936; September 1937; June,

July, December 1939; August, September, October 1940; February, May, June, September 1941; September, December 1942; January, February, July, December 1943; January, March, May, October, November 1945; May, August 1946; March, May, June, December 1947; February 1949; September 1951; January 1953; October 1954; June 1956; January, July, 1957; June, July 1958; January 1959; February 1960; January 1961; June, December 1962; September 1964; January, March 1965; February 1966; March 1968

HaPeles, Nisan, Av 1902

Rabbinical Council Record, April 1961

United Synagogue Review, December 1954

Yad Washem Studies, Vol 3, 1959

Dos Yiddishe Vort, Tammuz-Av 1954

Letters

From Charles Batt, Orthodox lay leader, to Rabbi David Silver: August 27, 1976

From Mrs. Louis Engleberg, daughter of an Orthodox lay leader, to the author: August 6, 1975

From Rabbi Mordecai Gifter, Telshe *Rosh Yeshivah*, to Rabbi David Silver, n.d.

From Herman Landau, *Vaad Hatzala* activist, to the author: August 19, 1973

From Rabbi Elisha Rosenfeld, London rabbi, to Rabbi David Silver: July 11, 1972

From Dr. Hillel Seidman, author and historian, to the author: May 9, 1977

Interviews

Bernstein, Louis, Rabbi, *Rabbinical Council of America leader,* January 29, 1975

Chill, Samuel, Rabbi, *Mir Yeshiva graduate and rabbi of the Kingsway Jewish Community Center of Flatbush,* February 26, 1974

Feinstein, Jehiel Michal, Rabbi, *Tel Aviv Rosh Yeshivah*, August 12, 1971

Gershuni, Bessie, Mrs, *daughter of Rabbi Eliezer Silver,* December 27, 1971

Gustman, Israel, Rabbi, *Jerusalem Rosh Yeshivah,* October 22, 1972

Hallerstein, Jacob, *Secretary of the Agudat Harabanim,* April 30, 1974

Horowitz, Moshe, Rabbi, *Torah educator,* August 6, 1973

Itamar-Wohlgelernter, Max J. E., Rabbi, *American and Israeli rabbi,* February 22, 1971

Kasher, Menahem, Rabbi, *Jerusalem Torah scholar and author,* July 16 and August 7, 1974

Kirshblum, Mordecai, Rabbi, *Mizrachi leader in New York and Jerusalem,* October 2, 1972

Lewin, Isaac, Rabbi, *American scholar and Agudat Israel leader,* August 12, 1974.

Lichtenstein, Tovah, Mrs, *daughter and wife of roshei yeshivah,* June 19, 1975

Morduchovitz, Joseph, Rabbi, *New York rabbi,* August 4, 1974

Pechenik, Aaron, Rabbi, *Rabbinic author and editor,* September 9, 1975

Reichman, Solomon, Rabbi, *Agudat Harabanim leader,* August 6, 1974

Shapiro, David, *affiliated with the Institute of Contemporary Judaism of Hebrew University,* February 28, 1971

Sher, Abraham, Rabbi, *Secretary of the Israeli Vaad ha-Yeshivot,* October 25, 1970

Silver, David L., Rabbi, *son of Rabbi Eliezer Silver,* October 4, 1972; July 10, 24, 1974; July 14, 1976

Sladowsky, Yitzhak, Rabbi, *American rabbi,* February 22, 1975

Teitelbaum, Simcha, Rabbi, *American Torah educator,* July 30, 1974

Weinberg, Charles, Rabbi, *Rabbinical Council of America leader,* August 19, 1975

Wohlgelernter, Solomon P., Rabbi, *American rabbi and Vaad Hatzala activist,* July 31, 1974

Zohar, Haim, *Israeli diplomat,* December 17, 1977

INDEX

Abramowitz, Dovber, 34
Abrams, Norman B., 261
Agudat Harabanim
vs. Conservative movement, 295
constitution of, 315-325
controversy within, 105-109
dinei Torah, 117-119
education, 290
and Ezras Torah, 63
founding of, 32
herem of, 115, 141-143
journal, 100
Kashrut, 72, 124-152
leadership changed, 292-294
march on Washington, 219-221
opposition to, 105
Presidency of Rabbi Silver, 95-120
publications, 63-64, 100
vs. Rabbinical Council of America, 294
vs. Reform movement, 295
relief activities, 188-189
roshei yeshivah and, 290, 292-299
Sabbath observance, 306
Silver's participation in, 57-58, 65, 95-120
survey of rabbinate, 97-101, 101-104
Talmud reprint, 63-65
and *Vaad Hatzala*, 189, 200-201
Yeshiva University and, 264-271
and Yiddish, 290
Agudat Israel
American Torah Foundation, 179
convention, 157-160, 166-169, 174-175, 176-179, 278, 279
Council of Torah Sages (*Mo'etzet Gedolei haTorah*), 155, 175
Joint Boycott Council and, 172-174
Mizrachi movement and, 169-172, 302
platform, 162-163

Agudat Israel (*continued*)
relief activities, 172
Youth Aliyah and, 180-182
Agunah, 114
Album, Tzvi Shimon, 36
Aliyah, 254-255, 276; *see also* Youth Aliyah
Alperstein, Abraham Eliezer, 21
Alter, Abraham Mordecai (Gurer rebbe), 159-160, 180, 194
American Jewish Joint Distribution Committee, 62
American Torah Foundation, 179
Amiel, Moshe Avigdor, 170
Anfei Erez, 259
Appointments, *see* Rabbinic appointments
Aranowitz, Bassia (Mrs. E. Silver), 51, 91
Ash, Abraham Joseph, 20
Assimilation, 15-22, 29-30
Austria, 242

Background of E. Silver, 43
Bar-Ilan (Berlin), Meyer, 156, 171
Belgium, 231
Belkin, Samuel, 271
Bengis, Selig Reuben, 256-257
Berkson, Pearl (Mrs. E. Silver), 92
Berlin, Hayyim, 26
Berlin (Bar-Ilan), Meyer, 156, 171
Bermuda Conference, 218
Beth Din Tzedek, 150
Bierut, Boleslaw, 238
Bloch, Elijah Meyer, 232, 273-274
B'nai Brith, 285-287
Braver, Yehudah, 125-126
Brisker Rav (Yitzhak Zev Soloveitchik), 200, 260, 296
Brit milah, 77
Bund, 16

ספר

עֲנְפֵי אר"ז

חלק ראשון

ערכי א-ב

פלפולי דאורייתא בסדרי זרעים, מועד, קדשים וטהרות

הרב אליעזר זילבר

הרב דסינסינעטי, אהיא

בהרה"ג ר' בונם צמח זצ"ל

נכד הגאונים בעל באר הגולה ועוד

ראש נשיאות אגודת הרבנים בארה"ב וקנדה

נדפס בסיוע ועד אגוה"ר ואחדים מידידי הרה"ג שליט"א

וכבר מוכן לדפוס רוב יתר החלקים מערכי ג — עד ת'

נדפס בדפום "בלשן"

ע"י מרדכי שוסטערמאן ושלום דובער פויזנגער

שנת ה' אלפים תש"ך

Title page of *Anfei Erez*, by Rabbi Eliezer Silver

זה השער לה' צדיקים יבאו בו

בעזהי"ת

ספר

צמח אר"ז

חידושים וביאורים בכמה מסכתות מתלמוד בבלי וירושלמי

מאת

הגאון הגדול רבי אליעזר זילבר ז"ל

ששימש אב"ד בהערים:

הריסבורג, פא.; ספרינגפילד, מאסס.; וסינסינטי, אהיו

ונשיא „אגודת הרבנים דארצות הברית וקנדה"

מחבר הספר „ענפי ארז", ג' חלקים

וביניהם גם חידושי תורה מאת אביו

הגאון ר' בונם צמח זילבר ז"ל

רב דעיר דוסאט, ליטא

◄ • ►

יוצא לאור על ידי בנו בכורו ותלמידו

דוד ליב זילבר, רבה של הריסבורג, פא.

בסיוע של חבר בעלי-בתים מוקירי רבנו ומעריציו של הגאון המחבר ז"ל

בסינסינטי והריסבורג ובני המשפחה

שנת תשל"ה

נדפס בבית דפום
סענדר דיימס
ברוקלין, ניו יורק

Title page of *Tzemah Erez*, by Rabbi Eliezer Silver